International Studies in Entrepreneurship

Volume 49

This series highlights cutting-edge research in entrepreneurship, small business/SMEs, economic development, and policy. Volumes in the series feature empirical studies, theoretical analyses, practical applications, and policy recommendations in regional and global contexts, and explore a wide variety of topics with regard to entrepreneurship, including demographics, new venture financing, research & development, business creation, labor dynamics, technology management, and education. Springer and Series Editors welcome proposals for research monographs, edited volumes and reference works in all areas of entrepreneurship research.

Magnus Henrekson · Christian Sandström ·
Mikael Stenkula
Editors

A Green Entrepreneurial State?

Exploring the Pitfalls of Green Deals

Springer

Editors
Magnus Henrekson
Research Institute of Industrial Economics (IFN)
Stockholm, Sweden

Christian Sandström
Linnaeus University
Växjö, Sweden

Mikael Stenkula
Research Institute of Industrial Economics (IFN)
Stockholm, Sweden

ISSN 1572-1922 ISSN 2197-5884 (electronic)
International Studies in Entrepreneurship
ISBN 978-3-032-15511-5 ISBN 978-3-032-15512-2 (eBook)
https://doi.org/10.1007/978-3-032-15512-2

This Springer imprint is published by the registered company Springer Nature Switzerland AG
The registered company address is: Gewerbestrasse 11, 6330 Cham, Switzerland

Preface

Until recently, there was broad consensus that free trade, domestic deregulation, and the removal of entry barriers—as well as other policies that curtail competition—were the keys to stimulating economic growth and societal welfare. In the business realm, the prevailing sentiment was that policy's primary objective was to create a level playing field for companies—regardless of age, industry, size, or the characteristics and nationality of their owners. This perspective significantly influenced the establishment of the internal market within the European Union.

However, consensus has shifted in recent years. Western governments are now launching expansive programs to rejuvenate their post-pandemic economies and to achieve ambitious goals such as sharply reducing, and eventually eliminating, CO_2 emissions. British-Italian economist Mariana Mazzucato was at the forefront of advocating this renewed policy direction, gaining widespread attention with her 2013 book *The Entrepreneurial State*. In the United States, eminent scholars such as Harvard professor Dani Rodrik have championed the resurgence of vertical industrial policies that address specific challenges and target select sectors.

Highlighting the purported immediacy of the problems they aim to address, these increasingly interventionist and specialized industrial policies are frequently termed "missions" or "moonshots."

The reemergence of state-driven strategies stems from several powerful dynamics: China's deployment of industrial policy possibly fueling its remarkable growth; the West's perceived stagnation juxtaposed with China's rapid technological advances; the unforeseen disruption of the COVID-19 pandemic; climate change concerns; and growing geopolitical tensions. The ripple effect of imitation is evident: the European Union, observing the recent surge in subsidies and interventions in the United States, has reciprocated with measures of its own. Intriguingly, this trend intensifies even as the inherent limitations of vertical industrial policy appear to be hindering China's economy.

Green Deals—broad strategies that aim to transform economies by making them climate-neutral, resource-efficient, and competitive all at once—are part of this trend. Nuclear power has been shut down prematurely in parts of Europe and replaced with intermittent energy sources such as wind and solar power. Public funds have been allocated to hydrogen initiatives, carbon capture technologies, and similar efforts to transform Western economies.

By 2025, it became increasingly evident that many of these efforts were faltering. Europe's flagship battery initiative, Northvolt, ended up as the largest bankruptcy in modern Swedish history. Attempts to produce steel using hydrogen were abandoned, despite billions of euros in support from the EU and its member states. In Germany, energy prices hit record highs, and the manufacturing sector was struggling. The blackout in Spain and Portugal raised questions about grid stability in countries increasingly dependent on solar and wind power.

These failures are neither small nor insignificant. They stand in stark contrast to the promises made by EU officials and renowned scholars. The President of the European Commission, Ursula von der Leyen, referred to the EU Green Deal as the Union's "man on the moon" moment, while the Commission's Executive Vice President in charge of the Green Deal, Frans Timmermans, stated in 2020 that "[t]he Green Deal is Europe's new growth strategy. A strategy where environmental, economic and social sustainability go hand-in-hand."

Awareness is gradually increasing that these policies are not working. As Mario Draghi emphasized in his 2024 report on EU competitiveness, Europe is falling behind the United States and China. According to Draghi, the core problem "is that new companies with new technologies are not rising in our economy … we are failing to translate ideas into commercial success." In particular, the "green transition" has not delivered on its promises to generate prosperity and sustainability. The purpose of this collective volume is to explore why this is the case, while also pointing to alternative paths forward.

In two earlier collective volumes, we questioned the ideas underpinning industrial policy and the notion of an entrepreneurial state,[1] as well as so-called moonshot policies.[2] By October 2025, these two volumes had been downloaded 420,000 times. While some voices have been raised in light of spectacular failures across the continent, Europe continues largely along the same path, underscoring the ongoing need for critical inquiry into these matters.

The current volume offers a combination of theoretical perspectives, in-depth case studies, and systematic assessments of policy outcomes across economies. Our findings show that these failures are not random, nor do they appear to be part of a long-term trajectory toward improved competitiveness. Rather, they stem from poorly designed policies that are now manifesting as poor outcomes.

Green Deal policies are politically enticing, casting policymakers as visionaries who courageously confront grand contemporary challenges. At the same time, major corporations reap the rewards of expansive support schemes and stimulus packages unfolding across Europe and the United States.

---

[1] Wennberg, K., & Sandström, C. (Eds.) (2022). *Questioning the Entrepreneurial State: Status-quo, Pitfalls, and the Need for Credible Innovation Policy*. Cham: Springer. https://doi.org/10.1007/978-3-030-94273-1

[2] Henrekson, M., Sandström, C., & Stenkula, M. (Eds.) (2024). *Moonshots and the New Industrial Policy: Questioning the Mission Economy*. Cham: Springer. https://doi.org/10.1007/978-3-031-49196-2

Some readers may find our analysis somewhat eurocentric. That is true—but also largely unavoidable. Among developed countries that have enacted legislation committing to become climate-neutral by 2050, only four—Australia, New Zealand, Canada, and South Korea—are outside Europe. In contrast, 31 European countries have made this commitment.

We are deeply grateful for the knowledge and effort each author has contributed to this volume, including their feedback on other chapters and on the overall framing.

Research funding from the Jan Wallander and Tom Hedelius Foundation and the Kamprad Family Foundation for Entrepreneurship, Research & Charity is gratefully acknowledged by Magnus Henrekson. Christian Sandström wishes to thank the Hamrin Foundation for supporting his research. Mikael Stenkula extends his gratitude to the Jan Wallander and Tom Hedelius Foundation and Anders Sandrews Stiftelse. The Open Access fee has been generously co-funded by the Hamrin Foundation.

Stockholm, Sweden — Magnus Henrekson
Växjö, Sweden — Christian Sandström
Stockholm, Sweden — Mikael Stenkula
October 2025

Praise for *A Green Entrepreneurial State?*

"In this important and illuminating volume, Magnus Henrekson, Christian Sandström, and Mikael Stenkula marshal a distinguished group of scholars to reassess the promise and perils of state-driven environmental policy. The contributors combine theoretical sophistication with international case evidence to reveal why government-led green innovation frequently falters and how more entrepreneurial, bottom-up dynamics can better advance sustainability. This book should be essential reading for policymakers and academics seeking to rethink the economic foundations of the green transition."

—David B. Audretsch, *Distinguished Professor, Ameritech Chair of Economic Development and Director, Institute for Development Strategies, Indiana University*

"An All-Star set of authors challenge the conventional wisdom that Europe's Green New Deal offers a Free Lunch that simultaneously decarbonizes and reboots European economic growth. The subtle analysis explores the intended and unintended consequences of launching deep subsidies for unproven technologies. Policy makers, analysts and students will gain from the book's insights about policy evaluation under uncertainty."

—Matthew E. Kahn, *Provost Professor of Economics at the University of Southern California*

"Green energy projects have been a 'darling' of policymakers worldwide. But despite the very real problems motivating these efforts and the good intentions of many political leaders, these efforts have frequently misfired (with rare exceptions, such as in China). This volume ably explores these important and very contemporaneous issues."

—Josh Lerner, *Jacob H. Schiff Professor at Harvard Business School*

"This volume offers a compelling and critical examination of the 'green entrepreneurial state' ideal. Through theoretical and historical inquiry, it reveals how well-meaning policy missions frequently become marches of folly, suppressing the decentralized discovery processes on which genuine innovation depends. The contributions collectively illustrate that the road to sustainability is paved with local learning, entrepreneurial diversity, and institutional humility—rather than grand designs imposed from above."

—Maria Minniti, *Louis A. Bantle Chair in Entrepreneurship and Public Policy, Director of the Institute for an Entrepreneurial Society, Whitman School of Management, Syracuse University*

"Green Transition has been the rallying cry for a new wave of industrial policy theorists, politicians and civil servants who champion the 'green entrepreneurial state.' This superb collection draws deftly on theory and evidence to question the coherence of this concept. It needs to be read by all those who believe that they have the wisdom to plan our future—whether green or otherwise."

—Mark Pennington, *Professor of Political Economy and Public Policy, King's College, University of London*

"Can a 'green entrepreneurial state' direct innovation and transform industries through green new deals and missions more cost effectively than more traditional approaches? Magnus Henrekson, Christian Sandström, and Mikael Stenkula have assembled a collection of essays from distinguished scholars arguing that for a broad range of industrial sectors these attempts have been extremely costly for consumers and have achieved limited environmental benefits. All the essays are written in manner that should be accessible to policymakers and students, with detailed examples of actual green new deals and their financial and environmental consequences taken mostly from the European experience. For this reason, these essays would be a welcome addition to the reading list of a course on entrepreneurship."

—Frank A. Wolak, *Holbrook Working Professor of Commodity Price Studies, Department of Economics, Stanford University*

Contents

About the Editors

Magnus Henrekson is a Professor of Economics and Senior Research Fellow of the Research Institute of Industrial Economics (IFN) in Stockholm, Sweden. He resigned as CEO of IFN in 2020 after 15 years of service. Until 2009, he held the Jacob Wallenberg Research Chair in the Department of Economics at the Stockholm School of Economics. He is also a member of the Royal Swedish Academy of Engineering Sciences (IVA)

He received his Ph.D. in 1990 from Gothenburg University with his dissertation *An Economic Analysis of Swedish Government Expenditure.* Throughout the 1990s, he conducted several projects that aimed to explain cross-country growth differences. Since the turn of the new millennium, his primary research focus has been entrepreneurship economics and the institutional determinants of the business climate. In this area, he has published extensively in scientific journals and contributed several research surveys to *Handbooks* in the field of entrepreneurship.

Henrekson also has extensive experience as an advisor, board member, and lecturer in many different contexts, in both the business and public sectors.

Christian Sandström is an Associate Professor of Technology Management from Chalmers University of Technology, where he also received his doctoral degree (2010). His research concerns innovation policy and the interplay between technological and institutional change. Sandström is one of the editors of *Questioning the Entrepreneurial State* (Springer) and *Moonshots and the New Industrial Policy* (Springer). He has published more than 30 papers in peer-reviewed academic journals, such as *Business History, Small Business Economics, Technological Forecasting & Social Change*, and *Industry & Innovation.*

Sandström wrote his thesis on the topic of disruptive innovation. He has been a visiting scholar at the University of Cambridge and ETH Zürich in Switzerland. Sandström has received several awards for his pedagogical skills and is a frequently invited public speaker on the topic of technological change and industrial transformation.

Mikael Stenkula is an Associate Professor of Economics and holds a PhD from the School of Economics and Management at Lund University. He received this degree in 2004 with his dissertation *Essays on Network Effects and Money*. After having worked for a year as a lecturer at Lund University, where he taught microeconomics, he joined the Research Institute of Industrial Economics (IFN) in 2005. His primary research areas are entrepreneurship economics and taxation. In addition to publishing in peer-reviewed journals, Stenkula has also co-edited several volumes, including *Moonshots and the New Industrial Policy* (Springer).

Stenkula has also taught at the Stockholm School of Economics and serves as the executive secretary of the award committee for the Global Award for Entrepreneurship Research, the foremost global award for research on entrepreneurship.

Introductory Essay

The Pitfalls of Green Deals: Introduction and Synthesis

Magnus Henrekson, Christian Sandström, and Mikael Stenkula

Abstract Green Deals have been introduced across Western economies as large-scale, mission-oriented innovation policies (MOIPs) intended to combine economic growth with environmental sustainability. Rooted in the concept of an "entrepreneurial state," these initiatives reflect renewed confidence in governments' ability to direct technological and industrial transformation. However, their outcomes have frequently diverged from expectations. This volume examines the theoretical foundations and empirical results of Green Deals, highlighting the institutional, economic, and behavioral factors that contribute to their shortcomings. Drawing on perspectives from evolutionary economics, public choice theory, and behavioral political economy, the contributors analyze a wide range of cases, including Germany's *Energiewende*, Italy's Superbonus, and the European Union's hydrogen and battery programs. Across these examples, recurring challenges such as rent-seeking, mission capture, optimism bias, and distorted incentives are identified. The findings indicate that while Green Deals have advanced ambitious sustainability goals, they often undermine competitiveness and fiscal stability while generating limited environmental benefits. The volume concludes by outlining alternative pathways that emphasize incremental, technology-neutral, and institutionally grounded approaches to sustainability—approaches that align more closely with long-term economic resilience and effective environmental policy.

Financial support from the Jan Wallander and Tom Hedelius Foundation (P2023–0186), and the Kamprad Family Foundation for Entrepreneurship, Research & Charity (P2022–0048) and Anders Sandrews Stiftelse is gratefully acknowledged.

M. Henrekson (✉) · M. Stenkula
Research Institute of Industrial Economics (IFN), Stockholm, Sweden
e-mail: magnus.henrekson@ifn.se

M. Stenkula
e-mail: mikael.stenkula@ifn.se

C. Sandström
Linneaus University, Växjö, Sweden
e-mail: christian.sandstrom@lnu.se

M. Henrekson et al. (eds.), *A Green Entrepreneurial State?*, International Studies in Entrepreneurship 49, https://doi.org/10.1007/978-3-032-15512-2_1

Keywords Entrepreneurship policy · Green deals · Green transition · Innovation policy · Moonshot policies · Public choice

JEL Codes H50 · L26 · L52 · O33 · O38 · P16

Introduction

Historically, environmental policy has depended on tools such as taxes, regulations, and bans to advance sustainability goals. In recent years, however, there has been an increasing convergence between environmental and industrial policy. Governments throughout the Western world are now implementing so-called Green Deals—broad industrial policy frameworks designed to achieve sustainability objectives.

This shift in policy direction has unfolded alongside a relative weakening of Europe's economic competitiveness. Since the 2008–2009 financial crisis, the European Union has gradually fallen behind both China and the United States. Although economic performance can be assessed through multiple indicators, Europe seems to be trailing on nearly all of them. The seriousness of this decline was underscored by Mario Draghi in a report commissioned by the European Commission and released in late 2024 (Draghi 2024).

Policymakers—particularly within Europe—have advanced Green Deals as a strategy to merge environmental sustainability with economic revitalization. This renewed focus on major state-led initiatives has gained further support from economists such as Mariana Mazzucato and Dani Rodrik, who advocate a more interventionist state role in shaping markets and directing economic progress (e.g., Mazzucato 2018a, 2021; Rodrik 2022).

As part of the concept of "mission-oriented innovation policy" (MOIP), governments are encouraged to steer economies toward overarching societal goals such as sustainability, inclusiveness, and resilience. Drawing on historical precedents like the US Apollo program, this perspective has reshaped how many policymakers and commentators understand the state's role in driving innovation.

These ideas have inspired leaders and institutions worldwide to launch ambitious green industrial strategies under banners such as Green Deals or Moonshots. European Commission President Ursula von der Leyen (2019) has even described the European Green Deal as Europe's "man on the moon moment," while US Secretary of Energy under the Biden administration, Jennifer Granholm (2022), has called the fight against climate change "our generation's moonshot."

In this volume, we rely on the OECD's (2021, p. 15) definition of a Mission Oriented Innovation Policy (MOIP) as "a co-ordinated package of policy and regulatory measures tailored specifically to mobilise science, technology and innovation in order to address well-defined objectives related to a societal challenge, in a defined timeframe."

Relatedly, we define a Green Deal as a comprehensive set of mission-oriented innovation policies (MOIPs) encompassing multiple domains and explicitly aimed at advancing sustainable development through a broad array of policy instruments, including industrial policy. Green Deals are frequently promoted as strategies to reconcile environmental objectives with economic competitiveness; however, some interpretations instead emphasize the necessity of economic sacrifice to achieve sustainability goals. This understanding broadly aligns with Mazzucato's (2021, p. 137ff) conceptualization, in which "Green New Deals" are presented as paradigmatic missions—ambitious, systemic initiatives particularly suited to large-scale political and economic intervention.

From this perspective, Green Deals have clearly given policymakers a pronounced role as primary agents behind desirable changes. Here is a typical formulation: "Moving to a greener low carbon economy means redirecting all sectors and all actors—public, private and civil society—towards economic growth in a sustainable and inclusive direction" (Kattel et al. 2021, p. 18).

Despite the scale and scope of these Green Deals and broad agreement on the urgency of the climate challenge, these extensive initiatives have so far been implemented across several Western countries with relatively limited critical scrutiny (Henrekson et al. 2024a, 2024b). Academic analyses remain scarce, particularly regarding the risks of failure and unintended consequences associated with MOIPs.

The absence of critical scrutiny is alarming. The EU's flagship battery venture, Northvolt in Sweden, ended in the country's largest bankruptcy since the 1930s. Across Europe, hydrogen projects are being cancelled despite the prospect of securing billions of euros in subsidies. Meanwhile, energy prices continue to rise, industrial output is falling in countries such as Germany, and electricity consumption is declining, even though electrification is meant to play a central role in the green transition. The blackout on the Iberian Peninsula in April 2025 further underscored growing concerns about the reliability of intermittent energy sources such as solar and wind power.

Are these setbacks simply part of the unpredictable and complex dynamics of economic development? After all, overinvestment, bubbles, and bankruptcies are integral features of a capitalist economy (Schumpeter 1934). Or do the cancellations, shutdowns, and foreclosures instead reflect the consequences of misguided policies? Since these policies have been implemented based on academic advice, our focus is directed toward the theories underpinning Green Deals and their effects on the economies where they have been adopted.

This introductory essay is organized as follows. The next section outlines the purpose of the volume and situates it within the broader literature on innovation policy and environmental sustainability. We then introduce the concept of Green Deals and trace its intellectual foundations. The essay continues with concise summaries of the individual contributions, presented in three parts. This is followed by a synthesis of the empirical evidence drawn from the case studies, highlighting recurring patterns of failure and the eight key takeaways identified. The final sections discuss alternative policy pathways and present the main conclusions of the volume.

The Purpose of This Collective Volume

As we will see, the literature on innovation systems and innovation policy has thus far paid relatively little attention to climate policy failures. This volume therefore focuses explicitly on the challenges surrounding Green Deals.

Its purpose is threefold. First, given the limited scholarly attention to the shortcomings of Green Deals, it seeks to document contemporary cases in which large-scale sustainability initiatives have failed to deliver the expected results. Second, it aims to identify and apply relevant theoretical frameworks that can help explain the mechanisms underlying such failures. Third, it explores alternative pathways for fostering economic recovery and advancing sustainable development.

Moonshots and Green Deals

The EU Green Deal is the Union's flagship strategy to reach climate neutrality by 2050 while fostering sustainable growth and protecting ecosystems (European Commission 2019a). It sets out sweeping reforms across energy, transport, manufacturing, agriculture, and finance, backed by a large-scale investment program designed to attract both public and private capital. At its core lies an ambitious financing framework. Through the European Green Deal Investment Plan, the EU has pledged to mobilize at least EUR 1 trillion in sustainable investments over the next decade (European Commission 2020a).

The Russian invasion of Ukraine in 2022 underscored the EU's dependency on fossil fuel imports and led to the launch of the REPowerEU Plan. This package builds on the Green Deal by focusing on energy savings, faster deployment of renewables, and diversification of energy supplies (European Commission 2022). The plan lays down concrete measures for scaling up renewable electricity production and reducing dependence on Russian fossil fuels.

Among the priority areas identified, renewable hydrogen has received particular emphasis. The Commission's Hydrogen Strategy outlines ambitions to install at least 40 GW of renewable hydrogen electrolysers in the EU by 2030, producing up to 10 million tonnes of renewable hydrogen (European Commission 2020b).[1] REPowerEU further strengthens this by calling for both 10 million tonnes of domestic production and an additional 10 million tonnes of imports by 2030 (European Commission 2022). Hydrogen is viewed as a key energy carrier for sectors where direct electrification is challenging, such as steel, chemicals, and heavy transport.

Offshore wind has been positioned as a cornerstone of Europe's clean energy transition. The EU's Offshore Renewable Energy Strategy sets ambitious targets, including 60 GW of offshore wind by 2030 and 300 GW by 2050, compared to

[1] 40 GW corresponds to the effect of roughly 25 state-of-the-art nuclear reactors. Producing 10 million tonnes of hydrogen through electrolysis requires approximately 550 TWh of electricity, corresponding to one-fifth of current total electricity production in the EU.

just 12 GW in 2020 (European Commission 2020c). To put this in perspective, the 2050 target would be nearly five times the total installed capacity of France's 57 nuclear reactors, which stood at around 63 GW in 2025. The strategy also emphasizes innovation in floating wind and marine energy technologies, alongside the need for cross-border cooperation on grid infrastructure. Progress reports published in 2023 note that while investment is gathering pace, achieving the 2050 goal will require sustained additional annual financing on the scale of hundreds of billions of euros (European Commission 2023a).

Solar energy deployment is advancing in parallel under REPowerEU, which includes measures to streamline permits, expand rooftop solar installations, and boost domestic panel manufacturing (European Commission 2022). Together, solar and wind are expected to form the backbone of the EU's renewable electricity system by mid-century.

Decarbonizing transport is a central pillar of the Green Deal. The EU has adopted new CO_2 emission standards for cars and vans, mandating that all new passenger vehicles and light commercial vehicles registered from 2035 must be zero-emission (European Commission 2023b). This regulation is part of the broader *Fit for 55* legislative package, which aims to cut greenhouse gas emissions by at least 55% by 2030 compared to 1990 levels.

Beyond regulation, the Green Deal signals a shift toward more interventionist industrial policies. The EU has embraced a mission-oriented approach, channeling support into strategic value chains such as batteries, solar panels, and electrolyzers. This industrial policy shift reflects not only the need to build domestic capacity for the energy transition but also a growing awareness of geopolitical vulnerabilities in global supply chains (European Commission 2024a).

Taken together, the Green Deal amounts to an extensive mix of legislation, tariffs, and supply-side measures in which certain technologies receive preferential treatment and targeted support. It represents a large-scale economic experiment endorsed by many scholars across several disciplines, but whose long-term implications for Europe's competitiveness and resilience remain uncertain.

Influences Behind the Green Deal

As noted earlier, the concept of a Green Deal is closely tied to the idea of mission-oriented innovation policies (MOIPs). Both MOIPs and the broader notion of an "entrepreneurial state" have been the subject of relatively limited but growing scholarly scrutiny in recent years (Wennberg and Sandström 2022; Muldoon and Yonai 2023; Kantor and Whalley 2025; Kirchherr et al. 2023). However, comparatively little attention has been devoted to examining the specific features and implications of Green Deals themselves.

Mariana Mazzucato's Impact

Mariana Mazzucato is widely regarded as one of the leading scholars shaping the EU's Green Deal and the growing convergence of environmental and industrial policy. While her influence is significant, it is also clear that she is part of a broader literature that lends intellectual support to these policy directions.

Few academics have played a more prominent role in defining the policy architecture of the Green Deal. Her concept of mission-oriented innovation has been explicitly adopted by EU institutions and woven into major policy frameworks. As the founding Director of the UCL Institute for Innovation and Public Purpose (IIPP), Mazzucato has a strong platform and ample resources for wielding influence. The IIPP is also quite explicit about this influence, e.g., writing that they are "working closely with the European Commission and the United Nations on the use of mission-oriented innovation to achieve growth that is more inclusive and sustainable" (Mazzucato and McPherson 2018, p. 6).

Mazzucato's ideas on Green Deals have been taken up and debated in a variety of international contexts. In the G20-commissioned report *Principles for an Inclusive and Sustainable Global Economy*, she argued for integrating mission-oriented strategies into global economic policy as a means to foster sustainable development and confront shared challenges (Mazzucato 2025). Her influence has also extended to Latin America, where she has promoted mission-oriented approaches to issues such as sustainable mobility and environmentally responsible commodity exports (Mazzucato 2023).

One of her most significant contributions remains the 2018 report to the European Commission, *Mission-Oriented Research & Innovation in the European Union: A Problem-Solving Approach to Fuel Innovation-Led Growth.* In the introduction, she recalls that:

> The European Commissioner for Research, Science and Innovation, Carlos Moedas, invited me to draft strategic recommendations on mission-oriented research and innovation in the EU, to guide the future European Union Framework Programme for Research and Innovation. (Mazzucato 2018b, p. 2)

Her role was not limited to thought leadership; she also served as special advisor to Commissioner Carlos Moedas. In 2019, he officially launched five "moonshot initiatives," explicitly inspired by the Apollo 11 mission, designed to tackle some of the world's most pressing challenges. These missions aimed to "deliver solutions to some of the greatest challenges facing our world, such as cancer, climate change, healthy oceans, climate-neutral cities and healthy soil and food."[2]

Taken together, Mazzucato's contributions as an academic writer, public intellectual, and advisor converge in a mission-oriented logic that has become deeply embedded in the European Green Deal. This influence stretches from the broader framing of the Green Deal as a transformative climate strategy, to the EU's main R&D funding program, Horizon Europe's research missions, and to the design agenda of

---

[2] European Commission (2019b).

the New European Bauhaus, a policy and funding initiative focusing on achieving a green transition in the built environments (European Commission 2024b, 2025).

Her ideas also gained traction through public commentary and media debate. In a widely cited *Financial Times* article, she argued that "[e]conomic growth has not only a rate but also a direction. … Europe has an opportunity to seal one of the most important deals of a generation" (Mazzucato 2019). Such statements provided not only intellectual scaffolding but also rhetorical momentum, reinforcing institutional narratives about the Green Deal's purpose.

At its core, her work reflects a renewed confidence in the capacity of governments to steer markets and mobilize change. This belief is captured in her assertive claim:

> Governments are the only actors capable of underwriting the scale of investments required; of coordinating multiple actors around the common goal of decarbonization; and of ensuring the costs and benefits of a green transition are distributed equitably across society so that social injustices are tackled alongside environmental crises. (Mazzucato 2022, p. 93)

Three Generations of Innovation Policy

Mariana Mazzucato's ideas capture a broader shift among European scholars toward a more hands-on role for the state in driving innovation. Over time, thinking about innovation policy has evolved through three main "generations" (Bergkvist et al. 2022).

First Generation: Fixing Market Failures

The earliest approach was rooted in neoclassical economics and the idea of *market failure*. Markets do not always provide enough investment in research and development (R&D), because knowledge is hard to own and easy to share. Firms therefore underinvest, knowing they cannot capture all the returns (Nelson 1959; Arrow 1962).

Governments were expected to step in and "fix the market" by funding R&D, supporting education and skills, and building strong intellectual property systems (Smith 2000). From the 1960s onward, this logic justified large public investments in universities, labs, and subsidies for private R&D (OECD 1998).

Second Generation: Building Innovation Systems

By the 1980s, scholars such as Nelson and Winter (1982) began to see innovation not as something that could be centrally directed, but as an evolutionary process shaped by learning, routines, and firm diversity. Policy, in this view, should focus less on control and more on creating fertile ground for experimentation and capability-building.

This inspired the innovation systems perspective (Freeman 1987; Lundvall 1992; Nelson 1993), which emphasized networks of firms, universities, public agencies, and users. The key challenge was no longer just market failure, but *system failure*, i.e., when the networks and institutions that support innovation are weak or poorly connected (Woolthuis et al. 2005).

Governments were now seen as facilitators who could strengthen these systems by promoting collaboration, supporting clusters, improving infrastructure, and encouraging knowledge exchange (Kline and Rosenberg 1986).

Third Generation: Missions and Directionality

As global problems like climate change and inequality grew more urgent, critics argued that second-generation policy lacked clear purpose. The third generation of innovation policy aims to give innovation direction—to steer it toward solving major societal challenges (Schot and Steinmueller 2018).

Left alone, markets and institutions tend to reinforce the status quo and incremental change (Geels 2004). Mission-oriented policies instead call on governments to take a proactive role: to set bold goals, coordinate actors, and guide investment toward sustainability. The goal is not only to fund innovation but to shape the markets where they can thrive.

This approach has been developed by scholars such as Jacobsson and Bergek (2006), Geels (2002), and Hekkert et al. (2007). They argue that policies must work at multiple levels—supporting experimentation, transforming established systems, and aligning innovation with wider social goals.

Yet, one issue often goes missing: government failure. A review of over 7,000 innovation-policy articles found that only 11% even mentioned problems such as rent-seeking, lobbying, or regulatory capture (Kärnä et al. 2023). Few explored them in depth. As a result, today's enthusiasm for Green Deals and mission-oriented innovation sometimes overlooks the risks and limits of expanding the state's role too far.

How to Read This Collective Volume

The volume is structured into three parts. Following this introduction, *Part I* provides an overview of Green Deals (Stenkula 2026), together with several theoretical perspectives employed throughout the volume (Cheang 2026; Muldoon and Yonai 2026; Schnellenbach 2026). *Part II* presents a set of empirical case studies highlighting failed MOIPs (Björnemalm and Sandström 2026; Deshaies 2026; Fahlén et al. 2026; Johansson and Kriström 2026; Henrekson 2026; Sandström 2026; Hellstrand and Gärdebo 2026; Capone and Stagnaro 2026). *Part III* turns to alternative approaches to environmental policy, discussing different strategies for achieving both sustainability and economic development (Grafström 2026; Mund 2026; Hjortsberg 2026).

Part I: Theoretical Perspectives

The contributions in Part I of this volume provide an overview of Green Deals and present theoretical perspectives that explain why missions related to Green Deals often fail.

Defining Features of Green Deals

In "Green Deals around the World," Mikael Stenkula (2026) outlines the defining features of Green Deals across several representative contexts. He argues that mission-oriented innovation policy (MOIP) has fundamentally reshaped both environmental and industrial strategies, steering them toward direct public investment and publicly supported financing. The analysis contrasts the European Union's Green Deal with the US approach, while also examining initiatives in the UK, Germany, and Sweden.[3] Green Deals mark a departure from more conventional environmental policies that emphasize regulation and taxation to come to grips with negative externalities while remaining neutral regarding which technologies that are most appropriate to achieve the desired goals.

Evolutionary Perspectives

In "The Incoherence of Modest Industrial Policy," Bryan Cheang (2026) critiques the revival of industrial policy debates, arguing that Green Deals and mission-oriented innovation policies (MOIPs) clash with the evolutionary and unpredictable nature of modern economies.

He focuses on the tension between Dani Rodrik's "modest" industrial policy and Mariana Mazzucato's more ambitious, mission-oriented approach. Cheang contends that modest industrial policy—balancing transformative goals with humility and

[3] In addition to the 29 countries covered by Stenkula (2026), a mere handful of developed countries have passed legislation imposing climate neutrality ("net zero") by 2050, namely Canada, Australia, New Zealand, South Korea, Switzerland, Lichtenstein, and Iceland. Among the other 160 countries in the world, only six (Armenia, Chile, Colombia, Fiji, Moldavia, and South Africa) have enacted a clear national statute mandating net-zero by 2050.

experimentation—is theoretically incoherent. The very uncertainties that justify modesty make large-scale structural transformation impossible, since transformation demands directionality, coordination, and strong state capacity.

Drawing on the literature on complexity and public governance (Hayek 1967; Colander and Kupers 2016; Page 2011), Cheang notes that economies are adaptive systems characterized by radical uncertainty (Henrekson et al. 2022). In such contexts, modest policies—favoring decentralized experimentation and open learning—are justified but inherently limited in transformative power.

Traditional industrial policy, by contrast, has always been transformative, involving structural reconfiguration, infrastructure, and institutional redesign (Hirschman 1958; Kuznets 1971; Lin and Monga 2017). Historical examples from East Asia (Chang 2006) and modernization theory (Rostow 1960; Myrdal 1970) show that transformation has required strong, directive states.

Rodrik's adaptive, network-based approach (Hausmann and Rodrik 2006; Aiginger and Rodrik 2020) acknowledges uncertainty but, according to Cheang, underestimates the coordination needed for transformation. Mazzucato's *entrepreneurial state* (2013, 2021) is more consistent, openly embracing mission-oriented intervention—but missions require convergence and alignment, which conflict with genuine pluralism.

Cheang's core claim is that industrial policy cannot be both modest and transformative. Real modesty limits ambition to incremental reforms; genuine transformation demands coherence and authority, risking illiberal outcomes (Scott 1998; Pennington 2010). The real divide, he concludes, lies not in policy tools but in first principles: whether to accept epistemic modesty in complex systems or pursue transformative state-led change despite its risks.

The Political Economy of Green Deals

In their contribution entitled "Raiders of the Entrepreneurial State: A Baptist and Bootlegger Analysis," Jeffrey Muldoon and Derek Yonai (2026) critically examine the notion of an "entrepreneurial state" (Mazzucato 2013), and reframe its implications for innovation, regulation, and rent-seeking through the lens of the "Bootleggers and Baptists" theory developed by public choice scholars. Muldoon and Yonai argue that instead of stimulating productive entrepreneurship, state-led industrial policy opens abundant opportunities for "plunder" by well-connected insiders ("Bootleggers") who exploit the state's moral legitimacy, often provided by well-meaning "Baptists" advocating the common good.

Drawing on Bruce Yandle's (1983) foundational work, and its later elaboration by Smith and Yandle (2014), the authors demonstrate how coalitions of moral advocates and opportunists often join forces to push for regulations and policies. In these counterintuitive alliances, Bootleggers secure rents and regulatory advantages under the cover of the Baptists' social legitimacy. Classic examples include blue laws on alcohol, as well as more recent large-scale environmental initiatives.

At the core of Muldoon and Yonai's study is an exploration of how coalition logic has shaped recent developments in environmental and industrial policy. Drawing on both historical and contemporary cases—the phasing out of incandescent lightbulbs (where manufacturers profited from promoting higher-cost alternatives), the US retreat from nuclear power (where fossil fuel interests and environmentalists found common cause), and the Paris Agreement (where multinationals positioned themselves to benefit from state-supported technologies)—they argue that well-intentioned interventions often end up enabling rent-seeking and crony capitalism at the public's expense. Their critique of Mazzucato's "entrepreneurial state" thesis centers on its neglect of standard public choice problems, particularly the friction and collective action failures inherent in real-world politics.

Muldoon and Yonai's central contribution is to demonstrate, through concrete empirical examples, that idealistic missions, whether aimed at green transition or industrial leadership, are regularly subverted by Bootlegger–Baptist coalitions. These dynamics not only fail to deliver the mission's intended social value but also routinely redistribute wealth to the politically powerful, undermining both innovation and market discipline.

Behavioral Aspects of Green Deals

In his contribution entitled "Behavioral Political Economy and Environmental Policy: Explaining Persistent Deviations from Efficient Policies," Jan Schnellenbach (2026) highlights that the design and implementation of Green Deals are almost never guided by neutral efficiency considerations alone. Instead, they are deeply shaped by behavioral dynamics—biases, heuristics, and expressive political behavior—which distort both citizen preferences and policy choices.

The behavioral political economy perspective stresses that voters, politicians, and bureaucrats systematically deviate from rationality in ways that undermine the efficiency of environmental policy. Following Downs' (1957) theory of rational ignorance, Caplan (2007) argues that individuals have incentives to indulge in "rational irrationality," since the marginal impact of a single vote is negligible. As a result, citizens often embrace "bliss beliefs" about the environment, views that signal virtue or identity rather than reflect careful cost–benefit assessments. By contrast, dissenting opinions are stigmatized as unvirtuous and carry high social costs that few are willing to bear.

Politicians, in turn, respond to these expressive preferences (Brennan and Lomasky 1993), amplifying availability cascades (Kuran and Sunstein 1999) and dread-risk perceptions (Slovic 1987). According to Schnellenbach, this dynamic renders Green Deals vulnerable to emotionally salient but economically inefficient outcomes. The German nuclear phase-out is a frequently cited case, where dread risk shaped policy design even at the cost of higher emissions. Likewise, public support for "degrowth" policies often rests on anti-market biases and neglect of innovation potential, despite evidence that technological change is central to sustainable growth.

In this view, behavioral distortions create "policy traps," resulting in policies that are symbolically resonant but economically counterproductive.

Part II: Empirical Evidence

Part II of the collective volume provides empirical illustrations of why Green Deal policies hardly ever work out as intended. In doing so, it addresses the underexplored theme of innovation policy failure.

The Ethanol Car Bubble

In "Exploring Failed Green Innovation Policy: The Rise and Fall of Ethanol Cars in Sweden 2003–2015," Rickard Björnemalm and Christian Sandström (2026) analyze Sweden's ethanol car bubble (2003–2015). Their case study shows how strong political backing, EU biofuel directives, and targeted subsidies such as the 2006 "pump law," green car rebates, and congestion tax exemptions created a temporary boom in ethanol cars—exceeding 20% of new sales in 2008—followed by a sharp decline.

The failure can be traced to three factors: weak technological and environmental fundamentals; consumer backlash fueled by poor performance and rising costs; and the capture of policy design by vested interests. Although formally technology-neutral, the pump law excluded electricity. Car manufacturers and the agricultural lobby exploited subsidies, while long-term transformative alternatives were neglected.

The study highlights the risks inherent in mission-oriented and so-called innovation policy 3.0 approaches. While rhetorically centered on transformation, such policies may in practice reinforce existing paradigms when shaped by powerful stakeholders. Echoing Kärnä et al. (2023), the authors argue that failure should be treated as a central concern in the study of innovation policy, not be relegated to an afterthought.

The German Energiewende

Launched in the early 2000s, Germany's *Energiewende* has long been seen as a model for large-scale renewable energy transitions. By rapidly expanding solar and wind power, Germany aimed to replace both nuclear and fossil fuels, inspiring the European Green Deal and its goal of EU-wide carbon neutrality by 2050. Germany itself pledged to reach neutrality by 2045.

In "The German *Energiewende*: A Green Deal Template or Planned Failure?", Michel Deshaies (2026) highlights several weaknesses. To replace stable nuclear and fossil-based generation with variable wind and solar, three key conditions are required: large overcapacity, extensive and costly grid expansion, and massive storage capacity. Yet Germany focused mainly on deploying renewables, giving far less attention to grids and storage. Even optimistic projections for hydrogen or other energy carriers cannot eliminate the need for huge renewable capacity.

Electricity makes up only about 20% of Germany's total energy use; the remaining 80%—mainly transport, heating, and industry—still depends on oil and gas. This means deep decarbonization must go far beyond the power sector.

The *Energiewende* has also driven sharp increases in household electricity prices, which doubled between 2001 and 2013 as renewable subsidies rose from EUR 5 billion to EUR 25 billion. Prices climbed further to EUR 0.458/kWh in 2023, leaving Germany with the highest household electricity costs in Europe, around 40% above the EU average. Industrial exemptions shift much of the burden onto households, prompting criticism of regressive redistribution and fears of deindustrialization as energy-intensive firms consider relocating abroad.

While the *Energiewende* has been influential in promoting renewables and shaping European policy, it also exposes the technical and economic constraints that complicate achieving net-zero emissions by mid-century.

The Costs of a Fossil-Free Future

Per Fahlén, Magnus Henrekson, and Mats Nilsson (2026) present a harsh critique of the EU's and UK's electrification-centric decarbonization strategy in their study entitled "In Pursuit of the Green Transition—Electricity at Any Cost?". By virtue of empirical analysis and comparative scenario modeling, they conclude that increasing shares of intermittent renewables are strongly and robustly associated with higher system costs, price volatility, and uninternalized externalities.

Their approach is grounded in recent system studies and cross-country cost comparisons (e.g., Manzolini et al. 2024; Idel 2022; Ueckerdt et al. 2013). They underline that advocates of weather-dependent electricity sources generally base their argument on the fact that the average cost per unit of electricity generated by a land-based wind mill or solar panel is quite low. However, this disregards system-level costs caused by the combined effect of intermittency and dispersed production. Adding these integration costs undermines the case for wind and solar power. Integration costs rise at an accelerated rate when a significant and growing share of electricity comes from intermittent sources. Integration costs include costs caused by the mismatch between supply and demand over time, balancing costs, and grid infrastructure costs. There are also a number of aspects that are seldom properly reckoned with such as far greater space requirements (several orders of magnitude), noise and microparticle pollution, disturbed and compressed biotopes, reduction in property values, greater need for metals and other materials in grids, and the need for extensive storage facilities.

The authors' analysis directly challenges the EU, individual member countries such as Spain and Germany as well as the UK, regarding their mission-oriented energy policies that neglect the operational and economic complexity involved. The authors also caution that "renewable" should not be conflated with "sustainable," contending that full system stability, cost, and societal impacts must be analytically integrated. Their evaluation shows that only scenarios prioritizing dispatchable resources and baseload power, chiefly nuclear power, consistently reconcile climate targets with reliability and affordability.

Green Industrial Megaprojects

In "Green Industrial Megaprojects: A Welfare Economics Perspective," Per-Olov Johansson and Bengt Kriström (2026) offer a stark and much-needed reminder that economics is not about money or markets for their own sake. The ultimate goal of economic activity is social welfare; prosperity only matters when it translates into better lives in terms of health, opportunity, dignity, and security. By means of cost–benefit analysis (CBA), they make a critical evaluation of large-scale, state-supported green transition projects. The authors emphasize the normative underpinnings of CBA, drawing attention to Hume's Law (an "ought" cannot be derived from an "is") and the need for explicit value judgments in policymaking. They highlight well-documented problems in the governance of megaprojects, including optimism bias, lack of transparent evaluation, and insufficient analysis of trade-offs.

Using the hydrogen-based steel plant investment in Boden in northern Sweden as a case study, the authors apply state-of-the-art general equilibrium CBA to the project and conclude that the plant may generate private profits under certain favorable conditions but its net social benefits are unlikely to be positive, given that the EU Emissions Trading System already internalizes most emissions-related costs. Without rejecting climate action or industrial policy more broadly, the analysis underscores the necessity for rigorous, transparent evaluation before committing large public resources to green industrial projects.

Hydrogen and Steel

In the essay "HYBRIT: A Hubristic Hydrogen-Based Steel Project," Magnus Henrekson (2026) analyzes a huge project aiming to make sponge iron production fossil-free by using hydrogen produced from renewable electricity. The project in question is HYBRIT, a high-profile Swedish initiative led by the state-owned mining company LKAB. Framed as a cornerstone of Sweden's green transition and the EU Green Deal, HYBRIT was promoted as a potential game-changer for global CO_2 reduction, yet it faced major technological, economic, and infrastructural hurdles.

HYBRIT's feasibility rested on a set of highly uncertain assumptions—including sustained low electricity prices, elevated carbon costs, and the availability of large-scale hydrogen storage—while simultaneously facing competition from international green steel producers and exerting pressure on northern Sweden's energy system.

In the end, growing criticism and shifting priorities prompted LKAB to indefinitely shelve its sponge iron ambitions and redirect its focus toward high-grade iron ore and rare earth metals extraction. The case illustrates how political enthusiasm can outpace technological and economic realities, reinforcing the need for independent and rigorous evaluation of large-scale green industrial projects.

Northvolt's Bankruptcy

In "Explaining Northvolt's Bankruptcy and the Dilemma of Green Deals," Christian Sandström (2026) examines the unintended consequences of green industrial policies by analyzing the bankruptcy of Northvolt, Europe's largest initiative to establish an independent battery manufacturing facility. Founded in 2017 and growing rapidly to nearly 6,000 employees by 2023, Northvolt struggled to scale production and remained dependent on Chinese suppliers—undermining EU's ambition of strategic autonomy. In March 2025, the company filed for bankruptcy.

The study identifies four main factors behind Northvolt's collapse: distortions in corporate incentives created by generous public support; excessive risk-taking; a fundamental mismatch between the long-time horizons needed to build industrial capabilities and the political and financial pressures for rapid expansion; and pervasive cognitive biases. The latter were amplified by a deeply entrenched societal consensus in Sweden on the urgency of the green transition.

Taken together, the case illustrates how even the most ambitious Green Deals can unintentionally foster systemic vulnerabilities in high-tech industrial ventures.

The Planetary Diet

In their study "The Planetary Diet: An Illusory Recipe," Stefan Hellstrand and Johan Gärdebo (2026) critically examine the Swedish Food Agency's 2025 dietary guidelines, which advocate a transition from meat and dairy to plant-based proteins in line with the global "planetary diet" framework. The authors argue that the guidelines rest on a weak scientific foundation and its application would compromise food security and agricultural stability in Sweden and elsewhere, particularly during geopolitical crises. It highlights the bureaucratic and ideological momentum underpinning the green transition, driven by the European Union, NGOs, a growing number of agenda-driven environmental research institutes, and academic counseling bodies such as the Swedish Climate Policy Council, which advocate phasing out animal husbandry despite its historical importance in Nordic diets.

The guidelines' proposed reductions in red meat (65–82%) and dairy (54–70%) consumption risk increasing import dependence and biodiversity loss. By contrasting historical Nordic dietary practices, shaped by harsh climatic conditions, with the planetary diet's ambitious targets, the authors contend that such policies are infeasible and could provoke political unrest, as evidenced by farmer protests and rising populist movements across Europe. The study criticizes the Swedish Climate Policy Council's reliance on the planetary boundaries framework, arguing that it overlooks practical agricultural constraints and risks exacerbating food insecurity and societal instability.

Italy's Superbonus

In their essay "Italy's Superbonus and the Capture of Climate Policy by Modern Monetary Theory," Luciano Capone and Carlo Stagnaro (2026) analyze how Italy implemented an environmental policy that produced the largest budget deficit in Europe since the Second World War. The program allowed households to claim a 110% tax credit for expenses incurred in improving the energy efficiency of buildings and enhancing their seismic resilience. These tax credits were fully transferable to third parties, such as construction companies or financial institutions. In total, the policy generated costs amounting to approximately EUR 220 billion, equivalent to about 10% of a single year's GDP, while delivering limited environmental benefits and fostering widespread tax fraud.

Capone and Stagnaro trace the origins of this policy to a small network of economists inspired by Modern Monetary Theory (MMT), a heterodox school of thought asserting that governments issuing their own currency are not financially constrained by taxation or borrowing, since they can create money to fund public spending. According to the authors, this group gained significant influence within the Italian government in 2020 and was able to advance the Superbonus policy in subsequent years. The measure was further facilitated by the temporary suspension of the European Union's fiscal rules during the pandemic, which effectively removed traditional budgetary constraints and enabled unprecedented fiscal expansion.

Part III: Alternative Paths Forward

Part III of this volume explores alternative approaches to reconciling economic growth with environmental sustainability. Under this heading, the three essays are only briefly summarized. Policy recommendations are further elaborated toward the end of this introductory essay.

In "A Silent Transition: Growth with Less Environmental Weight," Jonas Grafström (2026) presents empirical evidence showing how Western economies have historically combined environmental concerns with economic development. By reviewing data on emissions, energy use, and natural resource consumption, he argues that sustainability can be achieved through gradual, evolutionary change rather than through sweeping "green transition" initiatives.

Ernest Mund's (2026) essay, "Nuclear Technology Transition towards SMR and Generation-IV," examines technological advances in nuclear power, suggesting that some of the traditional risks and costs may be mitigated by next-generation reactor designs.

The section concludes with Jacob Hjortsberg's (2026) contribution, "'State-ification' of the Entrepreneur—or 'Entrepreneurialization' of the State? How Singapore Challenges both Mazzucato and Her Critics." Taking a broader institutional perspective, Hjortsberg argues that while entrepreneurial states are desirable, current efforts to create them often devolve into state-centric entrepreneurship. Drawing on evidence from Singapore, he outlines alternative ways of structuring entrepreneurial states.

Eight Takeaways

Having summarized the contributions of the volume, this section integrates and synthesizes the empirical findings in light of the theoretical perspectives outlined earlier—public choice, evolutionary economics, and behavioral political economy. Taken together, these lenses illuminate why mission-oriented policies so often fall short of their stated ambitions and provide the analytical foundation for the seven interrelated factors identified in the prequel to this volume (Henrekson et al. 2024a). The empirical studies in Part II demonstrate that these seven factors are equally applicable to Green Deals:

1. Wicked problems cannot be solved through missions.
2. Politicians and government agencies are not exempt from self-interest.
3. Missions distort competition.
4. Policymakers lack information to design missions efficiently.
5. Missions are subject to rent-seeking and mission capture.
6. Government support distorts incentives and creates moral hazard.
7. Missions ignore opportunity costs.

After discussing these seven takeaways and applying them to Green Deals, we then address an additional eighth aspect, namely the behavioral dimension of Green Deals.

Wicked Problems Cannot Be Solved Through Missions

Climate change and related environmental challenges are "wicked" in the sense Rittel and Webber (1973) and Richard Nelson (1977) used the term, referring broadly to complex and systemic problems. There are no simple solutions to this type of problem. Nelson and co-authors argued that moonshot policies "are not the right models for new programs aimed at the challenges we now face" (Foray et al. 2012, p. 1697).

The *Energiewende* (Deshaies 2026) and the premature shutdown of nuclear power in Germany (Schnellenbach 2026) can be regarded as green missions aimed to address a complex problem. The social and economic consequences are substantial, including declining industrial competitiveness, dependency on Russian gas, and sharply increased electricity costs. At the same time, climate change remains a global challenge where Germany's relative reduction of emissions is insignificant compared to increases taking place elsewhere, especially in China and India.

Politicians and Government Agencies Are not Exempt from Self-Interest

Political decision-making, much like business, is shaped by self-interest. The Northvolt case (Sandström 2026) illustrates this dynamic where former cabinet ministers served as advisors and shareholders in the company, with one moving on to a senior post within the European Union, while others became registered lobbyists for firms tied to the green transition. Similarly, the ethanol car case (Björnemalm and Sandström 2026) reveals how a serving cabinet minister maintained close ties to interest groups that profited from expanding the domestic ethanol industry.

Missions Distort Competition

Baumol (2005) characterizes mature capitalism as a system of oligopolistic competition, where a limited number of firms in each sector strive to outperform one another through innovation and renewal. Green Deals, however, often disrupt this process by privileging certain technologies and by disproportionately favoring some firms over others.

Renewables such as solar and wind power, for instance, have received substantial public support without being required to internalize all associated costs (Fahlén et al. 2026). At the same time, political decisions—rather than market dynamics—drove the premature closure of all nuclear power plants in Germany and half of those in Sweden, sidelining the underlying economic competitiveness of alternative energy sources.

Policymakers Lack Information to Design Missions Efficiently

As Cheang (2026) observes, mission-oriented innovation policies are, by design, anything but modest. They inevitably take the form of large-scale initiatives, carrying the inherent risk of being implemented with insufficient regard for prevailing conditions. Alves (2024) further emphasizes that building the necessary capabilities is a slow process, whereas missions are often launched in an atmosphere of urgency. This mismatch heightens the risk that mission-driven resources will be out of sync with labor markets, supply chains, and other critical institutional factors.

The empirical cases analyzed in this volume also indicate that policymakers do not possess the information required to craft Green Deals properly. One telling example is Hellstrand and Gärdebo's (2026) analysis of how "the planetary diet" is fed into the government bureaucracy and down the road is translated into misinformed and harmful policy guidelines.

This dynamic is also evident in the persistent quality problems that plagued Northvolt (Sandström 2026), as well as in the HYBRIT project to produce fossil-free sponge iron (Henrekson 2026). At full scale, HYBRIT would have required as much electricity as the entire Finnish economy. Yet, despite well-known challenges associated with large-scale hydrogen use, the project attracted enormous political prestige in both Stockholm and Brussels.

Missions Are Subject to Rent-Seeking and Mission Capture

Several of the empirical contributions illustrate how special interest groups capture Green Deals, shaping them in ways that will benefit themselves but may prove unsustainable both economically and environmentally.

The ethanol case (Björnemalm and Sandström 2026) demonstrates how the Federation of Swedish Farmers successfully lobbied for political backing. Parliamentary alliances, combined with EU regulations, gave ethanol a strong push, allowing social and political forces to override underlying technological and economic realities.

As Muldoon and Yonai (2026) point out, idealists and rent-seekers often find themselves aligned. They highlight the unlikely coalition of environmentalists and oil companies in the United States, both of which sought to undermine nuclear power.

Such dynamics are common in the context of Green Deals. In consensus-driven environments, rent-seeking tends to proceed largely unchallenged, with few voices willing to question initiatives—even when opportunity costs are high or projects may yield negative social value (Johansson and Kriström 2026).

Government Support Distorts Incentives and Creates Moral Hazard

When risks are increasingly borne by the public sector through government loans, credit guarantees, or subsidies for innovation, it may give rise to moral hazard. Firms will take on more risk because they know that another party will bear a large share of the costs of those risks. This effect is illustrated both by the Northvolt bankruptcy (Sandström 2026) and attempts to make steel using hydrogen (Johansson and Kriström 2026).

Missions Ignore Opportunity Costs

Several of the large-scale efforts toward sustainability described in this volume illustrate how opportunity costs are frequently ignored.

The financial, physical, and intellectual resources devoted to, e.g., hydrogen could have been allocated to alternative technologies or policies with greater potential impact. Upon assessing the effectiveness of hydrogen-supporting policies, these opportunity costs tend to be overlooked. By overlooking the opportunity costs, policymakers risk misallocating scarce resources and undermining the effectiveness of sustainability strategies.

Behavioral Aspects

Several of the empirical contributions in this volume highlight the importance of behavioral factors in explaining the dysfunctions of Green Deals. While numerous well-documented biases may apply, three stand out:

1. Rational irrationality, individuals rationally decide to hold beliefs that are not congruent with facts when the individual cost of irrationality is zero.
2. Expressive political behavior, actions are driven more by the desire to express identity, emotions, or moral beliefs than to achieve practical political outcomes, for example, voting, protesting, or posting to signal values rather than change policy.
3. Availability cascades, statements come to feel truer if they are often repeated (Schnellenbach 2024).

Together, these three biases help explain why voters and policymakers adopt policies that are ultimately misguided. Germany's premature closure of 23 nuclear power plants, paired with an increased reliance on intermittent energy sources, offers a striking example (Deshaies 2026).

These behavioral dynamics also shed light on the rapid political ascent of HYBRIT (Henrekson 2026) and the hydrogen-based steel mill project in Boden. As Johansson and Kriström (2026) observe, megaprojects are frequently shaped by optimism bias, with opportunity costs insufficiently weighed. Moreover, climate change and other environmental challenges have created a powerful "loss frame" (Tversky and Kahneman 1981), in which the perception of existential threat serves to justify the pursuit of large-scale projects whose practical feasibility may be limited.

Alternative Paths and Policy Recommendations

Having pointed out a collection of interrelated factors which explain the ongoing failure of Green Deal policies in Europe, this collective volume also points out alternative paths toward the ultimate goal of attaining carbon neutrality. These alternatives do not stray from the ambition to adhere to sustainability in the original wider sense that includes economic and social aspects (United Nations 1987).

Crafting effective sustainability policies ultimately requires aligning policy design with the dilemmas identified in this volume. Behavioral biases, evolutionary dynamics, and public choice challenges such as rent-seeking are not reasons to abandon environmental policy. Instead, they represent constraints that must be acknowledged and integrated into policy design.

More from Less?

As Grafström (2026) documents, environmental improvements can indeed be achieved alongside economic growth. Between 1990 and 2021, CO_2 emissions in the EU fell by 28% while the economy expanded by more than 50%. Over the same period, emissions of major pollutants such as lead (−95%), sulfur dioxide (−93%), and arsenic (−90%) declined sharply. Notably, electricity consumption has remained largely unchanged since 1990, even as the EU economy continued to grow.

These findings align with McAfee's (2019) argument, where he shows that the United States has undergone a process of dematerialization over the past half-century. McAfee identifies four interrelated drivers of how greater wealth can be generated from fewer resources, including capitalism, technological innovation, consumer responsibility, and regulation.

Capitalism, understood as a system of private, profit-maximizing firms, makes resource use costly and thus incentivizes efficiency. For instance, while a soft drink aluminum can weighed 85 g in the 1950s, today it weighs only about 13 g, an 85% reduction in material use for the same product. Similarly, design and material advances have reduced the raw plastic in a PET bottle by 80–85% over the past five decades.

Consumer demand has likewise played a central role. A prime example is how growing public awareness of the dangers of chlorofluorocarbons (CFCs) spurred demonstrations and pressure campaigns, contributing to the eventual global ban (Dugoua 2025).

The Role of Modesty

While each of the examples above represents significant improvement, they have unfolded incrementally over extended periods. The four factors identified by McAfee—capitalism, technological innovation, regulation, and consumer demand—have co-evolved in these cases. Similar dynamics are evident in the sharp reductions of pollutants such as sulfur dioxide (Schmalensee and Stavins 2009). In the case of leaded petroleum, for example, strong industry resistance delayed regulation, while consumer activism and regulatory agencies ultimately drove change (Newell and Rogers 2003).

As Cheang (2026) observes, mission-oriented innovation policies cannot afford to be modest in their implementation. Yet this very ambition carries the risk of drifting out of alignment with the technological and economic realities of a given context. By contrast, the approach outlined by McAfee does not rest on the government declaring sweeping visions such as net-zero targets for CO_2 emissions. This does not mean that public action toward sustainability is unnecessary. Rather, its role is to reinforce, guide, and complement the evolutionary interplay of markets, technology, regulation, and consumer behavior.

Adapting to Global Trends

Because many environmental challenges transcend national borders, no single country or even the EU can afford to diverge significantly from other major economies. This is especially true for CO_2 emissions. In 2023–2024, the EU-27 accounted for just 6% of global emissions, despite representing 14% of the global economy. Efforts in Europe to cut emissions will therefore have only limited global impact unless other regions follow suit.

Nor can the EU, the United States, or China stray too far from the rest of the world in emission controls, particularly if ambitious policies fail to deliver on their parallel promises of prosperity and industrial competitiveness.

Investments in Nuclear Power

An implication of Mund's analysis is that the EU and its member states should consider greater long-term investment in nuclear power. With proper maintenance, nuclear reactors built today are expected to generate electricity for close to a century, which is a time horizon well-suited to the kind of durable infrastructure investment required for the energy transition. This is particularly important given the substantial political risks associated with nuclear energy. In countries such as Sweden and Germany, reactors have been shut down prematurely as a result of political decisions rather than technical or economic considerations.

At the same time, the findings in this volume provide a cautionary perspective on such investments. Nuclear projects are not immune to the same challenges highlighted throughout this volume, including political capture, rent-seeking, optimism bias, and shifting societal preferences. These risks underscore the need to weigh carefully the governance and institutional conditions under which large-scale nuclear investments are undertaken.

Conclusion

Across Europe and the wider Western world, concerns are growing about the long-term competitiveness of mature economies. Green Deals have been launched in many countries with the ambition of combining sustainable development with continued economic growth.

Yet, six years into the EU's Green Deal, it has become increasingly evident that large-scale efforts to transform Europe into a clean, fossil-free, and prosperous economy are not delivering as intended. The contributions in this volume explore why this is the case and consider what alternative approaches might be more effective.

Our review of Green Deals and the academic literature underpinning them shows that these policy efforts have been shaped above all by perspectives rooted in innovation systems and mission-oriented approaches. Because this literature has paid limited attention to the dynamics of policy failure (Kärnä et al. 2023), policymakers have often been guided by scholars who placed considerable faith in government intervention while neglecting the constraints and challenges such interventions entail.

This collective volume introduces three complementary perspectives that help explain why Green Deals so often fall short of their ambitions: evolutionary economics (Cheang 2026), political economy and public choice (Muldoon and Yonai 2026), and behavioral economics (Schnellenbach 2026).

Taken together, these strands of literature provide much of the explanation for why Green Deals have failed to deliver on their promises. The empirical contributions in this volume cover a wide range of cases, such as the early ethanol car bubble (Björnemalm and Sandström 2026), Germany's *Energiewende* (Deshaies 2026), the hidden costs of wind power (Fahlén et al. 2026), hydrogen-based steel and iron ore projects (Johansson and Kriström 2026; Henrekson 2026), the Northvolt bankruptcy (Sandström 2026), the planetary diet (Hellstrand and Gärdebo 2026), and Italy's Superbonus (Capone and Stagnaro 2026).

Part III turns to possible alternative paths forward. It discusses more conventional approaches to environmental policy (Grafström 2026), examines the long-term potential of nuclear technology (Mund 2026), and considers alternative institutional models for cultivating a genuinely entrepreneurial state (Hjortsberg 2026). The contributions gathered under this heading are more limited in scope and are intended primarily as a platform for comparing and contrasting different policy approaches. Given the limited scholarly attention thus far to the shortcomings of existing Green Deals, an inquiry into the mechanisms underlying these disappointing outcomes is both timely and essential.

References

Aiginger, K., & Rodrik, D. (2020). Rebirth of industrial policy and an agenda for the twenty-first century. *Journal of Industry, Competition and Trade*, *20*(2), 189–207. https://doi.org/10.1007/s10842-019-00322-3

Alves, A. C. (2024). The cost of missions: The case of shipbuilding in Brazil. In M. Henrekson, C. Sandström, & M. Stenkula (Eds.), *Moonshots and the New Industrial Policy: Questioning the Mission Economy* (pp. 169–189). Cham: Springer. https://doi.org/10.1007/978-3-031-49196-2_10

Arrow, K. J. (1962). Economic welfare and the allocation of resources for invention. In R. R. Nelson (Ed.), *The Rate and Direction of Inventive Activity: Economic and Social Factors* (pp. 609–626). Princeton, NJ: Princeton University Press. https://doi.org/10.1007/978-1-349-15486-9_13

Baumol, W. J. (2005). Education for innovation: Entrepreneurial breakthroughs versus corporate incremental improvements. In A. B. Jaffe, J. Lerner, & S. Stern (Eds.), *Innovation Policy and the Economy, Volume 5* (pp. 33–56). Cambridge, MA: MIT Press. https://doi.org/10.1086/ipe.5.25056170

Bergkvist, J. E., Moodysson, J., & Sandström, C. (2022). Third-generation innovation policy: System transformation or reinforcing business as usual? In K. Wennberg & C. Sandström (Eds.), *Questioning the Entrepreneurial State: Status-quo, Pitfalls, and the Need for Credible Innovation Policy* (pp. 201–217). Cham: Springer. https://doi.org/10.1007/978-3-030-94273-1_11

Björnemalm, R., & Sandström, C. (2026). Exploring failed green innovation policy: The rise and fall of ethanol cars in Sweden 2003–2015. In M. Henrekson, C. Sandström, & M. Stenkula (Eds.), *A Green Entrepreneurial State? Exploring the Pitfalls of Green Deals* (pp. 113–130). Cham: Springer.

Brennan, G., & Lomasky, L. (1993). *Democracy and Decision: The Pure Theory of Electoral Preference*. Cambridge: Cambridge University Press.

Caplan, B. (2007). *The Myth of the Rational Voter*. Princeton, NJ: Princeton University Press.

Capone, L., & Stagnaro, C. (2026). Italy's Superbonus and the capture of climate policy by Modern Monetary Theory. In M. Henrekson, C. Sandström, & M. Stenkula (Eds.), *A Green Entrepreneurial State? Exploring the Pitfalls of Green Deals* (pp. 241–255). Cham: Springer.

Chang, H.-J. (2006). *The East Asian Development Experience: The Miracle, the Crisis and the Future*. London and New York, NY: Zed Books.

Cheang, B. (2026). The incoherence of modest industrial policy. In M. Henrekson, C. Sandström, & M. Stenkula (Eds.), *A Green Entrepreneurial State? Exploring the Pitfalls of Green Deals* (pp. 61–80). Cham: Springer.

Colander, D., & Kupers, R. (2016). *Complexity and the Art of Public Policy: Solving Society's Problems from the Bottom Up*. Princeton, NJ: Princeton University Press.
Deshaies, M. (2026). The German *Energiewende*: A Green Deal template or planned failure? In M. Henrekson, C. Sandström, & M. Stenkula (Eds.), *A Green Entrepreneurial State? Exploring the Pitfalls of Green Deals* (pp. 131–147). Cham: Springer.
Downs, A. (1957). *An Economic Theory of Democracy*. New York, NY: Harper.
Draghi, M. (2024). *The Future of European Competitiveness: A Competitiveness Strategy for Europe*. Brussels: European Commission.
Dugoua, E. (2025). Induced innovation and international environmental agreements: Evidence from the ozone regime. *Review of Economics and Statistics, 107*(6), 1–18. https://doi.org/10.1162/rest_a_01398
European Commission (2019a). The European Green Deal. COM(2019) 640 final. Brussels. https://eur-lex.europa.eu/legal-content/EN/TXT/?uri=CELEX:52019DC0640
European Commission (2019b). Commission launches work on major research and innovation missions for cancer, climate, oceans and soil. July 4. https://research-and-innovation.ec.europa.eu/news/all-research-and-innovation-news/commission-launches-work-major-research-and-innovation-missions-cancer-climate-oceans-and-soil-2019-07-04_en
European Commission (2020a). Sustainable Europe Investment Plan: European Green Deal Investment Plan. COM(2020) 21 final. Brussels. https://eur-lex.europa.eu/legal-content/EN/TXT/?uri=CELEX:52020DC0021
European Commission (2020b). A hydrogen strategy for a climate-neutral Europe. COM(2020) 301 final. Brussels. https://eur-lex.europa.eu/legal-content/EN/TXT/?uri=CELEX:52020DC0301
European Commission (2020c). An EU strategy to harness the potential of offshore renewable energy for a climate neutral future. COM(2020) 741 final. Brussels. https://eur-lex.europa.eu/legal-content/EN/TXT/?uri=CELEX:52020DC0741
European Commission (2022). REPowerEU Plan. COM(2022) 230 final. Brussels. https://eur-lex.europa.eu/legal-content/EN/TXT/?uri=CELEX:52022DC0230
European Commission (2023a). Offshore Renewable Energy Strategy—Progress report. COM(2023) 657 final. Brussels. https://energy.ec.europa.eu/publications/offshore-renewable-energy-strategy-progress-report_en
European Commission (2023b). Regulation (EU) 2023/851 of the European Parliament and of the Council of 19 April 2023 amending Regulation (EU) 2019/631 as regards strengthening the CO_2 emission performance standards for new passenger cars and new light commercial vehicles. OJ L 110, 25.4.2023. https://eur-lex.europa.eu/legal-content/EN/TXT/?uri=CELEX:32023R0851
European Commission (2024a). European Green Deal: Commission sets out 2040 climate target and opens a debate on the future policy framework. COM(2024) 63 final. Brussels. https://eur-lex.europa.eu/legal-content/EN/TXT/?uri=CELEX:52024DC0063
European Commission (2024b). New European Bauhaus: Investment Guidelines. https://new-european-bauhaus.europa.eu/system/files/2024-07/NEB%20Investment%20Guidelines.pdf
European Commission (2025). Horizon Europe 2028–2034. https://commission.europa.eu/document/download/a0ecf3f6-a964-4e00-9cb3-4be28833b386_en?filename=MFF_HORIZON%20EUROPE_v9.pdf
Fahlén, P., Henrekson, M., & Nilsson, M. (2026). In pursuit of the green transition—Electricity at any cost? In M. Henrekson, C. Sandström, & M. Stenkula (Eds.), *A Green Entrepreneurial State? Exploring the Pitfalls of Green Deals* (pp. 149–172). Cham: Springer.
Foray, D., Mowery, D. C., & Nelson, R. R. (2012). Public R&D and social challenges: What lessons from mission R&D programs? *Research Policy, 41*(10), 1697–1702. https://doi.org/10.1016/j.respol.2012.07.011
Freeman, C. (1987). *Technology Policy and Economic Performance: Lessons from Japan*. London: Pinter.
Geels, F. W. (2002). Technological transitions as evolutionary reconfiguration processes: A multi-level perspective and a case-study. *Research Policy, 31*(8–9), 1257–1274. https://doi.org/10.1016/S0048-7333(02)00062-8

Geels, F. W. (2004). From sectoral systems of innovation to socio-technical systems: Insights about dynamics and change from sociology and institutional theory. *Research Policy, 33*(6–7), 897–920. https://doi.org/10.1016/j.respol.2004.01.015

Grafström, J. (2026). A silent transition: Growth with less environmental weight. In M. Henrekson, C. Sandström, & M. Stenkula (Eds.), *A Green Entrepreneurial State? Exploring the Pitfalls of Green Deals* (pp. 259–271). Cham: Springer.

Granholm, J. (2022). Testimony of Secretary Jennifer M. Granholm, U.S. Department of Energy. Before the U.S. House Committee on appropriations subcommittee on energy and water development, April 28, 2022. https://www.congress.gov/117/meeting/house/114639/witnesses/HHRG-117-AP10-Wstate-GranholmJ-20220428.pdf

Hausmann, R., & Rodrik, D. (2006). Doomed to choose: Industrial policy as predicament. Working Paper. Cambridge, MA: Kennedy School of Government, Harvard University. https://drodrik.scholars.harvard.edu/sites/g/files/omnuum7106/files/dani-rodrik/files/doomed-to-choose.pdf

Hayek, F. A. (1967). The theory of complex phenomena: A precocious play on the epistemology of complexity. In *Studies in Philosophy, Politics and Economics* (pp. 22–42). London: Routledge.

Hekkert, M. P., Suurs, R. A. A., Negro, S. O., Kuhlmann, S., & Smits, R. E. H. M. (2007). Functions of innovation systems: A new approach for analyzing technological change. *Technological Forecasting and Social Change, 74*(4), 413–432. https://doi.org/10.1016/j.techfore.2006.03.002

Hellstrand, S., & Gärdebo, J. (2026). The planetary diet: An illusory recipe. In M. Henrekson, C. Sandström, & M. Stenkula (Eds.), *A Green Entrepreneurial State? Exploring the Pitfalls of Green Deals* (pp. 219–240). Cham: Springer.

Henrekson, M. (2026). HYBRIT: A hubristic hydrogen-based steel project. In M. Henrekson, C. Sandström, & M. Stenkula (Eds.), *A Green Entrepreneurial State? Exploring the Pitfalls of Green Deals* (pp. 187–201). Cham: Springer.

Henrekson, M., Kärnä, A., & Sanandaji, S. (2022). Schumpeterian entrepreneurship: Coveted by policymakers but impervious to top-down policymaking. *Journal of Evolutionary Economics, 32*(3), 867–890. https://doi.org/10.1007/s00191-022-00761-y

Henrekson, M., Sandström, C., & Stenkula, M. (Eds.) (2024a). *Moonshots and the New Industrial Policy: Questioning the Mission Economy*. Cham: Springer. https://doi.org/10.1007/978-3-031-49196-2

Henrekson, M., Sandström, C., & Stenkula, M. (2024b). Seven reasons why mission-oriented innovation policies seldom work in practice. *Economic Affairs, 44*(2), 354–362. https://doi.org/10.1111/ecaf.12654

Hirschman, A. O. (1958). *The Strategy of Economic Development*. New Haven, CT: Yale University Press.

Hjortsberg, J. (2026). State-ification of the entrepreneur—or entrepreneurialization of the state? How Singapore challenges both Mazzucato and her critics. In M. Henrekson, C. Sandström, & M. Stenkula (Eds.), *A Green Entrepreneurial State? Exploring the Pitfalls of Green Deals* (pp. 285–302). Cham: Springer.

Idel, R. (2022). Levelized Full System Costs of Electricity. *Energy, 259*(November), Article 124905. https://doi.org/10.1016/j.energy.2022.124905

Jacobsson, S., & Bergek, A. (2006). Innovation system analyses and sustainability transitions. *Environmental Policy and Governance, 16*(6), 297–307. https://doi.org/10.1002/eet.425

Johansson, P.-O., & Kriström, B. (2026). Green industrial megaprojects: A welfare economics perspective. In M. Henrekson, C. Sandström, & M. Stenkula (Eds.), *A Green Entrepreneurial State? Exploring the Pitfalls of Green Deals* (pp. 173–185). Cham: Springer.

Kantor, S., & Whalley, A. (2025). Moonshot: Public R&D and growth. *American Economic Review, 115*(9), 2891–2925. https://doi.org/10.1257/aer.20220540

Kärnä, A., Karlsson, J., Engberg, E., & Svensson, P. (2023). Political failure: A missing piece in innovation policy analysis. *Economics of Innovation and New Technology, 32*(7), 1037–1068. https://doi.org/10.1080/10438599.2022.2070843

Kattel, R., Mazzucato, M., Algers, J., & Mikheeva, O. (2021). The green giant: New industrial strategy for Norway. Report commissioned by Manifest Centre for Societal Analysis. London: UCL Institute for Innovation and Public Purpose, IIPP Policy Report (PR 21/01).

Kirchherr, J., Hartley, K., & Tukker, A. (2023). Missions and mission-oriented innovation policy for sustainability: A review and critical reflection. *Environmental Innovation and Societal Transitions*, *47*(June), Article 100721. https://doi.org/10.1016/j.eist.2023.100721

Kline, S. J., & Rosenberg, N. (1986). An overview of innovation. In R. Landau & N. Rosenberg (Eds.), *The Positive Sum Strategy: Harnessing Technology for Economic Growth* (pp. 275–306). Washington, DC: National Academies Press.

Kuran, T., & Sunstein, C. R. (1999). Availability cascades and risk regulation. *Stanford Law Review*, *51*(4), 683–768. https://doi.org/10.2307/1229439

Kuznets, S. (1971). *Economic Growth of Nations: Total Output and Production Structure*. Cambridge, MA: Harvard University Press.

Lin, J. Y., & Monga, C. (2017). *Beating the Odds: Jump-Starting Developing Countries*. Princeton, NJ: Princeton University Press.

Lundvall, B.-Å. (1992). *National Systems of Innovation: Towards a Theory of Innovation and Interactive Learning*. London: Pinter.

Manzolini, G., Binotti, M., Gentile, G., Picotti, G., Pilotti, L., & Cholette, M. E. (2024). Actual cost of electricity: An economic index to overcome levelized cost of electricity limits. *iScience*, *27*, Article 109897. https://doi.org/10.1016/j.isci.2024.109897

Mazzucato, M. (2013). *The Entrepreneurial State: Debunking Public vs. Private Sector Myths*. London: Anthem Press.

Mazzucato, M. (2018a). Mission-oriented innovation policies: Challenges and opportunities. *Industrial and Corporate Change*, *27*(5), 803–815. https://doi.org/10.1093/icc/dty034

Mazzucato, M. (2018b). *Mission-Oriented Research & Innovation in the European Union: A Problem-Solving Approach to Fuel Innovation-Led Growth*. Luxembourg: Publications Office of the European Union. https://op.europa.eu/en/publication-detail/-/publication/5b2811d1-16be-11e8-9253-01aa75ed71a1/language-en

Mazzucato, M. (2019). Europe's Green Deal could be the most important mission of our generation. *UCL News*, December. https://www.ucl.ac.uk/news/2019/dec/analysis-europes-green-deal-could-be-most-important-generation

Mazzucato, M. (2021). *Mission Economy: A Moonshot Guide to Changing Capitalism*. New York, NY: Harper Business.

Mazzucato, M. (2022). Financing the green new deal. *Nature Sustainability*, *5*, 93–94. https://doi.org/10.1038/s41893-021-00828-x

Mazzucato, M. (2023). Transformational change in Latin America and the Caribbean: A mission-oriented approach. Economic Commission for Latin America and the Caribbean (ECLA), UCL Institute for Innovation and Public Purpose, and German Agency for International Cooperation (GIZ).

Mazzucato, M. (2025). Principles for an inclusive and sustainable global economy: A discussion paper for the G20. London: UCL Institute for Innovation and Public Purpose. https://www.ucl.ac.uk/bartlett/ucl-institute-innovation-and-public-purpose/principles-inclusive-and-sustainable-global-economy-discussion-paper-g20

Mazzucato, M., & McPherson, M. (2018). The Green New Deal: A bold mission-oriented approach. London: UCL Institute for Innovation and Public Purpose Policy Brief (IIPP PB 04). https://www.ucl.ac.uk/bartlett/sites/bartlett/files/iipp-pb-04-the-green-new-deal-17-12-2018_0.pdf

McAfee, A. (2019). *More from Less: The Surprising Story of How We Learned to Prosper Using Fewer Resources—and What Happens Next*. New York, NY: Scribner Books.

Muldoon, J., & Yonai, D. K. (2023). A wrong but seductive idea: Public choice and the entrepreneurial state. *Journal of the International Council for Small Business*, *4*(4), 1–11. https://doi.org/10.1080/26437015.2023.2182730

Muldoon, J., & Yonai, D. K. (2026). Raiders of the entrepreneurial state: A Baptist and Bootlegger analysis. In M. Henrekson, C. Sandström, & M. Stenkula (Eds.), *A Green Entrepreneurial State? Exploring the Pitfalls of Green Deals* (pp. 81–91). Cham: Springer.

Mund, E. (2026). Nuclear technology transition towards SMR and Generation-IV. In M. Henrekson, C. Sandström, & M. Stenkula (Eds.), *A Green Entrepreneurial State? Exploring the Pitfalls of Green Deals* Exploring (pp. 273–284). Cham: Springer.

Myrdal, G. (1970). *The Challenge of World Poverty*. New York, NY: Pantheon.

Nelson, R. R. (1959). The simple economics of basic scientific research. *Journal of Political Economy, 67*(3), 297–306. https://doi.org/10.1086/258177

Nelson, R. (1977). *The Moon and the Ghetto*. New York, NY: Norton.

Nelson, R. R. (1993). *National Innovation Systems: A Comparative Analysis*. Oxford: Oxford University Press.

Nelson, R. R., & Winter, S. G. (1982). *An Evolutionary Theory of Economic Change*. Cambridge, MA: Belknap Press of Harvard University Press.

Newell, R. G., & Rogers, K. (2003). The U.S. experience with the phasedown of lead in gasoline. Washington, DC: Resources for the Future.

OECD (1998). *New Rationale and Approaches in Technology and Innovation Policy*. Paris: OECD Publishing.

OECD (2021). The design and implementation of mission-oriented innovation policies: A new systemic policy approach to address societal challenges. OECD Science, Technology and Industry Policy Papers No. 100. Paris: OECD Directorate for Science, Technology and Innovation.

Page, S. E. (2011). *Diversity and Complexity*. Princeton, NJ: Princeton University Press.

Pennington, M. (2010). *Robust Political Economy: Classical Liberalism and the Future of Public Policy*. Aldershot, UK and Northampton, MA: Edward Elgar.

Rittel, H. W., & Webber, M. M. (1973). Dilemmas in a general theory of planning. *Policy Sciences, 4*(2), 155–169.

Rodrik, D. (2022). *An Industrial Policy for Good Jobs*. Washington, DC: The Hamilton Project, Brookings.

Rostow, W. W. (1960). *The Stages of Economic Growth: A Non-Communist Manifesto*. Cambridge: Cambridge University Press.

Sandström, C. (2026). Explaining Northvolt's bankruptcy and the dilemma of Green Deals. In M. Henrekson, C. Sandström, & M. Stenkula (Eds.), *A Green Entrepreneurial State? Exploring the Pitfalls of Green Deals* (pp. 203–217). Cham: Springer.

Schmalensee, R., & Stavins, R. N. (2013). The SO_2 allowance trading system: The ironic history of a grand policy experiment. *Journal of Economic Perspectives, 27*(1), 103–122. https://doi.org/10.1257/jep.27.1.103

Schnellenbach, J. (2024). A behavioral economics perspective on the entrepreneurial state and mission-oriented innovation policy. In M. Henrekson, C. Sandström, & M. Stenkula (Eds.), *Moonshots and the New Industrial Policy: Questioning the Mission Economy* (pp. 61–76). Cham: Springer. https://doi.org/10.1007/978-3-031-49196-2_4

Schnellenbach, J. (2026). Behavioral political economy and environmental policy: Explaining persistent deviations from efficient policies. In M. Henrekson, C. Sandström, & M. Stenkula (Eds.), *A Green Entrepreneurial State? Exploring the Pitfalls of Green Deals* (pp. 93–110). Cham: Springer.

Schot, J., & Steinmüller, W. E. (2018). Three frames for innovation policy: R&D, systems of innovation and transformative change. *Research Policy, 47*(9), 1554–1567. https://doi.org/10.1016/j.respol.2018.08.011

Schumpeter, J. A. (1934) *The Theory of Economic Development*. Cambridge, MA: Harvard University Press.

Scott, J. C. (1998). *Seeing Like a State: How Certain Schemes to Improve the Human Condition Have Failed*. New Haven, CT: Yale University Press.

Slovic, P. (1987). Perception of risk. *Science, 236*(4799), 280–285. https://doi.org/10.1126/science.3563507
Smith, A., & Yandle, B. (2014). *Bootleggers and Baptists: How Economic Forces and Moral Persuasion Interact to Shape Regulatory Politics*. Washington, DC: Cato Press.
Smith, K. (2000). Innovation as a systemic phenomenon: Rethinking the role of policy. *Enterprise and Innovation Management Studies, 1*(1), 73–102. https://doi.org/10.1080/146324400363536
Stenkula, M. (2026). Green deals around the world. In M. Henrekson, C. Sandström, & M. Stenkula (Eds.), *A Green Entrepreneurial State? Exploring the Pitfalls of Green Deals* (pp. 35–59). Cham: Springer.
Tversky, A., & Kahneman, D. (1981). The framing of decisions and the psychology of choice. *Science, 211*(4481), 453–458. https://doi.org/10.1126/science.7455683
Ueckerdt, F., Hirth, L., Luderer, G., & Edenhofer, O. (2013). System LCOE: What are the costs of variable renewables? *Energy, 63*(December), 61–75. https://doi.org/10.1016/j.energy.2013.10.072
United Nations (1987). *Report of the World Commission on Environment and Development: Our Common Future*. New York, NY: United Nations.
von der Leyen, U. (2019). Press remarks by President von der Leyen on the occasion of the adoption of the European Green Deal Communication. https://ec.europa.eu/commission/presscorner/detail/fr/speech_19_6749
Wennberg, K., & Sandström, C. (Eds.) (2022). *Questioning the Entrepreneurial State: Status-quo, Pitfalls, and the Need for Credible Innovation Policy*. Cham: Springer. https://doi.org/10.1007/978-3-030-94273-1
Woolthuis, R. K., Lankhuizen, M., & Gilsing, V. (2005). A system failure framework for innovation policy design. *Technovation, 25*(6), 609–619. https://doi.org/10.1016/j.technovation.2003.11.002
Yandle, B. (1983). Bootleggers and Baptists: The education of a regulatory economist. *Regulation, 7*(3), 12–16.

Magnus Henrekson is a Professor of Economics and Senior Research Fellow of the Research Institute of Industrial Economics (IFN) in Stockholm, Sweden. He resigned as CEO of IFN in 2020 after 15 years of service. Until 2009, he held the Jacob Wallenberg Research Chair in the Department of Economics at the Stockholm School of Economics. He is also a member of the Royal Swedish Academy of Engineering Sciences (IVA).

He received his PhD in 1990 from Gothenburg University with his dissertation *An Economic Analysis of Swedish Government Expenditure*. Throughout the 1990s, he conducted several projects that aimed to explain cross-country growth differences. Since the turn of the new millennium, his primary research focus is entrepreneurship economics and the institutional determinants of the business climate. In this area, he has published extensively in scientific journals and contributed several research surveys to *Handbooks* in the field of entrepreneurship.

In addition to his academic qualifications, Henrekson has extensive experience as an advisor, board member, and lecturer in many different contexts, in both the business and public sectors.

Christian Sandström is an Associate Professor of Technology Management from Chalmers University of Technology, where he also received his doctoral degree (2010). His research concerns innovation policy and the interplay between technological and institutional change. Sandström is one of the editors of *Questioning the Entrepreneurial State* (Springer) and *Moonshots and the New Industrial Policy* (Springer). He has published more than 30 papers in peer-reviewed academic journals such as *Business History*, *Small Business Economics*, *Technological Forecasting & Social Change,* and *Industry & Innovation.*

Sandström wrote his PhD thesis on the topic of disruptive innovation. He has been a visiting scholar at the University of Cambridge and ETH Zürich in Switzerland. Sandström has received several awards for his pedagogical skills and is a frequently invited public speaker on the topic of technological change and industrial transformation.

Mikael Stenkula is an Associate Professor of Economics and holds a PhD from the School of Economics and Management at Lund University. He received this degree in 2004 with his dissertation *Essays on Network Effects and Money*. After having worked for a year as a lecturer at Lund University, where he taught microeconomics, he joined the Research Institute of Industrial Economics (IFN) in 2005. His primary research areas are entrepreneurship economics and taxation. In addition to publishing in peer-reviewed journals, Stenkula has also co-edited several volumes, including *Moonshots and the New Industrial Policy* (Springer).

Stenkula has also taught at the Stockholm School of Economics and serves as the executive secretary of the award committee for the Global Award for Entrepreneurship Research, the foremost global award for research on entrepreneurship.

Theoretical Perspectives

Green Deals Around the World

Mikael Stenkula

Abstract This essay examines the rise of "Green Deals" as large-scale state-sponsored active industrial policies to accelerate a transition toward climate neutrality. Building on the concept of mission-oriented innovation policy (MOIP), it documents how environmental and active industrial policies have converged across advanced economies, reshaping the policy toolkit toward direct public investment and publicly supported investment. The essay provides detailed accounts of the European Union's Green Deal and the U.S. counterpart, situating them in the broader political economy of climate policy. It also highlights initiatives in the United Kingdom, Germany, and Sweden, which additionally illustrate Green Deal initiatives and how the latter national strategies adapt EU-level frameworks and institutional constraints. A comparative analysis underscores key differences between the EU's fragmented, case-by-case approach and the more streamlined but fiscally uncertain U.S. model. The essay concludes by stressing the need for greater scrutiny of these policies, including their economic efficiency and fiscal sustainability.

Keywords Climate neutrality · Climate policy · Green Deal · Mission-oriented innovation policy · Industrial policy

JEL Codes H23 · O38 · P18 · Q58

I thank Elias Abrahamsson for excellent research assistance, Magnus Henrekson and Christian Sandström for useful comments, and the Jan Wallander and Tom Hedelius Foundation (P2023-0186) and Anders Sandrews Stiftelse for financial support.

M. Stenkula (✉)
Research Institute of Industrial Economics (IFN), Stockholm, Sweden
e-mail: mikael.stenkula@ifn.se

M. Henrekson et al. (eds.), *A Green Entrepreneurial State?*, International Studies in Entrepreneurship 49, https://doi.org/10.1007/978-3-032-15512-2_2

Introduction

Addressing climate change caused by rising greenhouse gas emissions has become a central concern for policymakers worldwide. Political leaders face growing demands from voters and media for decisive action, and climate policy has risen to the top of political agendas. Whereas environmental policy historically relied primarily on taxation, regulation, and prohibitions to promote sustainability, recent years have witnessed a convergence of environmental and industrial policy. Increasingly, governments initiate large-scale, state-sponsored industrial investments through an active industrial policy framework.

This renewed interest in industrial policy has been reinforced by economists such as Mariana Mazzucato and Dani Rodrik, who argue for a more proactive role for the state in shaping markets and directing economic development (e.g., Mazzucato 2018a, 2021; Rodrik 2022). Under the concept of "mission-oriented innovation policy" (MOIP), Mazzucato advocates for governments to guide economies toward socially desirable goals, including sustainability, inclusiveness, and resilience. Drawing on historical examples such as the American Project Apollo, she has succeeded in reshaping how many policymakers and public commentators conceive of the government's role in fostering innovation.

Mazzucato has also suggested that "Green New Deals" constitute a paradigmatic mission suitable for large-scale political intervention (Mazzucato 2021, p. 137ff). These ideas have inspired politicians and organizations worldwide to promote ambitious green industrial strategies under the labels of Green Deals or Moonshots.[1] Illustratively, European Commission President Ursula von der Leyen described the European Green Deal as Europe's "man on the moon moment," while U.S. Energy Secretary under the Biden administration, Jennifer Granholm, has called the fight against climate change "our generation's moonshot."[2]

Although the urgency of the climate challenge is widely acknowledged, these large-scale programs are being implemented across many Western countries with limited critical scrutiny (Henrekson et al. 2024). Academic analyses remain relatively scarce, particularly regarding the risks of failure and unintended consequences of MOIPs. To scrutinize these ideas and policies, a necessary first step is to map the scope, structure, and design of the emerging green industrial policies that fall under the umbrella of Green Deals.

Hence, the aim of this essay is to examine the structure and extent of Green Deals around the world. The analysis focuses in particular on the European Union and the United States, where Green Deal initiatives have expanded most rapidly and provided

[1] See, e.g., Mazzucato (2018b, 2019), which are two reports written for the European Commission recommending the European Union to use a mission-oriented research and innovation approach.

[2] See von der Leyen (2019) and Granholm (2022) for the quotes.

inspiration for other countries, but selected cases from other Western economies—the United Kingdom, Germany, and Sweden—are also briefly discussed.[3]

The essay proceeds with a brief theoretical discussion of the evolution of innovation policy, highlighting the shift from market- and system-failure perspectives to a broader societal-mission orientation. This is followed by a description of the European Green Deal and the U.S. case. Thereafter, examples from the individual countries are presented, before the essay concludes with a short comparative analysis and general conclusions.

Innovation Policy—A Historical Background

The recent surge in support for large-scale government intervention has not arisen in a vacuum. Before turning to the structure of Green Deals around the world, this section briefly reviews the evolution of innovation policy and explains how the renewed popularity of active industrial policy—of which Green Deals are a prime example—emerged.

The First Generation of Innovation Policy: Market Failure

The earliest approaches to innovation policy are often described as a "first generation" of thinking, grounded in neoclassical economics and the concept of market failures. In this perspective, markets were assumed to allocate resources efficiently under some ideal pre-determined conditions, but in the case of innovation such conditions often did not hold. Knowledge, in particular, was considered a public good. i.e., it was non-rivalrous and, at least partly, non-excludable, which meant private actors tended to underinvest in research and development (R&D), as they could not fully appropriate the returns (Nelson 1959; Arrow 1962). In other words, knowledge was characterized by having positive externalities, which meant that the social benefits of new knowledge were greater than the individual benefits for those who produced the knowledge.

The first generation of innovation policy thus viewed the role of government primarily as a corrective actor solving market imperfections. This entailed interventions such as subsidies for R&D, public funding of basic research, provision of education and skills, and the establishment of intellectual property rights regimes. The underlying linear logic was that the state should "fix the market" where it fails to

[3] Apart from the countries covered by this study, only a handful of other developed economies—namely Canada, Australia, New Zealand, South Korea, Switzerland, Lichtenstein, and Iceland—have enacted legislation committing to climate neutrality ("net zero") by 2050 (Energy and Climate Intelligence Unit 2025).

generate socially optimal levels of investment in knowledge production and diffusion (Smith 2000).

This market-failure perspective was highly influential in the postwar decades, shaping innovation policies in the OECD countries from the 1960s onwards. For example, large-scale public investments in research laboratories and universities, along with direct R&D subsidies to firms, were justified as mechanisms to correct for the under-provision of innovation in purely market-based systems (OECD 1998).

The Second Generation of Innovation Policy: System Failure

A second generation of thinking emerged in the 1980s inspired by Nelson and Winter's (1982) evolutionary economics perspective. Their perspective contrasted with the traditional neoclassical approach by emphasizing routines and firm heterogeneity. Central to their argument was the notion that technological change was path-dependent and shaped by prior investments, learning processes, and industrial structures.

Building on these insights, scholars began to criticize the narrow market-failure framework of first-generation innovation policy, instead advocating an "innovation systems" perspective—which can be considered a second generation of innovation policy theory (Freeman 1987; Lundvall 1992; Nelson 1993). This theory emphasized that innovation was not an isolated linear activity within firms, but the outcome of complex interactions among firms, universities, public agencies, users, and other institutions. Failures were thus not only about markets underproviding knowledge, but also about weaknesses in the systems that enable innovation. This approach gave rise to the concept of system failures, where governments were tasked with improving the structure and functioning of innovation systems (Woolthuis et al. 2005).

With this perspective, innovation policy was no longer narrowly limited to subsidizing R&D or correcting underinvestment, but expanded to encompass factors such as facilitating coordination, fostering linkages between knowledge creation and commercialization, and shaping institutions. In practice, this meant that policy instruments under the second generation stressed cluster programs, support for collaborative R&D projects, technology transfer offices, and networking platforms. The emphasis moved from correcting underinvestment in knowledge toward enabling interactive learning and fostering the institutional conditions under which innovation could thrive.

The Third Generation of Innovation Policy: Societal Failure

The third generation of innovation policy emerged in response to mounting global challenges such as climate change, biodiversity loss, and widening social inequalities. While the second-generation system-failure perspective focused on strengthening networks and institutions, it was criticized for lacking direction and failing to ensure that the innovations contribute to societal transformation addressing alleged societal challenges (Schot and Steinmueller 2018). This recognition has given rise to an orientation toward transformational and societal failures—problems that arise when innovation systems remain locked into unsustainable trajectories and fail to generate the radical changes needed for long-term sustainability.

At the heart of third-generation thinking lies the argument that markets and systems tend to reinforce existing structures only favoring incremental innovation, and thereby potentially locking-in societies in unsustainable regimes. Governments are therefore called upon not merely to correct market and system failures but to provide directionality—actively shaping innovation pathways and guiding economies toward sustainability.

With slightly different terminology and emphasis, several different strands of literature and a large number of scholars have—in line with the third generation—pointed to a pressing need for an expanded role of innovation policy, particularly in supporting the green transition. Mazzucato's work on Mission-Oriented Innovation Policy (MOIP), highlighted in the introduction, belongs to this intellectual tradition underscoring that solving the climate challenge requires more deep-seated political involvement in the economy. Jacobsson et al. (2017) is another example criticizing the European Commission's earlier emphasis on market failure, system weakness, and technological neutrality, arguing that such a narrow focus neglected the need for more transformative and directional policies. This type of criticism helped pave the way for the launch of the European Green Deal, which explicitly embraces a stronger political role in guiding innovation policy.

Summary

Over time, innovation policy scholarship has shifted from talking about correcting market failures, to addressing system failures, and finally to confronting societal failures. The trajectory reflects a growing emphasis on market creation and the proactive shaping of new industries and technological pathways. The literature on innovation policy has grown rapidly and over time and it has increasingly advocated a more interventionist approach to policy, where governments are expected not only to support innovation but also to steer it toward a sustainable future. The proliferation of Green Deals worldwide is a case in point, embodying a belief in the necessity of extensive state involvement to guide societies toward climate neutrality.

The European Green Deal

General Background

In December 2019, the European Commission announced the so-called European Green Deal, a set of goals, regulations, and policies aiming to combat climate change while keeping the EU competitive and ensuring social and political sustainability. The overall goal was to reduce greenhouse gas emissions and transform the EU into the first climate-neutral continent by 2050. In order to accelerate the process, an intermediate goal to reduce greenhouse gas emissions by 55% by 2030 (compared to the 1990 level) was laid down together with additional policies and regulation under the so-called *Fit for 55* package in July 2021.

The European Green Deal can be seen as an umbrella for all policies and regulations, including binding targets of national annual greenhouse gas emissions and of renewable energy in the energy-mix, deemed necessary to reach the overarching goal of climate neutrality ("net zero"). The initiatives have expanded over time, and it is impossible to give an exhaustive list of all policies covering different sectors, firms, technologies, and products. Examples include objectives such as expanding the use of decarbonized and sustainable fuels in aviation and shipping, achieving the complete phase-out of vehicles with tailpipe emissions, and advancing policies to improve energy efficiency in buildings. In 2024, the Net-Zero Industry Act was also adopted to ensure expedited administrative procedures and accelerated approval processes for clean technology industries located inside EU borders.

But the European Green Deal is more than just regulation and policies. An important part of the Deal is about spending. The investment pillar of the Green Deal is denoted the Green Deal Investment Plan. Initially, the EU drew up an ambitious plan of mobilizing funds of EUR 1 trillion through different forms of initiatives—and this amount refers only to funds needed for the first decade under the Green Deal (European Commission 2020a). Later assessments suggest that the Union must make climate-related investments amounting to EUR 1,200 to 1,300 billion annually until 2030, and even more thereafter, in order to achieve net-zero by 2050 (see, e.g., discussion in Pons and Madec 2024 or Andersson et al. 2025). It is important to note that this figure does not refer to direct public investment only; private investment must also be part of the solution, but its level is supposed to be increased through different forms of public guarantees and subsidies. Based on different estimations, the private share of the required increase of investment is appraised to be 50 to 75% (Pisani-Ferry and Tagliapietra 2024).

The Structure of Support

The European Union has traditionally taken a restrictive stance toward national state aid, given the risk that such support could distort competition among firms across member states. However, in response to the COVID-19 pandemic and the war in Ukraine, these constraints were temporarily relaxed. In pursuit of the EU's overarching sustainability and climate-neutrality objectives, the possibility to give state aid was later prolonged and modified, permitting member states to provide extensive public funding to support the green transition (a framework denoted the Temporary Crisis and Transition Framework, TCTF, which was extended in 2025 as the Clean Industrial Deal State Aid Framework, CISAF). As larger countries possess greater fiscal capacity, complementary industrial support at the EU level is seen as crucial to prevent distortion and fragmentation within the Single Market. Accordingly, spending at the federal EU level is considered essential and both the scope and scale of EU-level spending have recently expanded substantially. Much of the EU spending is supposed to trigger or require co-financing by member states. Public support for the green transition is therefore financed through a combination of national budgets and the EU budget. Estimates suggest that roughly one-third of green funding is centrally managed at the EU level, and the remainder being allocated nationally through member state plans (Pisani-Ferry and Tagliapietra 2024).

As a result of the rapidly increasing funds that are supposed to be spent on the green transition, a new agency, the European Climate, Infrastructure and Environment Executive Agency (CINEA), was established in 2021 in order to support, coordinate, and help implement the Green Deal. Today, the agency employs nearly 600 bureaucrats and experts and is projected to expand further.[4]

The funds are often paid out through different forms of programs, such as Horizon Europe. Horizon Europe is EU's key funding program for research and innovation. The program supports so-called moonshot scientific-driven projects, which underscores the connection to the concept of mission-oriented innovation policy with publicly targeted support discussed in the introduction.[5]

Highlighting the revitalized idea that politicians and bureaucrats have the ability to "pick the winners" by supporting what they see as key technologies necessary to succeed with the green transition, some of the support is directly targeted at specific solutions or companies. A prime application of this idea is the European Union's adoption of a hydrogen strategy in July 2020 to stimulate the use of hydrogen as a key means to achieve climate neutrality, and the subsequent launch in 2022 of the European Hydrogen Bank—an instrument designed to support the scale-up of hydrogen production by financing selected projects.[6]

Within so-called IPCEI (Important Projects of Common European Interest), member states can also cooperate and support specific projects that are deemed

---

[4] For more information see the homepage of CINEA at https://cinea.ec.europa.eu/index_en.

[5] For the period 2028–2034, the Commission has proposed a EUR 175 billion budget for Horizon Europe (European Commission 2025a). See European Commission (2025b) for possible EU moonshot projects that could be financed by these funds, and European Commission (2025c) for information about adapting to the climate change as an EU mission.

[6] See European Commission (2020b, 2023a) for more information. The trade body Hydrogen Europe estimated that it would require EUR 430 billion to scale up the EU's hydrogen sector by 2030. New estimates suggest that investments equaling at least EUR 320 billion are needed by 2030 (European Hydrogen Observatory, 2025).

to significantly benefit the EU. A centrally managed EU IPCEI fund does not exist, but the Commission has so far approved state-aid support for 11 IPCEIs, including funding for hydrogen and battery projects. Granted national state aid plus expected private investment within these projects added up to almost EUR 100 million by mid-2025 (European Commission 2025d).

To mobilize the necessary resources, the European Union has introduced a broad range of instruments—including grants, public co-financing, subsidies, and guarantees—designed to diversify the channels of support. In response to the pandemic, the EU established the Recovery and Resilience Facility (RRF), initially to assist member states in need but subsequently expanded its scope to include support for the green transition. At least 37% of RRF expenditure must be directed toward climate-related measures (Pisani-Ferry and Tagliapietra 2024; Pons and Madec 2024). To finance the RRF, the EU has, for the first time, borrowed jointly in capital markets (e.g., by issuing so-called green bonds). Part of the RRF is used to support other initiatives, such as NextGenerationEU and RePowerEU, with funds. A so-called Just Transition Mechanism is also part of the system and is supposed to alleviate the negative effect that might hit certain regions harder than others due to the transition. It should be noted that the treaties do not confer upon the European Union a general authority to impose taxes directly—the power to tax rests with individual member states. As a result, the EU cannot give tax credits to corporations or households to stimulate green investments.

Additional financing is provided through revenues from the EU Emissions Trading System (ETS), the cap-and-trade mechanism for greenhouse gas emissions. These revenues fund, *inter alia*, the Innovation Fund, which supports projects facilitating the transition to climate neutrality.

Beyond these funds, the European Investment Bank (EIB), formally a distinct body independent from other EU institutions, has designated climate and environmental sustainability as its primary priority. The EIB devotes more than 50% of its lending toward projects supporting the green transition and has committed to support green investments amounting to EUR 1 trillion until 2030 (Pisani-Ferry and Tagliapietra 2024; Pons and Madec 2024). Complementing this is the InvestEU program, which employs public funds and guarantees to lower the costs and risks of private investments in priority sectors, including green endeavors.

To get a grasp of the complexity of the system, Fig. 1 schematically maps the Green Deal and its public support system. The goals and funds of these sources are partly overlapping and summing up all the amounts spent that is reported within the different programs and budgets would result in double counting. However, the EU's seven-year budget together with the NextGenerationEU recovery plan includes investment totaling EUR 1.8 trillion and one-third of this amount is designated to Green Deal investments (European Commission 2024a). A more detailed description of the support system is presented in the Appendix.

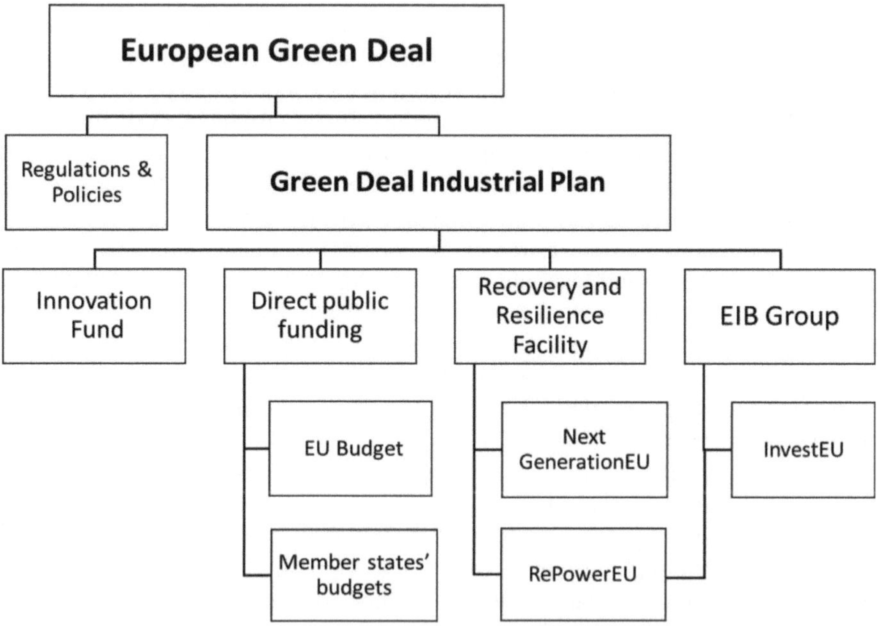

Fig. 1 The EU Green Deal and the most important parts of the public support system

The U.S. Green Deal: The Inflation Reduction Act (IRA)

General Background

In August 2022, the United States, under President Joe Biden, enacted the Inflation Reduction Act (IRA)—a somewhat misleading title for what was in fact the largest public climate-related investment initiative in U.S. history.[7] The U.S. climate target, established in April 2021, was to halve greenhouse gas emissions relative to their 2005 level by 2030.[8] Estimates suggest that the IRA would reduce national carbon emissions by approximately 1 billion metric tons until 2030, thereby closing about two-thirds of the gap toward the climate target that would persist without any further actions (Jenkins et al. 2022). Together with complementary regulations and policies, the legislation aimed not only to reduce national carbon emissions by 2030, but also to strengthen competitiveness, foster innovation, and raise productivity (Jiang et al. 2022; McKinsey 2024).[9]

[7] The IRA also includes other parts not associated with environmental challenges, notably measures related to the healthcare and medical system.

[8] Cf. EU's target of reducing greenhouse gas emissions by *55%* by 2030 relative to the *1990 level.*

[9] The whole Act is available at https://www.congress.gov/bill/117th-congress/house-bill/5376. Earlier initiatives, such as the Build Back Better Act, also aimed to reduce emissions, though on a smaller scale than the IRA.

The IRA provided approximately USD 500 billion in new spending and tax incentives, of which approximately USD 400 billion was earmarked for environmental projects to be implemented over a ten-year period. It should also be noted that the Biden administration advanced other major investment programs, most notably the Bipartisan Infrastructure Law (BIL) and the CHIPS and Science Act (CHIPS), which resulted in a total value of new commitments of more than USD 2 trillion (roughly 7.7% of U.S. GDP in 2022) over the same time period (McKinsey 2024).[10]

The IRA employs multiple instruments to address the climate challenge, including tax incentives, grants, and loan guarantees. The majority of the funds are directed toward tax credits designed to accelerate the deployment of renewable energy and energy-efficiency systems. Additional resources are allocated to clean energy financing and other targeted initiatives (Bertrand 2022). As will be described below, many of these programs were, however, halted or suspended following Donald Trump's assumption of office in 2025.

According to estimates by McKinsey (2024), roughly two-thirds of the public federal support under IRA is allocated to various tax incentives, of which most parts target corporations. Slightly more than 20% is directed toward grants, while just over 10% is provided through different forms of loan support.

To finance the Green Deal initiative, the Administration increased the minimum corporate tax on large corporations and initiated cost savings within the health care sector, among other things. According to the Congressional Budget Office's initial estimates, the IRA was not expected to be underfinanced—on the contrary, it was projected to generate a surplus contributing to deficit reduction (CRFB 2022).

Key Components of the IRA

Figure 2 provides a schematic overview of the key components of the IRA. Tax credits and deductions fall under the authority of the U.S. Department of the Treasury and encompass a wide range of instruments. Consumer-oriented credits include support for electric vehicles, rooftop solar panels, and heat pumps. Producer-oriented credits similarly target, e.g., manufacturers of renewable energy components, such as battery cells and solar or wind energy equipment.[11] Unlike many grant-based schemes,

[10] Other estimates suggest that IRA provides funds for climate and clean energy provisions amounting to around USD 370 billion (Dings and Sol 2025). The uncapped design of part of the support system (mainly tax credits) makes it difficult to predict the final level of expenditure, as it ultimately depends on the scale of production and investment, and on the amount of support claimed by firms and individuals. Credit Suisse estimates that public support could exceed USD 800 billion. Moreover, accounting for multiplier effects, they claim that the total investment stimulus could reach USD 1.7 trillion (Jiang et al. 2022). Other estimates suggest even higher figures.

[11] Tax credits existed well before the IRA was in place, but the scope and size increased substantially following IRA due to extensions, modifications, and new programs. In addition to tax credits, there is also a system of enhanced tax deductions linked to improvements in the energy efficiency of commercial buildings.

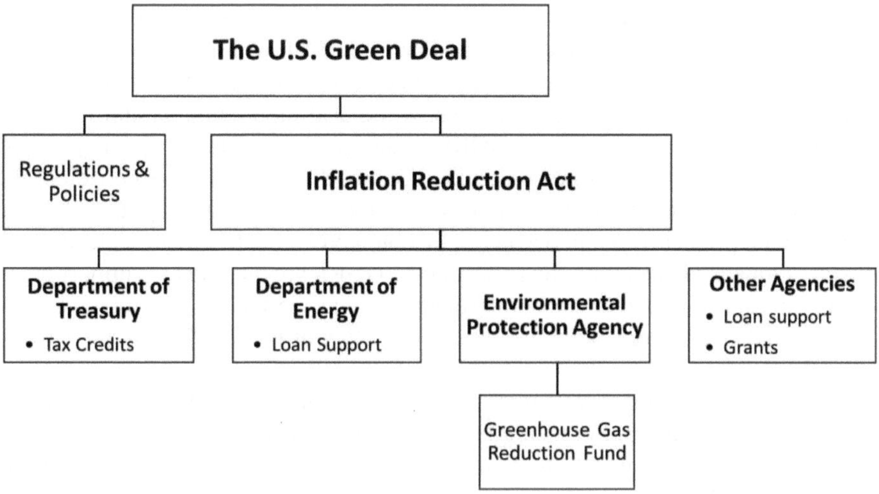

Fig. 2 The U.S. Green Deal and the most important parts of the public support system

manufacturers are not required to submit applications—if eligible, they can just claim the credits directly on their tax returns. (However, if requested, they must be able to present valid documentation). The credit amount is often based on the production output (production tax credits, PTC) or investment amount (investment tax credits, ITC).[12] The tax credit support system is not subject to the ordinary annual appropriations implying that the fiscal cost is uncapped and will vary with uptake (for information about tax credits, see EPA 2025a).

To incentivize domestic production, many forms of support require that eligible firms produce or assemble the subsidized items within the United States, and that they incorporate domestic inputs—such as American rare earth metals or batteries—into their production processes (Dings and Sol 2025).[13]

Even if the key component of the IRA is tax credits, there are other parts as well. The U.S. Department of Energy's Loan Programs Office (LPO) provides financial support for the green transition, primarily through subsidized direct loans and loan guarantees. The IRA expanded the LPO's lending authority more than tenfold, to over USD 350 billion. The LPO primarily targets *large-scale* projects that traditional lenders may be unable to finance due to debt-capacity constraints or may decline to support because of perceived risks. For example, the LPO gave a loan guarantee exceeding USD 500 million for a hydrogen and energy storage facility in Utah (Jiang et al. 2022; McKinsey 2024).

---

[12] Since 2025, the tax credit system no longer targets specific technologies or industries. Instead, the tax credits apply broadly to all generation facilities and energy storage systems with an anticipated greenhouse gas emissions rate of zero.

[13] In addition, there are often also wage and apprenticeship requirements implying that the supported corporations must pay prevailing wage rates and employ apprentices from registered apprenticeship programs in order to receive the maximum tax credit (IRS 2025).

The IRA also authorized the U.S. Environmental Protection Agency (EPA) to establish the Greenhouse Gas Reduction Fund (GGRF), with a budget of USD 27 billion, aimed at stimulating projects that reduce emissions and pollution, particularly in low-income and disadvantaged regions, while also mobilizing capital for green investments. Unlike the LPO, the GGRF is designed to support primarily *small-scale* investments, small businesses, and low-income communities. A portion of the funds is directed to nonprofit green banks, which leverage private capital to finance smaller green projects often underserved by commercial banks due to scale and risk considerations.[14] Hence, both the LPO and the GGRF are intended to support green projects that conventional financial intermediaries may view as too risky or unsuitable in scale—either too large, as in the case of the LPO, or too small, as in the case of the GGRF.

The IRA also encompasses a wide range of additional support programs administered by other agencies. For example, it allocates funds to the U.S. Department of Agriculture to provide grants and loans for rural electricity generation and storage projects. Funds have also been allocated to the National Oceanic and Atmospheric Administration (NOAA), which administers competitive grants to organizations engaged in, e.g., strengthening resilience to weather- and climate-related events. However, a detailed account of all these initiatives is beyond the scope of this essay.

IRA After Donald Trump Took Office

On his first day in office, January 20, 2025, President Trump issued an Executive Order which instructed all agencies to immediately stop disbursing funds associated with the IRA and to review the processes for issuing grants, loans, and other allowances. The White House Office of Management and Budget followed up by requiring all agencies to temporarily pause all grant, loan, and financial assistance programs.[15] Formal climate targets were also abandoned as the United States withdrew from the Paris agreement.

Furthermore, several individual programs were directly shut down. On March 20, 2025, a Trump-appointed EPA Administrator terminated the lion's share of the Greenhouse Gas Reduction Fund by closing down the National Clean Investment Fund and the Clean Communities Investment Accelerator Program (which constituted USD 20 billion of the 27 billion fund) claiming that those programs were associated with "fraud, waste and abuse" and that EPA should not be "a frivolous spender in the name of 'climate equity'" (EPA 2025c).

---

[14] The GGRF consists of three components: the National Clean Investment Fund, the Clean Communities Investment Accelerator, and the Solar for All program. For further information of GGRF, see EPA (2025b).

[15] Executive Order 14,154 ("Unleashing American Energy"), see https://www.whitehouse.gov/presidential-actions/2025/01/unleashing-american-energy/.

On July 4, 2025, President Trump signed the One Big Beautiful Bill Act, under which many environment-related tax credits were either repealed or phased out, particularly consumer-focused provisions such as the electric vehicle tax credit. However, some credit facilities were expanded—notably those related to clean fuel production and carbon dioxide sequestration (Tax Foundation 2025). Lawsuits and court decisions seeking to compel the Administration to unfreeze funds have followed President Trump's actions, and it remains uncertain what will happen with the IRA going forward.

Green Deals in Other Countries

The United Kingdom

In November 2020, the UK government under Prime Minister Boris Johnson announced the Ten Point Plan for a Green Industrial Revolution, aimed at supporting green jobs and accelerating the reduction of greenhouse gas emissions to achieve net-zero by 2050. The plan was to fund GBP 12 billion in government investment, with the expectation of mobilizing as much as three times that amount in private-sector funding, by 2030. To begin with, the goal was to reduce UK emissions by 180 million metric tons of carbon dioxide until 2032 (GOV UK 2020, 2021).

The Ten Point Plan encompasses targeted key areas with support to offshore wind, hydrogen, nuclear power, zero emission vehicles, green public transportation, sustainable aviation and maritime technologies, and carbon capture. The last two points of the plan referred to protecting the natural environment and establishing a green financing program. The latter program raises financing through different forms of green bonds issued by the government to fund green government expenditures in the form of direct investment, subsidies, or tax foregone (HM Treasury 2023).

The core ambition of the Ten Point Plan has largely been maintained under successive governments. Boris Johnson's successor as Prime Minister, Rishi Sunak, adopted a more pragmatic and cautious approach. By emphasizing affordability, scaling back certain goals, and reviewing costs, his government slowed the pace of regulatory initiatives and the rollout of grants. Under the Prime Minister at the time of writing, Keir Starmer, there has been stronger alignment with the original plan's ambition, accompanied by the goal of making the UK a "clean energy superpower" (GOV UK 2024a).

New initiatives have also been introduced. Most notably, the Great British Energy Act of 2025 established Great British Energy (GBE), a state-owned company with a mandate to invest in clean energy generation and expand "home-grown" clean power, capitalized with GBP 8.3 billion. In addition to pursuing its own projects, GBE is designed to act as a co-developer with private firms and local authorities, helping to de-risk projects—particularly at the development stage—with the aim of mobilizing private capital (GOV UK 2024b). To launch its activities, the company was allocated

GBP 25 million to establish its headquarters in Aberdeen (HM Treasury 2024). Its initial priorities covered projects such as offshore wind development, but it will also support nuclear power (including SMR technology).

Germany

In 2021, Germany amended the Climate Action Act (*Klimaschutzgesetz*) to introduce legally binding rules committing the country to achieve climate neutrality by 2045. The Act set intermediate targets of reducing greenhouse gas emissions by 65% by 2030 relative to 1990 levels, and by 88% by 2040. Achieving the 2045 climate-neutrality target is estimated to require total investment of around EUR 5 trillion, of which approximately EUR 500 billion is expected to come from public sources (European Parliament 2024a).

Germany's long-term strategy under the label *Energiewende* has been to shift away from fossil fuels and nuclear energy toward renewable energy and greater energy efficiency, with the overarching objective of achieving climate neutrality. Nuclear power was fully phased out in 2023, and coal is to be phased out no later than 2038.[16]

The German federal state employs a mix of regulatory instruments and financial support to promote the transition. As a member of the European Union, many of these instruments align with EU-level frameworks. Domestic measures include grants and investment support provided, e.g., through the Federal Office for Economic Affairs and Export Control (*Bundesamt für Wirtschaft und Ausfuhrkontroll*, BAFA), as well as loans and concessional financing from the state-owned development bank KfW (*Kreditanstalt für Wiederaufbau*), which plays a central role in funding green projects (BAFA 2025; KfW 2023).

A flagship role in the German government's financing of projects related to the country's energy and climate transition is held by the Climate and Transformation Fund (*Klima- und Transformationsfonds*, KTF). Originally created in 2010, it was substantially expanded under the Social Democratic led coalition government formed in 2021, investing in renewable energy and green technologies such as hydrogen and electromobility. Public funding through KTF is expected to be complemented by substantial private investment.

For the 2024–2027 period, the KTF was allocated more than EUR 200 billion (roughly 4.6% of German GDP in 2024), financed from federal sources (BMWE 2023). However, in November 2023 the Federal Constitutional Court ruled that the government's financing plan for KTF violated the constitutional "debt brake" and the constitutional limit on federal debt, forcing a substantial cutback in the size of the fund (European Parliament 2024a).[17] In 2025, the new Christian Democratic led government introduced a new EUR 500 billion Infrastructure and Defense Fund. To

[16] See Deshaies (2026) for more information about *Energiewende*.

[17] The problem with the KTF funding contributed to government's collapse in November 2024.

bypass the constitutional limit and secure sufficient parliamentary support, notably from the Green Party, the government agreed to earmark 20% of the fund for climate projects. As a result, EUR 100 billion was transferred to KTF, which supplied the fund with substantial resources to continue supporting green projects (Clean Energy Wire 2025; ESG Lore 2025).

Sweden

In 2017, Sweden adopted its current Climate Policy Framework (in force since January 1, 2018), which introduced the Climate Act with legally binding climate targets and the long-term objective of achieving net-zero greenhouse gas emissions by 2045. Intermediate targets require emission reductions of 63% by 2030 and 75% by 2040, relative to 1990 levels (Government Offices of Sweden 2021; European Parliament 2024b).

An important element of Sweden's support system is *Klimatklivet* ("the Climate Leap"), an investment grant program administered by the Swedish Environmental Protection Agency (*Naturvårdsverket*). Established in 2015, *Klimatklivet* provides subsidies covering up to 50% of investment costs for non-household projects that reduce greenhouse gas emissions. Since its inception, *Klimatklivet* has allocated nearly SEK 20 billion (≈ EUR 1.8 billion) to more than 27,500 green investments across the country (Naturvårdsverket 2025).

Industriklivet ("the Industry Leap"), launched in 2018, channels support more directly toward industrial technology transitions by financing research, development, pilot projects, and first-of-a-kind industrial decarbonization investments. Through 2024, *Industriklivet* had distributed SEK 7.4 billion in public grants. Together with co-financing from project partners, the total mobilized investment amounted to nearly SEK 100 billion (≈ EUR 9 billion) (Energimyndigheten 2025).

In addition to grants, Sweden employs other instruments. The National Debt Office (*Riksgälden*) was mandated in 2021 to issue credit guarantees for large industrial green investments, covering up to 80% of loan values, with a framework of SEK 80 billion (≈ EUR 7.7 billion; roughly 1.25% of Sweden's GDP in 2024) authorized by the end of 2024 (Riksgälden 2024). A prominent case was the EUR 1.2 billion loan guarantee for H2 Green Steel's new plant in Boden (Riksgälden 2023).[18] Publicly supported green loans are also available, for instance, through the state-owned company *Almi*, which may offer loans with amortization relief and lower interest rates to small and medium-sized corporations (Almi 2025).

[18] The project also received state aid financed partly through EU's Recovery and Resilience Facility (RRF) (European Commission 2024b). The H2 Green Steel project (renamed Stegra in 2024) is evaluated by Johansson and Kriström (2026).

In the same way as with Germany, the support aligns with the EU-level frameworks and often uses funds from the EU system. Both *Klimatklivet* and *Industriklivet* are partly financed through the EU's *NextGenerationEU* instrument, and *Almi* is supported by InvestEU funds, which are described above.

Comparative Analysis

Although the European and U.S. systems share the overarching goal of reducing greenhouse gas emissions and addressing climate change, they differ in several significant ways. Compared to the European Union, the U.S. Green Deal, as depicted by the IRA, is less fragmented and more output-oriented. Subsidies under the IRA are more rules-based and open-ended, not tied to project-specific viability assessments, whereas EU subsidies are more case-specific and often based on an alleged funding gap, designed (in theory) to prevent overcompensation and to comply with state-aid law. A substantial share of the IRA provisions is uncapped and operates outside the annual appropriations process, meaning that support is not constrained by pre-determined budgetary limits. The IRA is also strongly origin-based, requiring domestic production or assembly within the United States—or the use of domestic inputs—to qualify for support (or have higher support levels granted under such conditions). Both the EU's Temporary Crisis and Transition Framework (TCTF) and its Net-Zero Industry Act can be seen as a response to the IRA initiative.

The EU framework for green support has been criticized on several grounds, highlighting various shortcomings. The system is often regarded as overly complex and fragmented, as multiple overlapping and sometimes contradictory guidelines apply, forcing firms to navigate several parallel funding schemes with differing principles and conditions. The case-by-case negotiation-based approach lacks clear *ex ante* criteria. This creates incentives for rent-seeking behavior, as firms may strategically exploit the "funding gap" logic to secure subsidies for cost-inefficient projects. Moreover, the framework tends to favor large, well-established incumbents with the resources, networks, and administrative capacity to manage the process, thereby disadvantaging smaller and more dynamic entrants (Dings and Sol 2025).[19]

The U.S. system offers a more streamlined and output-based model, with automatic tax credits that can be claimed *ex post* through the tax system. This simplicity may reduce administrative burdens and accelerate deployment, but the IRA system entails its own problems. Critics have highlighted the escalating fiscal costs where the uncapped design makes total fiscal costs highly uncertain. Moreover, the reliance on subsidies rather than carbon pricing has raised concerns regarding cost-effectiveness. The support system is further criticized for its complexity and lack of neutrality, due to the inclusion of arbitrary clauses concerning location, labor requirements, and input use. It may also risk trade distortions and tensions with international partners (see,

---

[19] For further critique of and problems with the prevailing European system, see European Court of Auditors (2024).

e.g., critique from the Tax Foundation 2025). In this sense, the EU framework may lack efficiency and transparency, while the U.S. model achieves speed and scalability at the expense of fiscal predictability, neutrality, and international coherence.

While the comparative analysis primarily contrasts the European Union and the United States, national initiatives in the UK, Germany, and Sweden highlight further diversity. The UK's Ten Point Plan and the creation of Great British Energy (GBE) exemplify a centralized approach relying on a state-owned enterprise to co-develop projects and crowd in private investment. Germany's *Energiewende* and the Climate and Transformation Fund (KTF) demonstrate long-term institutionalization of climate goals, but also fiscal and constitutional constraints, which have led to creative financing mechanisms. Sweden represents a smaller open economy combining EU-level funding with domestic grant programs like *Klimatklivet* and *Industriklivet*. Together, these cases show that while all three countries pursue ambitious targets and the latter two also align with EU goals, their strategies diverge in institutional design.

Conclusion

Green Deals represent a profound shift in economic governance, blending industrial and environmental policy in ways that challenge traditional economic doctrines. The EU approach is expansive but fragmented, relying on overlapping instruments and complex state-aid rules, while the U.S. Inflation Reduction Act prioritizes scalability and simplicity through uncapped tax credits, though at the cost of fiscal unpredictability and non-neutrality. National cases such as the UK, Germany, and Sweden further illustrate how institutional contexts shape the design and delivery of support. Despite their differences, these policies share a common reliance on large-scale public intervention to catalyze private investment to achieve the green transition.

Yet critical questions remain regarding efficiency, fiscal sustainability, and international trade effects. Further academic scrutiny is essential to understand both the promise and the risks of mission-oriented industrial policy in addressing climate change.

Appendix: The EU Support System

Direct Public Funding—National Level

According to the EU treaties, the member states cannot unconditionally support corporations and sectors in the economy as that would risk distorting competition between companies in different countries of the Union. Therefore, there has been a general prohibition of state aid (with some exceptions). However, due to the COVID-19 crisis and the Ukraine war, this policy has been softened. By introducing temporary "crisis frameworks," the EU allows its member states to temporarily deviate from the principle of banning state aid. In March 2023, the framework was amended and the exception was prolonged, now allowing public funding to support the national transition to climate-neutral economies under the Temporary Crisis and Transition Framework, TCTF.[20] According to TCTF, state aid can always be granted to all renewable technologies, green hydrogen, and biofuel storage projects (TEPSA 2023). In July 2025, TCTF was replaced by the Clean Industrial Deal State Aid Framework (CISAF), simplifying and prolonging the possibility to give state aid focusing on green energy, industrial decarbonization, and clean-tech manufacturing (European Commission 2025e).[21]

Between 2012 and 2022, state-aid support for green endeavors amounting to EUR 630 billion was granted. These aid schemes were five times larger than aid targeted toward underdeveloped regions (the second most used objective referred to when circumventing the aid restriction), between 2017 and 2022 (European Commission 2025f).

Direct Public Funding—EU Level

One problem with national state aid is its skewed distribution between countries. There is a varying capacity and willingness to grant support to green industries across the member states. A dilemma for the EU is that large and rich countries—notably Germany and France—have greater interest and opportunities to support their industries. Providing support from the EU level to avoid the distortions and fragmentation of the Single Market that a highly skewed national funding can create is seen as important. Hence, it is argued that scaling up industrial support at the EU level while expanding its scope is required to facilitate the green transition across the Union and to create a level playing field for all companies acting inside EU borders.

To support the green transition at the union level, 30% of EU's long-term budget (Multiannual Financial Framework, MFF) is therefore earmarked to support different climate- and environment-related objectives by providing the European Green Deal Investment Plan with funds. In practice, this means that the EU is supposed to spend

[20] However, already in January 2022, the EU introduced new guidelines on state aid for climate, environmental protection, and energy (CEEAG), updating earlier rules from 2014, to assess when national aid for environmental and climate protection should be allowed in order to create a flexible framework to support the Green Deal objectives (European Commission 2022). Hence, there exist overlapping parallel EU state-aid rules, which complicate the support system.

[21] To speed up investment in line with the Green Deal industrial plan, the EU has also amended the General Block Exemption Regulation (GBER)—after 2023 denoted Green Deal General Block Exemption Regulation—which makes it possible for member states to provide certain types of—particularly climate- and energy-related—state aid without requiring prior approval from the European Commission.

more than EUR 500 billion between 2021 and 2027, taken directly from the EU budget for this issue. The EU funding is expected to be complemented with more than EUR 100 billion by the member states (Pons and Madec 2024).

Recovery and Resilience Facility

As a response to the COVID-19 pandemic, the EU did not only relax the state-aid rules, but they also launched the Recovery and Resilience Facility (RRF) as an instrument to support its member states. Based on the member states' national recovery and resilience plans—which outlined proposed reforms and investment projects requiring support—the EU was able to provide funding to its member states through the facility. Together with the changing state-aid rules, the RRF's objective has been widened, and funds are now also used to facilitate the green transition among its member states. At the time of writing, national recovery plans must allocate at least 37% of their recovery expenditure to climate-related investments (Pisani-Ferry and Tagliapietra 2024; Pons and Madec 2024).[22]

To build up the RRF, the EU raises funds by borrowing on the capital market (e.g., by issuing so-called green bonds). This is the first major instance of joint EU borrowing to finance member state spending. In the next step, these funds are made available by request to member states through grants and loans. However, payouts to member states are performance-based, and EU disburses the amount it has raised on the capital markets in arrears when specific pre-defined targets in line with the national recovery plans are met. The part of the funds that is used to give grants will in the final step be returned to the capital market over the EU budget (e.g., when the green bonds expire). RRF consists of EUR 650 billion available for investments, of which more than EUR 350 billion is earmarked as grants (European Commission 2025g). Member states are also allowed to use RRF funds to finance IPCEI.

NextGenerationEU

Besides funds allocated directly from the EU budget, the Green Deal Investment plan is complemented by loans and grants from an instrument called NextGenerationEU presented by the Commission in May 2020. The bulk of the NextGenerationEU is financed through the RRF as described above. In the same way as RRF, it was initially a temporary recovery instrument to dampen the economic downturn that member states were facing due to the COVID-19 crisis but is now also a way to support member states' green transition. Altogether NextGenerationEU decides over EUR 750 billion that should be spent before the end of 2026 when the instrument ends (European Commission 2025h).

[22] In addition, a minimum of 20% must be devoted to digital investments.

RePowerEU

In order to phase out the dependence on Russian fossil fuel, the RePowerEU plan was launched in May 2022. The goal was to speed up the green transition and promote massive investment in renewable energy. REPowerEU is used to promote the expansion of renewable energy sources such as solar, wind, and hydrogen, with the goal of substantially increasing the use of solar photovoltaic power and renewable hydrogen. The main financing source is the above-described Recovery and Resilience Facility (RRF). The EU has mobilized EUR 300 billion for these purposes (European Commission 2025i). The European Investment Bank Group will also support the objectives of RePowerEU with additional loans and equity (European Commission 2023b).

InvestEU

InvestEU is a program launched in 2021, with the general purpose of stimulating private investments in the Union by bringing together a multitude of earlier EU financial instruments. Within the program, public funds and guarantees are used to reduce the cost and risks of private investments in prioritized areas, including private initiatives in line with the Green Deal objective. At least 30% of the InvestEU program must support climate- and environment-related projects.

The program will provide EU budget guarantees to allow the European Investment Bank (EIB) or other implementing partners to invest in (and lend to) more high-risk green projects. EU guarantees of EUR 26.2 billion are supposed to spur private investment and it is claimed that it could mobilize additional private investment of at least EUR 370 billion by 2027. Funding comes partly from NextGenerationEU (Pons and Madec 2024; European Commission 2025j).

Innovation Fund

To further support the decarbonization of European industry and bringing cutting-edge technologies to the market, the EU has set up a specific innovation fund. It is said to be "the world's largest funding programmes for the deployment of net-zero and innovative technologies." The fund is financed through the EU Emission Trading System (EU-ETS). How much money that will be released through the fund will depend on the carbon prize, but it is estimated that the fund will raise approximately EUR 40 billion between 2020 and 2030. The fund can support up to 60% (or, in special cases, even 100%) of the capital and operational costs (minus revenues) during the first ten years. Innovation Fund projects are required to share knowledge to spur spillover effects to support other companies, sectors, projects, or future applicants. In early 2025, some 200 projects had been awarded support (European Commission 2025k).

EIB Group

The EIB group, i.e., the European Investment Bank (EIB) and the European Investment Fund (EIF), is an integral part when it comes to the Green Deal by supporting different initiatives, plans, or programs, such as InvestEU. Financing the green transition is nowadays the bank's first priority (Pisani-Ferry and Tagliapietra 2024). EIB is supposed to mobilize investments under the EU instruments (as described above) and through the EU budget amounting to around EUR 250 billion. In addition, 50% of their total lending should be directed toward activities related to climate change. They are on track to support green investment to a total value of EUR 1 trillion until 2030 (Pons and Madec 2024).

Miscellaneous

In order to alleviate the negative effects of the green transition that may disproportionately hit certain groups or regions, the EU has created a Social Climate Fund and a Just Transition Fund to support vulnerable groups (Social Climate Fund) or regions (Just Transition Fund) with resources and different forms of financial support. A so-called Just Transition Mechanism is mandated to support underprivileged regions with EUR 55 billion between 2021 and 2027, partly financed by the Just Transition Fund (Pons and Madec 2024; European Commission 2025l).

References

Almi (2025). Green Loan—when you want to invest sustainably. https://www.almi.se/en/loan/green-loan/

Andersson, M., Köhler-Ulbrich, P., & Nerlich Green, C. (2025). Investment needs in the EU and their funding. *ECB Economic Bulletin*, 1/2025.

Arrow, K. J. (1962). Economic welfare and the allocation of resources for invention. In R. R. Nelson (Ed.), *The Rate and Direction of Inventive Activity: Economic and Social Factors* (pp. 609–626). Princeton, NJ: Princeton University Press.

BAFA (2025). Energy & Climate Protection. https://www.bafa.de/EN/Energy/energy.html

Bertrand, S. (2022). How the Inflation Reduction Act and Bipartisan Infrastructure Law work together to advance climate action. Washington, DC: Environmental and Energy Study Institute. https://www.eesi.org/articles/view/how-the-inflation-reduction-act-and-bipartisan-infrastructure-law-work-together-to-advance-climate-action

BMWE (2023). Federal Cabinet adopts business plan for the Climate and Transformation Fund (CTF). https://www.bundeswirtschaftsministerium.de/Redaktion/EN/Pressemitteilungen/2023/08/20230809-federal-cabinet-adopts-business-plan-for-the-climate-and-transformation-fund-ctf.html
Clean Energy Wire (2025). Germany's new €500 bln fund—What's in it for climate and energy? https://www.cleanenergywire.org/factsheets/qa-germanys-eu500-bln-infrastructure-fund-whats-it-climate-and-energy
CRFB (2022). CBO Scores IRA with $238 Billion of Deficit Reduction. https://www.crfb.org/blogs/cbo-scores-ira-238-billion-deficit-reduction
Deshaies, M. (2026). The German *Energiewende*: A green deal template or planned failure? In M. Henrekson, C. Sandström, & M. Stenkula (Eds.), *A Green Entrepreneurial State? Exploring the Pitfalls of Green Deals* (pp. 131–147). Cham: Springer.
Dings, J., & Sol, X. (2025). State Aid 2.0: Lean, clean, European. Report from European Federation for Transport and Environment. https://www.transportenvironment.org/uploads/files/State-Aid-report-TE.pdf
Energimyndigheten (2025). Resultat från Industriklivet. https://www.energimyndigheten.se/forskning-och-innovation/forskning/industri/industriklivet/resultat-fran-industriklivet/
Energy and Climate Intelligence Unit (2025). Net Zero Scorecard. https://eciu.net/netzerotracker
EPA (2025a). Summary of Inflation Reduction Act provisions related to renewable energy. https://www.epa.gov/green-power-markets/summary-inflation-reduction-act-provisions-related-renewable-energy
EPA (2025b). About the Greenhouse Gas Reduction Fund. https://www.epa.gov/greenhouse-gas-reduction-fund/about-greenhouse-gas-reduction-fund.
EPA (2025c). Administrator Zeldin terminates Biden-Harris $20B 'gold bar' grants. https://www.epa.gov/newsreleases/administrator-zeldin-terminates-biden-harris-20b-gold-bar-grants
ESG Lore (2025). Germany approves €500 Billion fund with €100 billion for climate transition. https://esglore.com/news/germany-approves-e500-billion-fund-with-e100-billion-for-climate-transition/
European Commission (2020a). Sustainable Europe investment plan. European Green Deal investment plan. https://eur-lex.europa.eu/legal-content/EN/TXT/PDF/?uri=CELEX:52020DC0021
European Commission (2020b). A hydrogen strategy for a climate-neutral Europe. https://eur-lex.europa.eu/legal-content/EN/TXT/PDF/?uri=CELEX:52020DC0301
European Commission (2022). 2022 guidelines on State aid for climate, environmental protection and energy. https://eur-lex.europa.eu/EN/legal-content/summary/2022-guidelines-on-state-aid-for-climate-environmental-protection-and-energy.html
European Commission (2023a). On the European Hydrogen Bank. https://eur-lex.europa.eu/legal-content/EN/TXT/PDF/?uri=CELEX:52023DC0156
European Commission (2023b). A Green Deal Industrial Plan for the Net-Zero Age. https://eur-lex.europa.eu/legal-content/EN/TXT/PDF/?uri=CELEX:52023DC0062
European Commission (2024a). The European Green Deal. https://ec.europa.eu/commission/presscorner/api/files/attachment/879954/3%20European%20Green%20Deal.pdf
European Commission (2024b). Commission approves €265 million Swedish State aid measure partly funded under Recovery and Resilience Facility to support H2GS's green steel plant. https://ec.europa.eu/commission/presscorner/detail/en/ip_24_3468
European Commission (2025a). Horizon Europe 2028–2034. https://commission.europa.eu/document/download/a0ecf3f6-a964-4e00-9cb3-4be28833b386_en?filename=MFF_HORIZON%20EUROPE_v9.pdf
European Commission (2025b). EU long-term budget 2028–2034—Moonshot examples. https://research-and-innovation.ec.europa.eu/document/download/a64d902e-c508-4694-a0da-60504d071f82_en?filename=ec_rtd_mff-moonshots.pdf
European Commission (2025c). EU mission, adaptation to climate change. https://data.europa.eu/doi/10.2777/5725296

European Commission (2025d). Approved integrated Important Projects of Common European Interest (IPCEI). https://competition-policy.ec.europa.eu/state-aid/ipcei/approved-ipceis_en
European Commission (2025e). Clean Industrial Deal State Aid Framework (CISAF). https://competition-policy.ec.europa.eu/about/contribution-clean-just-and-competitive-transition/clean-industrial-deal-state-aid-framework-cisaf_en
European Commission (2025f). State aid Scoreboard 2023. https://competition-policy.ec.europa.eu/document/download/0b2037c5-c43f-4917-b654-f48f74444015_en
European Commission (2025g) Recovery and Resilience Facility (RRF). https://commission.europa.eu/business-economy-euro/economic-recovery/recovery-and-resilience-facility_en
European Commission (2025h). Recovery plan for Europe. https://commission.europa.eu/strategy-and-policy/recovery-plan-europe_en
European Commission (2025i). REPowerEU: Affordable, secure and sustainable energy for Europe. https://commission.europa.eu/topics/energy/repowereu_en
European Commission (2025j). InvestEU Fund. https://investeu.europa.eu/investeu-programme/investeu-fund_en
European Commission (2025k). What is the Innovation Fund? https://climate.ec.europa.eu/eu-action/eu-funding-climate-action/innovation-fund/what-innovation-fund_en
European Commission (2025l). The Just Transition Mechanism: Making sure no one is left behind. https://commission.europa.eu/strategy-and-policy/priorities-2019-2024/european-green-deal/finance-and-green-deal/just-transition-mechanism_en
European Court of Auditors (2024). *State Aid in Times of Crisis*. Special Report 21. Luxembourg: Publications Office of the European Union.
European Hydrogen Observatory (2025). EU Hydrogen strategy under the EU Green Deal. https://observatory.clean-hydrogen.europa.eu/eu-policy/eu-hydrogen-strategy-under-eu-green-deal
European Parliament (2024a). Germany's climate action strategy. https://www.europarl.europa.eu/RegData/etudes/BRIE/2024/767182/EPRS_BRI(2024)767182_EN.pdf
European Parliament (2024b). Sweden's climate action strategy. https://www.europarl.europa.eu/RegData/etudes/BRIE/2024/767174/EPRS_BRI%282024%29767174_EN.pdf
Freeman, C. (1987). *Technology Policy and Economic Performance: Lessons from Japan*. London: Pinter.
GOV UK (2020) The Ten Point Plan for a Green Industrial Revolution. https://assets.publishing.service.gov.uk/media/5fb5513de90e0720978b1a6f/10_POINT_PLAN_BOOKLET.pdf
GOV UK (2021). Net zero strategy: Build back greener. https://assets.publishing.service.gov.uk/media/6194dfa4d3bf7f0555071b1b/net-zero-strategy-beis.pdf
GOV UK (2024a). Boost for UK clean energy growth as PM arrives at COP29. https://www.gov.uk/government/news/boost-for-uk-clean-energy-growth-as-pm-arrives-at-cop29
GOV UK (2024b). Great British Energy founding statement. https://assets.publishing.service.gov.uk/media/66a235daab418ab055592d27/great-british-energy-founding-statement.pdf
Government Offices of Sweden (2021). *Sweden's Climate Policy Framework*. Stockholm: Government Offices of Sweden. https://www.government.se/articles/2021/03/swedens-climate-policy-framework/
Granholm, J. (2022). Testimony of Secretary Jennifer M. Granholm, U.S. Department of Energy. Before the U.S. House Committee on appropriations subcommittee on energy and water development, April 28, 2022. https://www.congress.gov/117/meeting/house/114639/witnesses/HHRG-117-AP10-Wstate-GranholmJ-20220428.pdf
Henrekson, M., Sandström, C., & Stenkula, M. (Eds.) (2024). *Moonshots and the New Industrial Policy: Questioning the Mission Economy*. Cham: Springer. https://doi.org/10.1007/978-3-031-49196-2
HM Treasury (2023). UK Green financing allocation and Impact report. https://assets.publishing.service.gov.uk/media/651446cdb1bad4000d4fd916/HMT-UK_Green_Financing_Allocation_Impact_Report_2023_Accessible.pdf
HM Treasury (2024). Autumn Budget 2024. https://www.gov.uk/government/publications/autumn-budget-2024/autumn-budget-2024-html

IRS (2025). Prevailing wage and apprenticeship requirements. https://www.irs.gov/credits-deductions/prevailing-wage-and-apprenticeship-requirements

Jacobsson, S., Bergek, A., & Sandén, B. (2017). Improving the European Commission's analytical base for designing instrument mixes in the energy sector: Market failures versus system weaknesses. *Energy Research & Social Science, 33*, 11–20. https://doi.org/10.1016/j.erss.2017.09.009

Jenkins, J. D., Mayfield, E. N., Farbes, J., Jones, R., Patankar, N., Xu, Q., & Schivley, G. (2022). Preliminary report: The climate and energy impacts of the Inflation Reduction Act of 2022. REPEAT Project, Princeton University. https://repeatproject.org/docs/REPEAT_IRA_Prelminary_Report_2022-08-04.pdf

Jiang, B., et al. (2022). *US Inflation Reduction Act—A Tipping Point in Climate Action.* Zurich: Credit Suisse.

Johansson, P.-O., & Kriström, B. (2026). Green Industrial Megaprojects: A Welfare Economics Perspective. In M. Henrekson, C. Sandström, & M. Stenkula (Eds.), *A Green Entrepreneurial State? Exploring the Pitfalls of Green Deals* (pp. 173–185). Cham: Springer.

KfW (2023). Sustainable finance. https://www.kfw.de/nachhaltigkeit/Dokumente/KEa4/ENG-sustainable-finance-project.pdf

Lundvall, B.-Å. (1992). *National Systems of Innovation: Towards a Theory of Innovation and Interactive Learning.* London: Pinter.

Mazzucato, M. (2018a). Mission-oriented innovation policies: Challenges and opportunities. *Industrial and Corporate Change, 27*(5), 803–815.

Mazzucato, M. (2018b). *Mission-Oriented Research & Innovation in the European Union: A Problem-Solving Approach to Fuel Innovation-Led Growth.* Luxembourg: Publications Office of the European Union.

Mazzucato, M. (2019). *Governing Missions in the European Union.* Luxembourg: Publications Office of the European Union.

Mazzucato, M. (2021). *Mission Economy: A Moonshot Guide to Changing Capitalism.* London: Penguin.

McKinsey (2024). *The Inflation Reduction Act: Here's What's in It.* Report, April 17. https://www.mckinsey.com/industries/public-sector/our-insights/the-inflation-reduction-act-heres-whats-in-it

Naturvårdsverket (2025). Klimatklivet. https://www.naturvardsverket.se/amnesomraden/klimatomstallningen/klimatklivet/

Nelson, R. R. (1959). The simple economics of basic scientific research. *Journal of Political Economy, 67*(3), 297–306. https://www.journals.uchicago.edu/doi/10.1086/258177

Nelson, R. R. (1993). *National Innovation Systems: A Comparative Analysis.* Oxford: Oxford University Press.

Nelson, R. R., & Winter, S. G. (1982). *An Evolutionary Theory of Economic Change.* Cambridge, MA: Belknap Press of Harvard University Press.

OECD (1998). *New Rationale and Approaches in Technology and Innovation Policy.* Paris: OECD Publishing.

Pisani-Ferry, J., & Tagliapietra, S. (2024). An investment strategy to keep the European Green Deal on track. Bruegel Policy Brief, 31/2024. https://www.bruegel.org/sites/default/files/2024-12/PB%2031%202024.pdf

Pons, J. F., & Madec, L. (2024). Financing the Green Deal: How are the EU and member states contributing? Note written for Eurofi, September 2024. https://www.eurofi.net/wp-content/uploads/2024/12/v.2-financing-the-green-deal-how-are-the-eu-and-member-states-contributing.pdf

Riksgälden (2023). Green credit guarantee for a loan to H2 Green Steel. https://www.riksgalden.se/fi/press-and-publications/press-releases-and-news/news/2023/green-credit-guarantee-for-a-loan-to-h2-green-steel/

Riksgälden (2024). Credit guarantees for green investments. https://www.riksgalden.se/en/our-operations/guarantee-and-lending/credit-guarantees-for-green-investments/

Rodrik, D. (2022). *An industrial policy for good jobs*. Washington, DC: The Hamilton Project, Brookings. https://www.brookings.edu/articles/an-industrial-policy-for-good-jobs/
Schot, J., & Steinmueller, W. E. (2018). Three frames for innovation policy: R&D, systems of innovation and transformative change. *Research Policy, 47*(9), 1554–1567. https://doi.org/10.1016/j.respol.2018.08.011
Smith, K. (2000). Innovation as a systemic phenomenon: Rethinking the role of policy. *Enterprise and Innovation Management Studies, 1*(1), 73–102. https://doi.org/10.1080/146324400363536
Tax Foundation (2025). How the One Big Beautiful Bill changes green energy tax credits. https://taxfoundation.org/blog/big-beautiful-bill-green-energy-tax-credit-changes/
TEPSA (2023). Next steps for the European Green Deal: Navigating economic and security challenges, keeping a focus on climate and justice. https://tepsa.eu/analysis/next-steps-for-the-european-green-deal-navigating-economic-and-security-challenges-keeping-a-focus-on-climate-and-justice/
von der Leyen, U. (2019). Press remarks by President von der Leyen on the occasion of the adoption of the European Green Deal Communication. https://ec.europa.eu/commission/presscorner/detail/en/speech_19_6749
Woolthuis, R. K., Lankhuizen, M., & Gilsing, V. (2005). A system failure framework for innovation policy design. *Technovation, 25*(6), 609–619. https://doi.org/10.1016/j.technovation.2003.11.002

Mikael Stenkula is an Associate Professor of Economics and holds a PhD from the School of Economics and Management at Lund University. He received this degree in 2004 with his dissertation *Essays on Network Effects and Money*. After having worked for a year as a lecturer at Lund University, where he taught microeconomics, he joined the Research Institute of Industrial Economics (IFN) in 2005. His primary research areas are entrepreneurship economics and taxation. In addition to publishing in peer-reviewed journals, Stenkula has also co-edited several volumes, including *Moonshots and the New Industrial Policy* (Springer).

Stenkula has also taught at the Stockholm School of Economics and serves as the executive secretary of the award committee for the Global Award for Entrepreneurship Research, the foremost global award for research on entrepreneurship.

The Incoherence of Modest Industrial Policy

Bryan Cheang

Abstract This essay argues that the notion of modest industrial policy, the idea that governments can lead structural transformation but remain modest, cautious, and adaptive, is incoherent and self-defeating. The very conditions that are said to demand modesty—radical uncertainty, complexity, and bounded knowledge—also render structural transformation implausible. If policymakers admit they are operating in unknown territory, then the idea that they can steer society in a coherent direction becomes less a policy strategy and more an article of faith. Yet this is precisely the tightrope today's leading theorists attempt to walk. Dani Rodrik advocates a learning-oriented industrial policy while still gesturing toward ambitious structural change, seemingly hoping that modest means will deliver immodest ends. Mariana Mazzucato, for her part, insists the state must "pick a direction" and align society accordingly, but assures us this will be done inclusively and experimentally—as if consensus and coordination might emerge spontaneously on command. These contradictions are not incidental; they strike at the heart of the project. Industrial policy cannot be both radically uncertain and confidently directional. In the end, one cannot promise a revolution with a shrug. Advocates must choose: either scale down their ambitions or be honest about the scale of authority their vision requires.

Keywords Industrial policy · Structural transformation · Entrepreneurial state · Complexity · Authoritarianism · Social engineering

JEL Codes P11 · B53 · O21 · O25

B. Cheang (✉)
London School of Economics, London, UK
e-mail: b.cheang@lse.ac.uk

M. Henrekson et al. (eds.), *A Green Entrepreneurial State?*, International Studies in Entrepreneurship 49, https://doi.org/10.1007/978-3-032-15512-2_3

Introduction

The Oxford English Dictionary defines the word "incoherent," when applied to abstract schemes, as "consisting of or forming a group or series of incongruous parts; not connected or unified by any general principle or characteristic; inconsistent, uncoordinated." In similar vein, an incoherent government policy is one where the "different parts of it do not fit together properly" (Collins Dictionary 2025). The purpose of this essay is to demonstrate the incoherence of modest industrial policy, an institutional proposal that seeks to combine the aims of structural transformation with a desire for liberal experimentation under conditions of complexity and uncertainty. I argue that if industrial policy seeks to seriously pursue structural transformation, then it cannot be modest, and must require ambitious policymaking and expansionary state power. A modest approach to industrial policy lacks the state capacity necessary to effectuate structural transformation, and therefore, ambitious industrial policy cannot become modest without losing its ability to steer the direction of economic production in desired ways.

While industrial policy is not new, it has seen a resurgence in recent policy discourse, with advocates claiming its necessity due to the alleged excesses of neoliberal governance, the problem of de-industrialization, and the need for a green transition in the face of a "climate emergency" (Mazzucato 2021b; Rodrik 2022; Krugman 2023). Industrial policies, to be clear, are policies that "explicitly target the transformation of the structure of economic activity in pursuit of some public goal," where such goals may include but are not exclusive to "climate transition," "good jobs," "lagging regions," "exports or import substitution" (Juhasz et al. 2024, p. 216). Importantly, since industrial policy is expected to achieve the structural transformation of an economy's production processes, this requires "the exercise of choice and discretion by the public authorities" (Juhasz et al. 2024, p. 216). So defined, industrial policies may include a range of tools, whether public subsidies, direct government investment, infant industry protection, public–private partnerships, and more, as long as they are aimed at structural transformation.

Despite this common definition of industrial policy, various theorists justify their position differently. One helpful classification is between modest and ambitious industrial policy. We may understand the former as an approach to industrial policy that is limited in scale, scope, and size, while the latter has a far more expansive reach across society. Perhaps the best exemplar of ambitious industrial policy is the theory of the mission-directed entrepreneurial state by Mariana Mazzucato (2013; 2021a). She argues that not only is industrial policy warranted, it also has to be done in a *mission-directed* manner, whereby the powers of the state are focused toward politically ambitious, large-scale goals and where social actors are marshaled around a common mission. In this perspective, the call is not merely for "more industrial policy" to be pursued, but for the institutionalization of a new form of governance where state–society relations are restructured toward one where the state acts as a central focal point in driving social change. Mazzucato's transformative ideal entails "changing the relationship between public and private sectors, and between them and civil society, so they all work symbiotically for a common goal. The reason for rethinking government is simple: only government has the capacity to bring about transformation on the scale needed" (2021a, p. 205). Just like the United States succeeded in the ambitious goal of sending a man to the moon, governments should similarly pursue grand state-led missions today, namely tackling the climate emergency.

While mission-oriented industrial policy is arguably the leading voice in the industrial policy agenda, there is a lesser-known strand of thinking, mostly associated with the writings of economist Dani Rodrik. In this view, industrial policy should not be ambitious, but rather modest. The concern is to create scope for bottom-up experimentation. As Rodrik writes: *"the more ambitious the goals of industrial policy are, the less government knows about the techniques available to solve them"* (Aiginger and Rodrik 2020, p. 202, emphasis mine). Rather than the traditional approach of industrial policy where state elites pick winners and losers ex ante, modest industrial policy likens it to a "search process in unknown territory, which should be open to new solutions, experiments, and learning" (ibid., p. 202). The implication is that public sector organizations should be restructured accordingly, to approach industrial policy in a much more modest manner, based on the principles of "open architecture, self-organization and transparency," and in so doing improve its epistemic capacity in an environment of uncertainty (Hausmann and Rodrik 2006, pp. 31–33).

Strangely enough, the language of complexity, experimentation and modesty is also incorporated within Mazzucato's ambitious plan for state-led social change. Denying that she wishes to simply pick winners and losers, Mazzucato (2021a, p. 53) instead claims that the entrepreneurial state's role is to "pick a direction, and within that direction take a wide portfolio approach," whereby private agents get to experiment but are somehow still expected to cohere with the pre-chosen direction of the state. Like Rodrik, she acknowledges that the problems society deals with today are complex "wicked" ones that defy "linear" solutions (ibid., p. 154), but unlike Rodrik, she explicitly endorses a muscular state.

Accordingly, I argue that modest industrial policy, whether of the Rodrik school or concerning Mazzucato's equivocation, is an incoherent position. If the concerns of uncertainty and complexity are taken seriously, then this translates into a polycentric structure of governance between decision-making entities that requires a public actor to give up any ambition to structurally transform society. Additionally, policies would need to be implemented in a piecemeal fashion, which renders it powerless to change the direction of production which is a dynamic by-product of the diverse choices of entrepreneurial agents. Conversely, if the aim of structural *transformation* is retained, then it requires an *ambitious* degree of state capacity, which is necessary to align the actions and aims of individual agents according to a cohesive plan of action. In other words, Mazzucato's mission-oriented entrepreneurial state approach, which precisely and explicitly calls for such cohesive alignment, is a far more authentic approach to industrial policy and one more faithful to the underlying goal of steering structural transformation.

The essay is structured as follows. The first section reviews the literature on complex systems and its implications on public policy. It shows that the challenge of radical uncertainty and complexity faced by human agents warrants policymaking that is modest, piecemeal and limited in scope. The second section investigates the theoretical foundations of structural transformation that industrial policy aims to achieve, through the works of theorists such as Paul Rosenstein-Rodan, Simon Kuznets, Walt Rostow, Gunnar Myrdal, and Albert Hirschman.[1] Fundamentally, achieving structural transformation requires interventions not only into the economic structure of production but also into non-economic policy domains, giving rise to an expansionary logic of state power. The third section demonstrates the implications of this expansionary logic on Dani Rodrik's proposal for modest industrial policy, showing it to be self-defeating. Moreover, Mazzucato's account also rests on an equivocation where open dissent and experimentation are said to be favored while cohesive alignment to a common mission is expected. In the end, industrial policy advocates cannot have their cake and eat it too.

Complex Systems and the Need for Modesty in Public Governance

The economy is best understood as a complex system—an interconnected whole composed of many agents, institutions, and interactions that evolve. A system is complex not merely because it is large or disordered, but because its components are interdependent. Each part reacts to local information and incentives, yet the aggregate outcomes are shaped by countless feedback loops, contingencies, and emergent effects that cannot be traced back to any single actor's intention. This makes the system fundamentally open-ended and resistant to reductionist explanations.

Complexity arises when the behavior of the whole is not simply the sum of its parts. Individual decisions, though purposeful, interact in structured but unpredictable ways, giving rise to emergent properties—regularities that exist only at the systemic level and cannot be deduced from the properties of constituent parts (Hayek 1967; Lewis 2012). These interactions are organized rather than random: Firms, consumers, and governments operate within a web of institutions, rules, and social practices that structure their choices. Yet, even within these entanglements, the outcomes are contingent, sensitive to initial conditions, and shaped by historical path dependencies.

In such systems, radical uncertainty is the norm. Agents are not merely ignorant of particular facts; they are unaware of the full space of possible outcomes. New technologies, preferences, or institutional changes emerge endogenously within the system, making future developments both unknowable and constantly evolving (Henrekson et al. 2022). Unlike calculable risks, which assume known distributions

[1] These are all thinkers who contributed to the early foundations of structuralism, see Monga and Lin (2019, introduction).

of outcomes, radical "Knightian" uncertainty implies that even the set of possibilities is fluid and open-ended. This makes predictive planning, in the strong sense, inherently limited.

Importantly, this uncertainty is not a result of poor measurement or insufficient data, but a structural feature of how knowledge is produced and used in complex social systems. Each economic actor holds only partial, local, and often tacit knowledge, and coordination emerges through interaction rather than imposition. As a result, the system evolves not through the execution of a master plan, but through a process of continuous adaptation and learning.

These characteristics are particularly pronounced in the structure of production, i.e., the sectoral composition of the economy, the distribution of firms, the technologies employed, and the processes through which goods and services are made. These are not fixed elements but constantly shifting outcomes of decentralized, adaptive behavior. Changes in relative prices, consumer demand, regulatory rules, and innovation all affect which sectors expand or contract, which business models succeed, and which production techniques are adopted. Moreover, these shifts are often the result of mutual adjustment: Producers and consumers respond not only to market signals but also to each other's evolving actions and expectations.

This complex economic order cannot be understood through simple aggregation or mechanical models. Attempts to represent the economy using fixed equations or steady-state equilibrium assumptions ignore the layered ontology of social systems—where higher-level properties emerge from lower-level interactions in ways that are not reducible to them. As some critics have argued, many formal models in macroeconomics impose inappropriate assumptions: they presume closed systems, equilibrium dynamics, and representative agents, effectively eliminating the very complexity they aim to explain (Paniagua 2023). The result is an analytical framework that abstracts from the causal structures, rules, and interactions that give rise to economic outcomes.

Crucially, this complexity is not chaotic. Social systems can exhibit order and pattern, but they do so through organized complexity, a structured web of relations governed by procedural rules. These rules—legal norms, market institutions, regulatory frameworks—do not determine outcomes, but they shape the space of possible interactions. In this way, stability and adaptation can coexist. The economy evolves not through the execution of a directive plan (mission-directionality) but through ongoing, decentralized experimentation within a rule-bound order.

The implication for public policy is the need for modesty. Because knowledge is dispersed, contextual, and often tacit, no single authority can acquire the information needed to direct the economy's evolution. This is not simply a matter of technical limitation but a structural feature of complex systems. As such, policy interventions must be modest in scope and epistemically humble in aspiration. They should focus not on steering outcomes but on maintaining general procedural rules that facilitate interactions. Reforming these procedural frameworks—improving the legal environment for contracts, creating space for innovation, and ensuring accountability can have broad system-level effects without requiring predictive control.

Public policy in complex systems must also be iterative and adaptive. Since no blueprint can reliably anticipate emergent outcomes, policies must be open to revision, grounded in local experimentation, and subject to continual feedback (Colander and Kupers 2016). The logic is akin to evolutionary learning: small-scale interventions allow for trial and error, limiting the risk of systemic failure and enabling successful strategies to proliferate beyond. Large, sweeping interventions, by contrast, are brittle. They presume a level of foresight and synoptic intelligence that is incompatible with the structure of the system itself. Taking complexity seriously means rethinking the role of public action. It suggests that effective governance is not about intelligent planning but about maintaining basic and general conditions under which self-organizing processes can flourish. The appropriate metaphor is not the "engineer" with a blueprint, but the "gardener" who maintains an evolving ecosystem (Feld and Nientiedt 2022).

The need for policy modesty, as grounded in the theory of complex systems, can be further clarified by examining socialism as a mode of social organization. Historically, the failure of central planning under socialism has been well documented, rooted in its inability to gather and process the vast and dispersed knowledge required for efficient resource allocation. The failure of socialism lies in its ambition, to *replace* the perceived chaos of market coordination with the supposed scientific order of centralized rational planning (Lavoie 2016). However, this critique applies primarily to large-scale socialism (Hodgson 2019). If socialism is pursued on a smaller scale, within intentional communities, cooperatives, or worker-owned enterprises, then many of these knowledge problems are significantly attenuated. Such arrangements have existed throughout history and may continue to function within the wider institutional setting of a liberal market order. In short, when socialist aspirations are reframed in more modest terms, they become more feasible and less prone to the epistemic and democratic failures of large-scale state planning.

Yet this move toward modest socialism necessitates significant concessions. Once socialists abandon the aim of transcending market-based pricing and competition altogether, they must accept that any non-market modes of organization must exist *within* a broader non-hierarchical meta-framework characterized by freedom of entry and exit. Indeed, any viable economic system must fall back on decentralized coordination mechanisms involving mutual adjustment among relatively autonomous agents. This includes the possibility that non-market arrangements (which may be established within the broader liberal order) may fail, dissolve, or be displaced by more successful alternatives. Modest socialism, therefore, implies not only accepting the procedural norms of liberal institutions but also relinquishing the classical Marxist ambition of *transforming* society wholesale. It must concede that even small-scale experiments in non-market governance are contingent, revisable, and subject to the pressures of the larger market order in which they are embedded. In this sense, modest socialism may survive, *but only by giving up the very project of systemic social transformation.* I will now proceed to elucidate that industrial policy advocates must similarly abandon the aim of structural transformation if modesty is taken seriously.

Why Care About Modesty?

What is at stake, in terms of the discussion of modest socialism, is not only a concern with efficient resource allocation but also its compatibility with the value of liberal democracy. Any goal which is pursued in an ambitious mission-oriented manner across society carries the significant risk of the loss of liberty, by licensing state elites to implement the mission at hand come what may (Cheang 2024). Historically, the logic of mission-directionality emphasized by Mazzucato has waxed and waned, but is most pronounced in times of emergencies, when a cohesive, directed approach to policymaking is warranted, such as in times of war or in the case of the recent pandemic response. The sweeping restrictions on civil liberties implemented after COVID-19 were perhaps understandable in the context of a "public health emergency," but they illustrate how totalizing policymaking can be inimical to freedom (Pennington 2021). Such responses can be tolerated only if they remain truly exceptional. The danger is if they become institutionalized or normalized as part of routine governance, thus eroding the open texture of democratic society.

The value of modesty is further associated with a healthy and sustainable liberal democracy because it reflects a disposition appropriate to governing in conditions of pluralism, fallibility, and moral disagreement. If liberal democracy is valued, then modesty, which may also be called "moderation," must be recognized not as a symptom of indecision, but as a positive virtue grounded in epistemic humility, respect for difference and a sober awareness of the limits of technocratic political knowledge (Craiutu 2023). It resists the temptation to subordinate society to any singular goal or ideology, recognizing instead that liberal democracy thrives on a diversity of ends and a multiplicity of voices. In this sense, moderation serves as the political expression of modesty: It tempers the zeal of ideological certainty with the discipline of institutional restraint.

Similarly, taking complexity concerns seriously has implications for contemporary climate policy. Like an economy, the climate system exhibits the hallmarks of a complex, nonlinear, and adaptive system, marked by feedback loops, tipping points, and irreducible uncertainties. Specifically, the climate system involves interactions among multiple subsystems, atmosphere, ocean, land, cryosphere, and biosphere, each with its internal variability and operating on different spatial and temporal scales (Curry 2023). As a result, there are emergent dynamics that make the overall environmental ecosystem highly sensitive to contingent shocks and which are impossible to model in a deterministic way. Any sensible response to climate risks must therefore be modest, adaptive, and context-sensitive, rooted not in grand global schemes of control, but in an ethos of epistemic humility and pluralism. However, much of contemporary climate policy remains narrowly focused on the *singular goal* of reducing carbon dioxide emissions, often structured by integrated assessment models and scientific consensus-building exercises that privilege one form of knowledge (Hulme 2023). While climate change does warrant a policy response, it does not follow that it needs to be ambitious and expansive, especially if one wishes to maintain an appreciation for democratic and epistemic pluralism.

Public policy that is sensitive to the challenge of complexity and its resulting uncertainty is modest, implying limits on scale, size, scope, and application. The key requirement is the existence of multiple decision-making centers that allow for trial-and-error and cross-movement. The question for our purposes is whether industrial policy may be modest in this way while retaining its macro-aim of structural transformation. The next section will explain the concept of structural transformation aimed at by industrial policy advocates, and the last section will show why such an objective cannot be genuinely modest.

The Essence of Industrial Policy: Structural Transformation

Before we evaluate whether industrial policy can incorporate modesty, it is necessary to first understand what it aims at, namely "structural transformation." At the heart of the theory of structural transformation is the belief that development policy must be seen from a "system-wide" perspective, specifically how different sectors, economic practices, and institutions all interconnect with each other to give rise to macro-level outcomes. Importantly, this means that economic policy is not an isolated domain but intimately tied with various other domains, as theorists of structural transformation (henceforth called "structuralists") have admitted. For them, they view the economy structurally, and such structures refer to:

> the composition of production activities, the associated patterns of specialization in international trade, the technological capabilities of the economy, including the educational level of the labor force, the structure of ownership of factors of production, the nature and development of basic state institutions, and the degree of development and constraints under which certain markets operate (the absence of certain segments of the financial market or the presence of a large underemployed labor force, for example). (Ocampo et al. 2009, p. 7)

To successfully engage in structural transformation is not merely to promote a new technology or industry but involves influencing the "social context in which economies operate" in a system-wide manner (Ocampo et al. 2009, p. xv). Theoretically, structuralist economic thinking is grounded in the concept of "wholeness" and strives to "account for a complete audit of the social setting" (Dutt and Ros 2003, pp. 57–59). Consequently, if such a complete auditing of the social setting is within its purview, structuralist policymaking naturally carries with it an inherent expansionary logic of state power that cannot be easily contained to one specific domain of human life.

A key conceptual pillar of structuralism is the recognition of internal rigidities and coordination failures that prevent development from occurring spontaneously. These include a nation's factor endowments, which may be unsuited to industrialization, or the absence of key sectors, institutions, or capabilities needed to sustain it. These are market failures that can persist over time. In response, structuralists argue that the state not only addresses such market failures in isolation but also rectify structural gaps that cut across society. An important task is to support industries with the strongest horizontal and vertical "linkages" to catalyze unbalanced growth strategies

(Hirschman 1958). For example, supporting manufacturing can produce spillovers both upstream and downstream in the production chain. Success hinges on the state's ability to "detect how one activity leads to another," sequencing interventions to create an expanding web of complementarities (Oqubay 2020, pp. 44–45). Such logic—once one thread is pulled—inevitably demands further action.

Structuralists have historically advocated transformation from an economy centered on low-productivity, often agricultural activity, into one characterized by capital intensity, scale economies, and sustained productivity growth. Today, however, there is recognition that services or some post-industrial structure may be the future. Yet, the underlying point shared in structuralism is that "all of today's high-income economies" have undergone this sort of deep structural transformation (from traditional to modern) converting "even the resource-poor, landlocked ones into dynamic performers and successful stories" (Lin and Monga 2017, p. 128). Coupled with the market failure paradigm, the implication is that absent a powerful activist state, poor nations may remain trapped in suboptimal equilibria.

Significantly, achieving structural transformation from a tradition-based to a modern production landscape implies an expansive logic, requiring the state to extend its reach and coherence across multiple policy domains. Consider the notion of linkage effects again. Manufacturing cannot develop in isolation. It depends on complementary capabilities such as transport infrastructure, engineering services, credit systems, educational institutions, and an educated labor force. Supporting one sector pulls a thread that draws others into the frame. Achieving coherent structural transformation, then, demands simultaneous and coordinated interventions, targeting not just individual firms, but whole ecosystems. Moreover, modern economies require access to land, credit, and labor markets that support industrial needs. This necessitates interventions in land-use planning, financial sector reform, and labor-market regulation. The state must first possess *extensive* state capacity, spanning multiple policy domains, to ensure that they all cohere with the planned objective, and second, *intensive* state capacity, the ability to enforce its will in any specific domain. Each intervention calls forth even more, to bring social actors into coherence and alignment with the desired mission.

Notably, this expansionary logic is not confined to the tangible economic sphere of production but can spill over into other intangible realms. Historically, the transformation from a tradition-based economy to a modern one is not merely a function of what is produced but implicates a range of social practices. Walt Rostow's (1971) "stages of growth" illuminate the contrast: traditional economies are agricultural, local, low-investment, and governed by rigid social structures and customary norms. In contrast, modern economies are marked by technological dynamism, capital accumulation, institutional complexity, and the proliferation of formal systems—law, banking, and education—that support innovation and growth. While many structuralists may reject Rostow's linear and normative "neoliberal" framing, they share the conviction that successful transformation involves radical changes not only in "what is produced" but also in the underlying systems of knowledge, social aspiration, and institutional order (ibid., Chaps. 2 and 3).

Two aspects of these broader shifts illustrate the expansive scope of state intervention implied. The first concerns human skills and cultural values. State-led industrialization required not just a technical matching of skills to industrial jobs but also the cultivation of an industrial culture valuing savings, discipline, innovation, and technical learning. East Asian experiences, often heavily praised by structuralists, are instructive. In Singapore, for example, the state pursued an aggressive campaign of linguistic and cultural engineering: the promotion of English over local languages and dialects, the systematic valorization of industrial virtues such as hard work and lifelong learning, and extensive moral suasion to inculcate norms of productivity and technical upgrading (Tremewan 1996; Cheang and Choy 2024). Similarly, in South Korea, industrial policy was not confined to subsidies but involved mass mobilization around educational achievement and engineering skills, coordinated through both formal schooling and cultural engineering (Ogle 1990; Oh 1999). Such cultural engineering had to be pursued to foster the sociological conditions favorable to modern industrial development. As Simon Kuznets, a chief theorist of structural transformation confirmed, "changes in the structure of production are usually associated with, indeed *require*, changes in other aspects of social structure—not only economic but also political and in the long run even ideological" (Kuznets 1971, pp. 75–76; emphasis added). Once the thread of sectoral change is pulled, it tugs on a web of interlinked social elements—language, norms, schooling, and identity—each reinforcing or constraining the other. What begins as an economic intervention quickly spreads across the cultural fabric, requiring transformations well beyond the factory floor.

Relatedly, structural transformation demands a reconfiguration of physical space. Industrial economies require urbanized, networked environments to support productive activity. This means not just building infrastructure but reshaping where and how people live. Moving from agriculture to manufacturing entails a "massive change" in housing and urban planning (Stiglitz 2019). Infrastructure investments, critical to structural transformation, are subject to indivisibilities and economies of scale—they must be large and coordinated, not piecemeal (Nurkse 1966; Gottschalk and Sampath 2021). In East Asia, this involved massive relocation programs, land consolidation, and urban redevelopment, often violating customary land use and private property norms (Chua 2018; Cheang 2024). Once state-led industrial development is set in motion, it triggers a cascade of spatial consequences: reshaping territory, displacing populations, and redrawing the administrative boundaries of everyday life.

Such patterns are not anomalies. History is replete with state-led structural transformation animated by visions of modernity. Whether they are successful is beside the point; what matters is their totalizing character. This can be exemplified by James Scott's (1998) account of "seeing like a state." From eighteenth-century Prussian forestry reform to Haussmann's Paris and blueprint colonial cities, these initiatives reflected a belief that societies could be rationally reordered through planning and statecraft. These were not narrow "economic policies" but involved the reorganization of land, labor, knowledge systems, and everyday life. Structural transformation, if pursued seriously to its logical conclusion, necessarily extends into the political and cultural domains. Once the transformation begins, coherence demands that no domain be left untouched.

To be clear, neither industrial policy advocates nor structural transformation theorists intentionally or explicitly endorse authoritarianism or coercion as the means to achieve their aims. Rather, the point is that successful structural transformation inevitably encounters deep-seated barriers, economic, institutional, and cultural, that require an ambitious and powerful state to overcome. Without confronting these obstacles, the process risks remaining partial or stalling altogether. One cannot isolate the economic structure of production from its corresponding social, cultural, and ideological foundations. As Kuznets reminds us, "some structural changes, not only in economic but also in social institutions and beliefs, are required, without which modern economic growth would be impossible" (Kuznets 1971, p. 348). Unsurprisingly, structuralists working within the modernization theory paradigm often diagnosed underdevelopment in cultural terms. Gunnar Myrdal, for example, condemned the "prevailing attitudes and patterns of individual performance in life and at work" as "deficient," citing what he saw as "low levels of alertness, adaptability, ambition, and general readiness for change and experiment; contempt for manual work; submissiveness to authority and exploitation; low aptitude for cooperation; low standards of personal hygiene; and so on" (Myrdal 1970, p. 226).[2] In this tradition, economic transformation is inseparable from cultural transformation. Each reinforces, and ultimately requires, the other.

Thus, the aspiration to achieve structural transformation demands far more than selective product-market interventions. It requires a deep and systematic reworking of the human, institutional, and spatial foundations of a society. It requires intervention across various domains of society: Macroeconomic stability, innovation systems, infrastructure, education, and cultural norms must all change in tandem (see papers in Monga and Lin 2019; Oqubay et al. 2020). Such planning proposals proceed from changing the "hardware" to engineering the "software"; it even entails "a definitive social, political and cultural victory of those who would modernize the economy over those who would…cling to the traditional society" (Rostow 1959, p. 7). A complete re-engineering of the social setting becomes imperative.

The ambitious nature of structural transformation is precisely why, according to its theorists, success has been hard to come by. It is said that "the main intellectual challenge for economics was (and remains) to understand why so few countries have managed to engineer such structural transformation" (Lin and Monga 2014, p. 278). Ironically, they have themselves provided the answer to this puzzle. Few nations can muster such robust "state capacity," let alone "engineer" the intimate details of private lives. The sheer difficulty of the task also helps one understand why structuralists have typically called for an expansive state. For them, development is not just about injecting a "missing ingredient" (such as more subsidies) but involves a "binding agent" to "bring together various scattered or hidden elements" (Hirschman 1958,

[2] Gunnar Myrdal's position within structuralism is established and confirmed in Monga and Lin (2019, p. 13).

pp. 6–7).[3] In comes the ambitious state, advocated by structuralists such as Alexander Gerschenkron, Ragnar Nurkse, and Paul Rosenstein-Rodan, to kickstart a "big push" (Taylor 2004; Cheang and Palmer 2023, Chap. 2). Structural transformation is not a matter of technical adjustment. It is *a far-reaching act of political, social, and institutional reconstitution driven by the state.*

You Cannot Have Your Cake and Eat It Too

As established, structural transformation is an ambitious task that calls for an ambitious state, with robust powers to impose its will on the population. Historically, this involved the transformation from an agrarian to a modern industrial economy. More recently, industrial policy advocates have envisioned new frontiers for structural transformation, including an innovation-led economy and one that is sustainable. The leading advocate of contemporary industrial policy is arguably Mariana Mazzucato, who has pushed the logic of "mission-directionality" in her work, and who thus personifies the spirit of ambitious structural transformation.

You're Free to Experiment—Inside the Mission Box

The logic of mission-directionality in Mariana Mazzucato's work takes center stage. The argument is not merely that governments should support specific industries through industrial policy, but that these tools should be integrated into a larger program to transcend the perceived limitations of neoliberal governance (Mazzucato 2021b). Specifically, industrial policy must serve politically ambitious goals. The state must focus its capacity on large-scale missions, mobilizing social actors to align with common objectives. In this way, what Mazzucato calls the "entrepreneurial state" is part of a broader normative vision: the creation of a mission-directed society. Consistent with the structuralist paradigm, she calls for a radical "transformation," involving "changing the relationship between public and private sectors, and between them and civil society, so they all work symbiotically for a common goal. The reason for rethinking government is simple: only government has the capacity to bring about transformation on the scale needed" (Mazzucato 2021a, p. 205). The totalizing nature of the project is evident. All sectors of society must work in line with a "common goal."

A careful reading of Mazzucato's proposals reveals that she is operating firmly within the structuralist tradition. As established above, this tradition favors a state powerful enough to overcome barriers and rigidities that prevent development. The

[3] Overall, Hirschman's vision of transformation is iterative yet encompassing. It may proceed one key sector after another but ultimately involves all aspects of the economy—industry, agriculture, infrastructure, human skills—and requires policy activism at each step.

only difference is context. Unlike the early industrializers of the twentieth century, Mazzucato's entrepreneurial state does not aim for catch-up growth. It operates in advanced, service-based economies. Yet the principle of structural transformation remains unchanged. The goal is no longer just economic development but a redirection of society toward progressive public missions, from tackling climate change to reducing inequality (Mazzucato 2024). Her model of a mission-directed state is thus a direct extension of structural transformation theory. It is not a modest reform proposal. It is a continuation of a longstanding belief in the state as a vehicle, a Hirschmanian "binding agent," for systemic change.

What is queer, however, is that Mazzucato simultaneously attempts to incorporate the language of complexity and uncertainty. She argues that the entrepreneurial state should not engage in central planning or heavy-handed interference but should instead embrace experimentation. This is because the problems she seeks to address are "wicked" in nature—complex and unsolvable in linear ways (Mazzucato 2021a, p. 154). She adds that the state operates in "open systems that are full of uncertainty and ambiguity" and must therefore be capable of "adapting to the underlying complexity" (ibid., p. 203). These claims are paired with a rejection of "mainstream economics," which she criticizes for focusing on "equilibrium and ideal outcomes" rather than dynamic, adaptive processes (ibid., pp. 202–203). She also insists that the state is not about command and control. To guard against such tendencies, she affirms the importance of "true participation," arguing that "open systems are more reactive to what can be seen as a countervailing power, i.e., dissension" (ibid., p. 202).

But this rhetorical embrace of dissension and complexity sits uneasily with the logic of mission-directionality. By definition, a mission hopes for convergence and alignment, but the countervailing forces she cites are *centrifugal*. They pull away from the center, introducing fragmentation and divergence. Yet the mission-directed state ultimately depends on *centripetal* forces—those that pull actors together toward a shared goal. While dissension is nominally welcomed, it can only be tolerated to the extent that it does not derail coherence. In practice, divergence must be absorbed, disciplined, or excluded. This is the price of attempting a systemic transformation. A state that asks all to work "symbiotically for a common goal" cannot, on pain of self-contradiction, simultaneously tolerate an environment where multiple, possibly incompatible goals flourish unchecked.

Mazzucato's incoherence becomes clearer when we examine her justification for state action. She claims that the state must not pick winners and losers in the traditional sense. Rather, "it should pick a direction, and within that direction take a wide portfolio approach. In other words, not pick one technology, or a random sector (usually one of those that lobbies hardest), or even a type of firm (SMEs) but a direction that can foster and catalyze new collaborations across multiple sectors and have as a key spillover the growth of firms that engage with it. In that sense it is not about picking winners, but picking the willing" (Mazzucato 2021a, p. 53). But this raises awkward questions. If a firm is already "willing"—meaning it shares the mission—then why does it need to be picked? Such collaborations can emerge organically.[4] If, on the other hand, a firm or actor pursues a contrary mission—say, continued fossil fuel investment—then the logic of coherence demands that this deviant be brought into line or be sidelined. Either way, the process ceases to be voluntary. Structural transformation, as she conceives it, cannot tolerate open-ended pluralism. It requires social actors to conform, not merely participate.

To illustrate this effect, consider a thought experiment. Imagine a group deciding which ice cream to buy. Everyone has different preferences, none of which are fixed. In a truly "open system," each person is free to choose, observe others, try alternatives, and revise their preferences over time. Preferences evolve through experience and comparison. This is how experimentation typically occurs. Now imagine the same group is told they must converge on one flavor. A committee is formed to debate and vote; after all, we desire "true participation" and "dissension." Yet, those who dissent must still eat what is collectively chosen. This is what mission-directionality, even with the incorporation of the deliberative process, amounts to: a process that mimics participation, but where adaptive, individual discovery is subordinated to a pre-agreed collective purpose. The rhetoric of openness masks a deeper requirement: coherence with the mission.

If one takes radical uncertainty seriously, as Mazzucato claims to do, then the institutional implication is clear. What is required is a fragmented political landscape with multiple jurisdictions. This would allow policy variation, inter-jurisdictional competition, and genuine experimentation through entry and exit. Social learning occurs not from centrally coordinated missions but from comparative feedback among diverse approaches (DeCanio 2014; Cheang 2024). Yet this is precisely what Mazzucato's vision cannot accommodate. Her mission-directed state simply cannot coexist with multiple missions. It must align, guide, and transform. The irony is sharp. She begins with the insight that uncertainty undermines markets, claiming that private actors behave like "pussycats" in the face of ambiguity, while only the state, the "real tiger," has the courage to act (Mazzucato 2013, p. 30). But this tiger does not create an open jungle. It marks out a path and expects others to follow.

Claiming to Wander, Determined to Direct

In contrast to Mariana Mazzucato, who equivocates between a mission-directed state and the rhetoric of open discussion, Dani Rodrik's proposal for industrial policy has a markedly different tone. There is much more explicit recognition of the problem of uncertainty and the attendant need for modesty, learning, and institutional flexibility. Yet, Rodrik's proposal, if taken seriously, lacks the force and coherence to overcome *the centrifugal tendencies in society that stand in the way of structural transformation.* In this sense, Mazzucato's entrepreneurial state remains a more authentic and consistent reflection of the structuralist tradition.

[4] For a similar critique of Mazzucato's justification for government action, the reader is referred to Elert and Henrekson (2022).

Importantly, while Mazzucato begins with a sweeping diagnosis of society's existential crises, such as the climate emergency and the concomitant sustainability goals, Rodrik instead places uncertainty at the center of his analysis. He acknowledges that industrial policy must operate as a "search process in unknown territory, which should be open to new solutions, experiments and learning" (Aiginger and Rodrik 2020, p. 202). Taking this premise seriously leads him to conclude that "the more ambitious the goals of industrial policy are, the less government knows about the techniques available to solve them" (ibid.). Such an admission points toward a conception of industrial policy that is modest, adaptive, and exploratory.

Rodrik's analysis, driven by the problem of uncertainty, leads him to outline institutional principles suited for such a context. Most notably, he insists that "industrial policy cannot rely on an omniscient government. It must rely on mechanisms that reveal information, wherever it may be" (Hausmann and Rodrik 2006, p. 30). The guiding principles he offers, open architecture, self-organization, and transparency, are to help the state interact more effectively with private actors and respond to dynamic information flows (ibid., pp. 31–33). However desirable such organizational reforms are for specific agencies, there is no reason to presume that they must be contained within centralized public authority. A genuinely open architecture is best embodied in a pluralist social order populated by multiple centers of decision-making, where actors, both public and private, self-organize, compete, and adapt in response to evolving circumstances. While Rodrik embraces these principles *within* the state apparatus, he cannot imagine a meta-social order *beyond* it, where the state itself is but one node among many, each capable of dissent and experimentation.

To his credit, Rodrik does not romanticize state capacity. He acknowledges that governments are hierarchical entities prone to "periodic reorganizations in search of simplicity followed by a gradual reversion back to a messier situation" (ibid., p. 34). As a potential remedy, he advocates exploring "network-like arrangements that may deliver what is required without any single node of the network being fully aware of all the things that are going on at any point in time" (ibid., p. 35). This is a promising direction. But its full implications are left unexplored. If one truly accepts "network-like" governance where no single node has a synoptic overview of the entire landscape, then it logically implies that no nodes have special over-arching authority over the rest. Other nodes within the network will possess genuine autonomy to make their own decisions and diverge, if they so choose, from the dominant mission. Such a vision is characteristic of the liberal polycentric tradition, where authority is divided across overlapping jurisdictions and no single actor possesses the final say over the rest (Aligica et al. 2019; Thunder and Paniagua 2024; Aligica and Murtazashvili 2025).

Embracing this logic would entail a radical shift in how the state's role is conceptualized. One would need to relinquish the notion of power as flowing from a single, hierarchical center, and instead recognize a system of dispersed authority (Kukathas 2003). However, Rodrik cannot entertain this conclusion at risk of undermining his proposals. His vision of a networked governance structure remains confined to familiar actors—trade associations, ministries, and development banks—all collaborating under the state's overall umbrella (Hausmann and Rodrik 2006, p. 35). There is no meaningful attempt to imagine how the traditional Weberian monopoly of decision-making over a territory may be fragmented or even transcended in toto. Most importantly, Rodrik continues to affirm structural transformation as a central goal. As discussed earlier, this concept is highly ambitious, given the scale of economic and social reordering it entails. Rodrik remains committed to the view that "poor countries remain poor because markets do not work as well as they could to foster the structural transformation that is needed" (Rodrik 2009, p. 5). If structural transformation is a public good that markets cannot provide, then it falls to the state to orchestrate it.

The coherence of Rodrik's proposals to take seriously the concern of uncertainty and the attendant need for learning may be called into serious question. On one hand, there is an explicit recognition that industrial policymakers operate in "unknown territory." Yet, in the same paper, the concept of directionality is also invoked, ostensibly because "support of structural change and productivity growth can no longer serve as a policy goal without any consideration of the direction of technological change" (Aiginger and Rodrik 2020, p. 193). Directionality, then, is still very much in play.

This gives rise to a contradiction. If policymakers are operating in genuinely "unknown territory," how can they determine a coherent direction for others to follow? Directionality presupposes some kind of synoptic view, a vantage point over the epistemic terrain from which the relevant paths can be charted and social actors "steered" into alignment. This is difficult to reconcile with the idea of a network-like arrangement where "no single node is fully aware of all the things going on at any point in time" (Hausmann and Rodrik 2006, p. 35). The tension is not merely semantic. It forces a choice between two conflicting visions where the state is either one *explorer* among many, wandering alongside others in a landscape of uncertainty, or it is a *leader* with privileged knowledge, charting the course for others to follow.

In the end, it is difficult to pin down exactly where advocates of modest industrial policy really stand. The literature on structural transformation and industrial policy is sprawling, encompassing a wide range of formulations. What this article has sought to do is assess the coherence of these competing visions. The key question is the following: Just how ambitiously will industrial policy advocates implement their proposals? On one hand, we are told that "the more ambitious the goals of industrial policy are, the less government knows about the techniques available to solve them" (Aiginger and Rodrik 2020, p. 202). Yet the same author, in a recent co-authored work with the advocate of arguably the most ambitious industrial policy theory, writes that we need a "different type of industrial strategy" that "not only catalyzes but also directs growth" (Mazzucato and Rodrik 2023, p. 4). This strategy includes "redesigning the direction of the economy from the ground up" (ibid., p. 35). Whether this is a case of admirable intellectual evolution or a quiet relapse into old habits is for the reader to judge.

Conclusion

Modest industrial policy is theoretically incoherent. The reasons stem from what industrial policy fundamentally aims to achieve, namely structural transformation. Structural transformation is inherently ambitious, requiring coordinated interventions across multiple domains that extend far beyond narrow economic policy. When pursued consistently, it requires a state with sufficient power to align private decisions with collective objectives and reshape the social setting of human life. Unsurprisingly, the theoretical foundations of structural transformation all point toward an expansive logic of state action. These structuralist thinkers understood that changing production structures pulls threads across society, necessitating interventions in domains spanning from finance and education to urban planning and cultural norms. Structural transformation is not confined to the production sphere and sealed off from other aspects of social life.

Contemporary industrial policy advocates face a Catch-22 choice. Either they embrace modesty, abandoning the desire to "steer" complex systems, or they persist with structural transformation. They cannot do both. Mariana Mazzucato's mission-oriented approach, despite its rhetoric of experimentation, remains more theoretically consistent with transformative ambitions. Her call for "all to work symbiotically for a common goal" reveals a logic that necessarily constrains the pluralism that genuine experimentation requires. Meanwhile, Rodrik's attempt to reconcile industrial policy with uncertainty ultimately falters on the same contradiction.

This is not to suggest that advocates of industrial policy harbor totalitarian ambitions. Rather, it clarifies the theoretical tensions in the literature and the logical implications of state-led structural transformation. East Asian developmental states did not achieve such transformation through modest means but through powerful and authoritarian social engineering. The challenge of complexity implies a modest state, but structural transformation requires an expansive and intrusive one. Industrial policy advocates cannot have it both ways.

References

Aiginger, K., & Rodrik, D. (2020). Rebirth of industrial policy and an agenda for the twenty-first century. *Journal of Industry, Competition and Trade*, *20*, 189–207. https://doi.org/10.1007/s10842-019-00322-3

Aligica, P. D., & Murtazashvili, J. B. (2025). *Governing Differences: Social Diversity, Polycentric Political Economy and Modus Vivendi*. Cheltenham: Edward Elgar Publishing.

Aligica, P., Boettke, P., & Tarko, V. (2019). *Public Governance and the Classical-Liberal Perspective: Political Economy Foundations*. New York, NY: Oxford University Press.

Cheang, B. (2024). Why mission-directed governance risks authoritarianism: Lessons from East Asia. *Journal of Institutional Economics*, *20*, e43. https://doi.org/10.1017/S1744137424000316

Cheang, B., & Palmer, T. (2023). *Institutions and Economic Development: Markets, Ideas, and Bottom-Up Change*. Singapore: Springer Nature.

Cheang, B., & Choy, D. (2024). Culture of meritocracy, political hegemony, and Singapore's development. *International Journal of Politics, Culture, and Society, 37*, 265–290. https://doi.org/10.1007/s10767-023-09458-x
Chua, B. H. (2018). *Liberalism Disavowed: Communitarianism and State Capitalism in Singapore.* Singapore: NUS Press.
Colander, D., & Kupers, R. (2016). *Complexity and the Art of Public Policy: Solving Society's Problems from the Bottom Up.* Princeton, NJ: Princeton University Press.
Craiutu, A. (2023). *Why Not Moderation? Letters to Young Radicals.* Cambridge: Cambridge University Press.
Curry, J. (2023). *Climate Uncertainty and Risk.* London: Anthem Press.
DeCanio, S. (2014). Democracy, the Market, and the Logic of Social Choice. *American Journal of Political Science, 58*(3), 637–652. https://doi.org/10.1111/ajps.12072
Collins Dictionary. (2025). Definition of "incoherent." Retrieved April 3, 2025, https://www.collinsdictionary.com/dictionary/english/incoherent
Dutt, A. K., & Ros, J. (2003). *Development Economics and Structuralist Macroeconomics: Essays in Honor of Lance Taylor*. Cheltenham: Edward Elgar.
Elert, N., & Henrekson, M. (2022). Collaborative innovation blocs and mission-oriented innovation policy: An ecosystem perspective. In K. Wennberg & C. Sandstrom (Eds.), *Questioning the Entrepreneurial State* (pp. 345–367). Cham: Springer. https://doi.org/10.1007/978-3-030-94273-1_18
Feld, L., & Nientiedt, D. (2022). Hayekian economic policy. *Journal of Economic Behavior & Organization, 204*(December), 457–465. https://doi.org/10.1016/j.jebo.2022.10.019
Gottschalk, R., & Sampath, P. G. (2021). Infrastructure for structural transformation: A comeback of planning? *Journal of Infrastructure Development, 13*(1), 53–64. https://doi.org/10.1177/09749306211023667
Hausmann, R., & Rodrik, D. (2006). *Doomed to Choose: Industrial Policy as Predicament.* Cambridge, MA: Kennedy School of Government.
Hayek, F. A. (1967). The theory of complex phenomena: A precocious play on the epistemology of complexity. In *Studies in Philosophy, Politics and Economics* (pp. 22–42). London: Routledge.
Henrekson, M., Kärnä, A., & Sanandaji, T. (2022). Schumpeterian entrepreneurship: Coveted by policymakers but impervious to top-down policymaking. *Journal of Evolutionary Economics, 32*(3), 867–890. https://doi.org/10.1007/s00191-022-00761-y
Hirschman, A. O. (1958). *The Strategy of Economic Development*. New Haven, CT: Yale University Press.
Hodgson, G. M. (2019). *Is Socialism Feasible? Towards an Alternative Future*. Cheltenham: Edward Elgar.
Hulme, M. (2023). *Climate Change Isn't Everything.* Hoboken, NJ: John Wiley & Sons.
Juhasz, R., Lane, N., & Rodrik, D. (2024). The new economics of industrial policy. *Annual Review of Economics, 16*, 213–242. https://doi.org/10.1146/annurev-economics-081023-024638
Krugman, P. (2023). How to think about green industrial policy. *New York Times.* May 9. https://www.nytimes.com/2023/05/09/opinion/climate-inflation-reduction-act-biden.html
Kukathas, C. (2003). *The Liberal Archipelago.* Oxford: Oxford University Press.
Kuznets, S. (1971). *Economic Growth of Nations: Total Output and Production Structure.* Cambridge, MA: Harvard University Press.
Lavoie, D. (2016). *National Economic Planning.* Arlington, VA: Mercatus Center (originally published 1985).
Lewis, P. (2012). Emergent properties in the work of Friedrich Hayek. *Journal of Economic Behavior & Organization, 82*(2–3), 368–378. https://doi.org/10.1016/j.jebo.2011.04.009
Lin, J. Y., & Monga, C. (2014). The evolving paradigms of structural change. In B. Currie-Alder, R. Kanbur, D. M. Malone, & R. Medhora (Eds.), *International Development: Ideas, Experience, and Prospects* (pp. 277–294). Oxford: Oxford University Press.
Lin, J. Y., & Monga, C. (2017). *Beating the Odds: Jump-Starting Developing Countries.* Princeton, NJ: Princeton University Press.

Mazzucato, M. (2013). *The Entrepreneurial State: Debunking Public vs. Private Sector Myths*. London: Penguin Books.

Mazzucato, M. (2016). From market fixing to market-creating: A new framework for innovation policy. *Industry and Innovation, 23*(2), 140–156. https://doi.org/10.1080/13662716.2016.1146124

Mazzucato, M., & Rodrik, D. (2023). Industrial policy with conditionalities: A taxonomy and sample cases. London: UCL Institute for Innovation and Public Purpose. https://discovery.ucl.ac.uk/id/eprint/10196231/1/Mazzucato_industrial_policy_with_conditionalities_a_taxonomy_and_sample_cases.pdf

Mazzucato, M. (2021a). *Mission Economy: A Moonshot Guide to Changing Capitalism*. London: Allen Lane.

Mazzucato, M. (Ed.). (2021b). *Public Purpose: Industrial Policy's Comeback and Government's Role in Shared Prosperity*. Cambridge, MA: Boston Review.

Mazzucato, M. (2024). Welcome to mission economics. https://marianamazzucato.substack.com/p/welcome-to-mission-economics

Monga, C., & Lin, J. Y. (Eds.) (2019). *The Oxford Handbook of Structural Transformation*. Oxford: Oxford University Press.

Myrdal, G. (1970). *An Approach to the Asian Drama: Methodological and Theoretical*. London: Vintage Books.

Nurkse, R. (1966). *Problems of Capital Formation in Underdeveloped Countries*. New York, NY: Oxford University Press (originally published in 1953).

Ocampo, J. A., Rada, C., & Taylor, L. (2009). *Growth and Policy in Developing Countries: A Structuralist Approach*. New York, NY: Columbia University Press.

Ogle, G. E. (1990). *South Korea: Dissent within the Economic Miracle*. London: Zed Books.

Oh, J. K.-C. (1999). *Korean Politics: The Quest for Democratization and Economic Development*. Ithaca, NY: Cornell University Press.

Oqubay, A., Cramer, C., Chang, H.-J., & Kozul-Wright, R. (Eds.) (2020). *The Oxford Handbook of Industrial Policy*. Oxford: Oxford University Press.

Oqubay, A. (2020). The theory and practice of industrial policy. In H. J. Chang, A. Oqubay, C. J. Cramer, & R. Kozul-Wright (Eds.), *The Oxford Handbook of Industrial Policy*. Oxford: Oxford University Press.

Paniagua, P. (2023). Complexity defying macroeconomics. *Cambridge Journal of Economics, 47*(3), 575–592. https://doi.org/10.1093/cje/bead002

Pennington, M. (2021). Foucault and Hayek on public health and the road to serfdom. *Public Choice, 195*, 125–143. https://doi.org/10.1007/s11127-021-00926-6

Rodrik, D. (2009). Industrial policy: Don't ask why, ask how. *Middle East Development Journal, 1*(1), 1–29. https://doi.org/10.1142/S1793812009000024

Rodrik, D. (2022). An industrial policy for good jobs. Washington DC: Brookings Institution. https://www.brookings.edu/research/an-industrial-policy-for-good-jobs/

Rostow, W. W. (1959). The stages of economic growth. *Economic History Review, 12*(1), 1–16. https://doi.org/10.1111/j.1468-0289.1959.tb01829.x

Rostow, W. W. (1971). *The Stages of Economic Growth: A Non-Communist Manifesto* (2nd ed.). Cambridge: Cambridge University Press (originally published in 1960).

Scott, J. C. (1998). *Seeing Like a State: How Certain Schemes to Improve the Human Condition Have Failed*. New Haven, CT: Yale University Press.

Smith, V. L. (2003). Constructivist and ecological rationality in economics. *American Economic Review, 93*(3), 465–508. https://doi.org/10.1257/000282803322156954

Stiglitz, J. (2019). Structural transformation, deep downturns, and government policy. In C. Monga & J. Y. Lin (Eds.), *Oxford Handbook of Structural Transformation* (pp. 35–44). Oxford: Oxford University Press.

Taylor, L. (2004). *Reconstructing Macroeconomics: Structuralist Proposals and Critiques of the Mainstream*. Cambridge, MA: Harvard University Press.

Thunder, D., & Paniagua, P. (2024). *Polycentric Governance and the Good Society*. Lanham, MD: Rowman & Littlefield.

Tremewan, C. (1996). *Political Economy of Social Control in Singapore*. London: Palgrave Macmillan.

Bryan Cheang is the Director of the Hayek Program at the London School of Economics. He is also a Senior Fellow at the Centre for the Study of Governance and Society at King's College London, where he received his PhD in Political Economy. He researches into the political economy of development, the role of culture and ideas in state-market interactions, liberalism in the Global South, and the challenges of industrial planning under conditions of uncertainty. He is the author of multiple academic articles and books, most recently *Southeast Asia's Development,* published by Oxford University Press.

Raiders of the Entrepreneurial State: A Baptist and Bootlegger Analysis

Jeffrey Muldoon and Derek K. Yonai

Abstract Rather than producing productive entrepreneurship, the entrepreneurial state creates opportunities for plunder by well-connected insiders. These insiders exploit the entrepreneurial state to rent-seek, to enrich themselves without producing anything of value to society. We argue that these opportunists behave according to the Bootlegger and Baptist theory of Public Choice. The opportunists attempt to legitimize their ill-gotten wealth by hiding in the shadows of perceived socially virtuous actors. The opportunistic actor (the Bootlegger) will partner with an idealistic, true believing party (the Baptist) to form a coalition which enables the latter party to correct a wrong that they believe needs righting, while providing the Bootlegger an opportunity to rent-seek and transfer wealth. We examine this scenario in terms of how these counter-intuitive coalitions form in environmental policy and extract wealth under the guise of protecting the environment. We will examine this behavior by analyzing the adoption of LED lightbulbs, the slowing of nuclear power development, and the incentives created in the Paris Agreement.

Keywords Rent-seeking · Bootleggers and baptists · Public choice · Entrepreneurship · Industrial policy · Entrepreneurial state

JEL Codes K00 · H10 · L26 · M10

J. Muldoon
Department of Management and Business Administration School of Business, Southeastern Louisiana University, Hammond, LA, USA
e-mail: jeffrey.muldoon@southeastern.edu

D. K. Yonai (✉)
School of Business, Flagler College, St. Augustine, FL, USA
e-mail: Dyonai@flagler.edu

M. Henrekson et al. (eds.), *A Green Entrepreneurial State?*, International Studies in Entrepreneurship 49, https://doi.org/10.1007/978-3-032-15512-2_4

Introduction

When Marianna Mazzucato published *The Entrepreneurial State* in 2013, she launched a major growth industry of works that argue that the way to grow the economy is through government-led innovation. This idea has since become orthodoxy in many countries, with the government becoming a major force investing in innovation—especially with what is known as the green economy.[1] Mazzucato (2013) builds on a long-standing tradition in economic discourse that highlights the role of the state in ensuring stability and handling market failures through regulation. Rather than just addressing issues from a regulatory or stimulus perspective, she argues that the government should invest in entrepreneurial companies. She builds on these ideas further in her work *Mission Economy* (2021)—where she refines her thesis that some projects (such as Project Apollo) are too large and too risky for public enterprise.

Mazzucato has performed a remarkable task by advancing a counter-intuitive argument that we need more rather than less government. In doing so, she challenges traditional narratives such as those of Philippon (2019) and Lindsey and Teles (2017), who argue that the United States and other countries have largely abandoned free markets since 2000. As evidence, they point to numerous regulations that have been enacted since then. However, Mazzucato and proponents of her work point to the lack of expenditures on growth projects (e.g., infrastructure and investment in new technology) in the West—especially compared with China. As a result, we have witnessed the emergence of a new orthodoxy; innovation produced by bureaucracy (Kattel et al., 2022).

This stands in direct opposition to the idealized notion of entrepreneurship, where it is often the result of entrepreneurs acting under conditions of uncertainty based on local information that creates innovation (Shane, 2004; Sarasvathy, 2009). As such, some entrepreneurship and business scholars have challenged this idea in two recently published edited collections (Wennberg and Sandström 2022; Henrekson et al., 2024). They challenged the basic assumptions of the entrepreneurial state through an examination of entrepreneurial and applied examples such as increased costs in higher education. Our contribution (Muldoon and Yonai 2023) to this debate has been to question the notions of the entrepreneurial state through the prism of Public Choice economics. We challenged two major assumptions of the entrepreneurial state framework. First, the state, as a collective, does not really exist; rather it is merely a combination of competing interests. Second, while goals help to align interests, even in conditions such as war, competing interests still oppose each other. Softening of these assumptions leads to rent-seeking, where firms are using the government to gain an advantage that they would not normally gain through normal market functioning.

We will examine a specific example in Public Choice theory, the Bootlegger and Baptist theory of regulation, with an application to the green energy transition. The Bootlegger and Baptist story was developed by Bruce Yandle (1983) to

[1] Where companies are devoted to improving the environment through innovation.

explain how true believers (Baptists) and opportunists (Bootleggers) partnered to create regulation.

Bootleggers and Baptists

Bruce Yandle, while working as the Executive Director of the Federal Trade Commission, first published the Bootlegger and Baptist (B&B) theory of regulation (Yandle, 1999, p. 5). The basic premise of B&B explains how diametrically opposed interest groups can form a coalition to promote self-serving regulations. The first group, the Baptists, supports regulation based upon moral/ethical grounds and seeks to act for the public good for its own sake. Bootleggers are groups who seek to intervene politically to distort the market for their benefit; they are not in it for altruistic reasons, but mere rent-seeking. The Bootleggers utilize the presence of the Baptists to provide moral support for their position because it would be unpopular with the general public and provides cover to politicians (Simmons et al., 2011). As Smith and Yandle (2014) note, the B&B theory provides a template to explain how politicians and corporations utilize public interest to gain private profit.

One example Smith and Yandle (2014) provide in their book on B&B is how big box stores and small main street stores joined forces to prevent Amazon from entering South Carolina.[2] The previous governor—during a period of high unemployment—provided various tax breaks to Amazon as a means of inducing them to build a distribution center in South Carolina. These tax breaks provided Amazon with an unfair advantage so other retailers, obviously, collaborated to prevent Amazon from building in the state. These retailers had a common desire "to reduce loss of market share to Amazon" (Smith and Yandle 2014, p. 1). In addition to big box stores and small mom and pop stores coming together was the presence of actual Baptists—who opposed Amazon due to the belief that Amazon did not provide sufficient controls on the distribution of pornographic materials.[3] The fact that customers could get their unrated material from some other physical locale was of little concern to the Baptists. Apparently, the retailers and the Baptists never met to develop a strategy—but the retail groups were more than willing to allow the Baptists to be the face of the anti-Amazon coalition; not only did the Baptists provide a sense of legitimacy, but they were also the largest religious denomination in South Carolina. Their gambit was initially successful as Amazon lost the support of the state, until they promised to build a second center in the state.

The Amazon case is merely one of many examples that occur in several different contexts. The thing each situation shares is the two separate (and normally opposed)

[2] Yandle's co-author Adam Smith is not the Adam Smith of the *Theory of Moral Sentiments* or *The Wealth of Nations*. This Adam Smith is Yandle's grandson, who is also an economist.

[3] The materials were unrated—and, as such, could have highly suggestive scenes.

groups, who come together to achieve a common goal. One party, the Baptists, operates on true belief; the other party, the Bootleggers, operates on basic opportunism. Smith and Yandle (2014, p. 207) describe it as:

> Baptist leaders lobby openly and enthusiastically for regulation of spirits; they prefer a world where less alcohol is consumed. Bootleggers, the illegal sellers of alcoholic beverages, happily support the laws as well; Sunday closings shut down legitimate sellers, thus expanding opportunities for bootleggers to sell their wares.

One of the common examples of this coalition of natural opposites would be the establishment of "blue laws" that banned selling alcohol on Sundays. Bootleggers (literal bootleggers and small liquor shops) wanted to limit the sale of alcohol to lower costs while Baptists wanted to limit alcohol sales on religious grounds (Yandle, 1983, p. 13).

This type of rent-seeking by Baptists and Bootleggers transfers wealth (benefits) from society to themselves. What generally happens is you have a coordination between two groups who prefer the same outcome for vastly different reasons. Generally, the Bootlegger will have an extensive lobbying network designed to effectively rent-seek. While the Baptists will have the moral high ground on the issue giving the Bootlegger's rent-seeking cover or an air of legitimacy by providing a moral or altruistic rationale for the policy. Given their competencies, Bootleggers can prime the political machine to enact the desired policy while Baptists can drum up voter and social support for the policy. In return, the Bootlegger receives the rent they were looking for, whether that is a subsidy, tax incentive, or regulatory prohibition of competition, etc., while the Baptist can take pride in doing "good," prohibiting the distribution of offensive material, saving the planet, making people behave "properly," and so forth. This is illustrated in Fig. 1.

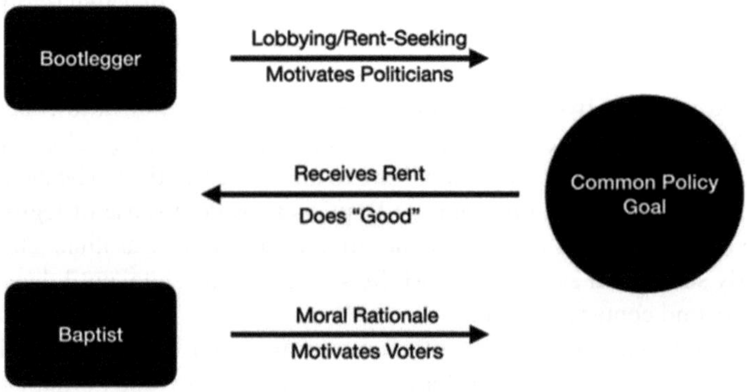

Fig. 1 Visualization of the B&B theory

Environmental Baptists and Bootleggers

The B&B theory of rent-seeking has been used in the recent environmental movement over the last few decades. In each case, the "Baptists" are environmentalists who want environmental regulation to turn back the tide of human impact on the environment.[4] Generally, the desire to preserve the environment and undo the damage human beings have done is seen as noble by many people. The environmental movement provides the moral high ground for environmental policy and inadvertently provides cover for the "Bootleggers." The "Bootleggers," on the other hand, are opportunistic industrial interests who only want to cash in on the goodies provided by the state through regulation, subsidies, tax credits, barriers to entry, and other benefits given by the government that one cannot obtain in a competitive market. This creates outcomes that transfer wealth from taxpayers to the "Bootleggers" while providing, at best, mixed results for the green "Baptists."

Illuminating Rents

The U.S. Energy Independence and Security Act of 2007 was designed "to increase the production of clean renewable fuels, to protect consumers, to increase the efficiency of products, buildings, and vehicles, to promote research on and deploy greenhouse gas capture and storage options, and to improve the energy performance" (EISA, 2007). One can see how the green "Baptists" would support the law given its aim at reducing human impact on the environment. However, EISA also had the support of many lightbulb manufacturers even though the law phased out incandescent lightbulbs. Testifying before a Senate committee, Kyle Pitsor from the National Electrical Manufacturing Association stated, "NEMA member manufacturers proposed, Mr. Chairman, to replace today's inefficient light bulbs [with products] 40 percent more efficient than today's companion incandescent bulb" (Receive Testimony of the Status of Energy Efficient Lighting Technologies and on S. 2017, The Energy Efficient Lighting for a Brighter Tomorrow Act, US Senate, Senate Hearing 110–195 (2007)).

While the lightbulb manufacturers sound like they are beating on the same drum as the green "Baptists," one needs to look beyond the obvious and see the unseen, like an economist. Philips Electronics, like the other lightbulb manufacturers, understood that there was money on the table to be had if they could team up with the green "Baptists." Philips informed the green "Baptists" "it was well positioned to capitalize on the transition to new technologies and wanted to get ahead of an efficiency movement that was gaining momentum abroad and in states like California" (Rice, 2011). The lightbulb manufacturers needed to find a way to pivot the market from incandescent lightbulbs to halogen, compact fluorescent lamps (CFL) and light emitting diodes (LEDs). The reason for the pivot was a "single 40 W LED bulb costs $7.50 or more,

[4] We do not address the merits of such a position.

while a traditional incandescent bulb goes for around 40 cents" (Regan, 2014). The decision to support the death of the incandescent bulb was a decision for potentially higher profit margins given "the profit margin on a bulb that sells for a quarter is negligible" (Rice, 2011).

The outcome on residential energy consumption since the enactment of the EISA has been negligible. The energy consumption of the residential sector in the United States in 2022 was 21.81 quadrillion British thermal units (BTUs) whereas in 2007 energy consumption was 21.52 quadrillion BTUs (Fernandez, 2023). Essentially, the death of the incandescent bulb resulted in the loss of affordable lightbulbs in favor of more expensive light bulbs while appearing to have no impact on residential energy consumption. The green "Baptists" did not seem to win much with the passage of the EISA but the "Bootlegger" lightbulb manufacturers captured higher prices at the expense of consumers.

The problem with the entrepreneurial state is the general assumption that people are angels wanting to do good and move society forward. The danger of the entrepreneurial state is its ripeness for pillaging by "Bootleggers." Once the "Bootleggers" identify the artificial government rent they want to capture, they have an incentive to engage in malinvestment to obtain it. In economics, this is illustrated as a wealth transfer from consumers to the "Bootleggers." Examples of this wealth transfer appear oblivious after the fact, like in the death of the incandescent lightbulb where consumers needed to pay in excess of 18 times more for lightbulbs.[5] Whatever the case, even if LED are superior, their superiority should be reflected in the market, not on the whims made by politicians influenced by interested parties who cloak their self-interest in the common good.

The Interesting Nuclear Bedfellows

In an age where people worry about carbon emissions and climate change, there was a viable energy source whose only immediate emission was steam. However, that source was de-railed in the United States by two groups that most people would not think of as having anything in common. The death of nuclear energy in the United States began in the 1960s when the fossil fuel industry and environmentalists teamed up to take down nuclear energy (Munger, 2019). Between these two groups, it is easy to see how environmentalists fill the role of the green "Baptist." They were concerned about the proliferation of nuclear power plants and the potential harm that could arise from a nuclear disaster. On the other hand, seeing environmentalists and the fossil fuel industry holding hands in a common effort appears mindboggling.

Our "Bootlegger," the fossil fuel industry, wanted to remove their most viable competitor for cheap clean energy, nuclear power. As F. William Engdahl (1993, p. 157) noted, "[b]y the early 1970s, nuclear technology had clearly established itself as the preferred future choice for efficient electric generation, vastly more efficient

[5] This is based on an incandescent bulb priced at USD 0.40 and an LED bulb priced at USD 7.50.

(and environmentally friendly) than either oil or coal." To take down its competitor, "[Robert] Anderson and his Atlantic Richfield Oil Co. funneled millions of dollars… to target nuclear energy" (ibid., p. 159). One such organization was "Friends of the Earth, established in this time with a $200,000 grant from Anderson" (ibid., p. 159). Not only was Anderson funding the Friends of the Earth but he also utilized the Aspen Institute for Humanistic Studies to function as "a major financial conduit for creation of the establishment's new anti-nuclear agenda in the early 1970s" (ibid., pp. 159–160).

With this B&B coalition in place, well-intentioned people like Jane Fonda, through the movie *The China Syndrome*, could be positioned to help strike a death blow to nuclear energy by creating "widespread panic" (Dubner and Levitt 2007). "[I]nstead of becoming a nation with clean and cheap nuclear energy… the United States kept building power plants that burned coal and other fossil fuels" (Dubner and Levitt 2007). Another example of a wealth transfer to "Bootleggers" would be the fossil fuels purchased to operate the fossil fuel power plants built instead of nuclear plants after that B&B coalition killed the expansion of nuclear power.

B&B Rent-Seeking and the Paris Agreement

The United Nations, starting with the 1992 Earth Summit, began to shift its focus to climate change. Originally, the United Nations was formed in 1945 over issues of collective security, human rights, or economic issues such as addressing poverty. However, the emergence of the green movement in the United States and Western Europe provided an impetus to shift the mission of the United Nations. The net result of this was the 1997 Kyoto Protocol, which aimed to reduce greenhouse gas emissions for certain countries from 2008 until 2012. The protocol was then extended until 2020 with the Doha amendments (Harrabin, 2012). However, there were numerous reasons why the Kyoto Treaty failed. One major reason was that many countries, including the United States, refused to sign the treaty and, in the process, created a series of distributional conflicts. To address this issue, countries embarked on a series of negotiations, including the 2009 Copenhagen Accord. This accord, although not legally binding and limited, did lead to the bottom-up approach that would form the basis of the Paris Agreement of 2015. One of the key aspects of the Copenhagen Accord era was that it created mitigation measures that could address further environmentally damaging acts.

The Paris Agreement of 2015 built upon the previous treaties in that rather than having legally binding accords, it used goals that were self-determined targets whereby a country would select the amount of CO_2 it would reduce (called Nationally Determined Contributions or NDCs).[6] However, unlike other agreements on climate, there were no legally binding protocols, rather the Paris Agreement would utilize the

[6] https://unfccc.int/process-and-meetings/the-paris-agreement/nationally-determined-contributions-ndcs#Taking-stock-and-informing-the-preparation-of-successive-NDCs_

force of social pressures on countries to either maintain or increase reductions in CO_2 emissions (United Nations Framework Convention on Climate Change, 2015). Another key aspect of the treaty is the idea of ever-increasing reductions in CO_2 emissions.

Although the NDCs are not legally binding, the processes around them, including reporting and review, are mandatory. Thus, the signatories of the Paris Agreement sought to create transparency as an ethical guidepost to encourage progress toward reaching goals. Countries are obligated through the treaty to provide evidence of their progress. The reports include Biennial Transparency Reports which detail greenhouse gas inventories and actions taken to address issues caused by emissions. Every five years, starting in 2023, countries are required to conduct a global stocktake, to help monitor each country's progress and maintain commitment (Hermwille et al., 2019). In addition, the global stocktake would also be a mechanism to assert pressure on laggards. In terms of cooperation, the Paris Accords provided provisions for technical and financial support to developing countries to help them achieve their NDCs. Another example of cooperative approaches would be the establishment of international carbon markets to allow polluters to offset their emissions.

The Paris Agreement became enforceable on November 4, 2016, when countries representing 55% of global emissions signed the agreement. The basic protocols are the following (United Nations Framework Convention on Climate Change, 2015):

(a) Holding the increase in the global average temperature to well below 2 °C above pre-industrial levels and to pursue efforts to limit the temperature increase to 1.5 °C above pre-industrial levels, recognizing that this would significantly reduce the risks and impacts of climate change;

(b) Increasing the ability to adapt to the adverse impacts of climate change and foster climate resilience and low greenhouse gas emissions development in a manner that does not threaten food production;

(c) Making finance flows consistent with a pathway toward low greenhouse gas emissions and climate-resilient development.

Countries with exceptionally large amount of emissions, such as the United States, signed the Paris Agreement (although the U.S. later both recanted and came back). Although the Paris Agreement could be critiqued because there are no strict provisions for non-compliance and requires cooperation between countries that simply cannot agree on major points.

As Yandle (2017, para. 2) notes, "[t]he fact that environmentalists supported the agreement is no surprise." However, Yandle points out their unexpected coalition partner in supporting the Paris Agreement, namely industrialists such as "Microsoft, Apple, Nike, the German industrial giant Siemens, and its Swiss counterpart ABB, to name a few" (Yandle 2017, para. 2). Again, while support for the Paris Agreement seems like a morally upstanding cause for some, it is an opportunity to reap economic rents emanating from regulation for others.

Microsoft and Apple are invested in developing software for electric vehicles, while Siemens and ABB develop more efficient electrical machinery. So where are the rents, you may ask. The investments made by these companies would experience a bump in profit if government regulation steered markets toward these technologies. While one could argue that this is what the entrepreneurial state should do, the problem is that the industrialists use the entrepreneurial state to guarantee these investments' pay off by changing the law to coerce consumers in the market to adopt this particular technology; the outcome is completely arbitrary given that the government and rent-seekers already determined what should happen rather than letting consumers in the market voluntarily vote with their money. This is not entrepreneurial; it is a rigged game. As Yandle (2017, para. 8) so eloquently puts it, "[w]ith firm-specific government subsidies for the development of clean technologies and a seat at the regulators' table, the environmental bootleggers, like their earlier counterparts, can laugh all the way to the bank." Thus, it is through the coercion of the entrepreneurial state that wealth ends up being transferred from consumers to the industrialist "Bootleggers."

Conclusion

Mazzucato and her followers depict government intervention in entrepreneurship as a frictionless machine, where the normal vagaries of politics, such as interest-group actions and self-interest, do not seem to reign. In doing so, she presents an idealized version of the political sphere, one that most economists have rejected since the 1970s. However, the role and influence of incentives determine the political process rather than abstract notions of the common good. As such, we cannot expect that politicians would make choices based on what works and what is good. The argument presented in the B&B theory of rent-seeking reveals the differing levels of self-interest in that we have groups with legitimate concerns (Baptists) conspiring with groups who merely pursue rent-seeking (Bootleggers). In fact, any government policy has the potential for rent-seeking by well-placed interest groups that will undermine the efficiency of government policy. This is true even when politicians can produce a perfect intervention. Mazzucato is aware of these arguments, but she largely dismisses them as irrelevant, because they are "theoretically based" rather than representations of actual government action. As we have demonstrated here and in our previous article, these are problems that simply cannot be dismissed. Whatever the rhetorical merits Mazzucato's work possesses, real life is more complex and difficult than she imagines.

The Hippocratic Oath binds physicians to do no harm to their patient. This should also be the attitude in political interventions in the economy; politicians should do no harm to their community. However, the opposite happens in government as politicians spend money on programs that often would not have occurred in a competitive market and may not have the support of the electorate. It is doubtful that the majority of these programs work, and they serve to undermine market efficiency with the net result being that insiders appear to win at the expense of the public. In the process, it produces crony capitalism, rather than true legitimate innovation.

References

Dubner, S. J. & Levitt, S. D. (2007). The Jane Fonda effect. *New York Times Magazine*. September 16. https://www.nytimes.com/2007/09/16/magazine/16wwln-freakonomics-t.html

Engdahl, F. W. (1993). *A Century of War, Anglo-American Oil Politics and the New World Order*. Wiesbaden: Dr. Bottiger Verlags-GmbH.

Energy Independence and Security Act 2007, 42 USC §17001 (2007).

Fernández, L. (2023). Energy consumption of the residential sector in the United States from 1975 to 2022. Retrieved from https://www.statista.com/statistics/183625/us-residential-sector-energy-consumption-from-2000/

Harrabin, R. (2012). UN climate talks extend Kyoto Protocol, promise compensation. *BBC News*, December 8. Archived from the original on July 16, 2018.

Hayek, F. A. (1988). *The Fatal Conceit*. Chicago, IL: University of Chicago Press.

Henrekson, M., Sandström, C., & Stenkula, M. (Eds.) (2024). *Moonshots and the New Industrial Policy: Questioning the Mission Economy*. Cham: Springer. https://doi.org/10.1007/978-3-031-49196-2

Hermwille, L., Siemons, A., Förster, H., & Jeffery, L. (2019). Catalyzing mitigation ambition under the Paris Agreement: Elements for an effective global stocktake. *Climate Policy*, *19*(8), 988–1001. https://doi.org/10.1080/14693062.2019.1611788

Kattel, R., Drechsler, W., & Karo, E. (2022). *How to Make an Entrepreneurial State: Why Innovation Needs Bureaucracy*. New Haven, CT: Yale University Press.

Lindsey, B., & Teles, S. M. (2017). *The Captured Economy: How the Powerful Enrich Themselves, Slow Down Growth, and Increase Inequality*. New York, NY: Oxford University Press.

Mazzucato, M. (2013). *The Entrepreneurial State*. New York, NY: Anthem Press.

Mazzucato, M. (2015). The green entrepreneurial state. In I. Scoones, M. Leach, & P. Newell (Eds.), *The Politics of Green Transformations* (pp. 134–152). New York, NY: Routledge.

Mazzucato, M. (2021). *Mission Economy: A Moonshot Guide to Changing Capitalism*. New York, NY: Allen Lane-Penguin.

Muldoon, J., Gould, A. M., & Yonai, D. K. (2023). Conjuring-up a bad guy: The academy's straw-manning of Milton Friedman's perspective of corporate social responsibility and its consequences. *American Economist*, *68*(2), 171–188.

Muldoon, J., & Yonai, D. K. (2023). A wrong but seductive idea: Public choice and the entrepreneurial state. *Journal of the International Council for Small Business*, *4*(4), 1–11.

Munger, M. (2019). Who is afraid of nuclear power? https://www.aier.org/article/who-is-afraid-of-nuclear-power/

Philippon, T. (2019). *The Great Reversal: How America Gave Up on Free Markets*. Cambridge, MA: Belknap Press.

Receive Testimony of the Status of Energy Efficient Lighting Technologies and on S. (2017), The Energy Efficient Lighting for a Brighter Tomorrow Act, US Senate, Senate Hearing 110–195 (2007).

Regan, S. (2014). Lights out for America's favorite light bulb. *Reason*, July 1. https://reason.com/2014/01/07/lights-out-for-americas-favorite-light-b/

Rice, A. (2011). Bulb in, bulb out. *New York Times Magazine,* June 3. https://www.nytimes.com/2011/06/05/magazine/bulb-in-bulb-out.html

Sarasvathy, S. D. (2009). *Effectuation: Elements of Entrepreneurial Expertise*. Northampton, MA: Edward Elgar Publishing.

Shane, S. (2004). *A General Theory of Entrepreneurship: The Individual-Opportunity Nexus*. Northampton, MA: Edward Elgar.

Simmons, R. T., Yonk, R. M., & Thomas, D. W. (2011). Bootleggers, Baptists, and political entrepreneurs: Key players in the rational game and morality play of regulatory politics. *Independent Review*, *15*(3), 367–381. https://www.independent.org/pdf/tir/tir_15_03_3_simmons.pdf

Smith, A., & Yandle, B. (2014). *Bootleggers and Baptists: How Economic Forces and Moral Persuasion Interact to Shape Regulatory Politics*. Washington, DC: Cato Press.

United Nations Framework Convention on Climate Change (2015). Paris Agreement, FCCC/CP/2015/L.9/Rev.1 [PDF]. UNFCCC Secretariat. Archived from the original on December 12, 2015. https://unfccc.int/documents/7682

Wennberg, K., & Sandström, C. (2022). *Questioning the Entrepreneurial State: Status-quo, Pitfalls, and the Need for Credible Innovation Policy*. Cham, CH: Springer.

Yandle, B. (1983). Bootleggers and Baptists—The education of a regulatory economist. *Regulation*, May/June, 12–16.

Yandle, B. (1999). Bootleggers and Baptists in retrospect. *Regulation, 22*, 5–7.

Yandle, B. (2017). When industries love regulation. *PERC*, July 27. https://www.perc.org/2017/07/27/when-industries-love-regulation/

Jeffrey Muldoon is an Associate Professor in the Department of Management and Business Administration at Southeastern Louisiana University. With a Ph.D., in Management from Louisiana State University, his scholarly interests focus on entrepreneurship, management history, and organizational behavior. He has published numerous peer-reviewed journal articles in outlets such as *Journal of Management History, Journal of Small Business Management, Journal of Business Research,* and *Entrepreneurship Education and Pedagogy*. His research has been recognized with multiple awards, including the John F. Mee Award for Best Management History Contribution at the Academy of Management. He is currently Chair of the Management of the Management History division and editor in chief of the *Journal of Management History*.

Derek K. Yonai is the Director of the Brown Innovation Center and the Peter and Sue Freytag Associate Professor of Economics in the School of Business at Flagler College and a Senior Research Fellow at the Institute for Faith, Work & Economics. He received his Ph.D., from George Mason University and his JD, with honors, from Whittier College School of Law.

His published research discusses the economic role of property rights and the law; his popular writings deal with the importance of economic freedom. Dr. Yonai's most recent research has been addressing how business and management scholars misunderstand the work of Milton Friedman and the free enterprise system.

Given his previous administrative roles, Dr. Yonai has given numerous radio interviews appearing on shows in Alaska, Colorado, Florida, Iowa, Kansas, North Carolina, Montana, and South Dakota. Dr. Yonai has written various Op-Eds that have appeared in various outlets including the *Dallas Morning News*, *Sun Sentinel*, *Orlando Sentinel*, *Detroit News*, and *Miami Herald*. He also has given many public talks on humanizing business education.

Behavioral Political Economy and Environmental Policy: Explaining Persistent Deviations from Efficient Policies

Jan Schnellenbach

Abstract This study examines why environmental policymaking often diverges from fact-based reasoning, drawing on insights from behavioral political economy. Concepts such as rational irrationality, expressive political behavior, and availability cascades explain why voters and policymakers systematically adopt biased beliefs and fail to update these beliefs in an unbiased way. Two cases are analyzed: Germany's nuclear exit and contemporary calls for degrowth. Both illustrate how heuristics, biases, and expressive motives shape public opinion and policy outcomes, often at the expense of efficiency.

Keywords Behavioral political economy · Heuristics and biases · Environmental policy · Expressive political behavior · Green transition

JEL Codes D72 · D78 · D91 · H11 · Q58

Introduction

In recent years, innovation policy has become closely intertwined with both industrial and environmental policy, frequently emphasizing regional development goals. Traditionally, environmental policy mainly revolved around regulating and limiting negative externalities. However, drawing on the work of scholars like Mariana Mazzucato (2021), policymakers at regional, national, and EU levels have shifted industrial policy toward a far more interventionist approach, which is sometimes described as "innovation policy 3.0." This approach assumes that governments can and should define ambitious goals ("missions") and steer the economy toward achieving these goals. Importantly, proponents of mission-oriented policymaking believe that this is not only to be achieved through general rules, but through discretionary government interventions and micro-management.

J. Schnellenbach (✉)
Chair for Microeconomics, Brandenburg University of Technology, Cottbus, Germany
e-mail: jan.schnellenbach@b-tu.de

M. Henrekson et al. (eds.), *A Green Entrepreneurial State?*, International Studies in Entrepreneurship 49, https://doi.org/10.1007/978-3-032-15512-2_5

Clearly, this requires a rather optimistic view of the capacities and incentives of policymakers. Even traditional public choice insights that follow from the analysis of incentives faced by self-interested policymakers are mostly ignored by the advocates for mission-oriented policymaking. But phenomena analyzed in behavioral economics are completely blanked out. Cognitive biases and the use of heuristics are, if mentioned at all, located in the private sector, where they lead to deficient decisions that must be corrected by governments that are, for some reason, believed to be endowed with superior rationality.

However, in behavioral political economy, it is well established today that such superior rationality is typically not present in political decision-making. Public debates about economic and environmental policy are rarely decided by factual evidence alone. While economists often assume that rational agents respond to incentives and information in predictable ways, political decision-making unfolds in a very different setting. In democratic systems, individuals face weak incentives to acquire and process information thoroughly, and political outcomes are shaped by collective choices, rhetoric, and identity rather than by narrowly instrumental reasoning. As a result, systematic biases and heuristics influence both voter preferences and policymaking.

Behavioral political economy provides a framework for understanding these deviations from fact-based decision-making. Concepts such as *rational irrationality* (Caplan 2001a, 2007), *expressive political behavior* (Hamlin and Jennings 2011), and the strategic use of *narratives* and *availability cascades* (Kuran and Sunstein 1999) help explain why policy outcomes often diverge from the prescriptions of economic expertise. The persistence of anti-market attitudes, skepticism toward technologies such as nuclear power, and recurring calls for degrowth illustrate how psychological mechanisms, moral heuristics, and expressive reasoning shape collective choices.

This study applies insights from behavioral political economy to analyze two prominent cases of environmental and economic debate: the German exit from nuclear power generation and contemporary growth skepticism. Both cases highlight how systematic biases, emotional narratives, and identity-driven expressive behavior can override factual evidence and efficiency considerations. By tracing these mechanisms, the study aims to improve our understanding of why well-intentioned policies may result in inefficient or counterproductive outcomes.

Why Policymaking is not Always Fact-Based

There are now a number of theoretical approaches in behavioral political economy that explain why the assumption of decision-making based on an unbiased assessment of all relevant information will often not be met in real-world politics. We will discuss some influential theories briefly in this section: rational irrationality, expressive political behavior, and narratives in economics (see Schnellenbach and Schubert 2015, 2025 for broader surveys). These explanations have in common that the peculiar incentives that are in place in the political sphere allow individuals to consume political beliefs, without significant material consequences. This has already been pointed out by Kliemt (1986), who has coined the term "veil of insignificance."

In private decisions in markets, individuals usually receive some negative feedback from making bad decisions. Sometimes, this negative feedback arrives immediately (e.g., as a disappointingly bland dinner at a randomly chosen restaurant), sometimes it comes with a substantial delay (e.g., as a result of making a bad financial investment decision), but individuals can in any case be certain that there is a direct link between their level of diligence in gathering and processing information and their individual outcome. That is clearly not the case in politics. The first difference is the indirectness of the decision. In representative democracies, we vote on parties or candidates, i.e., on bundles of positions concerning many different issues. The second difference is that we vote collectively.

Being one of thousands or millions of individuals involved in a municipal, state- or national-level election renders a single vote insignificant for the overall result, simply because the probability of being decisive is approximately zero, and so is the expected material consequence of voting in one direction or the other. On the other hand, the costs of collecting and processing information to rely on the most accurate factual assessment of a situation in making a political decision can be extremely high, especially if complex trade-offs and difficult assessments of risks are involved. A first knee-jerk reaction to this set of incentives by economists accustomed to working with rational expectations is that individuals may err, but that they do so randomly, so that on average, decision-making remains unbiased.

However, there are good reasons for this not to be the case. First of all, individual voting decisions are preceded by lengthy periods of public political debate, where rhetoric and narratives matter. Successful political entrepreneurs are in the business of turning errors in individual political decisions from random to correlated errors, in a way that serves special interests, be they ideologically or materially motivated. Second, for many individuals, positioning themselves in a given political or ideological spectrum is a matter of personal identity, and positions taken on single, specific issues depend on that position. Therefore, we can expect errors in political decision-making to be systematically biased, and there are different theories that elaborate on this fundamental problem from different perspectives.

Rational Irrationality

Caplan (2001a) proposes that individuals are willfully, or rationally, irrational in the political sphere. They can rationally decide to hold beliefs that are not congruent with facts precisely because they act behind the veil of insignificance. On markets, acting upon false beliefs leads to private costs. However, that does not imply that individuals are fully rational. If the costs of deviating from full rationality are sufficiently low, one can still maintain a cherished belief that is factually wrong. For example, in order to avoid cognitive dissonance, individuals may stick to the belief that their workplace is relatively safe, even if it is not, as long as the probability of a catastrophic outcome is still relatively low (as already pointed out by Akerlof and Dickens 1982). But in the political sphere, the individual cost of irrationality is zero, which allows individuals to hold their bliss belief (Caplan 2001a, p. 8).

Exactly how the bliss belief comes about remains, in Caplan's framework, theoretically undetermined. But if applied to real-world phenomena, the model proves fruitful. For example, Caplan (2001b, p. 318) argues that voters systematically underestimate the negative side effects of redistributive government subsidies aimed at supporting special interests. Therefore, they choose to ignore the detrimental effects of rent seeking on efficiency that are well-known to economists, and that generally could also be known by the general public. Instead, they want to believe that governments can and do identify worthy causes of government support.

Using a large set of survey data, Caplan (2002) shows that the beliefs regarding the economy and economic policy of economists and the general public systematically diverge. Caplan also demonstrates that this is neither due to differences in political ideology, nor to differing party loyalties or to the general level of education. In the meantime, *folk economics* has evolved as an empirical research branch that attempts to identify the beliefs that underlie the economic reasoning of laypeople. Distorted views on causal mechanisms governing the economy have, for example, been identified in housing policy, where many people resist the idea that building new housing will reduce rents (Nall 2025). Another area where laypeople think systematically differently than experts is the distributional and efficiency effects of protectionist policies (Swedberg 2018). Caplan (2007) also identifies some further policy issues where such divergences occur. For example, many people intuitively put more trust into deliberate political action than into the anonymous coordinating function of the price mechanism. Another example is the make-work bias, which leads individuals to focus on organizing economic activity such that jobs are preserved, even if this comes at a huge cost in terms of efficiency.

But how are bliss beliefs formed? To some degree, they likely rely on cognitive mechanisms that have been associated with some evolutionary advantage in the past, but that may have adverse effects in modern, highly complex societies. One salient example is people's tendency to affiliate in groups and to apply a zero-sum interpretive framework where the benefit of one group can only come at the expense of another group. If this is applied to nations engaging in trade, factually false beliefs on trade policy will inevitably emerge (Boyer and Bang Petersen 2018). Once in place, and if shared by many individuals, communication in peer groups and society as a whole can entrench such beliefs and questioning them may even be socially punished as deviating behavior (Schnellenbach 2005).

Expressive Political Behavior

Hamlin and Jennings (2011, p. 645) define expressive behavior as the opposite of instrumental political actions. The latter aim at maximizing the payoffs associated with a policy or a successful election of a preferred candidate, minus the individual costs invested into supporting this preferred political platform. Initially, the focus of theories of expressive behavior was on the act of voting itself. The paradox of voting describes the fact that in such an instrumental calculus, the act of voting itself is instrumentally irrational, simply because in modern mass elections, the probability of being decisive is approximately zero while the cost of going to the ballot box is positive (Downs 1957).

There are different explanations for the relatively high levels of voter participation nevertheless observed in most of the stable democratic countries. One example is the proposition that voters are morally motivated to participate, and that it is easy for them to do so, because while the costs of participation are positive, they are typically very low (Kirchgässner 1992). A Sunday walk to the voting booth is not perceived as particularly burdensome. However, a theory of low-cost moral behavior will have difficulties explaining why people occasionally line-up for hours in order to cast their vote. On the other hand, the consumption value associated with expressing one's political and social identity could motivate voters to carry these costs.

A somewhat surprising result is that, by choosing a political identity, individuals often willingly incur personal costs (Pickup et al. 2022). Such costs can result from adhering to social or other norms associated with having a certain political identity that are often enforced in peer groups. For example, being a very vocal climate activist should normally not be consistent with going on long-distance flights for private travel, or with driving a high-powered fossil-fueled private car. In this sense, restricting one's feasible set of consumption alternatives in order to be consistent with a self-imposed political identity can clearly be costly in terms of attainable private happiness. However, this insight is not in conflict with Caplan's framework sketched above: The choice of a bliss belief is made by taking possible private costs into account, but once a bliss belief is picked, it can be maintained without incurring additional political or private costs.

Clearly, it is not always possible to unambiguously separate non-instrumental, expressive motives from material incentives (Hamlin and Jennings 2011, p. 649). Individuals who have a concern for internal coherence may, for example, seek to choose a political identity that suits their economic interests, and then attempt to defend this identity and the beliefs associated with it regardless of objective evidence. If my income increases as a result of a certain policy, I may be inclined to defend the policy by claiming it to be efficient, even if the best available evidence casts doubts on its efficiency properties. But if I have (consciously or subconsciously) chosen my identity to align with my material interests, then such a public defense of dubious political beliefs may not even be the result of a cynical calculus but merely reflect my honest attempt to preserve internal, psychological coherence.

Expressive political behavior may result in expressive policy traps, which are potentially highly inefficient overall outcomes (Hillman 2010). While it is costless for every single individual to confirm her identity using expressive voting, pursuing non-instrumental concerns becomes costly if a sufficient number of individuals do so at the same time. The Brexit vote could be an example: At least some of the voters who cast a ballot in favor of Brexit would probably have had second thoughts if they had been decisive voters, i.e., if the outcome of the collective decision had depended on their individual vote. In that case, they would have taken into consideration the full material costs that Brexit had for themselves. But behind the veil of insignificance, simply consuming the expressive value of signaling discontent to the government was individually costless.

Exploiting Behavioral Biases in Policy Debates

As discussed above, one mechanism that can lead to policymaking based on systematically biased perceptions of the world is when individuals choose to stick to beliefs that are not factually accurate. But it is also possible that participants in the policy debate, be it politicians, bureaucrats, or interest groups, deliberately attempt to use behavioral mechanisms in order to manipulate the policy preferences of voters or of other politicians. A prominent example has already been discussed by Kuran and Sunstein (1999), namely so-called availability cascades.

The availability heuristic (Tversky and Kahneman 1973) is a well-known cognitive bias that leads to systematically distorted perceptions of small probabilities. These perceptions depend on the availability of recent examples in the memory of individuals. If I have recently read of a passenger plane crashing, I tend to overestimate the likelihood of plane crashes, as long as this news is still present in my memory. Repetitive exposure to similar pieces of information can compound the effect and create an illusory truth: statements feel truer if they are often repeated, even if individuals know that they are false (Fazio and Sherry 2020).

Kuran and Sunstein (1999) argue that availability cascades are often deliberately triggered when availability entrepreneurs feed distorted risk perceptions into the public debate. They also argue that often, the more a position becomes dominant, the costlier dissent becomes, further shrinking visible heterogeneity and reinforcing a perceived consensus on false risk perceptions. In such settings, people may publicly endorse views they privately doubt. Therefore, expectations are formed regarding the social reward for holding some belief, and these expectations allow a public consensus supporting false beliefs to be very stable. It requires some means of coordination in order to motivate a sufficiently large group of individuals to take the reputational risk associated with voicing public dissent against a belief that they privately know to be false. The echo chambers of social media are known to reinforce these kinds of effects (e.g., Cinelli et al. 2021).

Observing only public statements, it can be difficult to distinguish between a situation with preference falsification, where individuals voice different views in public than in private, and honestly held distorted beliefs. For the latter, other cognitive biases than the availability heuristic have also been shown to be important. For example, the anchor effect can be deliberately used to influence collective beliefs (Furnham and Boo 2011). Expectations about the consequences of a decision are then anchored in familiar contexts or memories with either positive or negative connotations. An argument in favor of a higher minimum wage can, for example, be anchored using a relatively high minimum wage in another country, even if the underlying conditions are very different there and the economic argument for taking this country as a benchmark is weak. Or an argument against a higher minimum wage can be anchored by reference to an experience of increasing unemployment, even if the current conditions are different.

An important issue regarding the scope of deliberately influencing beliefs is timing. Evidence indicates that once policy preferences and underlying beliefs are formed, they are not easily changed, at least not on the collective level (Schnellenbach 2023). Both an individual-level confirmation bias in filtering information and collective conservatism as a result of peer pressure to conform with prevailing beliefs likely play a role in stabilizing given beliefs. Thus, efforts to successfully influence belief formation are likely to be most successful when uncertainty is high and individuals simply do not have any good cues yet to evaluate policy proposals and their consequences.

Case 1: The German Exit from Nuclear Power

For countries where natural geographic conditions do not allow for a large potential of hydroelectric power, nuclear power remains the prime source of carbon–neutral energy. The prime example of such a country in Europe is France, where over twelve months between August 2024 and July 2025, 70.1% of electricity produced came from nuclear power plants, and only 2.1% from fossil sources of energy.[1] In neighboring Germany, on the other hand, 19.4% of electricity came from burning coal, 8.23% from burning gas, and 0.56% from burning oil. German electricity production emitted 314 g of CO_2 per kWh of electrical power, while French electricity production emitted only 25 g. Granted, Germany exhibited a much larger share of renewable energy from wind and solar power in this period. But missing large-scale batteries, it had to rely on burning fossil fuels (and on importing French nuclear power) whenever the wind did not blow and the sun did not shine. At different times, when wind and solar power production peaked and exceeded demand, Germany often had to export highly taxpayer-subsidized energy at negative prices.

We will return to the failure of fully accounting for the full costs of providing a stable energy supply with renewables in detail in the section discussing other examples of behavioral mechanisms in environmental policy. For now, it suffices to conclude that if the policy objective is to transform electricity generation to carbon neutrality as quickly as possible, using nuclear power clearly is an effective means and shutting down nuclear power plants induces significant costs and leads to increased CO_2 emissions (Jarvis et al. 2022) at least in the short- to medium run. If, on the other hand, the objective is to rely on renewables to as great an extent as possible, then Germany is ahead of France. However, it would not be able to pursue its current path if it were not bailed out by importing French nuclear power whenever domestic

[1] See https://app.electricitymaps.com/map/zone/DE/all_years/yearly for Germany and https://app.electricitymaps.com/map/zone/FR/all_years/yearly for France.

renewable production is lower than electricity demand. In this sense, Germany still relies heavily on nuclear power, even though it has entirely externalized this reliance.

We have arrived at the current state of affairs after decades of increasing skepticism toward nuclear power in the German policy debate. Wendland (2017) shows that starting with the earliest debates about the civil use of nuclear power in the 1960s, two parallel debates evolved. On the one hand, there was a pragmatic and sober debate among engineers and planners discussing different scenarios of energy supply and demand. On the other hand, from the very beginning, there was another debate with apocalyptic underpinnings among philosophers, public intellectuals, and (mostly left-wing) politicians. In the latter, the civil production of nuclear power was associated with the uncontrollable destructive forces unleashed by nuclear weapons. The 1980s saw children's books become bestsellers in Germany that described scenarios where children and teenagers had to cope with the apocalyptic nuclear disasters.

This created a strong, widespread sentiment of fear and hostility toward nuclear energy. A strong undercurrent in public opinion against using nuclear energy had always been present, and was emboldened by external events, particularly by the explosion of a reactor at the Chernobyl power plant in 1986, and later the 2011 Fukushima accident. However, until 1998 Germany was governed by conservative-liberal governments that consistently resisted public demands for an exit from nuclear energy. This changed when a coalition between Social Democrats and Greens came into office and made the abolition of nuclear energy a top item on their agenda. In 2000, a consensus was reached with the private firms running the still active power plants to phase out the service of existing plants and to prohibit the construction of new plants. This consensus was formalized into law in 2002.

In 2010, a conservative-led government acknowledged the general plan for the phase-out but extended the timeline and allowed existing plants to run longer than originally planned. The main argument for this step was the CO_2 neutrality of nuclear power. In order to facilitate a smooth transition to carbon–neutral electrical power, nuclear power would be an efficient bridge technology until a full shift to renewables with sufficient battery capacity could be achieved. However, this new policy stance was very short-lived. In an almost immediate, opportunistic response not even waiting for, but anticipating a strong response in public opinion, Chancellor Merkel reacted to the Fukushima incident by taking the political initiative to close down all active German nuclear sites. Eight reactors were subsequently closed already in 2011, and the remaining nine were gradually phased out. The final three plants were shut down in 2023.

Even though a tsunami striking a nuclear power plant is a strictly impossible event in Germany, the Fukushima incident led to another strong increase in anti-nuclear sentiment in Germany (e.g., Weiß et al. 2014). Evidence indicates that Germany's risk perception concerning nuclear power after the event was shaped by journalists who themselves were driven by strong personal concerns regarding the safety of nuclear power. In fact, German journalists reporting about the Fukushima incident were much more concerned and fearful than even their Japanese colleagues (Meißner 2019). These risk perceptions may therefore be an example of a case where availability cascades self-stabilize over the long run. Journalists had already grown up in a social environment that strongly exaggerated risks of nuclear power and even morally vilified its use and continued to reproduce these perceptions once they produced journalistic content themselves. However, such a self-stabilization is not inevitable. In other countries that previously also had strong anti-nuclear movements, a renaissance of nuclear power now seems possible.

One important difference may be that in Germany, the issue is an integral part of the Green Movement since its emergence in the 1970s, and it became a core policy stance among Social Democrats during the 1980s and 1990s (e.g., Joppke 1993). This is striking, because earlier, the latter had a decidedly pro-nuclear stance. Nuclear power was initially seen by Social Democrats as an opportunity for progress by supplying cheap and abundant energy. However, during the 1980s, an increasing number of prominent Social Democrats followed the Greens by associating themselves with the anti-NATO peace movement, which had huge overlaps with protest movements against the civil use of nuclear power. One could even argue that for the "Anti-Atom" movement, all things nuclear were seen as inherently unacceptable, be it military or civil. In countries where this strong anti-nuclear stance is less important for the core identity of political movements, a more pragmatic debate about nuclear policy is possible.

The patterns of decision-making we observe in the context of nuclear power in Germany therefore fit different mechanisms identified in behavioral political economy. There can be little doubt that positioning oneself on the issue of nuclear power has a high expressive value for many individuals. This is true in both directions. For proponents and adversaries of nuclear power alike, activism on the issue has been shown to be associated with the presence of a corresponding personal norm (de Groot and Steg 2010). It has also been shown that the mobilization of anti-nuclear movements largely relied on pre-existing networks of activism (Jasper and Poulsen 1995), indicating an expressive value of the issue to broader environmental and anti-war political movements.

Nuclear power is particularly susceptible to availability cascades because it is perceived to be associated with disastrous consequences and overall catastrophic outcomes, while the details of outcomes in the case of hazardous events are largely unknown among the population. It has been observed already almost 40 years ago that experts rank the risks associated with nuclear power much lower than lay people (Slovic 1987). The former know that accidents such as in Chernobyl or Fukushima can, for technical reasons, simply not happen in the modern nuclear facilities in use in Western European countries. The latter are led by the availability heuristic to gauge the risks of nuclear power in general by looking at cases such as Chernobyl and Fukushima. In addition to the availability heuristic, this is also explained by probability neglect: If people are characterized by strong emotional affect against a technology, they are likely to neglect issues of probability and instead focus on creating outrage by emphasizing catastrophic outcomes, even if their likelihood is basically zero (Sunstein 2002). Here, the expressive value of taking a moral stance against a dread risk and the unwillingness to acknowledge very low levels of risk reinforce each other.

A telling example from the German debate is again related to the Fukushima incident. Both media and prominent German politicians from the Green Party promoted the narrative that as a result of the incident, thousands of individuals died from the effects of exposure to high levels of radiation (Krämer 2013; Kulke 2013). In fact, almost all deaths associated with the incident were caused by flooding after the tsunami, not by radiation. Measured by the benchmark of expert reports commissioned by the UN (UNSCEAR 2021) which concluded that radiation had done very little damage at Fukushima even in the long run, the narratives promoted by anti-nuclear politicians and activists, and also some of the press, were blatant lies. Nevertheless, they stuck with significant parts of the population.

Even if they are explicitly informed of the dangers of climate change and the opportunity to use nuclear power to generate carbon–neutral electricity, respondents in surveys who are characterized by higher environmental values and concern for climate change are less likely to favor nuclear power (Corner et al. 2011). This is a stance that is easily explained by the veil of insignificance for voters—the individual costs of making expressive decisions are zero. But that is not the case for policymakers, who could be decisive in achieving carbon neutrality more quickly by promoting the use of nuclear power. One explanation may be that these policymakers are not primarily concerned with solving the problem, but with re-election, and that they are bound by the policy preferences of their electoral base. But given the urgency of the problem of stopping climate change, the question remains: Why do they prioritize re-election?

Hyperbolic discounting (Laibson 1997) may be one explanation. The benefits of controlling climate change immediately are delayed, and abstract. The reward of winning the next election by serving the demand for expressive policies from voters is relatively immediate and very concrete. Even if they have an honest preference for reducing CO_2 emissions, this incentive structure can easily tempt policymakers to delay actual emissions reduction by shutting off nuclear power in order to benefit from ideological utility and the material gains from securing office. This is particularly important, because we often associate hyperbolic discounting with market failure that needs to be corrected by rational politics. In contrast to this naive view, we see here that hyperbolic discounting in politics may lead to inefficient decisions where superior rationality is expected.

Case 2: Limits to Growth

Calls to end growth are not a novel phenomenon. Robert Thomas Malthus, who lived from 1766 to 1834, already argued that there were strict limits to population growth. He underestimated the extent to which later productivity gains in food production would be achieved, and how much scope this would create for further population growth. He also underestimated that population growth itself would become a trigger for further innovations in food production and increases in productivity.

In 1968, Malthus found a successor in the American biologist Paul R. Ehrlich, who in his bestseller *The Population Bomb* (Ehrlich 1968) predicted that humanity would soon have completely exhausted essential natural resources. However, in 1990, Ehrlich lost a wager he had made with the economist Julian Simon a decade earlier. Simon argued that if Ehrlich's prediction was correct, this would need to be reflected in steeply rising prices for natural resources. Ehrlich agreed, but was proven wrong: Between 1980 and 1990, real prices for all raw materials covered by the wager did not increase, but in fact declined (Gorelick 2009). Simon, who expected market participants to be highly flexible in adapting to any scarcities reflected in short-term price increases, was right.

In 1972, the Club of Rome predicted a collapse within one hundred years due to depleted resources (Meadows et al. 1972). But the trajectories of depleted resources predicted in the book did never materialize. In later updates of the report, among other things, it was urged that population growth be limited by paying out rewards to women for staying childless. Since the 1980s, peak-oil estimates have repeatedly placed the maximum in crude-oil production within the next few years—yet this has not occurred, and so far accessible oil reserves have not become extremely scarce. Although modern eco-apocalyptic thinking has invariably turned out to be wrong until this day, calls to restrict growth or even to initiate processes of degrowth have surfaced again and again (e.g., Kallis et al. 2018).

Doomsayers consistently underestimate two aspects. First, the efficiency of the price mechanism. Rising prices signal increasing scarcity, which induces market participants to look for alternatives or for opportunities to increase supply. The market—not the supposedly superior knowledge of political planners—creates efficient incentives. These incentives lead not only to substitution among raw materials but also to innovation. New resource-saving technologies are developed and deployed. Relative decoupling occurs when resource consumption (or the level of emissions) grows at a slower pace than production. By contrast, absolute decoupling occurs when the two curves move in opposite directions—that is, when resource consumption and emissions decline even though production is growing.

Solving the climate problem requires absolute decoupling. Net CO_2 emissions must fall in absolute terms and move toward zero in the foreseeable future. Absolute decoupling is observed in an increasing number of economies (e.g., Hubacek et al. 2021). And not only CO_2 decoupling is observed: Using the example of Sweden, Grafström (2026) shows how GDP growth is also absolutely decoupled from the use of air pollutants, energy intensity, and the use of hazardous chemicals. However, such trends can mostly be found in developed, more affluent economies. Regardless of how one judges this normatively, environmental and climate protection are luxury goods that only gain political acceptance once a threshold level of prosperity has been reached.

Developing and emerging countries that still rely to a large extent on fossil technologies often have other priorities than devoting resources to switching to non-fossil alternatives. Neither are emerging economies, such as India or China, likely to forgo further economic growth. Large parts of their populations are still too far from Western levels of prosperity to forgo catching up. But the use of resource-saving and emissions-avoiding technologies in such countries depends crucially on those technologies becoming more efficient and cheaper—that is, on continued technological progress. Proponents of degrowth strategies err not only in terms of assuming that prosperity can be capped, reduced, and redistributed at will globally. They also err in terms of underestimating the potential for resource-saving technological progress in market economies, and in assuming that such progress can be made at least as quickly in other institutional frameworks such as planned economies. However, there exists no historical evidence supporting these assumptions.

By shifting from the market to more planned, bureaucratically steered mechanisms in advanced economies—that is, switch from a growth model to a degrowth model—one would very likely reduce the chances of solving global environmental problems. As is so often the case, policy would, despite good intentions, lead to strongly negative outcomes—good intentions and noble goals alone are not enough. Absent rapid, resource-saving technological progress in emerging and developing countries, renouncing further growth in a few rich countries while growth continues elsewhere, would achieve virtually nothing for the global climate and the environment. By contrast, continued growth in rich countries together with efficient incentives such as CO_2 pricing will lead to progress that spills over into developing and emerging economies and enables early absolute decoupling there as well.

If growth is, to a significant extent, knowledge-driven, and in a modern market economy stems mainly from creativity and entrepreneurship rather than being material-intensive, then degrowth presupposes a radical restructuring of the entire economic order. That is precisely what almost all growth sceptics demand. However much various concepts differ in detail, they share the idea of a comprehensive, centrally planned control of the economy. The decision about what is allowed to be produced should no longer be left to market participants themselves. Consumption would also be rationed by the government. The transition to a centrally planned economy is often rhetorically described as a "democratization" of the economy, but in reality it would be associated with a radical loss of individual freedom. Powerful state planners would take the place of the many individual decisions coordinated through the market, and individuals would be submitted to their decisions.

All historical experience argues against such a system working in the long term. But why is it so popular in many environmentalist circles? To some extent, resorting to central economic planning as a response to environmental problems reflects the anti-market bias discussed by Caplan (2007). People believe that profit-seeking is socially harmful and fail to understand that proper price incentives direct entrepreneurial activity toward socially beneficial actions. For example, in some policy debates emissions trading is not understood as a mechanism that provides rational incentives to market participants but is framed akin to a medieval sale of indulgences to compensate for committed (environmental) sins. In contrast, efficient, fair, and moral outcomes are believed to be the result of deliberate planning that imposes some vision of a desirable future on society. The capacities of government actors to implement such a vision are often overestimated; there is a belief that governments can achieve any form of societal coordination, while markets and the price mechanism are inherently uncontrollable. Thus, governments are understood as magic black boxes that produce the desired outcome, if only they are endowed with sufficient resources and legal competencies. And a moral heuristic (Sunstein 2005) associates democratic government action with an interest in the common good, in contrast to the self-interest pursued in markets (e.g., Carden 2008).

Other Examples of Behavioral Mechanisms in Environmental Policy

Kirchherr et al. (2023) argue that many policy decisions are influenced by a normativity bias: If individuals agree that the stated goal of a policy is normatively appealing, they are often in favor of this policy even if it is not cost-efficient or efficient in other ways. Legitimacy spills over from the normative goal to the instrument, and a detailed cost–benefit analysis is not conducted. A policy instrument is favored simply because it is claimed to support some normatively appealing goal, even if it is not demonstrated that it is the most efficient instrument for pursuing (and achieving) that goal. And frequently, trade-offs between competing goals are also not considered. This can lead to situations where individuals ignore at least some fractions of the actual costs of policy measures that they prefer for normative reasons. Such a bias can also be deliberately exploited in order to influence policy preferences.

One example is the claim that the production costs of solar and wind energy are extremely low, often communicated together with the slogan that "sun and wind will never send us a bill" (Jeremy Rifkin in an interview, Moreau 2021). The problem with such a claim is that it is only true with regard to the marginal cost of power generation. These are indeed very low, once a solar or wind farm is set up. However, this claim ignores the significant systemic costs of renewable energy sources. Since renewables fluctuate with weather conditions often in a non-predictable way, a power system with a large share of renewables also requires high investments into backup and/or battery capacities (Heptonstall and Gross 2021). These backup capacities for power generation are not always CO_2 neutral. In a region that is geographically suitable, hydro power could play an important role, but in other regions, power generation using gas will be necessary.

The costs of stabilizing the energy system with a high fraction of renewables can be very high, precisely due to the naturally fluctuating supply of these energy sources. Extremely large battery capacities would be needed to bridge prolonged periods of bad, yet windless weather without relying on fossil or nuclear backups. Idel (2022) calculates a measure of the full systemic costs, the levelized full system costs of electricity (LFSCOE) and shows that systems that rely on renewables only will be much less cost-efficient than systems that also rely on nuclear energy. Fahlén et al. (2026) also provide a detailed account of full systemic costs. They provide estimates of the system integration costs depending on the degree of reliance on solar and wind energy. The results indicate that costs increase with the reliance on renewables. A recent German study (Bothe et al., 2025) estimates that for Germany alone, the costs of ensuring system stability on the current policy trajectory of relying on renewables and natural gas backups will amount to EUR 5,400 billion between 2025 and 2049.

Nevertheless, proponents of such a shift often only include the marginal costs of power generation and ignore the systemic costs when arguing in favor of a full shift to renewables. Similarly, indirect environmental costs associated with wind and solar energy are often absent from the political debate, such as the impossibility to fully recycle solar panels or windmills, noise pollution (e.g., Forlim et al. 2024), or the damage done to bird populations by wind farms.

The normativity bias is also frequently associated with a failure to take opportunity costs into consideration. A straightforward example would be a calculation of the capacity of carbon–neutral power generation that could be installed for the systemic costs estimated for a full shift to renewables. But one could also take a broader perspective and ask where given funds could produce the largest welfare gains for society. Cost–benefit analyses of alternative spending options often rank these options in a very different order than common political priorities. For example, investments into battling infectious diseases or malnutrition, or into improvements in education in poor countries, are likely associated with far higher returns than many climate policies (Lomborg 2023). Regardless, issue salience in political debates and ignorance of opportunity costs often lead to a prioritization of the latter instead of the former.

Finally, there also appears to be a widespread failure to account for the interaction of different policy measures that aim at the same goal. Take climate policy as an example again: With a credible commitment to include all relevant sectors in emissions trading and to reduce the quantity of available emissions rights along a pre-defined path, all market participants have an incentive to invest in emission-saving technologies. This is a straightforward reaction to the anticipated increase of emission prices over time, and trading ensures that emissions are always reduced where the costs of reduction are lowest. Adding an additional policy layer of sector-specific goals for emissions reduction counteracts the efficiency properties of emissions trading. It forces market participants in sectors with high reduction costs to nevertheless reduce their emissions to attain a politically defined goal. In an efficient world, these sectors would have the opportunity to reduce later, and to use the available time to develop cost-saving technologies of emissions reduction. However, policymakers frequently combine both policies. There appears to be a naive belief that the stacking of policies increases efficacy, while inefficient interactions between policies are ignored.

Conclusions

The discussion of German nuclear energy policy and the degrowth debate illustrates a central paradox of modern policymaking: while urgent global challenges such as climate change require efficient and fact-based responses, actual political decisions are often shaped by cognitive biases, expressive motives, and distorted narratives.

Behavioral political economy shows that these deviations are not random, but systematic. Voters can indulge in *rational irrationality* because individual political choices carry negligible material consequences. Politicians, in turn, face strong incentives to cater to expressive preferences, short-term emotions, and salient risks rather than to long-term efficiency.

The cases studied reveal how availability cascades, probability neglect, and moral heuristics reinforce public opposition to nuclear energy, despite its potential contribution to decarbonization. Similarly, degrowth narratives appeal to fairness intuitions and anti-market biases, while overlooking the historical role of technological progress and the effectiveness of market incentives in driving resource efficiency. These patterns demonstrate how well-meaning policy agendas can become trapped in expressive or symbolic gestures, producing outcomes that undermine their stated goals.

Recognizing the influence of behavioral mechanisms in political decision-making does not imply resignation, but it does call for humility and institutional awareness. Policies that rely on clear price signals, robust institutional frameworks, and transparent communication of trade-offs stand a better chance of aligning incentives with long-term social welfare. At the same time, economists and policymakers must account for the cognitive and emotional drivers of public opinion; ignoring them only leaves room for manipulation and narrative-driven policy traps.

Ultimately, behavioral political economy reminds us that the challenge of effective policymaking lies not only in designing efficient solutions, but also in overcoming the systematic biases that shape collective choices. Bridging the gap between expert knowledge and widespread voter perceptions is essential if democracies are to respond effectively to pressing environmental and economic challenges.

References

Akerlof, G., & Dickens, W. (1982). The economic consequences of cognitive dissonance. *American Economic Review, 72*(3), 307–319. http://www.jstor.org/stable/1831534

Bothe, D., et al. (2025). *Neue Wege für die Energiewende ("Plan B")*. Köln: Frontier Economics. https://www.frontier-economics.com/media/n0wmtjhk/frontier-dihk-energiewende-plan-b-08092025-stc.pdf

Boyer, P., & Bang Peterson, M. (2018). Folk-economic beliefs: An evolutionary cognitive model. *Behavioral and Brain Sciences, 41*, e158. https://doi.org/10.1017/S0140525X17001960

Caplan, B. (2001a). Rational Ignorance versus rational irrationality. *Kyklos, 54*(1), 3–26. https://doi.org/10.1111/1467-6435.00138

Caplan, B. (2001b). Rational irrationality and the microfoundations of political failure. *Public Choice, 107*(3–4), 311–331. https://doi.org/10.1023/A:1010311704540

Caplan, B. (2002). Systematically biased beliefs about economics: Robust evidence of judgmental anomalies from the survey of Americans and economists on the economy. *Economic Journal, 112*(479), 433–458. https://doi.org/10.1111/1468-0297.00041

Caplan, B. (2007). *The Myth of the Rational Voter. Why Democracies Choose Bad Policies.* Princeton, NJ: Princeton University Press.

Carden, A. (2008). Belief, bias, and regime uncertainty after Hurricane Katrina. *International Journal of Social Economics, 35*(7), 531–545. https://doi.org/10.1108/03068290810886939

Cinelli, M., De Francisci Morales, G., Galeazzi, A., & Starnini, M. (2021). The echo chamber effect on social media. *Proceedings of the National Academy of Sciences, 118*(9), e2023301118. https://doi.org/10.1073/pnas.2023301118

Corner, A., Venables, D., Spence, A., Poortinga, W., Demski, C., & Pidgeon, N. (2011). Nuclear power, climate change and energy security: Exploring British public attitudes. *Energy Policy, 39*(9), 4823–4833. https://doi.org/10.1016/j.enpol.2011.06.037

Downs, A. (1957). *An Economic Theory of Democracy*. New York, NY: Harper & Row.

Ehrlich, P. R. (1968). *The Population Bomb*. New York, NY: Ballantine Books.

Fazio, L. K., & Sherry, C. L. (2020). The effect of repetition on truth judgments across development. *Psychological Science, 31*(9), 1150–1160. https://doi.org/10.1177/0956797620939534

Fahlén, P., Henrekson, M., & Nilsson, M. (2026). In pursuit of the green Transition—Electricity at any cost? In M. Henrekson, C. Sandström, & M. Stenkula (Eds.), *A Green Entrepreneurial State? Exploring the Pitfalls of Green Deals* (pp. 149–172). Cham: Springer.

Forlim, C. G., Ascone, L., Koch, C., & Kühn, S. (2024). Resting state network changes induced by experimental inaudible infrasound exposure and associations with self-reported noise sensitivity and annoyance. *Scientific Reports, 14*, Article 24555. https://doi.org/10.1038/s41598-024-76543-2

Furnham, A., & Boo, H. C. (2011). A literature review of the anchoring effect. *Journal of Socio-Economics, 40*(1), 35–42. https://doi.org/10.1016/j.socec.2010.10.008

Gorelick, S. M. (2009), *Oil Panic and the Global Crisis: Predictions and Myths*. Hoboken, NJ: Wiley-Blackwell.

Grafström, J. (2026). A silent transition: Growth with less environmental weight. In M. Henrekson, C. Sandström, & M. Stenkula (Eds.), *A Green Entrepreneurial State? Exploring the Pitfalls of Green Deals* (pp. 259–271). Cham: Springer.

de Groot, J. I. M., & Steg, L. (2010). Morality and nuclear energy: Perceptions of risk and benefits, personal norms, and willingness to take action related to nuclear energy. *Risk Analysis, 30*(9), 1363–1373. https://doi.org/10.1111/j.1539-6924.2010.01419.x

Hamlin A., & Jennings, C. (2011). Expressive political behaviour: Foundations, scope and implications. *British Journal of Political Science, 41*(3), 645–670. https://doi.org/10.1017/S0007123411000020

Heptonstall, P. J., & Gross, R. J. K. (2021). A systematic review of the costs and impacts of integrating variable renewables into power grids. *Nature Energy, 6*(1), 72–83. https://doi.org/10.1038/s41560-020-00695-4

Hillman, A. L. (2010). Expressive behavior in economics and politics. *European Journal of Political Economy, 26*(4), 403–418. https://doi.org/10.1016/j.ejpoleco.2010.06.004

Hubacek, K., Chen, X., Feng, K., Wiedmann, T., & Shan, Y. (2021). Evidence of decoupling consumption-based CO_2 emissions from economic growth. *Advances in Applied Energy, 4*, Article 100074. https://doi.org/10.1016/j.adapen.2021.100074

Idel, R. (2022). Levelized full system costs of electricity. *Energy, 259*, Article 124905. https://doi.org/10.1016/j.energy.2022.124905

Jarvis, S., Deschenes, O., & Akshaya, J. (2022). The private and external costs of Germany's nuclear phase-out. *Journal of the European Economic Association, 20*(3), 1311–1346. https://doi.org/10.1093/jeea/jvac007

Jasper, J. M., & Poulsen, J. D. (1995). Recruiting strangers and friends: Moral shocks and social networks in animal rights and anti-nuclear protests. *Social Problems, 42*(4), 493–512. https://doi.org/10.2307/3097043

Joppke, C. (1993). *Mobilizing Against Nuclear Energy: A Comparison Between Germany and the United States*. Berkeley, CA: University of California Press.

Kallis, G., Kostakis, V., Lange, S., Muraca, B., Paulson, S., & Schmelzer, M. (2018). Research on degrowth. *Annual Review of Environment and Resources, 43*, 291–316. https://doi.org/10.1146/annurev-environ-102017-025941

Kirchgässner, G. (1992). Towards a theory of low-cost decisions. *European Journal of Political Economy, 8*(2), 305–320. https://doi.org/10.1016/0176-2680(92)90028-F

Kirchherr, J., Hartley, K., & Tukker, A. (2023). Missions and mission-oriented innovation policy for sustainability: A review and critical reflection. *Environmental Innovation and Societal Transitions, 47*, Article 100721. https://doi.org/10.1016/j.eist.2023.100721

Kliemt, H. (1986). The veil of insignificance. *European Journal of Political Economy, 2*(3), 333–344. https://doi.org/10.1016/0176-2680(86)90024-8

Krämer, W. (2013). *Unstatistik des Monats: Die Strahlentoten von Fukushima.* https://www.mpib-berlin.mpg.de/unstatistik-reaktorunglueck-von-fukushima

Kulke, U. (2013). Roth im Strudel der "Atomopfer“ von Fukushima. *Die Welt*, March 12. https://www.welt.de/politik/deutschland/article114366195/Gruenen-Chefin-Roth-im-Strudel-der-Atomopfer-von-Fukushima.html

Kuran, T. & Sunstein, C. R. (1999). Availability cascades and risk regulation. *Stanford Law Review, 51*(4), 683–768. https://doi.org/10.2307/1229439

Laibson, D. (1997). Golden eggs and hyperbolic discounting. *Quarterly Journal of Economics, 112*(2), 443–478. https://doi.org/10.1162/003355397555253

Lomborg, B. (2023). *Best Things First*. Copenhagen: Copenhagen Consensus Center.

Mazzucato, M. (2021). *Mission Economy. A Moonshot Guide to Changing Capitalism.* London: Allen Lane.

Meadows, D. H., Meadows, D. L., Randers, J., & Behrens III, W. W. (1972). *The Limits to Growth. A Report for the Club of Rome's Project on the Predicament of Mankind*. New York, NY: Universe Books.

Meißner, F. (2019). The Fukushima disaster and the “clash of risk cultures”: Japanese and German journalists' perceptions of a nuclear crisis. *Global Media Journal – German Edition, 9*(2). https://doi.org/10.22032/dbt.40623

Moreau, A.-S. (2021). “The sun and the wind will never send us a bill!”. Jeremy Rifkin on his “Green New Deal”. https://www.philonomist.com/en/interview/sun-and-wind-will-never-send-us-bill

Nall, C. (2025). Can economic fact-checking remedy incorrect beliefs about housing markets? *Housing Policy Debate, 35*(1), 118–123. https://doi.org/10.1080/10511482.2024.2418046

Pickup, M., Krimborough, E. O., & de Rooij, E. A. (2022). Expressive politics as (costly) norm following. *Political Behavior, 44*(4), 1611–1631. https://doi.org/10.1007/s11109-020-09667-6

Schnellenbach, J. (2005). Model uncertainty and the rationality of economic policy. *Journal of Evolutionary Economics, 15*(1), 101–116. https://doi.org/10.1007/s00191-004-0231-y

Schnellenbach, J. (2023). Public entrepreneurship in economic evolution. In K. Dopfer, R. R. Nelson, J. Potts, & A. Pyka (Eds.), *Routledge Handbook of Evolutionary Economics* (pp. 402–410). London: Routledge.

Schnellenbach, J., & Schubert, C. (2015). Behavioral political economy. *European Journal of Political Economy, 40*(B), 395–417. https://doi.org/10.1016/j.ejpoleco.2015.05.002

Schnellenbach, J., & Schubert, C. (2025). Belief consumption. In R. Jong-A-Pin & C. Bjørnskov (Eds.), *Elgar Encyclopedia of Public Choice* (pp. 86–92). Cheltenham, UK, and Northampton, MA: Edward Elgar.

Slovic, P. (1987). Perceptions of risk. *Science, 236*(4799), 280–285. https://doi.org/10.1126/science.3563507

Sunstein, C. R. (2002). Probability neglect: Emotions, worst cases, and law. *Yale Law Review, 112*(1), 61–107.

Sunstein, C. R. (2005). Moral heuristics. *Behavioral and Brain Sciences, 28*(4), 531–543. https://doi.org/10.1017/S0140525X05330093

Swedberg, R. (2018). Folk economics and its role in Trump's presidential campaign: An exploratory study. *Theory and Society, 47*(1), 1–36. https://doi.org/10.1007/s11186-018-9308-8

Tversky, A., & Kahneman, D. (1973). Availability: A heuristic for judging frequency and probability. *Cognitive Psychology, 5*(2), 207–232. https://doi.org/10.1016/0010-0285(73)90033-9

UNSCEAR (2021). *United Nations Scientific Committee on the Effects of Atomic Radiation 2020/2021 Report Volume II*. New York, NY: United Nations. https://www.unscear.org/unscear/en/areas-of-work/fukushima.html

Weiß, H.-J., Markutzyk, S., & Schwotzer, B. (2014). Deutscher Atomausstieg made in Japan? Zur Rolle von Fukushima als Schlüsselereignis in der Medienberichterstattung über die deutsche Atomdebatte 2011. In J. Wolling & D. Arlt (Eds.), *Fukushima und die Folgen: Medienberichterstattung, Öffentliche Meinung und politische Konsequenzen* (pp. 79–99). Ilmenau: Universitätsverlag Ilmenau.

Wendland, A. V. (2017). Reaktorsicherheit und Zukunftskommunikation: Nuklearpolitik, Atomdebatten und kerntechnische Entwicklungen in Westdeutschland und Osteuropa 1970–2015. In C. Kampmann, A. Marciniak, & W. Meteling (Eds.), *Zum Verhältnis von Sicherheit und Zukunft in der Geschichte* (pp. 305–352). Baden-Baden: Nomos.

Jan Schnellenbach is Professor of Economics at Brandenburg University of Technology in Cottbus, Germany and an Affiliated Fellow at the Walter Eucken Institute at Freiburg, Germany. He received his Ph.D., in economics in 2003 at the University of St. Gallen, Switzerland with his dissertation *Decentralized Fiscal Policy as a Discovery Procedure,* focusing on fiscal federalism from a political economy perspective. In 2009, he was awarded the venia legendi for economics by the University of Heidelberg.

His main research interests concern the understanding of the process of economic policy-making from a behavioral economic perspective, as well as more conventional issues such as sustainable public finances, regional structural change, and the economic analysis of fiscal federalism. He has published over 30 articles in refereed journals and 60 papers in edited volumes and non-refereed academic journals. He is also active in policy consulting, with a current focus on the political management of structural change in German regions where coal mining and lignite power plants are being phased out.

Empirical Evidence

Exploring Failed Green Innovation Policy: The Rise and Fall of Ethanol Cars in Sweden 2003–2015

Rickard Björnemalm and Christian Sandström

Abstract The literature on innovation policy has so far paid little attention to policy failure and the mechanisms leading to failure. We describe the Swedish bubble in ethanol cars 2003–2015 and explain why policy efforts failed. Ethanol was competitive in the political domain as the fuel was backed by the Center Party and the associated farmers' lobby group, but lacked economic, technological, and environmental competitiveness. Our findings suggest that green innovation policies aimed at supporting new technologies against vested interests may instead end up extending established interests as policies are put in place under the influence of various stakeholders other than the common good.

Keywords Ethanol cars · Green deals · Policy failure · Innovation · Technology

JEL Codes H50 · L26 · L52 · O31 · O38 · P16

Introduction

Innovation policy has increasingly merged with industrial policy and environmental policy, often with a focus on regional development. Environmental policy was traditionally concerned with imposing various emission controls on harmful substances. Inspired by economists such as Mariana Mazzucato (2021), policymakers on the regional and national levels, as well as the European Union, have reoriented industrial policies toward a new, more interventionist path, sometimes referred to as innovation policy 3.0 (Schot and Steinmuller 2018).

Literature on innovation systems has emphasized the importance of niche experiments to accomplish sustainable transitions across different sectors (Geels 2002).

R. Björnemalm
Department of Management and Engineering, Linköping University, Linköping, Sweden
e-mail: rickard.bjornemalm@liu.se

C. Sandström (✉)
Linnaeus University, Växjö, Sweden
e-mail: christian.sandstrom@lnu.se

M. Henrekson et al. (eds.), *A Green Entrepreneurial State?*, International Studies in Entrepreneurship 49, https://doi.org/10.1007/978-3-032-15512-2_6

Scholars have highlighted the importance of government support in the nursing phase when a new technology is still immature.

While state support for infant industries and novel technologies has been highlighted by many scholars as critical (e.g., Jacobsson and Bergek 2004), this policy recommendation is rarely questioned or scrutinized. A systematic review of the innovation literature showed that little attention is given to the mechanisms behind policy failure (Kärnä et al. 2023).

In this study, we explore how and why state innovation policies aimed at providing support for sustainability transitions may fail. We do this through a historical case study of Sweden's ethanol car bubble. Ethanol cars gained traction in the early 2000s, and demand peaked in 2008. By 2010, the bubble had burst as car engines broke down and there was a public outcry among consumers.

Our case description shows that state support for sustainability transitions faces an inherent risk of being captured by politically entrenched actors—those who are better at political maneuvering—rather than by the firms that develop the most promising technology. While previous research has argued that political support toward nascent industries is important in order to generate positive externalities (Bergek et al. 2008), our findings suggest that such political support may strengthen incumbent interests.

As policymakers and key interest groups tend to be well integrated into established technological and economic paradigms, efforts to support technological niche experiments may therefore become extensions of the current hegemony rather than contributing to its upheaval (Bergkvist et al. 2022). In Sweden, support for ethanol was backed by the farmers' lobby who regarded these innovation policies as an opportunity to obtain more government support.

The remainder of the study is organized as follows. First, we review some of the literature on sustainability transitions and the role of innovation policy. Then we present our method, which is followed by an empirical description of our data. We conclude by discussing these findings and relate them to the literature.

Background: Green Missions

As a consequence of path dependence, technological lock-in, regulatory capture, and collective action problems, scholars increasingly discuss not only market failure in the traditional sense, but also in the sense of system failure when entire technological systems may fail to accomplish anticipated levels of renewal and change (Bleda and del Rio 2013). The resulting outcome would then be an absence of necessary economic and environmental development.

Prevailing policy recommendations derived in the literature on innovation systems and technological systems emphasize the importance of creating technological niches and nursing markets (Jacobsson and Bergek 2004). In doing so, scholars argue that technology neutrality is not ideal as implementing them is "an elusive quest" that is not even to be preferred (Azar and Sandén 2011, p. 135).

These ideas have been popularized by scholars such as Mariana Mazzucato who advocate that the state ought to take on a more active role in advancing societal goals such as sustainability (Mazzucato 2021). As Mazzucato (2022, p. 93) argues:

Governments play a critical role in catalyzing and coordinating both public and private investment around common goals, not least transitioning to a green economy.

While Jacobsson and Bergek (2004) acknowledge that "policymaking is a political process," initiatives aimed at nursing technological niches are rarely questioned, neither in academia nor by policymakers. Broadly speaking, there is a lack of studies on failed innovation policy (Kärnä et al. 2023) and the trend toward Innovation Policy 3.0 and increased directionality has so far not been paralleled by a discussion of the boundary conditions of such policies. In their literature review covering 7,161 papers published from 2010 to 2019 in major innovation journals such as *Research Policy*, *Technological Forecasting and Social Change*, *Industrial and Corporate Change*, *Technovation*, the *Journal of Technology Transfer*, and *Economics of Innovation and New Technology*, Kärnä et al. (2023) showed that analyses and even mere mentioning of policy failure is exceedingly rare in the literature on innovation policy.

Kärnä et al. (2023) search for the occurrence and frequency of terms associated with various aspects of policy failure, including rent-seeking, pork barrel, median voter, special interest groups, regulatory capture, lobbying, budget maximizing, political failure, and political economy. A mere 11% of the papers studied contained any mention of the terms related to failure and out of these 11%, less than half did so at any length beyond merely mentioning a term, e.g., rent-seeking.

In sum, we observe on the one hand that academic research has become increasingly optimistic regarding the possibilities for policymakers to intervene in the market economy and tilt it toward outcomes that are socially and environmentally desirable. On the other hand, echoing the results of Kärnä et al. (2023), little academic effort has been devoted to studying how and why interventionist innovation policies may and often do fail.

We are therefore interested in the failure of policies aimed to support technological niche experiments and attempts at industrial renewal. Specifically, we set out to answer the following research question: What are the mechanisms behind failed innovation policy?

Method and Data Collection

To study the mechanisms behind failed innovation policies, we looked for a historical case where policies failed, either due to not fulfilling the original goals of the policy or due to undesired side effects. Moreover, a fairly recent example would be more suitable as policy lessons are probably more applicable if this is the case.

The Swedish ethanol car bubble constitutes a case where these criteria are fulfilled. It began in the early 2000s, peaked in 2008, experienced a massive and persistent decline during the 2009–2015 period, and has never recovered. Our results also show that the origin of the ethanol car bubble was a product of innovation policies and support structures where the instituted policies failed to overcome ethanol cars' economic, technological, and environmental limitations.

Our data collection and analysis consists of two parts. We first identified and reviewed secondary literature and primary sources in the form of newspaper articles from the Swedish Media Archive (*Mediearkivet*), reports from government agencies and parliament using online archives (*Riksdagens öppna data*), the Swedish National Audit Office (*Riksrevisionen*), and a limited number of academic articles of relevance. In addition, we also reviewed parliamentary motions and questions as well as election debates. These sources provided a baseline and helped us identify key policy decisions and documents. Following the advice of Langley (1999), we visualized the policy process by constructing a timeline of events.

Second, we iterated the timeline throughout our research, triangulating using data from multiple sources. We complemented the timeline using statistical data from Statistics Sweden, Transport Analysis (the government agency for transport policy analysis), and Mobility Sweden (the Swedish trade association for manufacturers and importers of passenger cars, trucks, and buses), concerning market share, number of cars sold, new registrations, and number of vehicles in operation. These data were used to illustrate the scale and scope of the ethanol car bubble. We reviewed the newspaper articles from *Mediearkivet* multiple times, gathering data that reflected public opinion and public debate (as expressed in newspapers and by politicians). Finally, we combined these different data sources to try and identify influential interest groups and their connection to the policy process.

Case Description: The Ethanol Car Bubble

State support for ethanol as a fuel has varied over time in Sweden. Ethanol could be produced domestically from grain and potatoes. Thus, farmers and their organizations have been consistent proponents of ethanol as a fuel. Traditionally, the farmers' party in Sweden, the Center Party, had therefore been advocates for ethanol. Since the late 1970s, every party leader had at some point written motions in parliament advocating state support for ethanol as a fuel.

Despite being present in public discussions for decades, ethanol never gained that much traction as a fuel until the early 2000s. At its peak in 2008, roughly 20% of all cars sold in the country used ethanol as a fuel. A few years later, very few ethanol cars were sold, and the vehicles gradually left the fleet (see Fig. 1).

In 2007 sales of ethanol cars increased by 36% and in 2008 by 66%. The decline in the following years was equally steep: −32% in 2009, −11% in 2010, −57% in 2011, and −61% in 2012. In 2015 the number of decommissioned ethanol cars exceed the number of newly registered ones, and from then on, the total number of ethanol cars has declined year by year.

Figure 2 illustrates the overall timeline of events on three levels: the levels of policy, interest groups, and public opinion and debate. In our case description, we summarize what our analysis identifies as the most significant elements of the ethanol

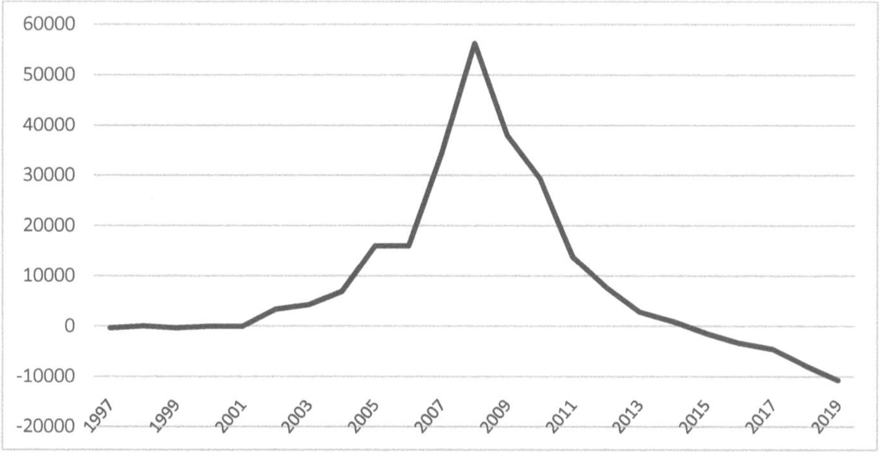

Fig. 1 Annual change in the number of ethanol cars in traffic in Sweden, 1997–2020. *Note* Data before 2002 do not include ethanol hybrids. Data before 2005 include cars with the following fuels: kerosene, liquefied petroleum gas, producer gas, ethanol, methanol, motor gas, rapeseed oil, paraffin oil, natural gas, and biogas in hybrids. *Source* Statistics Sweden (2003, 2007, 2025)

car bubble. First, we briefly provide the relevant historical and political context, which partly explains the background of the ethanol car bubble. We then summarize three important policy initiatives—the so-called pump law, the green car rebate, and the exemption from congestion tax—which led to the rise of the ethanol car bubble. The role of bipartisan political support is then explored. Finally, we describe the decline and discuss the effects of the ethanol car bubble.

Political Background

In the 1990s, the Center Party was joined by the Social Democrats in supporting ethanol. Göran Persson, the then Prime Minister, declared a green vision where biofuel production constituted an important part (Eklöf et al. 2012). With this change in political conditions, ethanol enjoyed bipartisan support. This enabled investments in domestic biofuel production and several reforms to incentivize the purchase and use of ethanol cars. In the years 1998–2002, Persson's Social Democratic government was dependent upon support from the Center Party, and he was keen to pander to the party in different ways. Providing support for ethanol turned out to be one such activity.

By the early 2000s, the European Union (EU) enacted a Directive (EC 2003) specifying guidelines to increase the use of biofuels in member countries to specified levels by 2005 and 2010. The Swedish government commissioned a public inquiry into how these goals could be achieved.

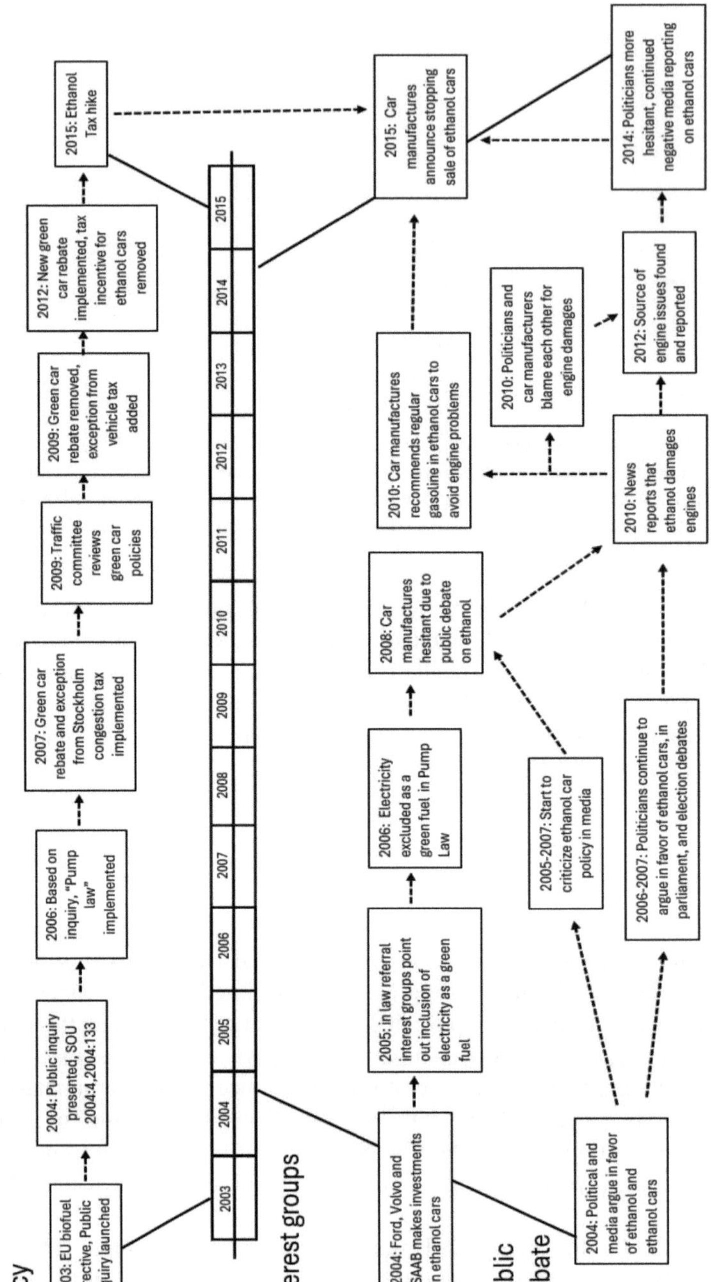

Fig. 2 Ethanol car bubble timeline, 2003–2015

In its first report (SOU 2004:4), the inquiry found that ethanol was the best possible option to reach the 2005 goal.[1] The report concluded that 150,000–300,000 cars using fossil fuels needed to be replaced by ethanol cars. Notably, the inquiry, per the government's instructions, proposed a law that mandated filling stations to provide at least one "renewable" transport fuel.[2] This would later become known as "the pump law." The author asserted that the proposed law, while being *prima facie* technology neutral, would in practice lead to ethanol being almost exclusively used over alternatives, including other biofuels. The EU Directive and the subsequent public inquiry marked the starting point of the ethanol bubble. The various policy efforts imposed in the coming years can be viewed as product of the EU Directive and the Swedish government's desire to comply.

The Pump Law

Taking effect in 2006, "the pump law" is a law that mandated filling stations over a certain size to provide pumps with "renewable" fuels. Notably, the law contains an exception that specifically excludes green electricity from being considered as a "renewable fuel." Absent the exemption, filling stations could have provided electric outlets to be compliant with the pump law. However, since the intent behind the law was to increase the use of biofuels, the law excluded electricity.

The stated reason was that one of the biggest obstacles for widespread adoption of biofuels in cars was that there would not be enough filling stations offering them. Following unsuccessful attempts in 2004 to persuade the fuel industry to voluntarily invest in biofuel pumps (SOU 2004:4; Swedish Parliament 2009), the government reverted to the original proposal in the public inquiry's first report. This proposal would be revised and eventually implemented.

Interestingly, the first version of the law did not exclude electricity. It was also heavily criticized by Hans Sandebring, the principal author of the public inquiry. Among other things, he warned that the bill would in practice favor ethanol-based technology over alternatives despite being ostensibly "technology neutral." The Swedish Legislative Council (*lagrådet*) also criticized the bill for lacking analysis of its consequences.

The decision to exclude green electricity was taken as a result of the referral process. Biofuel-related interest groups noted that including green electricity as a renewable fuel would defeat the purpose of the bill as filling stations would just add a couple of charging slots or power outlets to comply with the letter of the law, but

[1] The inquiry's reference group included, but was not limited to, various biofuel and biofuel-related interest groups such as Agrarian Ethanol (*Agroetanol*), the BioAlcohol Fuel Foundation, Green Motorists (*Gröna bilister*), Sekab, Svebio, and the Swedish Biogas Association (*Svenska biogasföreningen*).

[2] According to the inquiry (SOU 2004:4, p. 11) "[a] renewable transport fuel is defined as encompassing both fuels derived from biomass and fuels produced from renewable energy sources other than biomass," Original in Swedish; translated by authors.

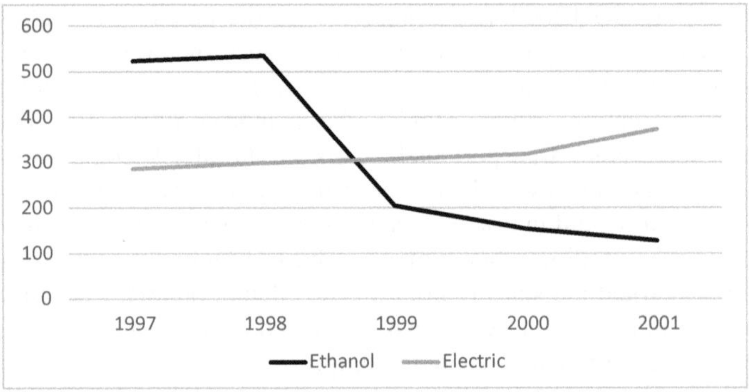

Fig. 3 Electric cars and ethanol cars in traffic in Sweden, 1997–2001. *Note* Data include cars using the following fuels: kerosene, liquefied petroleum gas, producer gas, ethanol, methanol, motor gas, rapeseed oil, paraffin oil, natural gas, and biogas. Ethanol hybrids are not included. *Source* Statistics Sweden (2003, 2007)

not the intent of the law. While criticism of the revised proposal was expressed at the time, criticism of the green electricity exemption was notably absent. The likely reason is that the market for electric cars was understood to be "negligible" at that point in time. The exclusion of electricity from the pump law was thus not considered a major issue.

However, as shown in Fig. 3, the market for both electric and ethanol cars was negligible in the late 1990s and early 2000s. Before the start of the ethanol car bubble, both technologies were still in their infancy. In fact, in 1999–2001, electric cars outsold ethanol cars, though the market was very small and would vary greatly year by year.

The Green Car Rebate

In 2006, the Swedish center-left government was replaced by a center-right government. One of the new government's priorities was to enact a rebate that would incentivize consumers to buy environmentally friendly cars.[3] The green car rebate amounted to SEK 10,000 (≈ EUR 900) and was directed toward individuals who bought a new "green" car. The green car rebate, in effect, functioned as a subsidy for ethanol cars. By providing a direct financial incentive, the rebate contributed to the further expansion of the ethanol bubble by stimulating demand. Both the number of ethanol cars and their relative market share increased when the rebate was introduced.

[3] See Huse and Lucinda (2014) for an in-depth analysis of its effects.

Exemption from Congestion Taxes

The Stockholm congestion tax, instituted on a trial basis in 2006 and permanented in 2007, refers to time-dependent tolls levied on cars traveling across the city during peak traffic hours.

The main purpose of the congestion tax is reflected in its name: to reduce congestion. However, it was argued that these congestion taxes could also be used to stimulate the demand for green cars and thus reduce emissions (SOU 2013:84). However, as Hultkrantz and Liu (2012) found, the exemption for green cars undermined the goal to reduce congestion. Consumers responded to the exemption by buying green cars. While this did have a positive effect on emissions (Hultkrantz and Liu 2012), it contributed to inflating the ethanol bubble by stimulating demand for green cars.

Bipartisan Support

Ethanol as a fuel enjoyed bipartisan support as both the center-left governments and center-right governments implemented policies to stimulate demand: the pump law, the green car rebate, and the exemption from congestion taxes. There were some politicians that went further in their support for ethanol, highlighting it as a potential savior of Sweden's deindustrialized rural north.

Some Center Party politicians, notably Maud Olofsson, Minister of Industry and Enterprise from 2006, stood out in their early and long-standing support for ethanol. Olofsson had an ethanol-driven Ford as early as 2001 and said the following in a parliamentary debate in 2005 (Olofsson 2005, p. 3):

> But within a few years it will be commercially viable to extract ethanol from cellulose, i.e., from forest raw materials and waste from the forest industry. This will mean lower production prices and higher competitiveness for Swedish-produced ethanol.[4]

Ethanol is also mentioned in the 2006 election as Swedish Prime Minister Göran Person also expressed support for ethanol (Persson 2006): "Therefore, we should not try to attract people with lower gas prices but instead get something else to pour into the tank on which the cars can be driven."[5]

Prime Minister Persson would also legitimize his government's policy efforts to increase the use of ethanol cars, by referring to Sweden's international industrial competitiveness. Specifically, rhetorically linking domestic car manufacturing and policies to promote "green cars" (Persson 2006):

> No absolutely I don't think so because what we are seeing now, because of our [the government's] policies and the international development, people are moving towards the energy efficient alternatives, environmentally friendly cars are increasing rapidly, we are getting a

---

[4] Original in Swedish; translated by the authors.

[5] Original in Swedish; translated by the authors.

new infrastructure for this, produced in Sweden. We are developing new engines. We are at the forefront of the world.[6]

Göran Persson would also tour ethanol factories and inaugurate the municipally owned company Sekab, which was supposed to do research in order to develop efficient methods for producing ethanol from cellulose (Sandström and Alm 2022). The breakthrough innovations in ethanol production that were envisaged never materialized. Although there was political support for any alternative green fuels, ethanol was the only alternative fuel that benefited from the enacted policies.

The Decline of Ethanol

An array of factors contributed to the downfall of ethanol from 2009 and onwards. Research by David Pimentel at Cornell University showed that, when all resource inputs are considered, ethanol production requires 29% more energy than it yields. Put differently, using ethanol as a fuel is unsustainable, as it consumes more energy to produce than it delivers (Pimentel and Pimentel 2008).

An important aspect of ethanol production concerns all the inputs required for growing the crops. Fertilizers require nitrogen, which emits two tonnes of CO_2 per hectare. Put differently, already when growing the crops, ethanol would have a worse net CO_2 impact compared to alternatives.

An expert group within the Ministry of Finance in Sweden published a report in 2010 which showed that CO_2 emissions would have been 20 million tonnes less if the same transportation had instead been done using gasoline. Sören Wibe, professor of forest economics, was commissioned by the Ministry of Finance to investigate the environmental effects of using ethanol as a fuel. Wibe argued that ethanol production was harmful for both the environment and the global economy as increased usage implied a conversion of farmland to ethanol production, which in turn contributed to deforestation in developing economies and increased CO_2 emissions. In his report, Wibe also ranked ethanol from agricultural products as the worst alternative (Wibe 2010).

By early 2009, oil prices declined sharply. The price of gasoline dropped below the price of ethanol, resulting in ethanol car owners refueling with gasoline. From an environmental standpoint, this was bad news as ethanol cars could run exclusively on gasoline. However, they were less efficient in terms of fuel consumption. When driven exclusively on gasoline, ethanol cars emitted more CO_2 than a standard gasoline car. This damaged the ethanol cars' "green" reputation as many people had bought an ethanol car because they had been persuaded that it was a more environmentally friendly alternative.

Ethanol cars had been a subject of public debate and media coverage throughout the 2000s (see Fig. 2). While media coverage until 2004 had been positive, criticism began to emerge as early as 2005 and continued during the implementation

[6] Original in Swedish; translated by the authors.

of the ethanol-friendly policies in 2006 and 2007. Despite this initial criticism, the bipartisan political support persisted. By 2010, public sentiment was characterized by mounting negativity, with engine problems emerging as a focal point of criticism. It would later be revealed that some ethanol contained high levels of sulfur, which caused car engines to clog and break. While not necessarily the fault of the ethanol car itself, car owners were upset as they had to pay for repairs. That sentiment reinforced the increasingly negative perception of ethanol as a fuel and ethanol cars as "green" alternatives.

As already described, several policy measures provided financial incentives to buy ethanol cars, which significantly boosted demand. Partly due to the increasingly negative public opinion toward ethanol cars, and their inherent limitations as a green alternative, previously implemented policy measures began to be rolled back.

A series of important events in 2008 and 2009 made diesel cars the preferred environmentally friendly alternative. First, a 2008 EU Directive changed the rules regarding the highest allowed CO_2 emission per kilometer, which effectively resulted in diesel cars being considered low-emission cars (SOU 2013:84). In 2009, diesel cars were also exempted from vehicle tax. In addition, the green car rebate was discontinued and was not reintroduced until 2012 (National Audit Office 2020). In 2010, it was announced that tax deductions for ethanol cars would be abolished; it was enacted in 2012 (SOU 2013:84).

It could be argued that these policy changes are the cause of the decline of ethanol cars. However, it is evident that the negative perception of ethanol cars among consumers was rooted, at least partly, in inherent limitations of the ethanol car as a "green" alternative. Thus, it is hardly surprising that consumers seemed to prefer diesel cars as a green alternative when incentives were similar.[7] Yet, the bipartisan political support for ethanol coupled with the incentives provided by policy efforts could boost demand for a time but ultimately not overcome the inherent limitations of the technology.

Effects of the Ethanol Bubble

When considering the rise of the ethanol car in the Swedish market, domestic car manufacturers were able to disproportionately take advantage of it. As Fig. 4 shows, Volvo, Saab, and Ford jointly controlled slightly more than 10% of the market for green cars in 2005. One year later, these three companies together made up almost 40% of all sales of "green cars" and at the height of the ethanol bubble in January 2008, they had grabbed 75% of the market for "green cars."

Importantly, Volvo was owned by Ford in 1999–2010. Ford introduced ethanol cars to the Swedish market in 1994. Through agreements with a consortium of local authorities, companies, and individuals, Ford secured a large order of at least 3,000

---

[7] Diesel cars are not considered environmentally friendly today, but at the time they were. This highlights how perceptions of what is considered "green" changes over time.

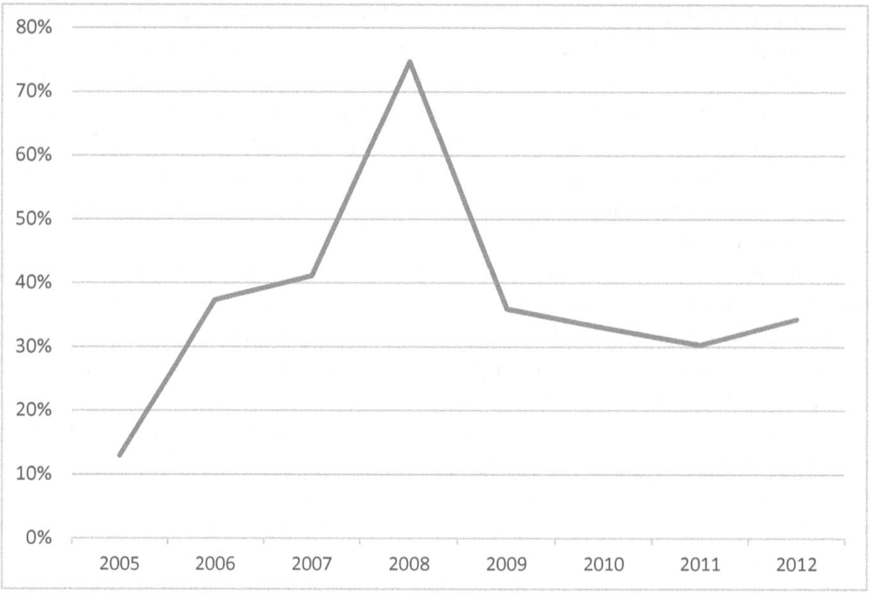

Fig. 4 Volvo's, Ford's, and Saab's market share of green cars in Sweden, 2005–2012. *Note* The market share data pertain to January of each year. *Source* Mobility Sweden (2023)

cars tailor-made for the Swedish market in 2001 (Pedersen and Hagman 2010). Ford was alone in the ethanol car market until 2005 when, following signals from policymakers about the pipeline of future policy measures, Saab and Volvo presented ethanol car models to be released in 2005 (Ny Teknik 2004a; Dagens Nyheter 2004; Ny Teknik 2004b). While there is evidence to suggest that Volvo was hesitant to focus on ethanol cars (Ny Teknik 2004a), the relatively low cost of converting gasoline cars to ethanol cars combined with a potentially strong market demand for green cars—following implementation of the communicated policy measures—meant that even hesitant car manufacturers offered ethanol car models. As stated by an information executive at Saab Automobile: "We have not previously seen that there exists a market" (Ny Teknik 2004b).

The fuel industry was another important interest group affected by the rise of ethanol cars. Ethanol did not represent a major threat to the fuel industry. For one, it was easy to adjust. Ethanol had already been mixed with gasoline to gradually replace lead since the 1980s (Bladh 2020). Furthermore, several policy efforts in the 1990s made it more attractive for the fuel industry to embrace domestic ethanol production. This included tax incentives and tariffs (National Audit Office 2011, 2020). Thus, the fuel industry was familiar with ethanol and viewed the efforts to create a market for ethanol cars as a positive (Swedish Parliament 2009). Moreover, ethanol car policy efforts and engagement from the fuel industry went hand in hand, as explained by a CEO of a filling station chain at the time:

> Nobody wants to buy ethanol cars until there are filling stations, but nobody wants to sell ethanol until there are ethanol cars. But now there are ethanol cars, and more are on the way. The investment in ethanol has also made it easier to get permission from the municipalities. (Göteborgs-Posten 2004).

Thus, one of the important effects of the ethanol car bubble was that it created both supply and demand for ethanol cars, but it only did so temporarily and artificially. Despite bipartisan political support, aligning car manufacturers with the fuel industry and incentivizing consumers, the inherent limitations of the technology could not be overcome. The extent of these efforts was unique in the European context (National Audit Office 2011, p. 110): "Sweden is, essentially, the only country in the EU which has created a market for E85." While some would argue that the creation of a new and relatively unique market could be considered a policy success, the ethanol car bubble was still a policy failure. It did not create a viable long-term market for ethanol cars and—as a follow-up report by the Parliamentary Traffic Committee found—hindered the development of alternatives:

> There are indications that the passing of the pump law, to a certain extent, has contributed to hampering the emergence of other alternative renewable fuels. (Swedish Parliament 2009, p. 25).

Another important effect was that the pump law had a considerable impact on filling station availability. In the eight years from 2006 to 2014, the number of filling stations in Sweden declined from 3,700 to 2,700; a 27% decline which affected rural areas disproportionately. According to the interest group Swedish Gasoline Distributors (*Svensk Bensinhandel*), the pump law led to the immediate closure of several hundred filling stations. However, this overall 27% decline was also shaped by concurrent macroeconomic and societal trends, including urbanization.

Analysis and Discussion

A Case of Policy Failure

As the case description shows, ethanol did not turn out to be a viable alternative to fossil fuels. In this sense, it is a failure as the government measures to support ethanol effectively led consumers, car manufacturers, and the fuel industry to a dead end.

The technology was launched artificially and prematurely, which resulted in a backlash among consumers. Its environmental benefits were limited or non-existent and it grew largely because generous, targeted support policies were put in place to favor ethanol. The pump law, tax deductions for green cars, and several other measures were implemented in 2005–2008, resulting in rapid growth of ethanol car sales. Sales peaked in 2008 and declined sharply thereafter, a trend largely attributable to policy shifts that promoted the emergence of "green diesel" cars as substitutes.

The various policies put in place to support ethanol also had negative economic effects in a broader sense. Congestion taxes in the Stockholm area were largely stripped of their positive effects for the economy (Hultkrantz and Liu 2012), filling stations were negatively affected, especially in rural areas, and the measures encouraging ethanol cars seem to have prevented the diffusion of superior alternatives.

Explaining the Failure of Innovation Policy

Policymakers adopted several of the measures touted by innovation system scholars. They successfully identified a technological niche experiment and provided extensive supportive measures paving the way for its diffusion into the socio-technical (ST) regime (Geels 2002).

Jacobsson and Bergek (2004) acknowledge that policy-making is fundamentally a political process and many scholars in innovation studies draw upon both institutional theory, economics, and sociology to argue that the ST regime tends to have the upper hand and often tends to be captured by incumbent institutions and political processes. But these domains of research largely fail to acknowledge that any political support to various technological niche experiments faces the same risk of being captured by powerful interest groups.

Political attempts to support niche experiments may be intended to empower institutional entrepreneurs and dismantle an established ST regime; however, during implementation such policies are often pushed in different directions as they become influenced by various interest groups.

Our case study shows that political support directed toward a certain niche experiment is indeed inherently political; in hindsight, the economic and technological viability appears to have been secondary. As interest groups exert pressure on the political process, the end result may instead be counter productive support measures that do not facilitate innovation. As the effects of the policy efforts unfold, even initially skeptical industry actors perceive a risk of missing out on the lucrative, but artificially created, market and feel obliged to invest and produce products they would not have produced otherwise, thus hurting themselves in the long term.

The impact of regulations is hard to predict. The pump law was originally supposed to be technology neutral. In practice, it subsidized ethanol cars as the only alternative, and over time the law grew out of date as it excluded what is currently seen as the most attractive alternative solution, namely electric cars. Thus, the pump law became a support scheme for combustion engine vehicles rather than incentivizing novel solutions. Documents from the referral process concerning the design of the pump law show that several interest groups, including the Swedish Petroleum Institute, backed the decision to exclude electricity as a "renewable" fuel. Hence, the ability of vested interests to capture the regulatory process implied that, in reality, what was supposed to function as an incubator for new technologies became an extension and entrenchment of existing solutions and companies. Ethanol cars were also referred to as flexifuel cars as they ran on both gasoline and ethanol. In effect, ethanol cars became an extension of the existing automotive technology, albeit with a few modifications.

To conclude, innovation policies aimed at supporting various novel technologies were justified by arguing that the established technology is dominant politically and economically and policies should be designed to address such path dependence. However, the policies suffered from the logical inconsistency of ignoring the risk that the design of policies is influenced by both economic and political special interests groups.

Conclusion

In this study, we have uncovered some of the mechanisms behind the failure of innovation policies. Innovation policy failure is a subject hitherto understudied by innovation scholars (Kärnä et al. 2023).

We have described and explained the emergence, rapid growth, and downfall of ethanol cars in Sweden. Support for ethanol was firmly rooted in the Center Party and as the Social Democrats became progressively more in favor of ethanol considerable political support was mobilized by the early 2000s. EU Directives prompted policymakers to take immediate action; the pump law was instituted in 2006 and disproportionately benefited ethanol relative to alternative fuels. The pump law was influenced by several interest groups, including the Swedish Petroleum Institute. Ethanol cars gained in popularity in the following years, and their adoption was further accelerated by additional policy measures. At the 2008 peak, more than 20% of all new cars sold in Sweden were ethanol cars.

This was followed by a rapid decline. Negative perceptions among consumers were reinforced as engines ran poorly on sulfur-heavy ethanol and often broke down. New research concerning the negative environmental effects of ethanol became available and spread quickly after 2008. As a consequence of this change in public opinion, policy efforts were altered to favor other alternative fuels at the expense of ethanol. In hindsight, it is clear that the fuel industry and domestic car manufacturers Saab and Volvo, together with Ford (which owned Volvo at the time), ultimately embraced the policy efforts—albeit with some hesitancy on the part of Volvo—and benefited in the short term from the rise of ethanol cars.

The Swedish ethanol car bubble constitutes an illustrative example of how political connections and political capabilities determine the outcomes of policy support for innovations rather than informed assessments of their long-term technological and economic viability. The Swedish ethanol car bubble clearly illustrates how support efforts directed toward technological niche experiments face the inherent risk of being captured by special and already entrenched interest groups. Choices regarding what technology to support and the design of these support schemes do not take place in a vacuum. On the contrary, they are subject to influence from vested interests, in the form both of firms and political parties backed by various interest groups. Moreover, even hesitant actors may find it hard to resist the short-term opportunity to benefit from politically backed technologies and artificially created markets, resulting in large-scale malinvestment.

We welcome further research on other aspects of ethanol policies in Sweden. This paper is largely based on primary data from online media, parliamentary archives, and aggregate statistics. We would appreciate further studies based on interviews with policymakers but acknowledge the difficulty in obtaining access to former cabinet ministers and other decision-makers who are willing to speak their mind concerning a policy failure.

This study has focused exclusively on policies geared toward ethanol cars. However, considerable efforts were also expended to develop domestic ethanol production and to develop ethanol from cellulose (Sandström and Alm 2022; Sandström and Björnemalm 2022). Research focused on these aspects of ethanol would make a valuable contribution to deepen insights regarding the rapid rise and downfall of ethanol as a building block in the green transition. We would also welcome more studies into the failure of innovation policies. To what extent has the ongoing revival of interventionist industrial policies been inspired by research that has put a blind eye to the risks of policy and lack of critical enquiry? This is a fundamental question that merits further research.

References

Azar, C., & Sandén, B. A. (2011). The elusive quest for technology-neutral policies. *Environmental Innovation and Societal Transitions, 1*(1), 135–139. https://doi.org/10.1016/j.eist.2011.03.003

Bergek, A., Jacobsson, S., & Sandén, B. A. (2008). 'Legitimation' and 'development of positive externalities': Two key processes in the formation phase of technological innovation systems. *Technology Analysis and Strategic Management, 20*(5), 575–592. https://doi.org/10.1080/09537320802292768

Bergkvist, J. E., Moodysson, J., & Sandström, C. (2022). Third generation innovation policy: System transformation or reinforcing business as usual. In K. Wennberg & C. Sandström (Eds.), *Questioning the Entrepreneurial State: Status-quo, Pitfalls, and the Need for Credible Innovation Policy* (pp. 201–217). Cham: Springer. https://doi.org/10.1007/978-3-030-94273-1_11

Bladh, M. (2020). *Vägskäl i svensk energihistoria: Den ena omställningen efter den andra.* Stockholm: Books on Demand.

Bleda, M., & del Rio, P. (2013). The market failure and the systemic failure rationales in technological innovation systems. *Research Policy, 42*(5), 1039–1052. https://doi.org/10.1016/j.respol.2013.02.008

Dagens Nyheter (2004). Volvo satsar på etanol. November 9. *Mediearkivet.*

EC (2003). Directive 2003/30/EC of the European Parliament and of the Council of 8 May 2003 on the promotion of the use of biofuels or other renewable fuels for transport. https://eur-lex.europa.eu/eli/dir/2003/30/oj/eng

Eklöf, H., Ekerholm, H., & Mårald, E. (2012). Promoting ethanol in the shadow of oil dependence: 100 years of arguments and frictions in Swedish politics. *Scandinavian Journal of History, 37*(5), 621–645. https://doi.org/10.1080/03468755.2012.725677

Geels, F. W. (2002). Technological transitions as evolutionary reconfiguration processes: A multi-level perspective and a case-study. *Research Policy, 31*(8–9), 1257–1274. https://doi.org/10.1016/S0048-7333(02)00062-8

Göteborgs-Posten (2004). Finska bensinkedjan St1 till Sverige. September 30. *Mediearkivet.*

Hultkrantz, L., & Liu, X. (2012). Green cars sterilize congestion charges: A model analysis of the reduced impact of Stockholm road tolls. *Transport Policy, 2*(May), 110–118. https://doi.org/10.1016/j.tranpol.2012.03.001

Huse, C., & Lucinda, C. (2014). The market impact and the cost of environmental policy: Evidence from the Swedish green car rebate. *Economic Journal, 124*(578), 393–419. https://doi.org/10.1111/ecoj.12060

Jacobsson, S., & Bergek, A. (2004). Transforming the energy sector: The evolution of technological systems in renewable energy technology. *Industrial and Corporate Change, 13*(5), 815–849. https://doi.org/10.1093/icc/dth032

Kärnä, A., Karlsson, J., Engberg, E., & Svensson, P. (2023). Political failure: A missing piece in innovation policy analysis. *Economics of Innovation and New Technology, 32*(7), 1037–1068. https://doi.org/10.1080/10438599.2022.2070843

Langley, A. (1999). Strategies for theorizing from process data. *Academy of Management Review, 24*(4), 691–710. https://doi.org/10.2307/259349

Mazzucato, M. (2021). *Mission Economy A Moonshot Guide to Changing Capitalism.* New York, NY: Harper Business.

Mazzucato, M. (2022). Financing the green new deal. *Nature Sustainability, 5,* 93–94. https://doi.org/10.1038/s41893-021-00828-x

Mobility Sweden (2023). Här kan du ladda ner tidigare publicerad nyregistreringsstatistik. https://mobilitysweden.se/statistik/arkiv-nyregistreringar_1

National Audit Office (2011). *Biodrivmedel för bättre klimat – Hur används skattebefrielsen?* RiR 2011:10. Stockholm: Riksrevisionen.

National Audit Office (2020). *Statliga åtgärder för fler miljöbilar.* RiR 2020:1. Stockholm: Riksrevisionen.

Ny Teknik (2004a). Etanoldrift i ny miljöbil från Volvo. November 9. *Mediearkivet.*

Ny Teknik (2004b). Saab tillverkar sin första miljöbil. September 23. *Mediearkivet.*

Olofsson, M. (2005). Landsbygdsutveckling i norra Sverige. Motion till riksdagen 2005/06: N482. Stockholm: Riksdagens öppna data, Sveriges riksdag.

Pedersen, M. B., & Hagman, O. (2010). Encouraging environmental driving: The journey towards a definition of environmentally classified vehicles in Sweden. *Icon, 16*, 159–175. http://www.jstor.org/stable/23791381

Persson, G. (2006). Valet 2006 – Slutdebatten. https://youtu.be/m19Z2pxCRn0?t=1837

Pimentel, D., & Pimentel, M. (2008). *Food, Energy and Society.* 3rd edition. Boca Raton, FL: CRC Press.

Sandström, C., & Alm, C. (2022). Directionality in innovation policy and the ongoing failure of green deals: Evidence from biogas, bio-ethanol, and fossil-free steel. In K. Wennberg & C. Sandström (Eds.), *Questioning the Entrepreneurial State: Status-quo, Pitfalls, and the Need for Credible Innovation Policy* (pp. 251–269). Cham: Springer. https://doi.org/10.1007/978-3-030-94273-1_14

Sandström, C., & Björnemalm, R. (2022). Hur uppstår gröna bubblor? Lärdomar från etanolbubblan som sprack. *Ekonomisk Debatt, 50*(5), 65–71. https://www.nationalekonomi.se/wp-content/uploads/2022/08/50-5-csrb.pdf

Schot, J., & Steinmueller, W. E. (2018). Three frames for innovation policy: R&D, systems of innovation and transformative change. *Research Policy, 47*(9), 1554–1567. https://doi.org/10.1016/j.respol.2018.08.011

SOU 2004:4. *Förnybara fordonsbränslen – nationellt mål för 2005 och hur tillgängligheten av dessa bränslen kan ökas.* Stockholm: The Swedish Government Offices. https://www.regeringen.se/rattsliga-dokument/statens-offentliga-utredningar/2004/01/sou-20044/

SOU 2013:84. *Fossilfrihet på väg: Betänkande av Utredningen om fossilfri fordonstrafik.* Stockholm: The Swedish Government Offices. https://www.regeringen.se/rattsliga-dokument/statens-offentliga-utredningar/2013/12/sou-201384/

Statistics Sweden (2003). *Fordon vid årsskiftet 2002/2003.* Stockholm: Statistiska centralbyrån.

Statistics Sweden (2007). *Fordon vid årsskiftet 2006/2007.* Stockholm: Statistiska centralbyrån.

Statistics Sweden (2025). *Fordonsbestånd 2001–2023*. https://www.scb.se/hitta-statistik/statistik-efter-amne/transporter-och-kommunikationer/vagtrafik/fordon/pong/tabell-och-diagram/fordonsbestand/

Swedish Parliament (2009). *Pumplagen – uppföljning av lagen om skyldighet att tillhandahålla förnybara drivmedel*. Report from the Swedish Parliament. 2009/10:RFR7. Stockholm: Riksdagens öppna data, Sveriges riksdag.

Wibe, S. (2010). *Etanolens koldioxideffekter: En översikt av forskningsläget [Carbon Dioxide Effects of Ethanol: A State-of-the-Art Review]*. Report 2010:1. Expertgruppen för miljöstudier. Stockholm: Ministry of Finance.

Rickard Björnemalm is a PhD student at the Department of Management and Engineering, Business Administration Division, at Linköping University. He holds an MSc in Economic History from Stockholm University. Rickard's master's thesis, "Strategy in Swedish state-owned enterprises: Managing market-orientation in energy, post, and telecommunications, 1980–1988", won the 2024 Håkan Lindgren Prize for best economic history undergraduate thesis in Sweden. His research concerns the interplay between corporate strategy and public policy from a historical perspective. He has published research on the behavior of government agencies and how state-owned enterprises strategically manage competition over time.

Christian Sandström is an Associate Professor of Technology Management from Chalmers University of Technology, where he also received his doctoral degree (2010). His research concerns innovation policy and the interplay between technological and institutional change. Sandström is one of the editors of *Questioning the Entrepreneurial State* (Springer) and *Moonshots and the New Industrial Policy* (Springer). He has published more than 30 articles in peer-reviewed academic journals such as *Business History, Small Business Economics, Technological Forecasting & Social Change*, and *Industry & Innovation*.

Sandström wrote his PhD thesis on the topic of disruptive innovation. He has been a visiting scholar at the University of Cambridge and ETH Zürich in Switzerland. Sandström has received several awards for his pedagogical skills and is a frequently invited public speaker on the topic of technological change and industrial transformation. He is an affiliated researcher at Linnaeus University and a columnist in Sweden's leading business magazine *Affärsvärlden*.

The German *Energiewende*: A Green Deal Template or Planned Failure?

Michel Deshaies

Abstract The highly proactive policy of developing renewable energies that Germany implemented from the beginning of the 2000s has been taken as a model to follow to achieve the energy transition by substituting renewable energies for fossil fuels. The increase in the production of renewable energies has offset the sharp drop in production from nuclear and coal-fired power stations. This apparent success of the *Energiewende* partly inspired the Green Deal aimed at decarbonizing the European economy by 2050, by replacing fossil fuels with renewable energies. Germany has also set itself very ambitious targets for the development of renewable energies and makes it possible to achieve carbon neutrality by 2045. However, achieving such goals in the foreseen time frame is likely to prove particularly difficult, as several major obstacles have been greatly underestimated. In the absence of sufficient energy storage capacity, it is then necessary to build even larger capacity of intermittent renewable energy. But even in the hypothesis of the production of an energy vector allowing storage such as hydrogen, it would be necessary to build large renewable capacity. The challenge to be met is all the greater since electricity represents only 20% of the country's final energy consumption. The rest, corresponding mainly to the production of fuels and residential heating and industrial and tertiary activities, is provided mainly by gas and oil which, together, constitute approximately 60% of final energy consumption.

Keywords Energiewende · Intermittent renewable energy · Energy scenario · Saturation of space

JEL Codes: L52 · L70 · O38 · P18 · Q42 · Q58

M. Deshaies (✉)
University of Lorraine, Nancy, France
e-mail: michel.deshaies@univ-lorraine.fr

M. Henrekson et al. (eds.), *A Green Entrepreneurial State?*, International Studies in Entrepreneurship 49, https://doi.org/10.1007/978-3-032-15512-2_7

Introduction

Germany's vigorous promotion of renewable energy since the early 2000s has often been hailed as a model for achieving the energy transition (*Energiewende*), with renewables intended to replace fossil fuels. The Renewable Energy Act of 2000 enabled the rapid expansion of large-scale wind and solar photovoltaic capacity and set the ambitious goal of phasing out nuclear power by 2023 and coal by 2030. This apparent success of the *Energiewende* partly inspired the European Green Deal, which aims to decarbonize the European Union by 2050 through the substitution of fossil fuels with renewable energy. Germany has also committed itself to even more ambitious goals, pledging to reach carbon neutrality by 2045. Yet these targets will be all the harder to achieve given that several significant obstacles were long underestimated.

This essay examines the challenges Germany has faced in implementing its energy transition. The first section shows that while the expansion of electricity generation from renewable sources has partly offset the decline in output from nuclear and coal plants, the rapid rise of intermittent renewables has created significant difficulties for the stability and management of the electricity grid.

The growth of renewable capacity, together with the infrastructure required to support it, has already had a marked impact on electricity prices and environmental outcomes. Moreover, the *Energiewende* has focused primarily on electricity production, even though most energy consumption in Germany comes from transport, residential heating, and industrial or service activities—sectors still largely dependent on gas and oil, which together account for about 60% of final energy use. Until 2022, hydrocarbon consumption remained unchanged: Germany's usage in 2021 was identical to that of 1990.

The war in Ukraine, which first reduced and then cut off Russia's natural gas exports, exposed Germany's and Europe's enduring reliance on imported hydrocarbons. In this context, the idea of replacing hydrocarbons through an unprecedented expansion of renewable electricity production—supplemented by large-scale use of hydrogen—has emerged as the new guiding purpose of both the *Energiewende* and the European Union's Green Deal.

After reviewing the many problems created by the intermittency of new electricity sources over the past 25 years, this analysis demonstrates that the surge in renewable generation has done little to reduce Germany's reliance on hydrocarbons. This dependence explains why the German economy has been so severely affected by the war in Ukraine and the subsequent halt to Russian energy imports.

Ambitious projects to drastically expand renewable production as a substitute for hydrocarbons appear unrealistic. They risk saturating available land and driving energy prices sharply higher—developments that would only deepen the threat of deindustrialization. Given the geographical and economic constraints on renewable expansion, it is legitimate to question whether these objectives are attainable at all—or whether they risk leading Germany, and by extension the European Union, toward economic and energy disaster.

An *Energiewende* Based on Massive Development of Renewable Energies

The Accelerated Development of Renewable Energies in Germany

Since the entry into force of the Renewable Energies Act (*Erneuerbare Energien Gesetz*) of April 1, 2000, which set up a system of advantageous feed-in tariffs for twenty years for producers of renewable energy, Germany has become the European country where these energies have expanded the most. In barely twenty years, renewable energy production increased by 400%, which resulted in an increase in its share of final energy consumption from 4% to 19% between 2002 and 2023.

However, this increase has been uneven among the different sources. Although the use of biomass for heat production remains the main source of renewable energy and has increased sharply since 2000, its relative share nevertheless fell, from 56% to 40% in 2023. This is explained by the much greater growth in biofuels and especially in the production of electricity by wind turbines and photovoltaic cells. Wind and solar power production constituted 40% of renewable energy in 2023, compared to a mere 10% in 2000. The progress of renewable energies has been by far the most significant in the production of electricity. The share of electricity from renewables increased from 6.5% in 2000 to 52% in 2023.

Since 2000, the production of electricity from renewable energies has increased by 222 TWh (Fig. 1), which partially offset the fall in production from nuclear power (−161 TWh) and from coal and lignite (brown coal) (−173 TWh). In quantitative terms, we can see that the challenge of substituting renewable energies for nuclear and coal has been partially met. The policy of the *Energiewende*, formulated in the aftermath of the Fukushima disaster and aiming to fully phase out nuclear power in 2023 while accelerating the expansion of renewables, seems to be materializing. This is what encouraged the German government in 2019 to also consider phasing out coal by 2038,[1] a target brought forward to 2030 by the coalition that assumed power in September 2021. However, this hides the fact that despite the huge investments in new wind (72 GW in 2024) and solar power capacity (89 GW in 2024),[2] these power sources must be permanently supported by "controllable" power stations due to their intermittency.[3]

---

[1] Decision announced following the report of the *Kohlekommission* responsible for establishing recommendations for the exit from coal (BMWi 2019).

[2] To put these numbers in perspective, it can be noted that the effect of a state-of-the-art nuclear reactor is 1.6 GW.

[3] See also the analysis in Fahlén et al. (2026).

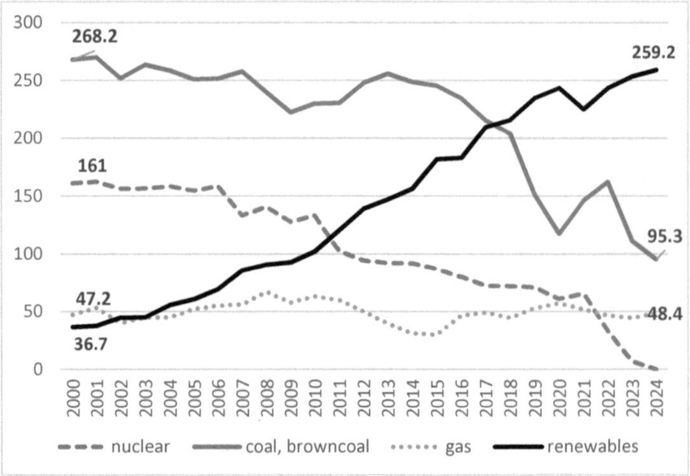

Fig. 1 Evolution of electricity production by source, Germany (TWh) 2000–2024. *Source* Energy Charts: Die Seite für interaktive Grafiken zu Stromproduktion und Börsenstrompreisen, https://www.energy-charts.info/index.html

Limits and Problems Resulting from the Intermittency of New Renewable Capacities

While wind power can provide up to 80% of the country's electricity consumption for a few hours, most of the time, especially during periods of cold winter weather or hot summer weather, lignite, coal or gas-fired thermal power stations provide the bulk of production. This was starkly illustrated in January 2025. During the first two weeks of January, when the weather was relatively mild and windy, wind turbines contributed 47% of the country's electricity production and for several days its share exceeded 65%, while lignite, coal, and gas power plants produced only 35%.

On the other hand, from January 13 to 19, a cold spell along with a drop in the wind reduced wind power production to one-third of its average level, suddenly contributing a mere 16% of electricity production. This made it necessary to run the thermal power stations at maximum capacity to supply 53% of electricity demand and to cover the remaining 10% through imports. Every winter there are several periods of cold and windless weather that can last two weeks or more. Hence, it is impossible to do without a fleet of reserve power plants to compensate for such periods of greatly reduced renewable electricity production. This also explains why, despite the growing share of renewable energies, the production capacity of controllable power plants has been maintained at almost the same level as in the early 2000s. An illustration of this necessity is the current situation of Germany's electricity supply. Since April 2023 and the shutdown of the last nuclear reactors, Germany has become a massive importer of electricity (around 10% of its consumption), in order to limit utilization of the coal and lignite power plants. Their production has also fallen substantially.

In the current state of technology, it is therefore not possible to completely replace fossil fuels with renewable weather-dependent energy sources. The considerable fluctuations in production over the course of the day and the year, especially from wind turbines, are almost never the same as the fluctuations in consumption. This is why, without sufficiently large energy storage systems (Sinn 2017), grid operators must constantly adjust the production of thermal power plants to variations in demand and production from intermittent renewable energies.

However, the growth of the installed capacity of these energy sources inevitably amplifies the already apparent problems. It happens more and more often that the wind and solar farms produce electricity in excess of domestic demand (Deshaies 2014; Sinn 2017). Due to the extent of this production and the geographical location of the country, this development has repercussions on the electricity systems of neighboring countries, with exchanges of increasing volumes of electricity causing a collapse in electricity prices and jeopardizing the profitability of thermal power stations, which are crucial for the ability to cope with peak consumption. Until now, moreover, the German *Energiewende*, which involves these immense intermittent production capacities, has only been possible because neighboring countries have abstained from radically expanding their wind and solar power capacity (Maisonneuve 2014).

Until 2020, problems were mainly caused by peaks in wind power production, thus requiring thermal power plants to reduce output or export electricity to neighboring countries during unusually windy periods. But over the past five years, the strong growth in solar capacity, which rose from 45 GW in 2019 to 95 GW in 2025, has caused a sharp increase in production peaks. While they were less than 30 GW in 2019, they have permanently exceeded 40 GW since 2024, reaching a record of 52.8 GW in June 2025 (Fig. 2). Solar power production during sunny days from April to September is now so high that it can provide 100% of domestic consumption.

This requires not only shutting down almost all thermal capacity, but also drastically reducing wind power production and even exporting large quantities of electricity to neighboring countries. However, since most European countries have also greatly increased their solar power capacity, significant peaks in solar production are becoming increasingly difficult to absorb. The blackout that occurred in Spain and Portugal on April 28, 2025, at 12:36 p.m. could well be an expression of these problems in managing solar power production, since it occurred precisely at the time when this reached its 2025 peak. It should be noted that the incident resulted from Spain's inability to export sufficiently to France. Indeed, at the time the incident occurred, France itself was forced to import large quantities of electricity from Germany, where photovoltaic production was also at its peak. Hence, it was the combined influx of excess solar production from both Spain and Germany, which France was unable to absorb, that ultimately caused the blackout.

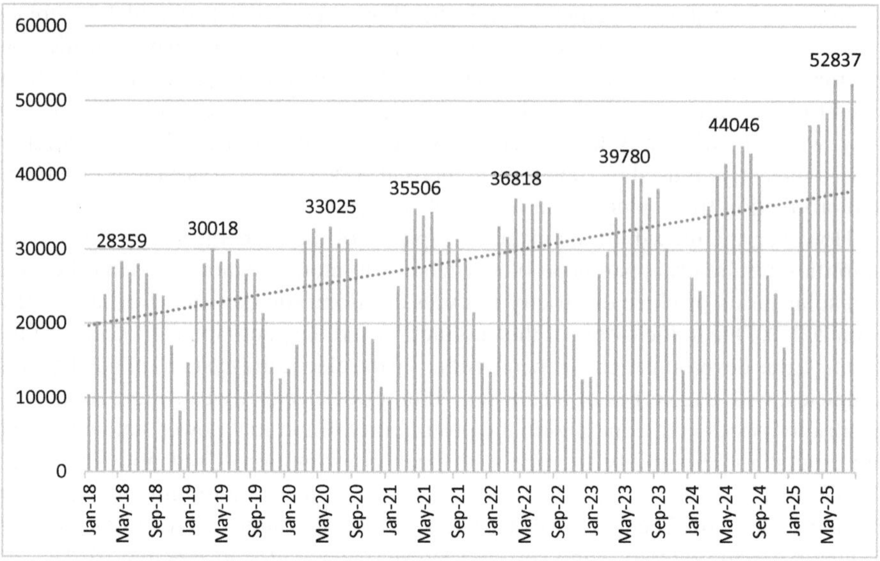

Fig. 2 Evolution of monthly maxima of photovoltaic electricity production in Germany from 2018 to June 2025. *Source* Energy Charts: Die Seite für interaktive Grafiken zu Stromproduktion und Börsenstrompreisen, https://www.energy-charts.info/index.html

A Heavier Energy Bill for Consumers

Neighboring countries have refrained from building comparable renewable capacities, in part because the cost of developing such infrastructure has driven electricity prices sharply upward for German households. Between 2001 and 2013, household electricity prices doubled, largely due to rising taxes imposed to finance renewable energy investments. Under the Renewable Energies Act, payments from consumers to renewable producers soared from EUR 5 billion in 2009 to more than EUR 25 billion in 2013 (BDEW 2014).

Because large industrial firms were exempt from these surcharges, the burden fell disproportionately on households. Critics have therefore described the system as a form of regressive redistribution: wealth flowed upward from ordinary consumers to renewable energy investors, who often belonged to the most privileged social classes (Smil 2017).

In response to this criticism concerning the increase in the price of electricity, reforms attempted to reduce the disadvantages resulting from the accelerated expansion of renewable energy sources, namely the uncontrolled growth of new installed capacities and the sharp increase in payments to producers of renewable electricity. However, despite these efforts to try to control the development of renewable energies, the price paid by the consumer has continued to increase, although more slowly. It nevertheless rose from EUR 0.2914 in 2014 to EUR 0.3216 in 2021, before the big increase following the war in Ukraine. The cost of electricity paid by German households was the highest in Europe ahead of Denmark in 2020, with an average price 50% higher than the European Union average (EUR 0.20/kWh) and higher still compared to France (EUR 0.19/kWh). Electricity prices paid by households soared to EUR 0.4575/kWh in 2023 (Strom-Report 2025). Even if the average price of electricity fell in 2024 (to EUR 0.409/kWh), it remains the highest in Europe (EU average = EUR 0.289/kWh). Needless to say, these high electricity and gas prices constitute a considerable competitive disadvantage for German firms.

The *Energiewende* and Energy Supplies from Russia

Germany Remains Highly Dependent on Hydrocarbons

The central limitation of Germany's *Energiewende* lies in its narrow focus on electricity production—already burdened by the technical shortcomings noted above. Yet electricity accounts for only about 20% of final energy consumption, which continues to be dominated by fuels, raw materials, and heat for households, industry, and services. Although renewables have made some progress in these sectors, their contribution remains modest: just 16.5% of heat generation for homes and industry and only 6.8% of fuels in 2021. Hydrocarbons still supply the overwhelming share of energy needs.

Over the past three decades, hydrocarbon consumption has barely declined: in 2021 it stood at 176 million tonnes, compared with 187 million tonnes in 1990. The most notable change has been a reduction in oil consumption—from 132 to 99 million tonnes—offset by a sharp rise in natural gas use, from 55 to 77 million tonnes. This shift occurred despite structural changes in the economy toward services, as overall final energy consumption has declined only marginally and has remained essentially stable since the early 2000s. Industry, which alone accounts for about 40% of energy demand, has been a major factor in this stability.

Thus, despite the dramatic expansion of renewable electricity generation, Germany's reliance on hydrocarbon imports remains almost unchanged from the period immediately following reunification.

The Loss of Energy Supplies from Russia Places the Country in a Delicate Situation

In 2021, Germany imported 34% of its oil, 55% of its gas, and 57% of its coal consumption from Russia. Therefore, the sanctions imposed on Russia by the EU, in particular the embargo on energy exports to Europe, have placed Germany in a particularly delicate situation. Moreover, replacing the gas imported from Russia was all the more difficult because it was delivered through pipelines. At the start of the war in Ukraine, Germany had no methane terminal allowing the import of LNG.[4] In 2022, oil imports from Russia only dropped by 15%, and despite the September 2022 sabotage of gas pipelines, 48% of the gas was still Russian in 2022. Since exports from Norway and LNG imported via the ports in the Netherlands and Belgium increased sharply, German gas requirements could be satisfied, and the storage tanks were also filled to get through the winter of 2022/2023 and 2023/2024. Another reason ensuring sufficient energy supply was a decline in gas consumption by 20% in 2023 and 2024 compared to 2021. This sharp decline resulted from a reduced consumption both by industry and households, reflecting an impoverishment of part of the population and the industrial sector.

Very Ambitious Energy Scenarios

Over the longer term, the German government is banking on a rapid acceleration in renewable energy expansion. This is deemed essential to lock in the nuclear phase-out and to complete the coal exit by 2030, as announced in autumn 2021.

Yet the decision to pursue such a swift withdrawal from coal directly conflicts with the equally urgent need to reduce dependence on natural gas for power generation—a challenge made all the more acute by the cessation of Russian imports. Projections by the World Energy Council (2022) suggest that if coal is phased out by 2030, oil would still provide about 25% of primary energy consumption, while the share of gas would climb to 35% (up from 25% in 2019). Even under the optimistic assumption that total energy demand falls by 10% by 2030, Germany would still need 110 billion cubic meters of gas—compared with 90 billion in 2019.

In an alternative scenario, if Germany were to delay the coal phase-out until 2038—as initially planned under Chancellor Merkel—gas would provide only about 10% of primary energy consumption. This, however, would necessitate maintaining coal and lignite at 25% in 2030, leading to far higher greenhouse gas emissions than those envisaged under the Green Deal.

Both scenarios, it must be stressed, rest on the bold—and likely unrealistic—assumption that renewable energy's share will soar from 15.7% in 2019 to 40% by 2030.

[4] A temporary solution in the form of a floating terminal was implemented in a hurry in the port of Wilhelmshaven. It should be noted, however, that its maximum capacity is 7.5 billion m^3, which is quite insufficient in relation to the country's needs. This is why four other terminals of this type are under construction in 2023 (Euractive 2022a, b).

Unreasonable Objectives for the Development of Renewable Energies

Develop Renewable Energies at a Forced March

As soon as it ascended to power in 2021, the new government coalition made up of the Social Democrats, the Greens, and the Free Democratic Party planned to considerably expand the development of renewable energies, increasing their share in electricity production from 45% in 2021 to 80% in 2030. According to the Federal Ministry for Economic Affairs and Climate Action (*Bundesministerium für Wirtschaft und Klimaschutz*, BMWK), it would therefore be necessary to increase the production of renewables from 240 to 600 TWh (Nunez & Quitzow 2024). An increase of this magnitude corresponds almost to the sum of current total electricity production from all energy sources.

To achieve this goal, the plan was to accelerate the deployment of huge new onshore and offshore wind and solar power plants. In eight years, the government wanted to double the onshore wind turbine fleet (from 56 to 115 GW), increase offshore wind power capacity from 8 to 30 GW and photovoltaic solar power capacity from 59 to 215 GW. There were also plans to step up the effort after 2030 to reach a capacity of 157 GW of onshore wind power in 2035. A revision of the Renewable Energies Act in 2023 aimed to lift as many aeronautical and environmental restrictions as possible to allow the installation of wind turbines. Thanks to this regulatory "relaxation" and by reducing vetoed spaces to a minimum, the government wanted to extend the areas that can accommodate wind farms by up to 2% of the territory and above all oblige all Bundesländer to apply this measure.

To achieve the announced objectives, an unprecedented annual development rate would be needed. For photovoltaics, 17 GW would have to be added each year, equaling all capacity added from 2016 to 2021. With regard to wind power, it would be necessary to build 6.5 GW of new capacity every year, which implies an expansion rate that is more than 60% higher than during the so far most expansive period from 2012 to 2017.

This is why, in a report published on March 7, 2024, the Federal Court of Auditors leveled an implacable indictment against the government's *Energiewende* policy. The critique is structured around three points: the lack of realism of the development objectives of new renewable energy capacities and reserve power plants by 2030; the cost of the necessary infrastructure and its effect on the electricity price; and the environmental consequences of development of renewable energies. The Court notes that the pace of development of wind and solar power is well below government forecasts and therefore it will be impossible to meet the announced objectives of 215 GW of solar and 115 GW of wind power in 2030 (Bundesrechnungshof 2024).

Germany now appears to have reached a stage of spatial saturation in wind power development, largely due to stark regional disparities. The bulk of capacity is concentrated in the northern and eastern *Länder*: two-thirds of all installed wind power is located in just five *Länder*—Lower Saxony, Brandenburg, Schleswig-Holstein,

North Rhine-Westphalia, and Saxony-Anhalt (see Table 1). By contrast, Baden-Württemberg and Bavaria, which together account for 30% of Germany's land area, host less than 8% of installed capacity.

These imbalances are explained not only by differences in wind potential, but even more by landscape concerns and the way such issues are perceived in the southern *Länder*. At the same time, suitable sites for further turbine installation in the north are becoming increasingly scarce.

This evolution reminds us that one of the main limits to the development of renewable energies is their low power density (Dp). According to Smil (2015, 2017), a major restriction is the amount of energy that can be produced per unit of area by an energy source. This is calculated by taking the ratio of the quantity of energy (E) produced by an energy converter (thermal power plant, hydroelectric, wind turbine, solar panel, etc.) and the surface (S) necessary for the operation of the energy system:

$$Dp\ (Wh/m^2) = E\ (Wh)/S\ (m^2).$$

For solar energy, consideration must be given to the land occupied by photovoltaic fields or semi-parabolic mirrors. In the case of wind energy, the calculation involves the total area covered by turbines, which must be spaced at minimum intervals from

Table 1 Installed capacity and wind power density by Land in MW (2024)

Länder	Capacity (MW)	Area (km^2)	Windpower density (MW/100 km^2)
Lower Saxony	12,950	47,709.8	27.1
Brandenburg	8997	29,654	30.3
Schleswig-Holstein	8973	15,801	56.8
North Rhineland-Westphalia	7778	34,112	22.8
Saxony-Anhalt	5503	20,456	26.9
Rhineland-Palatinate	4151	19,858	20.9
Mecklenburg-Western Pomerania	3797	23,295	16.3
Bavaria	2675	70,541	3.8
Hesse	2639	21,116	12.5
Baden-Württemberg	1889	35,748	5.3
Thuringia	1739	16,202	10.7
Saxony	1361	18,450	7.4
Saarland	553	2571	21.5
Bremen	203	419	48.4
Hamburg	125	755	16.6
Windpower onshore Germany	**63,333**	**357,581**	**17.7**

Source Bundesverband WindEnergie (2025)

Table 2 Power densities of renewable energies

Type of energy and installation	Plant power (MW)	Power densities (W/m^2)
Photovoltaic park	5 to 800	2–10
Concentrated solar park	10 to 400	5–10
Wind farm	10 to 500	2–5
Hydroelectricity	100 to 18,000	1–3
Biogas plant	2 to 150	0.1–0.2
Biofuels	–	0.1–0.4

Source Based on data from Smil (2015)

one another. Technical constraints require that turbines be placed at distances of five to ten times the diameter of the area swept by their blades (Hau 2005). The resulting power densities of the various renewable energy sources are presented in Table 2.

Among renewable energy sources, wind power is the least land-intensive in terms of direct infrastructure, since it primarily requires the installation of towers and access roads, while the surrounding areas can often continue to be used for agriculture or forestry. Yet deploying substantial wind capacity still demands vast tracts of land. Several constraints limit potential sites: minimum required distances from inhabited areas, as well as restrictions related to forests, wetlands, or ecological corridors used by migrating birds and bats. These factors cause the effective power density of wind farms to vary according to geographic conditions.

Studies by Denholm et al. (2009) and Smil (2015) indicate that the characteristic power density of wind farms in the United States and Europe lies between 0.5 and 1 W/m^2, reflecting a relatively low load factor of around 20%. This translates into an average land requirement of 100–200 hectares per installed megawatt (Smil 2015; Deshaies 2022). Consequently, generating large volumes of renewable energy necessitates land areas several orders of magnitude greater than those required for fossil-fuel production.

The Rising Opposition to Wind Power

The vast land requirements of wind energy help explain the mounting opposition to new projects, particularly in southern regions where far fewer turbines have been installed. This fierce resistance makes it unlikely that the pace of wind power expansion will return to the levels seen in the years immediately following the Fukushima disaster.

Opposition has multiplied through local associations, many of which are now united under the *Vernunftkraft* network.[5] On its website, the network advances not only technical and economic critiques of wind power but also socio-environmental

[5] https://www.vernunftkraft.de/

arguments, emphasizing the ecological damage and aesthetic disruption caused by large-scale turbine installations.

With wind turbines now reaching over 200—and in some cases more than 300—meters in height, forests are increasingly being targeted as potential sites for wind power installations. Forests cover roughly one-third of Germany's territory, often situated on elevated, windy terrain and at some distance from residential areas, making them highly attractive to developers. Several regional Red–Green coalition governments, including those in Hesse and Rhineland-Palatinate, view forest siting as an effective way to achieve ambitious renewable energy targets. In Hesse, the most forested *Land* (42% of its surface area), as much as 80% of the forest has been classified as suitable for wind projects, with only one-third designated as protected from exploitation.

Opponents, however, highlight the contradiction between advancing climate goals through renewable development and the destruction of natural habitats that shelter protected wildlife. Another key objection concerns the landscape: since these forests are located on elevated ground, the towering turbines are visible from surrounding populated areas, dramatically altering and, in the eyes of many, disfiguring the scenery.

Hydrogen, a Miracle Solution for the Energiewende?

What is most striking about the German government's renewable energy plans is their disregard for the very technical and spatial limits described above. The construction of vast intermittent generation capacity does not eliminate the continued need for fossil-fuel backup plants, given the absence of large-scale storage systems with sufficient capacity. Despite profound uncertainties over Germany's future energy supply, the principle of replacing nuclear and coal-fired plants with new reserve gas-fired stations has been maintained. Between 2022 and 2025, 11 GW of coal and lignite capacity were still scheduled to close, while 3 GW of new gas-fired plants were to be commissioned. Looking ahead to 2030, and the planned closure of the last coal plants, the Bundesnetzagentur (2025) anticipates the need for 17 to 21 GW of new gas-fired capacity.

To reconcile this apparent contradiction—especially in light of the interruption of Russian gas supplies—these new plants are presented as "hydrogen-ready." Hydrogen has been promoted as a future "miracle" energy carrier, central to the ambition of full decarbonization. The hydrogen strategy unveiled in 2020, later adopted by the European Union within the framework of the Green Deal, envisions producing large quantities of "green" hydrogen by electrolyzing water with surplus electricity from wind power (BMWi 2020). This hydrogen would serve as a form of energy storage, supplying fuel cell vehicles with heat or being converted back into electricity during periods of low wind and solar output. Advocates also highlight its potential use in the chemical and steel industries—sectors that remain particularly difficult to decarbonize.

As a result, the German government, which has estimated hydrogen needs to reach between 90 and 110 TWh in 2030, plans to invest around EUR 9 billion in 5 GW of electrolytic production capacity supplied by wind turbines, to which an additional 5 GW should be added by 2035. Several projects have been launched by the federal government to test the possibilities for producing and using hydrogen. These projects include AquaVentus, led by a consortium of roughly one hundred companies.[6] Based on the island of Heligoland in the North Sea, this project aims to develop 10 GW of hydrogen production capacity from offshore wind farms by 2035 (Tagesspiegel Background 2023). The one million tonnes of green hydrogen thus produced annually would be transported to the continent by a hydrogen pipeline capable of supplying the industrial areas of Hamburg and other North Sea ports.

However, this hydrogen strategy encounters two major obstacles. The first one is of an economic nature; the second one, and probably the most formidable, is geographic and relates to the space needed to produce the quantities of hydrogen that this strategy would require (Deshaies 2021). Indeed, today almost all of the hydrogen in the world is made through steam methane reforming ("blue hydrogen"), because it is by far the least expensive process (Maggio et al. 2019; Damette et al. 2020). The advantage of this process is that it requires approximately 85% less energy compared to electrolysis to produce a given amount of hydrogen (Furfari 2020). In the EU, hydrogen is produced in this way at a cost of around EUR 1.5/kg. If we include the capture and storage of carbon dioxide, this rises to EUR 2/kg. As for "renewable" hydrogen by electrolysis, the cost estimated by the IEA (2019) varies between EUR 3.2 and 7.7/kg, and even EUR 3.5 to 6 (van Renssen 2020).

It is reasonable to question whether offshore wind power can ever provide the vast quantities of hydrogen required to decarbonize Germany's economy. In 2020, offshore capacity stood at 7.7 GW, with targets of 20 GW by 2030 and 40 GW by 2040. These installations produced 30 TWh of electricity in 2020; at the same pace, output could reach 80 TWh in 2030 and 160 TWh in 2040. Yet only a fraction of this electricity could realistically be devoted to hydrogen production, since offshore wind must first replace coal-fired power plants. Under these constraints, no more than a quarter of offshore production—around 40 TWh by 2040—might be available for hydrogen, equivalent to roughly one million tonnes.

This shortfall explains why Germany has already turned to foreign partners to secure hydrogen supplies. Countries such as Morocco, Australia, Namibia, and India are being courted to produce large volumes of hydrogen from solar energy, generated in vast desert-based solar farms (RWE 2020). In theory, such imports could offset Europe's lack of available production space.

Initially, hydrogen for thermal power plants is to be produced from natural gas ("blue hydrogen"), before eventually shifting to "green hydrogen" generated through electrolysis powered by renewable electricity, including offshore wind. One striking proposal, advanced by Belgian investors (Tree Energy Solution), envisions producing hydrogen from vast solar farms in the Arabian Peninsula, converting it into "green"

[6] https://aquaventus.org/en/

methane, liquefying it, and transporting it to a terminal in Wilhelmshaven.[7] There, the methane would be reconverted into hydrogen for local industries, while the resulting carbon dioxide would be shipped back to the Gulf to synthesize more methane.

The promotional video for this project depicts two spheres: one, a desert blanketed with solar panels; the other, a lush, densely populated region—both linked across the sea. The imagery encapsulates a vision of energy neocolonialism: just as in the oil age, Europe would rely on massive inflows of energy from the Persian Gulf, only now in the guise of "green" power.

That such colossal intercontinental energy chains are seriously contemplated speaks volumes about the loss of realism prevailing in Europe's ruling circles. In their pursuit of decarbonization, fundamental constraints of nature and economic scarcity are too often ignored.

Conclusion

Since the beginning of the twenty-first century, Germany has committed itself to phasing out nuclear power while rapidly expanding renewable energy. Yet these choices have left the country in a precarious position. The inherent limitations of renewables, coupled with the need for a reliable, always-available energy supply, have compelled Germany to maintain a substantial fleet of coal and lignite plants while at the same time deepening its dependence on natural gas imports.

Mounting protests against the environmental and climate impacts of lignite mining and coal use more broadly led to the adoption of a coal phase-out target for 2030. Yet this commitment can only be met by ramping up natural gas consumption. The challenge became far greater when Russian deliveries—Germany's principal source of gas and oil—were halted as a direct consequence of the war in Ukraine. Confronted with what increasingly resembled an impasse, the previous left-leaning government embarked on what many viewed as a desperate course of action. First, it sought to accelerate renewable energy investments to unprecedented—and likely unrealistic—levels, despite the country's limited available space. At the same time, it pursued the substitution of coal with gas, with Russian supplies replaced by liquefied natural gas (LNG), primarily imported from the United States. In a later phase, natural gas was to be replaced by hydrogen, produced partly through electrolysis powered by offshore wind farms.

Because Germany lacks the domestic potential to supply the needs of the world's fourth-largest industrial economy, large quantities of hydrogen would inevitably have to be imported from distant regions. Even setting aside doubts about the feasibility of these goals, one consequence is clear: the twin pursuit of decarbonization and independence from Russian energy will drive up costs and create new dependencies—on hydrogen imports as well as on the metals required for wind turbines and solar

[7] https://tes-h2.com/ and https://www.cleanthinking.de/energiepark-wilhelmshaven-erneuerbares-methan/

panels. Energy prices, already soaring for natural gas in 2022 and 2023, are likely to remain high, since producing hydrogen with renewable energy is far more expensive in Germany than in the United States, Russia, or the Middle East. In this light, the *Energiewende* must be regarded as both a technical and economic failure.

Consequently, there is a growing concern that Germany's policy of forced decarbonization—pursued within the framework of the European Green Deal—may accelerate deindustrialization. Energy-intensive industries, such as chemicals and battery manufacturing, are already signaling their intention to shift investments to the United States, where energy costs are substantially lower.

The new government, in office since April 2025, appears increasingly aware of the risks posed by this trend. While not yet questioning the overall objectives of decarbonization, the Minister for Economic Affairs and Energy presented in September 2025 a ten-point energy policy plan aimed at making the transition both more efficient and more cost-effective. She described this moment as a "crossing point" in the energy transition.[8] The plan builds on findings from the government's energy transition monitoring (BMWE 2025), a meta-study summarizing and evaluating existing analyses. Among other measures, it envisages scaling back the pace of renewable expansion and commissioning new gas-fired power plants.

Whether this marks a genuine turning point in the *Energiewende*, capable of halting Germany's deindustrialization, remains uncertain. A wave of deindustrialization, similar to what has unfolded since 2000 in France, the United Kingdom, and Southern Europe, would indeed reduce emissions sharply—potentially enabling the EU to meet or even exceed its Green Deal targets (−55% by 2030 compared to 1990 levels). Yet achieving decarbonization in this way would amount to an economic and social calamity—and an environmental one as well. Much of Europe's industrial production, carried out on a continent where per-capita emissions have already fallen significantly since the early 1990s, would instead be relocated to North America and Asia, regions with far higher carbon footprints.

References

Tagesspiegel Background (2023). Grüner Offshore-Wasserstoff—viel mehr als nur Vision. https://background.tagesspiegel.de/energie-klima/gruener-offshore-wasserstoff-viel-mehr-als-nur-vision

BDEW (2014). Erneuerbare Energien und das EEG: Zahlen, Fakten, Grafiken. https://www.bdew.de/media/documents/20140224_Foliensatz-Energie-Info-Erneuerbare-Energien-und-das-EEG-2014.pdf

BMWE (2025). Energiewende. Effizient. Machen. https://www.bundeswirtschaftsministerium.de/Redaktion/DE/Publikationen/Energie/energiewende-effizient-machen.html

BMWi (2019). Kommission "Wachstum, Strukturwandel und Beschäftigung." https://www.bmwk.de/Redaktion/DE/Downloads/A/abschlussbericht-kommission-wachstum-strukturwandel-und-beschaeftigung.pdf?__blob=publicationFile

[8] https://www.bundeswirtschaftsministerium.de/Navigation/DE/Home/home.html.

BMWi (2020). Die Nationale Wasserstoffstrategie. https://www.bundeswirtschaftsministerium.de/Redaktion/DE/Publikationen/Energie/die-nationale-wasserstoffstrategie.pdf

Bundesnetzagentur (2025). Kraftwerksliste. https://www.bundesnetzagentur.de/DE/Fachthemen/ElektrizitaetundGas/Versorgungssicherheit/Erzeugungskapazitaeten/Kraftwerksliste/start.html

Bundesrechnungshof (2024). Energy transition not on track: Readjustments urgently needed. https://www.bundesrechnungshof.de/SharedDocs/Kurzmeldungen/EN/2024/energiewende-en.html

Damette, O., Cremel, M., Demaie, H., & Lemoine, F. (2020). Les enjeux économiques de la filière hydrogène: Une solution pour la transition énergétique? *Mondes en Développement, 192*(4), 89–101. https://doi.org/10.3917/med.192.0089

Denholm, P., Hand, M., Jackson, M., & Ong, S. (2009). *Land-Use Requirements of Modern Wind Power Plants in the United States.* Golden, CO: National Renewable Energy Laboratory. http://www.nrel.gov/docs/fy09osti/45834.pdf

Deshaies, M. (2014). Ambiguïtés et limites de la transition énergétique en Allemagne. *VertigO—la revue électronique en sciences de l'environnement, 14*(3). https://doi.org/10.4000/vertigo.15515

Deshaies, M. (2021). Pacte vert et enjeux énergétiques dans l'UE: L'étrange ambiguïté de la politique énergétique allemande. *Allemagne d'aujourd'hui, 2*(239), 43–57. https://shs.cairn.info/revue-allemagne-d-aujourd-hui-2021-2-page-43?lang=fr

Deshaies, M. (2022). Problèmes géographiques des transitions énergétiques: Quelles perspectives pour le système énergétique? In H. Gérardin, O. Damette, & J. Brot (Eds.), *Transitions Énergétiques et Développement: Modalités et Études de Cas* (pp. 35–56). Louvain-la-Neuve: Mondes Méditerranéens, EME éditions.

Euractive (2022a). L'Allemagne inaugure son premier terminal méthanier flottant. https://www.euractiv.fr/section/energie/news/lallemagne-inaugure-son-premier-terminal-methanier-flottant/

Euractive (2022b). L'Allemagne acquiert quatre terminaux GNL flottants dans une course effrénée pour remplacer le gaz russe. https://euractiv.fr/news/lallemagne-acquiert-quatre-terminaux-gnl-flottants-dans-une-course-effrenee-pour-remplacer-le-gaz-russe/

Fahlén, P., Henrekson, M., & Nilsson, M. (2026). In pursuit of the green transition—Electricity at any cost? In M. Henrekson, C. Sandström, & M. Stenkula (Eds.), *The Green Entrepreneurial State? Exploring the Pitfalls of Green Deals* (pp. 149–172). Cham: Springer.

Furfari, S. (2020). *The Hydrogen Illusion.* Self-published.

Hau, E. (2005). *Wind Turbines: Fundamentals, Technologies, Applications, Economics.* Heidelberg: Springer-Verlag.

IEA (2019). Global average levelised cost of hydrogen production by energy source and technology, 2019 and 2050. https://www.iea.org/data-and-statistics/charts/global-average-levelised-cost-of-hydrogen-production-by-energy-source-and-technology-2019-and-2050

Maggio, G., Nicita, A., & Squadrito, G. (2019). How the hydrogen production from RES could change energy and fuel markets: A review of recent literature. *International Journal of Hydrogen Energy, 44*(23), 11371–11384. https://doi.org/10.1016/j.ijhydene.2019.03.121

Maisonneuve, C. (2014). L'Europe de l'énergie: Un contrat à refonder d'urgence. *Note de l'Ifri.* https://www.ifri.org/sites/default/files/migrated_files/documents/atoms/files/notecmpolitiqueeuropeenne284revcm.pdf

Nunez, A., & Quitzow, R. (2024). Germany's hydrogen strategy: Securing industrial leadership in a carbon–neutral economy. In R. Quitzow & Y. Zabanova (Eds.), *The Geopolitics of Hydrogen. Studies in Energy, Resource and Environmental Economics* (pp. 49–66). Cham: Springer. doi:https://doi.org/10.1007/978-3-031-59515-8_3

RWE (2020). Deutschland schmiedet weltweite Wasserstoff-Allianzen. https://www.en-former.com/deutschland-schmiedet-weltweite-wasserstoff-allianzen/

Sinn, H.-W. (2017). Buffering volatility: A study on the limits of Germany's energy revolution. *European Economic Review, 99*(October), 130–150. https://doi.org/10.1016/j.euroecorev.2017.05.007

Smil, V. (2015). *Power Density.* Cambridge, MA: MIT Press.

Smil, V. (2017). *Energy Transitions.* 2nd edition. Santa Barbara, CA: Praeger.

Strom-Report (2025). Strompreise Europa: Was Strom in der EU kostet. https://strom-report.com/strompreise-europa/
van Renssen, S. (2020). The hydrogen solution? *Nature Climate Change, 10*, 799–801. https://doi.org/10.1038/s41558-020-0891-0
Bundesverband WindEnergie (2025). Die deutschen Bundesländer im Vergleich. https://www.wind-energie.de/themen/zahlen-und-fakten/bundeslaender
World Energy Council (2022). Energie für Deutschland. https://www.weltenergierat.de/wp-content/uploads/2022/07/EnergiefuerDeutschland2022_final.pdf

Michel Deshaies is a Professor of Geography at the University of Lorraine and member of the research laboratory LOTERR. After studying at the University of Le Mans and obtaining the agrégation in geography in 1989, he worked as a teaching and research assistant at University Nancy-2 between 1991 and 1995. He earned his doctorate in 1994 with a dissertation on incised meanders in the limestone plateaus of eastern France and completed his Habilitation in 2005 with a thesis on mining exploitation and landscapes. Since 2006, he has served as Professor and Director of the CERPA, and in 2012 he became Director of LOTERR. His research focuses on the exploitation of mining and energy resources, their environmental impacts, the energy transition, and the geographic transformations of Germany and Central Europe. He teaches courses on the exploitation of planetary resources, the geography of Europe, Germany, and Central Europe, as well as mountain geography. Deshaies has published extensively on mining landscapes, the transformation of lignite basins such as in Lower Lusatia, and the societal and environmental challenges linked to resource use.

In Pursuit of the Green Transition—Electricity at Any Cost?

Per Fahlén, Magnus Henrekson, and Mats Nilsson

Abstract This study critically examines the European Union's and the United Kingdom's plans for achieving a fossil-free energy system by 2050, centered on massive electrification and large-scale deployment of wind and solar power. Using empirical trends, cost analyses, and system-function assessments, the authors argue that current strategies underestimate real economic, technical, and social challenges. Three scenarios for meeting 2050 electricity demand are compared: full reliance on renewables; a 50/50 split between wind-solar and nuclear; and predominantly nuclear with limited renewables. Evidence from cross-country data shows that higher shares of weather-dependent generation strongly correlate with higher electricity prices, greater volatility, and increased system integration costs. High renewable shares require extensive backup, storage, and grid reinforcement, raising complexity and environmental impacts. The analysis highlights overlooked costs, such as reduced capacity value, transmission expansion, balancing services, and social externalities including property value losses and biodiversity effects. The authors contend that sustainability must encompass environmental, economic, and social dimensions, warning against equating "renewable" with "sustainable." They conclude that a technologically diverse, dispatchable-power-based strategy—especially with expanded

Magnus Henrekson gratefully acknowledges financial support from the Jan Wallander and Tom Hedelius Foundation (P2023-0186) and the Kamprad Family Foundation for Entrepreneurship, Research & Charity (P20220048).

P. Fahlén
Entro Nova, Resele, Sollefteå, Sweden

Chalmers University of Technology, Gothenburg, Sweden

P. Fahlén
e-mail: per.fahlen@telia.com

M. Henrekson (✉)
Research Institute of Industrial Economics (IFN), Stockholm, Sweden
e-mail: magnus.henrekson@ifn.se

M. Nilsson
Södertörn University, Stockholm, Sweden
e-mail: mats.a.nilsson@sh.se

M. Henrekson et al. (eds.), *A Green Entrepreneurial State?*, International Studies in Entrepreneurship 49, https://doi.org/10.1007/978-3-032-15512-2_8

nuclear power—offers a more robust, cost-effective, and socially acceptable pathway to climate neutrality than a predominant reliance on intermittent renewables.

Keywords Climate change · Dispatchable electricity · Green transition · Mission-oriented policy · Renewable electricity · Rent-seeking

JEL Codes L26 · L52 · L70 · O38 · P11 · Q48 · Q58

Introduction

The European Union and several of its key institutions, and by implication its 27 member countries, have explicitly identified wind and solar power as essential for transitioning to a fossil-free economy.

The European Green Deal sets a binding target to reduce net greenhouse gas emissions by at least 55% by 2030. It underscores the need for higher shares of renewable energy and greater energy efficiency, aiming to make Europe the first climate-neutral continent by 2050 (European Commission 2019).

The amended Renewable Energy Directive (RED III) sets binding national and EU targets for the share of renewable energy sources; to meet these targets the share of renewable energy in gross final consumption of energy needs to increase to 40% by 2030 (European Parliament 2023). The energy transition mandate has been accelerated through the REPowerEU Plan (European Commission 2022a) in response to a perceived need to reduce the EU's dependence on Russian fossil fuels following Russia's war on Ukraine.

Achieving net-zero emissions will require a dramatic shift in the electricity generation mix toward fossil-free sources. Renewables, particularly wind and solar,[1] are expected to dominate, with 2020 projections indicating that renewables could provide 75% to 100% of electricity, with at least 60% coming from wind and solar (European Commission 2020).

Until February 2022, nuclear power was not included in the EU Green Taxonomy, and it was thus not expected to be part of the EU's long-term energy mix despite being fossil free. This was changed with the adoption of the Complementary Climate Delegated Act (European Commission 2022b). Hence, the EU no longer considers that nuclear energy causes more harm to human health or the environment than other electricity production technologies already considered sustainable.

The European Union's stance on nuclear power has evolved over the past few years, particularly in the context of its green transition strategy. While nuclear energy has long been a component of the EU's energy mix, its role in achieving climate neutrality has been subject to extensive debate and policy shifts.

[1] Photovoltaic (PV) is the precise technical term for the technology that converts sunlight directly into electricity using semiconductor cells. Since our essay has a clear policy orientation, we have chosen to use the broader and more accessible term solar throughout.

Although no longer a member of the EU, the United Kingdom has adopted similarly stringent goals having committed to fully decarbonizing the electricity system by 2035 (GOV UK 2021a, 2021b) and having a legally binding target to achieve net-zero greenhouse gas emissions by 2050 (GOV UK 2021a, 2021b). The Biden administration in the United States adopted exactly the same goals (White House 2024), goals that were instantly revoked by the Trump administration in early 2025.

The challenge is greatly enhanced by the fact that the generated electricity is not only required to be fossil free; a sharp increase in electricity consumption is key to achieving the transition. Total electricity consumption in the EU is expected to increase from some 2,700 TWh in 2024 to close to 7,000 TWh by 2050 (Dickson 2021).[2] While EU bodies acknowledge that short-term price volatility is a concern, they suggest that, with appropriate measures, the long-term average electricity prices may not necessarily increase (European Commission 2024).

The purpose of this essay is to critically review the current plans by the EU and the UK to achieve a full green energy transition by 2050 where a key component is a huge expansion of the consumption of fossil-free electricity.

Our analysis shows that key system functions are largely ignored, that the cost models underestimate real economic consequences, and conclusions are not supported by empirical evidence or theory.[3]

The essay is organized as follows. In the next section, we present the empirical trends in electricity consumption and production in the EU, the UK and the USA, illustrating the divergence between political ambition and actual development. We then turn to the economic consequences of different technology mixes, focusing first on electricity prices and their correlation with weather-dependent power, and then on neglected but crucial system functions. This is followed by an analysis of system-level costs, demonstrating that levelized cost comparisons conceal major integration and balancing costs. After that, we discuss the economics at the power-plant level, showing that actual costs are higher than often reported and that profitability is undermined by market design and intermittency. In the subsequent sections, we review broader societal consequences, including external costs related to land use, biodiversity, and property values. We also stress that the concept of sustainability should not be narrowly defined but encompass system-level analysis and a broader understanding of sustainability that includes environmental, social, and economic dimensions.[4] The final section contains our main conclusions.

Our objective is *not* to dispute the goal of climate neutrality. Rather, we argue that the transition must be pursued in a manner that is technologically robust, economically viable, and socially acceptable. This requires a sober analysis of how

---

[2] For the UK, an approximate doubling is expected in order to achieve net zero by 2050 (NESO 2025).

[3] Concerning the system function and system-related costs we will to a great extent rely on studies and experiences from our native country, Sweden. Considering that the share of weather-dependent electricity production is significantly greater in large countries such as Germany, the UK, and Spain, Swedish experiences are highly likely to be applicable in most other European countries.

[4] For a more thorough elaboration on this point, the reader is referred to Fahlén (2023a) and Harjanne and Korhonen (2019).

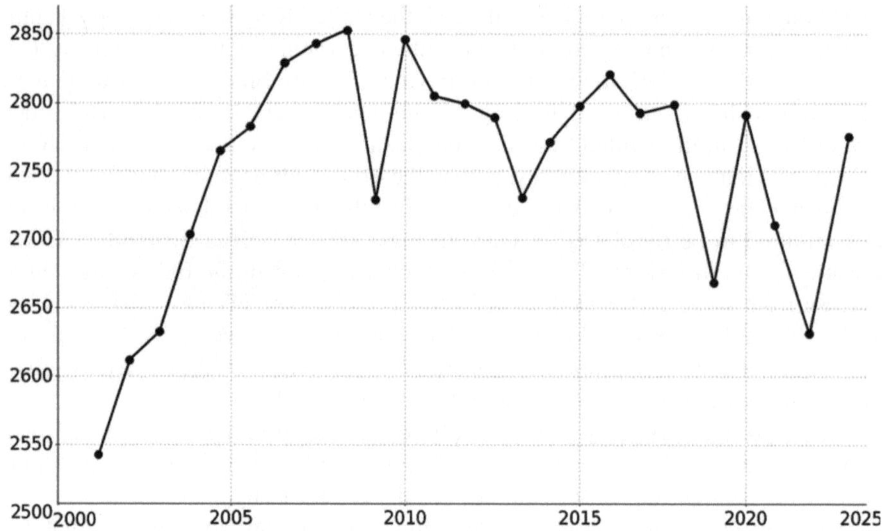

Fig. 1 Net electricity production in the EU, 2001–2024 (TWh). *Source* Eurostat

different electricity generation technologies contribute—or fail to contribute—to the functionality, resilience, and cost-effectiveness of the power system as a whole.

The Empirical Picture

In its "Fit-for-55" package the European Commission envisages that Europe's electricity will be almost completely zero carbon-based by 2050. They project that electricity will be 57% of the EU's energy mix and that a further 18% will be electrified indirectly via renewable hydrogen and its derivatives (Dickson 2021).

At the time of writing, four years have elapsed since these plans were launched but as shown in Fig. 1, net electricity production has fallen in the EU since the 2008 peak. In 2024 it was 5% lower than in 2008 and in 2023 consumption was the lowest in two decades. Despite an increase in 2024, total EU power demand remained almost 5% below the level just before the onset of the pandemic. The development in Germany is particularly noteworthy: From the peak in 2008 to 2023 German electricity consumption fell by 17% from 618 to 514 TWh.[5]

Although the EU's net electricity generation has remained relatively stable, fluctuating between 2,700 and 2,800 TWh, Table 1 shows that there has been a significant change in the composition of production. In EU-27, the shares of coal, natural gas, oil, and nuclear power have fallen substantially, while the share of wind, solar, and

[5] The development is even more dramatic in the UK: From the peak in 2007 to 2023, UK electricity consumption fell by 23% from 373 to 283 TWh.

biomass have increased sharply to almost 32% in 2023. The change in the UK is even more dramatic, where coal has been almost totally phased out and replaced by wind power; wind, solar, and biomass were close to 40% in 2023. The fossil-fuel share has fallen by 44 percentage points in the UK since 2008 compared to 34 percentage points in EU-27. The fossil-fuel share has fallen far less in the United States since coal has been largely replaced by natural gas.

If we take the EU projection of a need for 7,000 TWh in 2050, let us see what that requires in terms of electricity generation from different sources in the case of 100% renewable electricity and in two alternatives where it is sufficient that the electricity is fossil free. This exercise is presented in Table 2 based on the following three scenarios:

2050: I. The entire (except for some increase in hydro and biomass) increase in electricity consists of intermittent renewables, which was EU policy until early 2022. This means that all nuclear energy will be phased out.
2050: II. Wind and solar will make up 50% of the total in 2050 and the remainder (except for some increase in hydro and biomass) will be picked up by nuclear energy.
2050: III. Wind and solar will make up 20% of the total in 2050 and the remainder (except for some increase in hydro and biomass) will be picked up by nuclear energy.

In all scenarios fossil-fuel sources are set to zero and we assume that hydro and biomass can increase by approximately 50% from current levels. The item "Others"

Table 1 The electricity generation mix in EU-27, the UK, and the US, 2008 and 2023. (%)

	EU-27		**United Kingdom**		**United States**	
Source	**2008**	**2023**	**2008**	**2023**	**2008**	**2023**
Coal	29.0	11.7	31.0	1.0	48.0	16.2
Natural Gas	20.0	17.0	45.0	31.2	21.0	43.1
Nuclear	28.0	22.8	13.0	14.8	19.0	18.6
Wind	1.3	18.5	1.5	28.8	1.3	10.2
Solar	0.1	9.1	0.0	4.6	0.1	3.9
Biomass	2.0	4.1	1.0	4.9	1.0	1.1
Hydro	11.0	13.5	1.0	1.2	6.1	5.7
Geothermal	0.2	0.2	–	–	0.4	0.4
Oil	5.0	1.4	–	–	1.1	
Other	1.7	1.6	7.5	13.4*	2.0	0.8
Fossil share	54.0	30.1	76	32.2	70.1	59.3

* The bulk of this share consists of net imports (12.4%)
Source Eurostat, National Energy System Operator (NESO), and the U.S. Energy Information Administration

Table 2 Rough electricity mix share (%) in EU-27 in 2022 and potential mixes totaling 7,000 TWh in 2050

	2022		2050: I		2050: II		2050: III	
Source	**Share**	**TWh**	**Share**	**TWh**	**Share**	**TWh**	**Share**	**TWh**
Wind	~ 15	~ 420	59.0	4,130	33.3	2,333	13.3	933
Solar	~ 8	~ 210	29.6	2,070	16.7	1,167	6.7	467
Nuclear	~ 22	~ 610	0	0	38.6	2,700	68.6	4,800
Natural gas	~ 19	~ 540	0	0	0	0	0	0
Coal	~ 17	~ 475	0	0	0	0	0	0
Hydro	~ 11	~ 305	6.4	450	6.4	450	6.4	450
Bioenergy/ Waste	~ 7	~ 185	4.0	280	4.0	280	4.0	280
Others	~ 2	~ 55	1.0	70	1.0	70	1.0	70
Total	100	~ 2,800	100	7,000	100	7,000	100	7,000

Source Eurostat

is set to 1%. We also assume that the share of wind will be double that of solar (which was roughly the case in 2023).

The table clearly shows that the demand for wind and solar is very large in the first two scenarios, requiring expansion of roughly 900 and 450%, respectively. In scenario III, where wind plus solar is restricted to 20% of the total, the required expansion is roughly 120% from the 2022 level. Instead, a huge expansion of nuclear electricity is needed; by roughly 2,100 TWh (+243%) in scenario II and by 4,200 TWh (+586%) in scenario III.

To achieve the projected expansion of electricity production, the required expansion of installed power will differ greatly across scenarios. This will have substantial effects on system costs and stability. Assuming a capacity factor[6] of 0.3 for wind, 0.1 for solar, 0.85 for nuclear, 0.45 for hydro, and 0.7 for bioenergy/waste/others, scenario III, heavy on nuclear power, requires a mere 1.75 times the installed capacity in 2022 to achieve the projected 2.5-fold increase in electricity output. Scenario II, with a greater reliance on renewables, requires 2.8 times the 2022 capacity, and scenario I, where renewables predominate, requires 4.2 times the 2022 installed capacity (Fahlén et al. 2025, p. 6, Table 3). In addition to the larger capacity, the greater number of generators being spread over a much wider area will require an oversized transmission, stabilizing and balancing system and this simple comparison does not even include the larger required gross supply of energy to cover the given net demand due to the increasing system losses resulting from a greater share of renewable production (Fahlén 2023b). The assumed capacity factors are based on current data. Thus, they do not consider that these factors will decline as the share of renewables goes

[6] The capacity factor is the ratio of the actual electricity generated over a given period to the electricity it could have generated had it operated at its full capacity the entire time.

up. This is especially so for wind and solar generators, as the need for curtailment rises due to the installed overcapacity.

If we translate this into a need for new reactors, let us use the recently built reactor in Olkiluoto in northern Finland, OL3, as a benchmark. The OL3 power plant has an installed capacity of 1.6 GW. Assuming a capacity factor of 0.85 it will produce 11.9 TWh annually. Hence, 176 and 353 additional reactors of that size would be needed in scenarios II and III, respectively. There are many proponents for covering most of the need using small modular reactors (SMRs) instead. SMRs are projected to produce somewhere in the range 0.4 to 2.4 TWh per year. Assuming an average size of half the maximum, we are talking about 1,750 and 3,500 SMRs in scenario II and III, respectively.

The remainder of this essay will be devoted to discussing the consequences of each of the three 2050 scenarios outlined above, focusing on their implications for electricity prices, and system functionality. We begin by examining the current relationship between electricity prices and the share of weather-dependent electricity production, using cross-country data to highlight the economic consequences of large-scale wind and solar deployment. We then turn to core system functions—such as capacity adequacy, grid stability, and system inertia—and assess how these are affected by an increasing reliance on intermittent power. Particular attention is given to the growing complexity and cost of securing a stable electricity supply when dispatchable generation is replaced by variable renewables.

A central challenge in scenarios with high shares of wind and solar is the need for vast amounts of storage, such as hydrogen or batteries, to compensate for periods with little or no wind and sun. We show that storage needs, and associated costs, differ dramatically between scenarios: a system dominated by intermittent sources may require orders of magnitude more storage than one based on dispatchable, fossil-free baseload. Finally, we discuss the broader system-level and economic implications of each pathway, arguing that any viable strategy must consider the full set of system requirements, not just nominal production targets or power plant-level cost estimates.

The Price of Electricity

European Union institutions acknowledge that the rapid integration of intermittent renewable energy sources, such as wind and solar, introduces challenges related to electricity price volatility and grid stability. Flexibility solutions are said to be essential to address these challenges (ACER 2023). However, they do not assert that this transition will necessarily lead to increased average electricity prices over the long term. Instead, they emphasize the need for strategic investments and market reforms to mitigate potential cost impacts.

The European Union Agency for the Cooperation of Energy Regulators (ACER) has highlighted that the expansion of renewable energy sources contributes to increased price volatility in electricity markets. One suggestion is to use enhanced forecasting methods to support the EU's energy policies by stabilizing electricity markets and reducing financial risks associated with price fluctuations (Cerasa and Zani 2025).

However, while short-term price volatility is a concern, EU bodies suggest that, with appropriate measures, the long-term average electricity prices may not necessarily increase. Although most of the challenges are caused by the rapidly growing share of weather-dependent electricity sources, it is striking that the European Parliament and the Commission continue to focus primarily on reducing the influence of fossil fuels on electricity prices and on promoting investments in renewable energy projects (European Commission 2025). These changes are intended to enhance the EU's energy security and stabilize prices in the long term.

Is there any evidence that this will work? Since there are large cross-country variations in the share of electricity from weather-dependent sources, an indication can be obtained by studying the correlation between the share of wind + solar electricity and the average electricity price paid by households. This relationship is shown in Fig. 2 for EU countries plus the UK and the United States. A correlation coefficient of $r = 0.60$ shows a strong positive relationship, i.e., countries with higher shares of wind and solar tend to have higher electricity prices. The inserted trend line has a slope of 0.0050, indicating that each percentage point increase in wind + solar share is associated with an estimated increase of EUR 0.005/kWh in household electricity prices. A recent German study supports the view that the cost of electricity increases sharply as the share of renewables goes up (Begemann et al. 2025).

If Denmark is excluded from the dataset, the correlation coefficient increases to 0.71, indicating an even stronger positive relationship between wind + solar share and electricity price. The slope also increases to 0.0083. Denmark's extreme share of wind + solar of almost 70% would not have been possible without access to baseload power from Sweden and Germany.

Admittedly, Fig. 2 is based on a small number of countries due to data availability, and it can sometimes be difficult to compare prices between countries as prices vary due to different forms of support.[7] Despite these differences, the positive correlation remains robust. Hannesson (2025) finds a nearly identical relationship using averaged data from 2019–2021 for OECD countries. She reports a correlation similar to what we observe when Denmark is excluded from our dataset, with a slope coefficient of 0.65. This means that each percentage point increase in the share of wind and solar is associated with an estimated increase of USD 0.0065/kWh in household electricity prices.

The empirical evidence presented above shows a clear correlation between the share of intermittent renewables and higher average electricity prices. It is therefore relevant to revisit the three 2050 scenarios introduced above in order to assess their respective exposure to long-term price pressures.

Scenario I assumes that the entire increase in electricity demand is met with renewable sources, mainly wind and solar. This is the scenario with the highest share of intermittency; the resulting share exceeds 88%, which is far higher than any other

[7] Germany is an obvious case in point where the average electricity price for households was roughly EUR 0.40 per kWh in 2024 despite extensive direct subsidies to producers (Karlsson 2025a).

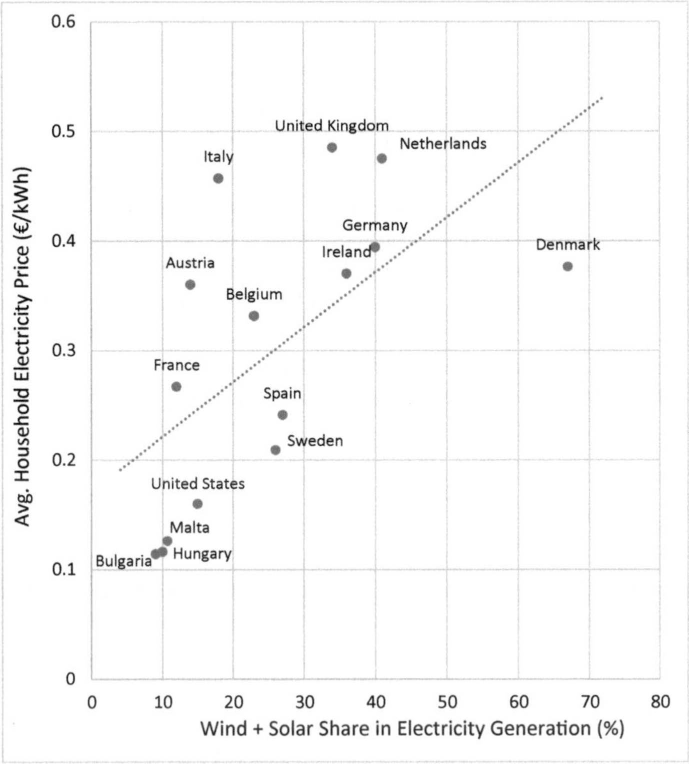

Fig. 2 The share of wind + solar electricity and household electricity price (EUR/kWh) in 2023. *Source* Eurostat and https://ember-energy.org/data/electricity-data-explorer/

country today. The strong positive correlation and steep slope documented in Fig. 2 strongly suggest that such a high share of intermittency would result in average prices far above levels experienced by the UK and Germany today. This observation is consistent with the documented correlation between the share of wind and solar power and household electricity prices. Scenario I is therefore likely to involve high costs for balancing, storage, and system stabilization, which in turn would lead to higher electricity prices.

Scenario II reduces the share of wind and solar and replaces it with nuclear power, which is dispatchable and thus not weather-dependent. Although this configuration lowers the volatility and the need for balancing services compared to Scenario I, it still includes a substantial amount of intermittent generation. In fact, countries that already have similar shares of weather-dependent electricity, such as Denmark and Germany, tend to experience elevated average electricity prices and frequent price spikes. Thus, the associated integration costs are likely to be substantial also in Scenario II.

Scenario III reduces the share of wind + solar to 20% and relies primarily on nuclear power to meet the projected demand increase. This significantly lowers the need for large-scale storage and short-term balancing measures. The dependence on external stabilization mechanisms is also much smaller. If implemented, this scenario would resemble systems that rely on stable baseload production and therefore tend to show lower and more predictable electricity prices.

In conclusion, current empirical data suggest that scenarios with large shares of weather-dependent electricity, such as Scenario I, are more likely to result in high electricity prices unless large-scale and costly countermeasures are introduced. A system based on fossil-free but dispatchable baseload, such as Scenario III, offers a more robust foundation for price stability and long-term cost control. Scenario studies by Fahlén (2023b) and Begemann et al. (2025) support these findings.

In sum, there is little evidence to date that the EU will be able to find efficient measures that hinder a rise in long-term average electricity prices if the share of electricity from intermittent sources continues to increase.

System Functions

Ensuring proper system functionality is fundamental to a reliable electricity supply. A well-functioning electricity system requires four things: delivery of sufficient energy, sufficient instantaneous power, high power quality, and robust security of supply. These requirements must be met in real time and in concert.

Sweden provides a striking example. In 2023, the Swedish National Audit Office (2023) delivered scathing criticism of the Swedish energy policy's lack of impact assessment for these basic needs. Svenska kraftnät, the national grid operator responsible for the secure operation, development, and maintenance of Sweden's high-voltage electricity transmission system, has for many years warned of the rapidly increasing problems with the expansion of wind power. In its 2025 report, the operator estimated that in the winter of 2025/26, there may be a lack of planned capacity equivalent to seven nuclear power plants (Svenska kraftnät 2025). However, increasing the share of wind power will not address the capacity adequacy issue. On the contrary, due to its weather dependency and limited dispatchability, it may exacerbate the challenge of ensuring firm capacity during peak demand periods.

Increasing the amount of wind power also means more transmission infrastructure. But the larger the transmission network and the more distributed the electricity generation, the more difficult it will be to maintain the stability of the system. This is clearly demonstrated by the Spanish blackout in April 2025. The more uneven production spread over larger areas requires transmission networks that are not only longer but also of higher capacity. This creates a high additional cost and is negative for the environment. To a large extent, these transmission costs are avoided with nuclear power. The operator's evaluation of the Spanish blackout (Red Eléctrica 2025, p. 8) presents a number of important lessons:

> [i]t is important to highlight the rate at which generation output can change within the system. New technologies based on power electronic inverters are capable of adjusting their output within a matter of seconds. While this capability is highly beneficial for the economic

optimisation of individual generating plants, it is not necessarily ideal from a power system stability perspective in general.

A clear example of this is the rapid schedule changes in photovoltaic generation driven by price fluctuations in electricity markets. From an electrical standpoint, such abrupt changes in inverter-based generation introduce significant imbalances into the system, because regulation mechanisms haven't operated yet. These imbalances must be compensated mainly through interconnections, particularly the one with France.

Severe imbalances lead to drastic shifts in power flows across the network, which in turn alter the capacitive and inductive behavior of the grid. Consequently, system voltages can vary rapidly. This effect is further exacerbated when such generation operates under power factor control and does not provide dynamic voltage control, as it limits the dynamic reactive power support that could otherwise help stabilize voltage.

Fuel-based power, such as nuclear power, can act as baseload, balancing, and regulating power and the fuel itself functions as storage. It can also be located close to high-consumption areas, whereas wind power is generally built far from users and requires additional external systems in the form of balancing power/storage, transmission networks, and grid stabilization systems. Synchronous generators in hydro and nuclear power plants, due to their large rotating mass, are proactive, i.e., prevent disturbances from occurring. In contrast, "synthetic" inertia, which is often promoted as a solution for wind power, is reactive and must constantly correct disturbances that have already occurred. This adds both complexity and cost to the system. To assist wind power, large rotary converters are also installed to stabilize the grid and manage reactive power.[8] They basically act as synchronous generators but without producing any electricity; instead, they consume electricity and incur an additional cost.

A reliable electricity system must be able to deliver sufficient energy and power at the right time and place, maintain frequency and voltage within narrow margins, and uphold a high level of security of supply. These requirements must be met continuously and simultaneously. The three 2050 scenarios differ markedly in how well they support these fundamental system functions.

Scenario I, which relies almost entirely (88.6%) on wind and solar power, presents the greatest challenges. Weather-dependent production cannot be dispatched on demand and often requires extensive backup in the form of balancing power, synthetic inertia, frequency control systems, and large transmission networks. The expansion of transmission infrastructure becomes necessary because wind and solar installations are typically located far from consumption centers. These additions increase both cost and vulnerability, while also having environmental consequences. In this scenario, large investments would be needed in grid stabilization and reserve capacity to ensure system reliability, especially during periods of low wind and solar output.

[8] Reactive power is the difference between active power—i.e., the useful power—and the total power consumed. In electric power systems with a high share of weather-dependent solar and wind generation, there are few synchronous generators, which traditionally provide intrinsic control of reactive power. As a result, active power is controlled but reactive power probably not. This may lead to severe problems in voltage control, which was the case in the Spanish blackout (Red Eléctrica 2025). Additional, often costly, equipment may be required to manage reactive power. Excessive reactive power reduces system efficiency, limits transmission capacity, and increases losses.

Scenario II reduces the share of weather-dependent power and introduces a significant amount of nuclear energy. While still dependent on wind and solar for a substantial portion (50%) of production, this configuration allows for a greater degree of dispatchability and reduces the strain on ancillary systems. Nuclear power can provide both baseload and balancing services, and its contribution to system inertia improves frequency stability. However, the share of wind + solar in Scenario II is almost double the 2023 share in EU-27 (Table 1). Thus, the system will still require substantial investments in backup capacity and advanced control technologies to manage fluctuations in renewable output.

Scenario III, with its emphasis on nuclear power and a limited share of wind + solar (20%), offers the most favorable conditions for robust system operation. Dispatchable power is available in large quantities, and system inertia is inherently provided by synchronous generators. The need for additional stabilization mechanisms, fast-reacting reserves, and external balancing resources is much lower. This reduces both the technical complexity and the operating cost of the system, while also enhancing resilience during periods of stress.

In summary, from a system functionality perspective, Scenario III is clearly the most robust. Scenario II represents an improvement over full reliance on renewables but still entails significant integration demands. Scenario I appears to be the most fragile, requiring comprehensive and expensive support systems to ensure reliable operation.

As the European Union accelerates its transition toward weather-dependent electricity generation, the structural demands placed on the electricity system grow accordingly. The increasing reliance on weather-dependent sources such as wind and solar introduces variability that must be managed in real time. This puts pressure on the system to provide sufficient flexibility—both in terms of supply and demand—to uphold operational reliability. But this flexibility comes at a high cost and results in a less efficient society with loss of production and services.

According to the European Commission's Joint Research Centre (JRC), the need for system flexibility will more than double by 2030 and increase sevenfold by 2050, compared to 2021 levels. This steep rise is directly linked to the variable nature of renewable power and the current shortage of large-scale, cost-effective storage solutions (Joint Research Centre 2023). Without adequate flexibility, the power system becomes more vulnerable to imbalances, frequency deviations and price spikes, particularly during periods of low wind and solar output (cf. the Spanish blackout).

The EU Agency for the Cooperation of Energy Regulators (ACER) emphasizes that the rapid phase-out of conventional thermal generation, combined with the growth of intermittent renewables, intensifies the challenge of ensuring security of supply. Maintaining a stable system under these conditions requires both technical and market-based mechanisms that can deliver rapid balancing services (ACER 2023).

In parallel, there are growing concerns regarding the physical infrastructure required to support this transformation. The European Parliamentary Research Service (EPRS) notes that much of the existing electricity grid in Europe is outdated and poorly adapted to the decentralized production patterns introduced by wind and solar power. Significant investment is needed to modernize transmission and distribution systems, integrate digital control technologies, and increase the grid's ability to handle bidirectional and fluctuating flows of electricity (EPRS 2023). Without these upgrades, congestion costs and curtailment rates are likely to rise, eroding both efficiency and public acceptance of the transition.

Together, these developments point to a fundamental system challenge: the move toward high shares of variable renewables demands not only new generation capacity, but a deep transformation of how the electricity system operates and is governed. Flexibility, redundancy, and infrastructure resilience must become central design criteria, not afterthoughts.

To manage the intermittency of wind and solar power, there must be other power sources, currently fossil-based power, that can be switched on and off whenever needed to balance supply and demand. The more wind and solar power in the system, the more capacity must be available in balancing power plants to replace solar and wind power when the sun is not shining and/or when there is insufficient or no wind. The capacity utilization of these balancing power plants will be lower the more wind and solar power is installed, which means that their revenue will be lower. To compensate for this fact, either balancing power prices have to be higher, or the owners of the balancing power plants have to be paid for availability and not only for electricity produced. Therefore, even if intermittent power were cheaper than traditional baseload power, it will not only lead to more volatile prices but also to higher electricity prices overall. Average household electricity prices have therefore increased in countries with high shares of wind and solar power.

The System-Level Economy

It is reasonable to require that system-level externalities be internalized, ideally down to the power plant level. However, such internalization must be based on accurate and comprehensive cost assessments. Cost estimates that omit key system services—such as frequency control, reactive power, inertia, and regulating capacity—fail to capture the true economic and operational impact of electricity production.

The LCOE is defined as the average cost required to build and operate a power plant over its expected lifetime, expressed per unit of electricity produced. While useful under conditions of stable demand and dispatchable generation, the LCOE fails to account for a number of key factors. These include financing conditions, real operational lifetimes, availability, and maintenance costs. Importantly, it does not include any allowance for system-level impacts such as grid integration costs, profile effects, or balancing requirements. The International Energy Agency (IEA) has noted that this metric is particularly misleading in systems with a high share of intermittent generation, where system interaction effects are substantial.

The Levelized Cost of Electricity (LCOE), commonly used to compare base-load generation technologies, does not include these system-level costs. It only reflects the average cost of building and operating a plant over its lifetime. This metric ignores integration costs, which become significant when a high share of electricity comes from intermittent sources. These costs include profile costs (which capture the mismatch between supply and demand over time), balancing costs, and grid infrastructure costs.[9] To address these omissions, alternative indicators such as system LCOE, Actual Cost of Electricity (ACOE), and Levelized Full System Costs of Electricity (LFSCOE) have been developed.

Ueckerdt et al. (2013) show that when wind power reaches around 20% of the electricity market, the costs of integrating it into the system become significant. The main reason is that production does not always coincide with demand. Often a great deal of electricity is generated at the same time, which pushes down prices and reduces the value of the electricity. At a 40% market share, these costs are roughly twice as high. The OECD-NEA (2012) reaches similar conclusions and emphasizes that integration costs rise rapidly as the share of weather-dependent electricity increases. The ACOE framework expands on the traditional LCOE by factoring in the reduced market value of intermittent generation and the lower capacity utilization that occurs as overcapacity increases. Based on real data from 2022, Manzolini et al. (2024) report that as wind power's market share rises from 0 to 50%, the cost per kWh increases from EUR 0.09 to 0.12 in Denmark, from EUR 0.09 to 0.15 in Germany, and from EUR 0.12 to 0.15 in the Netherlands. At a 50% share, curtailment is as large as 20–40% due to the high overcapacity. The study also shows that irrespective of market share, the use of battery storage for the excess capacity will always make wind power more expensive.

A more radical approach is the LFSCOE, which estimates the full cost of a system in which electricity is produced entirely by one type of technology. Idel (2022) calculates that for Germany, the LFSCOE is USD 0.106 per kWh for nuclear, USD 0.504 for wind, and USD 1.55 for solar power. These figures illustrate the sharp cost escalation associated with high shares of weather-dependent electricity sources.

In some countries, hydropower has historically played a key role as balancing power. However, its flexibility is now fully utilized in many systems. In Sweden, for example, balancing costs increased by more than SEK 5 billion (almost EUR 0.5 billion) from 2021 to 2023, during which time wind power production rose by roughly 7 TWh. While not all the cost increase can be directly attributed to wind, it remains the principal factor. The marginal balancing cost in this case exceeded the assumed LCOE of wind power by a wide margin, pointing to a systematic underestimation of its full cost.

A growing challenge arises from the increasing use of fixed-price Power Purchase Agreements (PPAs) in the wind sector. These contracts provide producers with a guaranteed price per kWh, regardless of market conditions. As long as the negative market price is not in absolute terms greater than the guaranteed price set by the PPA,

[9] The term "profile effects" refers to the fact that wind and solar power produce electricity according to weather conditions rather than consumption needs. When production is high, prices fall, and when production is low, other capacity must cover the gap. In the academic literature this is also called "profile costs" (Hirth 2013).

it is rational for producers to continue generating power even when the electricity is not needed. Such electricity is typically excluded from exchange trading and is often exported, thereby bypassing domestic consumers. In Sweden, this dynamic has coincided with a long-term decline in domestic electricity consumption—not due to reduced demand, but as a result of higher costs and limited ability to connect new users, largely caused by insufficient dispatchable capacity following nuclear phase-outs (Sandström 2025).

High shares of wind power give rise to periods with insufficient electricity generation. A commonly proposed solution is battery storage. To illustrate the scale of this challenge, consider a scenario in Sweden with one week of low wind in winter leading to a shortfall of 2 TWh. If half the shortfall must be compensated through storage and weekly electricity demand in mid-winter is roughly 4 TWh, then 1 TWh of battery capacity would be needed. This corresponds to roughly one-third of the storage capacity of all batteries produced in the world in 2024.

At world market prices, this would require an investment of approximately SEK 3.7 trillion (59% of Sweden's GDP in 2024).[10] With a battery lifespan of ten years, this entails annual depreciation of SEK 370 billion, plus financing costs of about SEK 74 billion per year at an interest rate of 4%. Combined, this represents more than 7% of Sweden's GDP. The climate impact is also significant: manufacturing this storage would emit around 150 million tonnes of carbon dioxide. Over ten years, this equates to 15 million tonnes annually, which is roughly one-third of Sweden's current total emissions. These estimates strongly suggest that large-scale battery storage is not a viable solution for managing week-long periods of insufficient wind with current technology.[11]

Finally, the economic viability of other generation types is also undermined in systems with high shares of intermittent power. According to the OECD-NEA (Keppler et al. 2018), nuclear power revenues fall by 24% when wind power reaches 10% of the market and by 55% at a 30% share. For open-cycle gas turbines, which are important for balancing, the losses are even greater—54 and 87%, respectively (Keppler et al. 2018), and these losses require compensation. These findings underscore the high and often overlooked system costs associated with maintaining stable and reliable electricity supply in systems dominated by variable renewables.

The Power-Plant-Level Economy for Wind Power

A widely accepted principle in electricity market design is that costs and benefits should, to the greatest extent possible, be attributed to the level where decisions are made, typically the power plant. This principle is consistent with European guidelines for grid connection and market participation. However, in systems with a high share of

[10] The EUR/SEK exchange rate was approximately 11.20 in August 2025.

[11] Calculations are based on data from Ask (2025).

variable renewables such as wind and solar, the most used cost metric, the Levelized Cost of Electricity (LCOE), becomes increasingly inadequate.

Reported production costs for onshore wind power in Northern Europe typically range from EUR 0.03 to 0.04 per kWh and the presumption is that the cost will continue to decline. However, market data and project tenders suggest considerably higher figures. For example, the guaranteed strike price requested by developers in recent UK auctions for onshore wind was around GBP 0.071 ($\approx$ EUR 0.082) per kWh in 2024, a figure similar to reported contract levels in Germany. This is more than double the typical assertions regarding the plant-level production cost.

Financial performance data from Sweden further illustrates the challenge. Wind power companies in the country lost an average of 0.35 cents for every euro of electricity sold between 2017 and 2023 (Sandström and Steinbeck 2025). Thus, just to break even, these firms would have needed average selling prices that were 35% higher. These losses suggest that the actual levelized production costs are closer to SEK 0.70 or more per kWh, roughly double the typically cited figure (Energiforsk 2021). The economics of wind power has also deteriorated due to technical trends. Newer turbine generations, while larger and more powerful, have proven more expensive to operate and maintain. Hughes (2021) documents that wear and tear substantially reduce the capacity factor and that the actual economic life spans are closer to 15 years for onshore and just 12 years for offshore wind, in contrast to the 25 to 30 years typically used in investment models. This is confirmed by significant losses among major wind turbine manufacturers and growing warranty obligations due to performance issues (Matthis 2023) and it will also increase the LCA (life cycle analysis) environmental impact.

These technical and financial constraints are further compounded by the declining market value of wind power as its share increases. This profile cost, caused by production clustering during high-wind periods when prices are low, weakens the economic return on new investments. Sandström and Steinbeck (2025) show that this effect has already contributed to protracted losses in the Swedish wind power sector. The market in northern Sweden has all but collapsed; installations that were valued at EUR 1.5 million per MW a couple of years ago may be for sale at less than EUR 10 per MW (Berg 2025).

International comparisons reinforce these findings. A detailed review by Hughes (2020) reported average production costs in the UK of GBP 0.091 per kWh for onshore wind and GBP 0.152 for offshore wind, while the average market value was only GBP 0.0013 per kWh. These figures are consistent with guaranteed prices in Germany and recent long-term contracts across Europe.

Ownership and market structure also play an important role. In Sweden, many wind power assets are owned by foreign entities and financed through publicly guaranteed loans, either at the national or EU level. As already mentioned, electricity is often sold through fixed-price power purchase agreements (PPAs) directly to foreign buyers, bypassing the domestic electricity market. As a result, this electricity does not affect local prices and is not available to Swedish consumers, who instead face higher prices and reduced supply flexibility (Fahlén 2023a; Sandström and Steinbeck 2024).

Examples from across Europe reveal recurring challenges in systems with high shares of wind and solar. In Germany, installed capacity of variable renewables already exceeds twice the maximum hourly demand, yet over half of electricity production still comes from dispatchable fuel-based sources (Karlsson 2025a). Finland, which has expanded wind capacity rapidly, is together with Spain the European country with the highest share of hours with negative electricity prices (Karlsson 2025b).

Such systems tend to require substantial overcapacity. In some cases, total installed capacity exceeds 300% of peak demand.[12] As a consequence, operators are frequently compensated to curtail production during periods of excess supply. In Sweden, hydropower producers are paid to spill water, and wind operators are paid not to produce. At the same time, fossil-based balancing plants are compensated for remaining idle when wind production is high. This constellation of support mechanisms lowers utilization rates, raises system costs, and increases the environmental footprint of the power system.

Social Benefits and Costs of Externalities

While wind power is often framed as a clean and socially acceptable form of energy, its negative effects tend to receive less attention. These include local disturbances, environmental degradation, and increasing demands on system stability. Although each European country faces unique circumstances, this section focuses on the Swedish case, where the interplay between wind power expansion and local impacts is particularly well documented.

In southern Sweden, there are estimates suggesting that the combined cost of compensating local residents for disturbances and of incentivizing municipalities to approve wind power projects amounts to approximately SEK 0.02 (i.e., less than 0.2 cents) per kWh of electricity produced (Tangerås et al. 2025, p. 142; leaning on Lundin 2024). However, this figure does not include any fall in property values, reduced agricultural productivity, or broader land-use conflicts. Importantly, the structure of these compensation schemes matters. Compensation provided directly to affected households is more transparent and legitimate than indirect transfers to local governments.

The reduction in property values linked to proximity to wind turbines has been quantified in several studies. Estimations based on Westlund and Wilhelmsson (2021) estimate that the total loss in property values due to wind power development in

[12] By the end of 2024, Germany's installed capacity of wind and solar power was 72 (of which 9 offshore) and 99 GW, respectively. To this should be added the installed capacity of non-renewable power of 92 GW. Peak demand during the busiest winter hour in 2023 was 73 GW. Hence, installed capacity of solar + wind was 234% of peak demand, while total installed capacity was 360% of peak demand (Bundesnetzagentur 2025).

Sweden exceeds SEK 100 billion (≈ USD 10 billion).[13] This sum is roughly equivalent to the total wind power investment in Sweden between 2017 and 2024, and around ten times the annual market value of the electricity generated by these installations. If distributed over the total electricity production from wind during the last decade (about 230 TWh), this implies a hidden cost of approximately SEK 0.43 per kWh—well above commonly cited production costs (LCOE).

Additional effects on rural sectors, such as agriculture, forestry, and fishing, have not been systematically quantified but are often reported to be substantial by local stakeholders. These impacts may include habitat disruption, loss of visual landscape value, and operational restrictions due to turbine placement.

Another key externality is the increased need for balancing power as the share of intermittent electricity grows. Holmberg (2024) estimates that if wind and solar power together expand to 240 TWh annually, the producers should pay a surcharge of about SEK 0.01 (≈ 0.1 cent) per kWh to compensate for the added stress on system balance. However, this estimate significantly underestimates the full economic burden, and it is unclear how it was derived.[14] System support costs for balancing power are already today in the same range as the production cost of wind power and continue to grow disproportionately as variability increases.

In addition to balancing costs, increasing shares of weather-dependent electricity also entail higher profile and transmission costs. These include the cost of overcapacity during periods of strong winds, reduced market value of generation, and the need to reinforce transmission infrastructure to accommodate geographically dispersed production.

Taken together, both the compensation levels for local impacts and the assumed balancing cost estimates by Holmberg (2024) fall short of empirical realities. More comprehensive and location-specific assessments are required to ensure that wind power expansion aligns with broader objectives of economic efficiency, social acceptance, and environmental integrity.

Environmental and System Impacts of Wind Power

Large-scale wind power differs from dispatchable sources such as nuclear and hydro power in that it does not contribute to critical system services like inertia and frequency control. This reduces overall grid stability. Life-cycle analyses also suggest that wind and solar energy have higher carbon emissions per unit of electricity than nuclear power (Vattenfall 2018; Ask 2025).

[13] In a follow-up study, Westlund and Wilhelmsson (2025) analyze over 600,000 real estate transactions from 2005 to 2018. Their main finding is that property values within 2 km of wind turbines decrease by 10 to 15%. It should be noted that this study concerns transactions that took place when total wind power production was less than half of the current level.

[14] This estimate is some two orders of magnitude less than the estimates we cited above.

In terms of energy return on investment (EROI), wind power performs significantly worse once the need for storage and backup is considered (Weissbach et al. 2013). Wind turbines require extensive amounts of non-renewable materials, including rare earth elements (Department of Energy 2015). The environmental footprint includes large land requirements, noise, and biodiversity impacts, as well as challenges related to decommissioning and waste management. Recent studies have pointed to problems such as noise emissions (Garcia Forlim et al. 2024; Mattsson et al. 2026), microplastics, and toxic chemicals near wind farms (Karlsson 2024).

Taken together, these factors underline that environmental and system costs increase sharply with large-scale deployment of wind power, and that these costs must be assessed alongside potential climate benefits.[15]

Conclusions

Official scenarios for a fossil-free "green" transition in Europe assume a huge increase in electricity consumption, driven by the electrification of transport, industry, heating, and other activities relying on fossil fuels. However, since policymakers began to talk about a massive increase in electricity consumption as key to a green transition, electricity consumption has decreased in the European Union and even more so in the UK. This is not due to reduced economic activity, but rather a consequence of supply-side constraints, market uncertainty, and high average and volatile prices.

The rapid expansion of wind and solar power in Europe as a key driver of the green transition lacks proper consideration of its cumulative effects on system functionality, economic viability and environmental sustainability. With wind and solar power approaching 30% of electricity production in the European Union and 35% in the UK, the system is already experiencing growing challenges related to balancing, infrastructure needs and capacity value.

Our analysis shows that the long-term socio-economic value of weather-dependent electric power has been overstated in assessments guiding long-term strategic policy decisions. These assessments rely on narrow production cost metrics that do not sufficiently account for real-world wind power cost, system integration costs, environmental externalities or lifecycle material demands. These include increased use of non-renewable resources, land use conflicts, and waste management concerns, as well as diminished reliability in systems with a high share of weather-dependent electricity.

A more diversified approach relying on known technologies would have been prudent. A viable alternative would have been investment in nuclear power; a technology first used in submarines in the mid-1950s. This would have provided dispatchable, fossil-free baseload electricity with much lower integration costs. In the short

[15] Such a holistic approach is consistent with the Brundtland Commission's definition of sustainable development, which emphasizes the need to balance environmental, economic and social objectives in all planning decisions (United Nations 1987).

term, gas-fired generation could have served as a transitional balancing resource until additional nuclear capacity became available. This would have maintained system stability, reduced emissions from coal and oil, and improved the ability to meet new demand in the medium term. Despite being fossil-free and widely used, it was not until 2022 that the European Union repealed its policy of phasing out all nuclear power from its energy system.

What we have described here is a clear-cut example of a mission-oriented policy containing both an unequivocal goal to be attained at a pre-specified point in time and how it should be achieved: (i) A goal of zero CO_2 emissions to be attained by 2050; (ii) identification of the key means to achieve this goal: massive electrification of virtually all activities currently relying on fossil fuels; and (iii) pinpointing by which technologies the required electricity should be produced.

This strategy was laid down in the European Union and its member countries as well as the UK at odds with existing evidence and practical experience. In an area pinpointed as key to the green transition, decisive policy decisions were not based on relevant empirical experience, comprehensive system-level analysis and a broad understanding of sustainability that includes environmental, social, and economic dimensions.

References

ACER (2023). *Market Monitoring Report 2023: European Wholesale Electricity Market Integration*. European Union Agency for the Cooperation of Energy Regulators. https://www.acer.europa.eu/progress-eu-electricity-wholesale-market-integration-2023-market-monitoring-report

Ask, P. (2025). Solkraftens skuggsida [The dark side of solar power]. *Kvartal*, March 25. https://kvartal.se/artiklar/solkraftens-skuggsida/

Begemann, U., von Branconi, C., & Frewer, T. (2025). Simulationsgestützte Analyse von Einflussfaktoren auf die Stromkosten für unterschiedliche Szenarien der Energiewende [Simulation-supported analysis of influence factors on the cost of electricity for alternative scenarios of the *Energiewende*]. https://www.ihk.de/nordwestfalen/energie-und-umwelt/energie/ihk-energiewendebarometer-4980902

Berg, M. (2025). Avgrundsdjup kris för vindkraften i norr: "Ingen tjänar pengar". [Abyssmal crisis for windpower in the north: "Nobody makes money"]. *Affärsvärlden*, July 28. https://www.affarsvarlden.se/artikel/avgrundsdjup-kris-for-vindkraften-i-norr-ingen-tjanar-pengar

Bundesnetzagentur (2025). KEY FINDINGS: Developments in the electricity and gas markets. Bonn: Bundesnetzagentur für Elektrizität, Gas, Bundeskartellamt Telekommunikation, Post und Eisenbahnen and Bundeskartellamt. https://www.bundesnetzagentur.de/SharedDocs/Downloads/EN/Areas/ElectricityGas/Monitoring/key_monitoringreport2024.pdf?__blob=publicationFile&v=3&utm_source=chatgpt.com

Cerasa, A., & Zani, A. (2025). Enhancing electricity price forecasting accuracy: A novel filtering strategy for improved out-of-sample prediction. *Applied Energy*, *383*, Article 125357. https://doi.org/10.1016/j.apenergy.2025.12535

Department of Energy (2015). An Assessment of Energy Technologies and Research Opportunities, Chapter 10: Concepts in Integrated Analysis. *Quadrennial Technology Review*, September. Washington, DC: US Department of Energy.

Dickson, G. (2021). Electrifying Europe with wind energy—towards net-zero by 2050. *The European Files,* October 21. https://www.europeanfiles.eu/environment/electrifying-europe-with-wind-energy-towards-net-zero-by-2050?utm_source=chatgpt.com

Energiforsk (2021). El från nya anläggningar [Electricity from new plants]. Report 2021:714. Stockholm: Energiforsk.

EPRS (2023). *Decarbonisation of the EU Energy System: Infrastructure and Investment Needs.* European Parliamentary Research Service. https://www.europarl.europa.eu/thinktank/en/document/EPRS_BRI(2023)739388

European Commission (2019). Delivering the European Green Deal: On the path to a climate-neutral Europe by 2050. https://commission.europa.eu/strategy-and-policy/priorities-2019-2024/european-green-deal/delivering-european-green-deal_en?utm_source=chatgpt.com

European Commission (2020). Towards net-zero emissions in the EU energy system by 2050: Insights from scenarios in line with the 2030 and 2050 ambitions of the European Green Deal. https://publications.jrc.ec.europa.eu/repository/bitstream/JRC118592/towards_net-zero_emissions_in_the_eu_energy_system_-_insights_from_scenarios_in_line_with_2030_and_2050_ambitions_of_the_european_green_deal_on.pdf?utm_source=chatgpt.com

European Commission (2022a). REPowerEU: Affordable, secure and sustainable energy for Europe. https://commission.europa.eu/topics/energy/repowereu_en

European Commission (2022b). EU taxonomy: Complementary Climate Delegated Act to accelerate decarbonization. https://finance.ec.europa.eu/publications/eu-taxonomy-complementary-climate-delegated-act-accelerate-decarbonisation_en

European Commission (2024). Questions and Answers on the revised electricity market design. https://ec.europa.eu/commission/presscorner/api/files/document/print/en/qanda_24_2260/QANDA_24_2260_EN.pdf?utm_source=chatgpt.com

European Commission (2025). Action Plan for Affordable Energy: Unlocking the true value of our Energy Union to secure affordable, efficient and clean energy for all Europeans. https://energy.ec.europa.eu/publications/action-plan-affordable-energy-unlocking-true-value-our-energy-union-secure-affordable-efficient-and_en

European Parliament (2023). The Renewable Energy Directive 2023/2413. https://eur-lex.europa.eu/eli/dir/2023/2413/oj

Fahlén, P. (2023a). *Omställningen av Sveriges elsystem—Konsekvenser för funktion, ekonomi, miljö och samhälle* [*Transformation of the Swedish electricity system—Consequences for Function, Economy, Environment, and Society*] EN-R2023:01. Resele: Entro Nova.

Fahlén, P. (2023b). *Sveriges eltillförsel 2050: 100 % eller 0 % "förnybart"? En jämförelse mellan fyra scenarier avseende funktion, kostnad och miljöpåverkan [Sweden's Electricity Supply in 2050: 100% or 0% "Renewable"? A Comparison of Four Scenarios Regarding Function, Cost and Environmental Impact].* EN-R2023:02. Resele: Entro Nova.

Fahlén, P., Henrekson, M., & Nilsson, M. (2025). *In pursuit of the green transition—Electricity at any cost?* IFN Working Paper No. 1542. Research Institute of Industrial Economics (IFN).

Garcia Forlim, C., Ascone, L., Koch, C., & Kühn, S. (2024). Resting state network changes induced by experimental inaudible infrasound exposure and associations with self-reported noise sensitivity and annoyance. *Scientific Reports, 14*(1), Article 24555. https://doi.org/10.1038/s41598-024-76543-2

GOV UK (2021a). Press release: Plans unveiled to decarbonise UK power system by 2035. https://www.gov.uk/government/news/plans-unveiled-to-decarbonise-uk-power-system-by-2035

GOV UK (2021b). UK becomes first major economy to pass net zero emissions law. https://www.gov.uk/government/news/uk-becomes-first-major-economy-to-pass-net-zero-emissions-law

Hannesson, R. (2025). An electricity market model with intermittent power. *Energies, 18*(6), Article 1435. https://doi.org/10.3390/en18061435

Harjanne, A., & Korhonen, J. (2019). Abandoning the concept of renewable energy. *Energy Policy, 127*, 330–340. https://doi.org/10.1016/j.enpol.2018.12.029

Hirth, L. (2013). The market value of variable renewables: The effect of solar wind power variability on their relative price. *Energy Economics*, *38*(July), 218–236. https://doi.org/10.1016/j.eneco.2013.02.004

Holmberg, P. (2024). Den svenska elmarknaden [The Swedish electricity market]. Background report to the memorandum Financing and risk sharing for investments in new nuclear power. Stockholm: Ministry of Finance. https://www.ifn.se/media/wkwj1cdv/2024-holmberg-den-svenska-elmarknaden.pdf

Hughes, G. (2020). Wind power economics: Rhetoric and reality. School of Economics, University of Edinburgh and Renewable Energy Foundation (REF). https://www.ref.org.uk/ref-blog/365-wind-power-economics-rhetoric-and-reality

Hughes, G. (2021). Costs, performance and investment returns for wind power. School of Economics, University of Edinburgh, and Renewable Energy Foundation. https://www.ref.org.uk/attachments/article/369/GH20210621.pdf

Idel, R. (2022). Levelized Full System Costs of Electricity. *Energy*, *259*(November), Article 124905. https://doi.org/10.1016/j.energy.2022.12490

Joint Research Centre (2023). *Flexibility Needs in the Future EU Power System*. Publications Office of the European Union. https://joint-research-centre.ec.europa.eu/publications/flexibility-needs-eu-power-system_en

Karlsson, H. (2024). Vindkraft och hälsoproblem: Forskningsläget gällande effekter på människor och djur av exponering för ljudföroreningar, kemikalier och partiklar från vindkraftverk [Wind power and health problems: The state of research on the effects on humans and animals of exposure to noise pollution, chemicals and particles from wind turbines]. In M. Henrekson (Ed.), *De norrländska stålsatsningarna: Frälsare eller gökunge?* Stockholm: Samhällsförlaget. https://www.samhallsforlaget.se/wp-content/uploads/2024/02/Karlsson-Vindkraft-och-halsoproblem.pdf

Karlsson, S. (2025a). Enorma kostnader för förnybart i Tyskland [Enormous costs for renewables in Germany]. *Second Opinion*, January 2. https://second-opinion.se/enorma-kostnader-for-fornybart-i-tyskland/

Karlsson, S. (2025b). Finska vindkraften på väg att blåsa bort [Finnish wind power about to blow away]. *Second Opinion*, February 17. https://second-opinion.se/finska-vindkraften-pa-vag-att-blasa-bort-sig-sjalv/

Keppler, J. H., et al. (2018). *The Full Costs of Electricity Provision*. NEA No. 7298. Paris: Nuclear Energy Agency, OECD. https://www.oecd-nea.org/upload/docs/application/pdf/2019-12/7298-full-costs-2018.pdf

Lundin, E. (2024). Wind power and the cost of local compensation schemes: A Swedish revenue sharing policy simulation. *Energy Economics*, *135*, Article 107632. https://doi.org/10.1016/j.eneco.2024.107632

Manzolini, G., Binotti, M., Gentile, G., Picotti, G. Pilotti, L., & Cholette, M. E. (2024). Actual cost of electricity: An economic index to overcome levelized cost of electricity limits. *Science*, *27*, Article 109897. https://doi.org/10.1016/j.isci.2024.109897

Matthis, S. (2023). Därför ber vindkraftsindustrin om mer allmosor [Why the wind industry is asking for more handouts]. *Energinyheter.se*, March 15. https://www.energinyheter.se/20230329/28767/darfor-ber-vindkraftsindustrin-om-mer-allmosor

Mattsson, K., Eriksson, G., Persson, L., Chilo, J., & Tatar, K. (2026). Efficient finite difference modeling of infrasound propagation in realistic 3D domains: Validation with wind turbine measurements. *Applied Acoustics*, *243*, Article 111156. https://doi.org/10.1016/j.apacoust.2025.111156

NESO (2025), Future energy scenarios: Pathways to net zero—Executive summary. London: National Energy System Operator. https://www.neso.energy/document/364546/download

OECD-NEA (2012). Nuclear energy and renewables: System effects in low-carbon electricity systems. NEA No. 7056. Paris: Nuclear Energy Agency, OECD. https://www.oecd-nea.org/upload/docs/application/pdf/2019-12/7056-system-effects.pdf

Red Eléctrica (2025). Black out in Spanish peninsular electrical system the 28th of April 2025. Madrid: Red Eléctrica. https://d1n1o4zeyfu21r.cloudfront.net/WEB_Incident_%2028A_SpanishPeninsularElectricalSystem_18june25.pdf

Sandström, C. (2025). Mer vindkraft är rena självmordet—hur tänker Vattenfall? [More wind power is suicide—how does Vattenfall think?]. *Affärsvärlden*, April 27. https://www.affarsvarlden.se/kronika/vilket-land-forlorar-mest-pa-svensk-vindkraft-kina-eller-luxemburg

Sandström, C., & Steinbeck, C. (2024). Vilket land förlorar mest på svensk vindkraft—Kina eller Luxemburg? [Which country loses most from Swedish wind power—China or Luxembourg?]. *Affärsvärlden*, May 20. https://www.affarsvarlden.se/kronika/vilket-land-forlorar-mest-pa-svensk-vindkraft-kina-eller-luxemburg

Sandström, C., & Steinbeck, C. (2025). Grön bubbla inom svensk vindkraft? [The green bubble in Swedish wind power?]. *Ekonomisk Debatt*, *53*(3), 63–68. https://www.nationalekonomi.se/wp-content/uploads/2025/04/53-3-Sandstrom-Steinbeck.pdf

Svenska kraftnät (2025). Kraftbalansen på den svenska elmarknaden, rapport 2025. Dnr 2025/2726. Sundbyberg. Svenska kraftnät. https://www.svk.se/49bb53/siteassets/om-oss/rapporter/2025/kraftbalansen-pa-den-svenska-elmarknaden-rapport-2025.pdf

Tangerås, T., Holmberg, P., & Le Coq, C. (2025). *Investeringar i elproduktion för en hållbar energiomställning [Investments in Electricity Generation for a Sustainable Energy Transition]*. Annual Report of the SNS Economic Council 2025. Stockholm: SNS Förlag. https://snsse.cdn.triggerfish.cloud/uploads/2025/01/konjunkturradets-rapport-2025-investeringar-i-elproduktion-for-en-hallbar-energiomstallning.pdf

Ueckerdt, F., Hirth, L., Luderer, G., & Edenhofer, O. (2013). System LCOE: What are the costs of variable renewables? *Energy*, *63*(December), 61–75. https://doi.org/10.1016/j.energy.2013.10.072

United Nations (1987). *Report of the World Commission on Environment and Development: Our Common Future*. New York, NY: United Nations. https://sustainabledevelopment.un.org/content/documents/5987our-common-future.pdf

Vattenfall (2018). Livscykelanalys—Vattenfalls elproduktion i Norden [Life cycle analysis of Vattenfall's electricity production in the Nordic countries]. Stockholm: Vattenfall.

Weissbach, D., Ruprecht, G., Huke, A., Czerski, K., Gottlieb, S., & Hussein, A. (2013). Energy intensities, EROIs (energy returned on invested), and energy payback times of electricity generating power plants. *Energy*, *52*, 210–221. https://doi.org/10.1016/j.energy.2013.01.029

Westlund, H., & Wilhelmsson, M. (2021). The socio-economic cost of wind turbines: A Swedish case study. *Sustainability*, *13*(12), Article 6892. https://doi.org/10.3390/su13126892

Westlund, H., & Wilhelmsson, M. (2025). Capitalisation of onshore wind turbines on property prices in Sweden: The need to compensate for negative externalities. *Economic Analysis and Policy*, *87*, 1452–1468. https://doi.org/10.1016/j.eap.2025.07.025

White House (2024). President Biden Sets 2035 Climate Target Aimed at Creating Good-Paying Union Jobs, Reducing Costs for All Americans, and Securing U.S. Leadership in the Clean Energy Economy of the Future. https://bidenwhitehouse.archives.gov/briefing-room/statements-releases/2024/12/19/fact-sheet-president-biden-sets-2035-climate-target-aimed-at-creating-good-paying-union-jobs-reducing-costs-for-all-americans-and-securing-u-s-leadership-in-the-clean-energy-economy-of-the-future/

Per Fahlén is Professor Emeritus, Energy and Environment, Chalmers University of Technology, member of the Royal Swedish Academy of Engineering Sciences (IVA), and active in his own consultancy firm ENTRO NOVA. He has an M.Sc. in applied physics and electrical engineering as well as a PhD and a Dr. Sc. in heating, ventilating and air-conditioning engineering and has been the Swedish representative in many national and international organizations and a member of various technical, research and editorial boards. In 2023 he was awarded the von Rittinger medal by the International Energy Agency Heat Pump Centre, which is considered to be the most prestigious distinction in this field of research and development.

Prior to becoming Full Professor and Head of Department at Chalmers University of Technology, Fahlén had a professional background as design and development engineer in the electrical industry as well as Head of Research and Quality at the Department of Energy at the Swedish National Testing and Research Institute.

Fahlén's research covers heating, cooling, refrigeration and ventilation systems, heat recovery, heat exchangers, heat pumps, control systems, electric supply and demand, commissioning, quality assurance, modeling, and simulation. In addition to a large number of national projects, he has participated in several EU and IEA projects and has been co-author of a number of international handbooks.

Magnus Henrekson is a Professor of Economics and Senior Research Fellow of the Research Institute of Industrial Economics (IFN) in Stockholm, Sweden. He resigned as CEO of IFN in 2020 after 15 years of service. Until 2009, he held the Jacob Wallenberg Research Chair in the Department of Economics at the Stockholm School of Economics. He is also a member of the Royal Swedish Academy of Engineering Sciences (IVA).

He received his PhD in 1990 from Gothenburg University with his dissertation *An Economic Analysis of Swedish Government Expenditure.* Throughout the 1990s, he conducted several projects that aimed to explain cross-country growth differences. Since the turn of the new millennium, his primary research focus has been entrepreneurship economics and the institutional determinants of the business climate. In this area, he has published extensively in scientific journals and contributed several research surveys to *Handbooks* in the field of entrepreneurship.

Henrekson also has extensive experience as an advisor, board member, and lecturer in many different contexts, in both the business and public sectors.

Mats Nilsson is Associate Professor of Environmental Economics, Department of Social Sciences, Södertörn University. He received his PhD in 2000 from Luleå University of technology with his dissertation *Five essays on Forest Raw Materials Use in an International Perspective.*

After his dissertation, Mats Nilsson has primarily conducted research on the electricity market and its functioning. In addition to his academic research, he has extensive experience working in both the private sector and government agencies on electricity market issues and electricity market design, including at the Swedish Energy Markets Inspectorate and Vattenfall. He is also an active commentator on matters concerning the development of the Swedish and Nordic electricity markets.

Green Industrial Megaprojects: A Welfare Economics Perspective

Per-Olov Johansson and Bengt Kriström

Abstract The growing popularity of large-scale, state-supported investments, especially those that are connected to the green transition, raises difficult normative and analytical questions. In this essay we address the welfare dimension of these initiatives by revisiting the foundations of cost–benefit analysis (CBA) in public decision-making. We begin by outlining the normative rationale for CBA, including the implications of Hume's Law and the necessity of explicit value judgments. We then turn to the main problems associated with megaprojects, such as optimism bias and a lack of transparent analysis of the pros and cons. As an illustration, we examine the case of a major hydrogen-based steel plant by the Stegra company (formerly H2 Green Steel) in Boden in northern Sweden. We suggest a blueprint to evaluate such investments using contemporary economic theory (general equilibrium CBA). We find that the investment in Boden—a municipality with a total population of 28,000 inhabitants and 17,000 in the urban area—is not likely to be socially beneficial, partly because existing EU policy already internalizes most of the climate impact that largely motivates the subsidies the project has received. The project may be privately profitable, although this requires a very particular set of favorable conditions. It is important to stress that we do not argue against climate action or industrial policy per se. Rather, we call for rigorous evaluation.

Keywords Green transition · Cost–benefit analysis · Megaprojects · Hydrogen steel · General equilibrium · Industrial policy

JEL Codes D61 · Q01 · H43 · Q58

We thank the editors for helpful comments.

P.-O. Johansson (✉)
Department of Economics, Stockholm School of Economics, Stockholm, Sweden
e-mail: per-olov.johansson@hhs.se

B. Kriström
The Swedish University of Agricultural Sciences (SLU), Umeå, Sweden
e-mail: bengt.kristrom@slu.se

Center for Environmental and Resource Economics (CERE), Umeå University, Umeå, Sweden

M. Henrekson et al. (eds.), *A Green Entrepreneurial State?*, International Studies in Entrepreneurship 49, https://doi.org/10.1007/978-3-032-15512-2_9

Introduction

The green transition, as outlined in policy documents such as the European Union's Green Deal (European Commission 2019) and Sweden's national environmental policy (Government Offices of Sweden 2021) involves significant public and private investment. Yet, the projects involved are seldom scrutinized by rigorous cost–benefit analysis (CBA). Historical experience with large-scale industrial projects—what we here refer to as megaprojects—often ends in disappointment. As extensively documented by Flyvbjerg (2009) and further explored in the volume by Henrekson et al. (2024), these projects are frequently plagued by systemic issues beyond simple optimism bias. They are vulnerable to political agendas, rent-seeking, lack of relevant information, and bureaucratic inefficiencies.

This study examines green megaprojects from a welfare economic perspective, using cost–benefit analysis as the guiding framework. While CBA has been subject to criticism—sometimes justifiably—it remains a transparent and systematic tool for assessing whether a project enhances social welfare. When resources are scarce, opportunity costs should not be overlooked, not the least when public funds are involved.

CBA provides a practical way to weigh the pros and cons of (mega-)projects, offering information about how such initiatives may affect the economy and overall welfare. Yet, the outcomes are informative, not prescriptive. This assertion follows inter alia from Hume's law. We begin, therefore, in the next section with a brief discussion of the normative foundations of CBA and the logical impossibility of deriving policy prescriptions from facts alone. We then turn to an overview of why megaprojects often fail, before illustrating these themes with a case study of hydrogen-based steel production in northern Sweden. A final section concludes.

Normative Foundations of Cost–Benefit Analysis

Scottish philosopher David Hume famously observed:

> In every system of morality, which I have hitherto met with, I have always remarked, that the author proceeds for some time in the ordinary way of reasoning... when of a sudden I am surprised to find, that instead of the usual copulations of propositions, is, and is not, I meet with no proposition that is not connected with an ought, or an ought not. (Hume 1739, 2000], Book III, Part I, Section I)

The passage highlights that one cannot derive an "ought" from an "is" without invoking value judgments. This has direct implications for policy evaluation: any recommendation about what should be done rests on ethical assumptions. CBA is no exception. It takes individual preferences as inputs and uses them to estimate changes in well-being. Since most public projects involve both winners and losers—that is, some individuals gain while others incur losses—any overall assessment requires aggregation.

A commonly used aggregation rule is the Kaldor–Hicks (KH) compensation test, which loosely states that a project is socially desirable if the winners can compensate the losers. If compensation was made—so that no one is worse off and at least one person is better off—the project would satisfy the stricter Pareto criterion. The KH test requires less information and is more flexible in practice, which makes it useful in applied work. However, it clearly rests on assumptions that involve value judgments.

The KH criterion is sometimes defended using trickle-down arguments: if all projects that pass the test are implemented, total resources will grow, and over time everyone will benefit (see, e.g., Dasgupta and Pearce 1972, p. 92, as quoted in Cornwall 1984, p. 613). Cornwall hints at the difficulties involved in establishing such a proposition. We refrain from a detailed discussion of this rather technical issue. For an introduction to welfare criteria, see Chapters 2 and 3 in Johansson (1991); for a more advanced treatment, see Johansson and Kriström (2016).

We use the KH criterion in the section where Stegra is evaluated. If a project passes a cost–benefit test under this criterion, the result provides potentially useful information. One way to justify KH is to assume that the existing distribution of welfare is optimal in a well-defined sense. But even under this strong assumption, the so-called Boadway paradox may be relevant (for large projects); even if the sum of benefits exceeds the costs, it does not follow that the winners can compensate the losers and still be better off. The Boadway paradox reinforces the point that moving from "is" to "ought" always requires assumptions that should be made explicit.

Hume's insight is not always observed in practice. A recent example is the open letter published by over 1000 researchers in the Swedish daily Dagens Nyheter (April 25 2025), in which scientific evidence on climate change was used to call for specific policy actions. While the underlying research may be sound, the leap from descriptive findings to normative conclusions is precisely what Hume cautioned against.

Before turning to megaprojects more generally, we conclude this section with a brief comment on the role of CBA. It is beyond the scope of this study to review the extensive literature on its strengths and weaknesses. Suffice it to say that CBA has been used for nearly a century to inform public decision-making. Its intellectual roots can be found in the early eighteenth century. Writers such as the French engineer Charles Dupuit pointed out that what is profitable for the private investor is not necessarily beneficial for society. For an overview of how the method has developed, including international applications and underlying assumptions, see Johansson and Kriström (2016, 2018). The earlier volume offers a more advanced treatment; the latter is a more accessible introduction.

Green Megaprojects and CBA

Several factors contribute to public megaprojects becoming disappointments. First, cost overruns are common, often caused by overly optimistic forecasts and selection bias in project decisions. European infrastructure projects provide many examples, such as the tunnel between England and France (1988–1994). To secure financing, traffic forecasts were inflated—only to be downgraded after completion. Insiders, with incentives to paint a positive picture, shaped the projections. Second, political considerations often influence the use of economic analyses, where results are sometimes applied selectively. Third, many megaprojects lack sufficient anchoring in decision-making bodies. In summary, research shows that large public investments carry substantial risks of taxpayers' money being misallocated.

The ongoing green transition illustrates several of these dilemmas. Advocates often attribute project failures to factors beyond anyone's control. A clear example is the default of the Northvolt battery factory in northern Sweden, announced on March 12, 2025. This is the largest default in Swedish industry since 1932, according to several sources (e.g., NyTeknik 2025). While it will take years before the precise extent of the default is known, the scale of the losses is into the billions of USD, around six billion USD (not counting losses by the equity investors) according to NyTeknik (2025).

Northvolt's difficulties can arguably not be blamed on declining demand for electric vehicles or foreign subsidies. Despite grants, loans, and investments exceeding SEK 100 billion (around USD 10 billion), a large share of which came from public sources, the company has not succeeded in large-scale battery production. The problems appear to be internal.

Sandström (2025) puts forward five major reasons for the collapse of Northvolt:

(i) Lack of industrial competence,
(ii) financial and political competence,
(iii) "impossibly difficult" Chinese competition,
(iv) politized capital markets, and
(v) a short-circuiting of society's control mechanisms.

According to Sandström, the key individuals behind Northvolt did not possess the necessary industrial competence. Conversely, they had exceptional financial acumen and political connections. Furthermore, they did not realize that China controls the entire value chain for battery production, from raw materials and rare earth elements to their refinement, production equipment, and full-scale manufacturing. This constitutes an "impossibly difficult" competitor. What is more, Sandström argues that capital markets ceased to function properly. For various reasons, there was a lack of due diligence. Finally, he claims that society's scrutinizing functions, such as media and academia, failed in their responsibility. In all, Sandström's analysis is a reminder that megaprojects are not by default destined to succeed.

The Northvolt case highlights a broader dilemma in the green transition: Projects attract capital based on promises of rapid, large-scale results, but these promises often end up unfulfilled. Similar consequences are now visible across Europe, where green steel projects are being shut down or postponed (see Johansson and Kriström 2025, Table 1). This raises important questions: What decision-making processes underpinned these investments? What forms of evaluation, risk analysis, or due diligence informed the allocation of subsidies, loans, or equity?

Bent Flyvbjerg, a leading scholar on infrastructure megaprojects, calls this pattern the "survival of the un-fittest" (Flyvbjerg 2009, p. 348): The projects most likely to be approved are those whose promoters excel at understating costs and overstating benefits. His research shows that such tendencies often lead to suboptimal outcomes. The Northvolt case is, one could reasonably argue, a case in point. Stegra, launched with substantial public support, could follow suit. Without rigorous, transparent evaluation, such initiatives risk conforming to Flyvbjerg's iron law of megaprojects: "over budget, over time, over and over again."[1]

The Henrekson et al. (2024) volume argues that mission-oriented innovation policies (MOIPs) are particularly vulnerable to a range of behavioral biases. These include overconfidence and the sunk cost fallacy, which lead policymakers to commit excessive resources to initiatives with limited potential even when early indicators suggest otherwise. Moreover, a public choice perspective reveals that self-interest among politicians and government agencies often influences project selection and continuation, with agencies presenting overly positive self-evaluations and ignoring critical assessments to safeguard their budgets and influence.

Finally, periods of exceptionally low interest rates, such as in Sweden 2015–2021 and in the euro area for more than ten years,[2] can contribute to reduced stringency in due diligence processes, not only for individual companies such as Northvolt, but more generally for large investment projects. When capital is cheap and readily available, lenders' and investor's incentives to scrutinize projects are blunted compared to an environment where capital costs are higher. Low interest rates can create a "hunt for yield" where investors are more willing to take on higher risks in pursuit of better returns. Furthermore, such an environment can foster overconfidence in future growth and profitability, thereby reducing critical scrutiny of business models and market conditions. This can result in projects with dubious viability receiving financing, and potential problems not being discovered until it is too late, as was possibly the case with Northvolt.

We now turn to our application of cost–benefit analysis: the hydrogen-based steel plant in Boden, Sweden—a green megaproject that has received both political acclaim and substantial financial support.

CBA of Green Steel: The Stegra Project

Stegra, formerly H2 Green Steel (H2GS), is a large-scale hydrogen-based steel plant under construction in Boden, northern Sweden. The project has been promoted as a flagship of Europe's green industrial transition, aiming to eliminate most fossil fuel inputs in steel production by using hydrogen produced from (fossil-free) electricity. The environmental ambition is substantial: to reduce CO_2 emissions by 95% relative

[1] For further discussion, see Johansson and Kriström (2016, pp. 211–212) and Flyvbjerg and Garner (2023).

[2] The Swedish Central Bank deposit rate was either negative or zero from November 2014 through February 2022, The ECB deposit rate was either negative or zero from July 2012 until September 2022.

to conventional methods. Yet even under optimistic scenarios, the plant is projected to place itself among the top emitters in the country. Because of ETS, these emissions will, of course, not have any effect on EU's total emissions. Interestingly, in December 2024, the Swedish Environmental Protection Agency (*Naturvårdsverket*) rejected Stegra's request for SEK 1.65 billion (about EUR 150 million) from the Climate Leap (*Klimatklivet*) program. The primary reason appears to be that the initial phase of Stegra's steel production would rely on natural gas, leading to estimated emissions of approximately 500,000 tonnes of CO_2 annually until the company achieves its goal of fossil-free operations.

To achieve its goals of producing 5 million tonnes of "green" steel annually, the plant requires roughly 20 TWh of electricity per year, equivalent to almost 15% of electricity use in Sweden.[3] The project is expected to directly employ around 2,000 people. Guarantees, loans, and subsidies have flowed from multiple levels of government.[4] The question that needs to be asked is whether this investment is a good idea from society's perspective, but that has not, as far as we can tell, been answered by granting institutions.

Our evaluation of Stegra employs a general equilibrium-based cost–benefit framework. This allows us to capture both direct and indirect effects in a simple way. Theory shows that we can focus on the project itself, if it is "small enough." Unfortunately, it is difficult to provide a simple definition of what is meant by a project being small in this context. Intuitively, think of it as a case when all prices are not significantly impacted (alas, "small can be large," as shown in Johansson and Kriström (2016), but we ignore this complication here). If the price changes are small enough, changes in consumer and producer surpluses can be set to zero. Consequently, we can use observed market prices in our welfare evaluations. When Stegra is in full operation, production will be about 4% of Europe's steel consumption (EUROFER 2024), which is unlikely to have any significant effect on steel prices. More on this below.

It is important to state some of the key assumptions upfront. While some of the parameters are based on the Stegra project, we do not include the necessary infrastructure investments that Boden is currently undertaking. Boden has made significant investments to support the establishment of Stegra's green steel facility. These investments include infrastructure development, land preparation, and other municipal commitments. As there is still considerable uncertainty regarding the project's viability, the municipality faces a substantial financial risk. If the project fails, it could have negative consequences for the municipality's finances and its taxpayers. According to Tegström (2022)

> [...] the municipality expects that 10,000 more people will be working in the Boden–Luleå area by the latter part of the 2020s, and that Boden's population will reach 33,000 by 2030. Compared to today, this will require, among other things, 3,200 additional housing units, accommodations for contractors, an entirely new preschool with eight sections,

---

[3] According to H2GS's (Stegra's) application to the Swedish Environmental Protection Agency for a permit to construct and operate a new steel mill, 20 TWh of electricity is needed annually. Refer to Naturvårdsverket (2022, p. 2).

[4] See Henrekson (2024) for details. See also European Commission (2024).

new infrastructure, expanded emergency services, and English-language education. (our translation)

Mäki (2025) claims that Boden faces significant debt problems due to Stegra-related investments.

We now turn to benefits and costs, the reader interested in the details is referred to Section 4 in Johansson and Kriström (2025).

Benefits

The projected price for green steel is anchored in cost estimates from conventional blast furnace-basic oxygen furnace (BF–BOF) production in Germany—approximated at EUR 540 per ton, based on 2019 data, excluding updated permit costs. Adjusting for a higher long-term permit price (EUR 85 per ton CO_2 versus EUR 15 in 2019), the estimated upper bound for the output price becomes EUR 645 (if a ton of conventional steel requires 1.5 permits). A lower-bound estimate, assuming China as the marginal producer, yields EUR 575, incorporating a similar carbon tariff.

Costs

On the cost side, the baseline estimate for green steel production is EUR 544 per ton, to which electricity costs are added (4 MWh per ton, at EUR 71 per MWh), giving a total of EUR 828 per ton. This base cost aligns reasonably well with external estimates by Pawelec and Fonseca (2022) and others, with some variation depending on assumed electricity prices. Regarding electricity, we use an official forecast price for 2027 at EUR 71 per MWh. Additional investment in electricity transmission is assumed to cost EUR 5.48 billion in present value terms, based on 20 TWh annual consumption. This corresponds to EUR 18.4 per MWh when regulated transmission line owners (natural monopolies) use a 3% discount rate.

Net Benefits

To assess net social value, the study computes net present values (NPV) using two discount rates (3 and 7%). Across all scenarios, NPV is substantially negative: ranging from –15.2 to –24.3 billion EUR. This conclusion holds even if the electricity production cost were zero, once transmission infrastructure is accounted for. The 7% discount rate is justified on the basis that the investment crowds out alternative investments. A sensitivity analysis is also conducted using a 3% discount rate. This follows common EU guidelines (itself based on a Ramsey framework according to which a (tax-financed) project displaces private consumption, see Johansson and Kriström (2016) for details). The results are, as indicated, robust across this range.

Our calculations do not include a price premium for green steel. Possibly, altruism might motivate a price premium, but we find no compelling reason to include it, as discussed further below.

Furthermore, Hasanbeigi et al. (2024) show that the Levelized Cost of Steel (LCOS) produced using green hydrogen in direct reduced iron (H_2-DRI) combined with electric arc furnaces (EAF) can become competitive with conventional blast furnace–basic oxygen furnace (BF–BOF) methods in countries such as Brazil and Australia—*even without carbon pricing*—when hydrogen prices fall to around USD 1 per kg. In contrast, green steel remains more expensive in regions such as the European Union and Japan. A recent report by Sundén (2024) provides a detailed profitability assessment of Stegra, comparing its cost structure to both traditional and low-emission alternatives. He finds that Stegra's hydrogen-based production—which uses DRI and EAF technology (assumed to be) powered by renewable electricity—will be among the most expensive globally. It faces stiff competition not only from conventional BF–BOF steel, but also from scrap-based steel produced in electric arc furnaces, which is widely available and significantly cheaper to make. Sundén concludes that Stegra's product is unlikely to set prices in a global market marked by overcapacity. This assertion is not inconsistent with our assumptions that the Stegra project is "small." Furthermore, Sundén argues that its profitability is uncertain unless carbon prices rise sharply and competitors fail to decarbonize. In short, Stegra appears to face the highest projected production costs among major global alternatives.

Finally, Russel (2025), in a report from the Singapore International Ferrous Week 2025, asserts that the consensus view is that the total cost of green steel at scale would be twice that of the conventional BF–BOF method. While the vision for green steel is shared, the consensus from the Singapore International Ferrous Week is sobering: Who will bear these significantly higher costs remains an open and challenging question for the industry.

Summing up

Our cost–benefit analysis of the Stegra case is instructive in several respects. Perhaps the most notable result is not that the project passes a cost–benefit test only under strong assumptions, but that our framework demonstrates how projects of this kind can be assessed within prevailing institutional settings—such as current climate policy. Indeed, if the green plant displaces conventional steel produced within the EU Emissions Trading System (EU ETS), total emissions remain largely unaffected; permits and emissions are simply reshuffled. Hence, if end-users of green steel pay a premium, they might be paying for an illusion (Johansson and Kriström 2022, p. 383). This phenomenon is a direct consequence of MOIPs often ignoring opportunity costs and relying on evaluations that do not employ rigorous cost–benefit analysis, as highlighted in the Henreksson et al. (2024) volume. Our basic point is that EU's emissions cap system weakens the rationale for subsidizing Stegra as a climate initiative. This is also true even if the plant displaces conventional steel plants abroad, as we explain below. We acknowledge that there may be other, perhaps more compelling, justifications for public support of green steel projects. We return to these below. Still, our analysis suggests that subsidizing Stegra may not be the most efficient use of scarce public resources.

The Counterarguments

There are certainly viable arguments in favor of subsidies to efforts like the Stegra initiative. Such arguments will typically, in our context, come under the rubric of market failures. And the market failures should be beyond those associated with climate, at least if we discuss projects within the EU.

A possible example of a relevant market failure is information failures. For example, unclear policy may make it difficult for firms to know where the ETS market is heading. This uncertainty could make firms wary of investing and therefore there could be underinvestment in green technologies from society's point of view. An illustration might be recent developments within the so-called HYBRIT project, a Swedish competitor to Stegra. It is a joint venture between SSAB, LKAB, and Vattenfall, three (mostly) state-owned public companies. The project also uses hydrogen instead of coal, although at a larger scale (requiring up to 70 TWh of electricity). The recently announced (early 2025) postponement of the project seems to be partly related to carbon prices; the price of carbon dioxide is far too volatile, according to company management. In an interview in the Swedish daily Dagens Industri (2025), LKAB's chairman Anders Borg claims that (our translation) "At present, there is no political clarity on where prices are heading. The EU must provide more reassuring guidance." To explore this point more concretely, we have simulated how Stegra's (social) profitability would be affected by a sustained increase in the EU ETS carbon price. If the carbon price grows by 5% annually for 20 years, it reaches approximately EUR 225 per ton. A 10% annual increase leads to a price of about EUR 572 per ton. In our high steel price scenario, and assuming a 7% discount rate, the present value of Stegra's loss falls to around EUR 12 billion and EUR 5 billion, respectively.

Another market failure of relevance is related to innovation; the Stegra project might spur innovations that otherwise would not have materialized. Arguably, one could make the case for an interaction between the two market failures. Information failure increases the financial risks for projects like Stegra, potentially hindering their development and thus slowing down the innovations they could spur.

Additionally, one could point to the effects on employment. The project arguably reduces unemployment in the region. However, that argument loses some of its bite since unemployment is already very low in Boden and its surroundings. Indeed, in

June 2025, unemployment was 3.8% in the county of Norrbotten which, together with the island of Gotland, was the lowest in Sweden on a per county basis.[5]

Finally, one could argue that Stegra displaces conventional steel mills in countries that do not have CO_2 prices. If green steel production in Sweden displaces high-emission steel produced in regions without carbon pricing, then a global social cost of carbon—say EUR 80–100 per tonne—could justify additional climate-related benefits. However, under EU's Carbon Border Adjustment Mechanism (CBAM, European Commission (2023)), imported steel is subject to tariffs reflecting its embedded carbon content. These tariffs generate revenue for the EU, and if Stegra crowds out imports from outside the EU, emissions abroad may indeed fall—but so too will CBAM tariff revenues. Hence, even under optimistic assumptions about displacement, the net welfare benefits are ambiguous. For simplicity, we assume that the net benefits are zero.

Concluding Remarks

The Stegra case highlights a set of challenges in green industrial policy. Such projects, especially in the climate domain, often attract widespread support. But good intentions do not substitute for careful evaluation. After all, one euro spent in Boden is one euro not spent elsewhere. Ensuring careful evaluation also requires a clear understanding of the distinction between scientific findings and policy prescriptions. Whether we like it or not, we cannot get an "ought" from an "is," as Hume reminds us. For additional discussion on the challenges of evaluating state-led entrepreneurial initiatives and their counterfactuals from a somewhat different perspective, see the volume by Wennberg and Sandström (2022), in particular Larsson's (2022) essay in that volume.

Furthermore, cost–benefit analysis (CBA) helps dealing with prevailing institutional arrangements in a rigorous manner. The outcome of our evaluation is in no small measure contingent upon the existence of the EU Emissions Trading System (EU ETS) and the Carbon Border Adjustment Mechanism (CBAM). Thus, if we undertake a similar analysis outside of the EU where there are no carbon prices, the outcome might be different, even if the numbers that describe the investment itself are the same.

It is important to stress that we do not argue against climate action or industrial policy. Indeed, modern research on industrial policy, marked by more rigorous methods and causal inference, has begun to alleviate traditional economic skepticism toward these market interventions, as detailed in a recent review by Juhász et al. (2024). However, despite this growing body of research, the Henrekson et al. (2024) volume highlights fundamental challenges to the efficacy of large-scale, state-led industrial policies.

[5] https://www.ekonomifakta.se/sakomraden/arbetsmarknad/arbetsloshet/arbetsloshet-per-lan_1211212.html.

We argue for careful evaluation of any project that uses substantial public resources. In a review of the empirical literature of mission-oriented innovation policy, Batbaatar et al. (2024, p. 137) claim that "[n]one of the 49 mission evaluations included a cost–benefit analysis or an attempt to assess opportunity costs. This calls into question the standard by which 33% of the missions were rated as 'successful'." CBA is a useful and time-tested approach to obtain information about how society is affected by alternative ways of using scarce resources. The approach is based on a number of assumptions that should be stated upfront without forgetting Hume's insight. Even so, CBA does not guarantee wisdom, but it helps prevent folly.

References

Batbaatar, M., Larsson, J. P., Sandström, C., & Wennberg, K. (2024). The state of the entrepreneurial state: Empirical evidence of mission led innovation projects around the globe. In M. Henrekson, C. Sandström, & M. Stenkula (Eds.), *Moonshots and the New Industrial Policy: Questioning the Mission Economy* (pp. 125–143). Cham: Springer. https://doi.org/10.1007/978-3-031-49196-2_8

Cornwall, R. R. (1984). *Introduction to the Use of General Equilibrium Analysis*. Amsterdam and New York, NY: North-Holland.

Dagens Industri (2025). LKAB tvekar om Hybrit—igen: "Har inte bråttom". April 28. https://www.di.se/nyheter/lkab-tvekar-om-hybrit-igen-har-inte-brattom/

Dagens Nyheter (2025). Vår forskning kan inte viftas bort som åsikter. April 25. https://www.dn.se/debatt/var-forskning-kan-inte-viftas-bort-som-asikter/

Dasgupta, P., & Pearce, D. W. (1972). *Cost-Benefit Analysis: Theory and Practice*. London: Macmillan.

EUROFER (European Steel Association) (2024). *European Steel in Figures 2024* (Version 2). https://www.eurofer.eu/assets/publications/brochures-booklets-and-factsheets/european-steel-in-figures-2024/European-Steel-In-Figures-2024-v2.pdf

European Commission (2019). *The European Green Deal*. Brussels. https://commission.europa.eu/strategy-and-policy/priorities-2019-2024/european-green-deal_en

European Commission (2023). *EU Carbon Border Adjustment Mechanism (CBAM)*. https://taxation-customs.ec.europa.eu/carbon-border-adjustment-mechanism_en

European Commission (2024). *State Aid: Commission Approves €265 Million Swedish Measure to Support the Establishment of a Large-scale Green Steel Plant in Boden*. https://ec.europa.eu/commission/presscorner/detail/sv/ip_24_3468

Flyvbjerg, B. (2009). Survival of the un-fittest: Why the worst infrastructure gets built—and what we can do about it. *Oxford Review of Economic Policy*, *25*(3), 344–367. https://doi.org/10.1093/oxrep/grp024

Flyvbjerg, B., & Garner, D. (2023). *How Big Things Get Done: The Surprising Factors that Determine the Fate of Every Project, from Home Renovations to Space Exploration and Everything in Between*. New York, NY: Crown Currency.

Government Offices of Sweden (2021). *Sweden's Climate Policy Framework*. Stockholm: Government Offices of Sweden. https://www.government.se/articles/2021/03/swedens-climate-policy-framework/

Hasanbeigi, A., Zuo, B., Kim, D., Springer, C., Jackson, A., & Heo, E. H. (2024). Green steel economics: Comparing the economics of green H2-DRI and traditional steelmaking around the world. Report by Global Efficiency Intelligence, TransitionAsia, and Solutions for Our Climate.

Henrekson, M. (2024). Utvärderingen av de norrländska stålsatsningarna – sammanfattning och slutsatser. In M. Henrekson (Ed.), *De norrländska stålsatsningarna – frälsare eller gökunge*

(pp. 9–37). Stockholm: Samhällsförlaget. https://www.ifn.se/media/oyebba5z/2024-henrekson-de-norrl%C3%A4ndska-sta-lsatsningarna-fra-lsare-eller-go-kunge.pdf
Henrekson, M., Sandström, C., & Stenkula, M. (Eds.) (2024). *Moonshots and the New Industrial Policy: Questioning the Mission Economy*. Cham: Springer. https://doi.org/10.1007/978-3-031-49196-2
Hume, D. (1739 [2000]). *A Treatise of Human Nature* (Book III). Oxford: Oxford University Press.
Johansson, P.-O. (1991). *An Introduction to Modern Welfare Economics*. Cambridge: Cambridge University Press.
Johansson, P.-O., & Kriström, B. (2016). *Cost–Benefit Analysis for Project Appraisal*. Cambridge: Cambridge University Press.
Johansson, P.-O., & Kriström, B. (2018). *Cost–Benefit Analysis*. Elements in Public Economics. Cambridge: Cambridge University Press.
Johansson, P.-O., & Kriström, B. (2022). Paying a premium for "green steel": Paying for an illusion? *Journal of Benefit-Cost Analysis, 13*(3), 383–393. https://doi.org/10.1017/bca.2022.20
Johansson, P.-O., & Kriström, B. (2025). "Green" steel investments in the EU: Pie in the sky? *Resource and Energy Economics, 82*, 101494. https://doi.org/10.1016/j.reseneeco.2025.101494
Juhász, R., Lane, N., & Rodrik, D. (2024). The New Economics of Industrial Policy. *Annual Review of Economics, 16*(1), 213–242. https://doi.org/10.1146/annurev-economics-081023-024638
Larsson, J. P. (2022). Innovation without entrepreneurship: The pipe dream of mission-oriented innovation policy. In K. Wennberg & C. Sandström (Eds.), *Questioning the Entrepreneurial State: Status-quo, Pitfalls and the Need for Credible Innovation Policy* (pp. 77–91). Cham: Springer. https://doi.org/10.1007/978-3-030-94273-1_5
Mäki, S. (2025). Kommunens skuld växer – nu är den 1,5 miljarder. *Norrländska Socialdemokraten*, April 30. https://www.nsd.se/nyheter/boden/artikel/kommunens-skuld-vaxer-nu-ar-den-15-miljarder/lzz5xwzl
Naturvårdsverket (2022). Utkast – underrättelse till regeringen H2GS 17:5 MB. https://www.naturvardsverket.se/contentassets/922cf967308c472b9d9bebc8915a0209/2022-02-03-underrattelse-till-regeringen-h2gs.pdf
Ny Teknik (2025). Northvolts konkurs den största i Sverige i modern tid – miljarder upp i rök. March 12.
Pawelec, G., & Fonseca, J. (2022). *Steel from Solar Energy: A Techno-Economic Assessment of Green Steel Manufacturing*. Brussels: Hydrogen Europe. https://hydrogeneurope.eu/wp-content/uploads/2022/06/Steel_from_Solar_Energy_Report_05-2022_DIGITAL.pdf
Russel, E. (2025). Green steel is distant and expensive, but teal steel is coming. *Reuters*, May 13. https://www.reuters.com/markets/commodities/green-steel-is-distant-expensive-teal-steel-is-coming-2025-05-13/
Sandström, C. (2025). *Northvoltkraschen*. Stockholm: Timbro Förlag.
Sundén, D. (2024). Lönsamhetsbedömning av de svenska satsningarna på fossilfritt stål i Norrland. Malmö: Scandinavian Institute for Public Policy.
Tegström, L. (2022). Stålverk i Boden: Skuldsättning blir skyhög – "Skattebetalarna tar den stora risken". *Norrländska Socialdemokraten*, April 4. https://www.nsd.se/nyheter/boden/artikel/stalverk-i-boden-skuldsattning-blir-skyhog-skattebetalarna-tar-den-stora-risken/jnkommnj
Wennberg, K., & Sandström, C. (Eds.) (2022). *Questioning the Entrepreneurial State: Status-quo, Pitfalls, and the Need for Credible Innovation Policy*. Cham: Springer. https://doi.org/10.1007/978-3-030-94273-1

Per-Olov Johansson is Professor Emeritus at the Department of Economics, Stockholm School of Economics. He has published around 125 articles and 15 books. He has been adjunct Professor at the University of Oslo and consultant to the World Bank, the European Commission, and the European Investment bank. He has teaching experience from the Stockholm School of Economics, Stockholm University, the University of Oslo, and various Swiss Universities.

Bengt Kriström is Professor of Resource Economics (1994) at the Department of Forest Economics, SLU-Umeå and Senior Advisor at CERE. He has published widely in applied welfare economics, mostly environmental economics. He is currently Editor-in-Chief, *Journal of Forest Economics*. He has been consultant to the European Investment Bank, the OECD, the Swedish Government, and the World Bank. He has taught, inter alia, at the Stockholm School of Economics, SLU, Umeå University, Universitat Autònoma de Barcelona, and Universidad de Las Palmas de Gran Canaria.

HYBRIT: A Hubristic Hydrogen-Based Steel Project

Magnus Henrekson

Abstract This study critically examines HYBRIT (Hydrogen Breakthrough Ironmaking Technology), a Swedish flagship project—led by the government-owned iron ore company LKAB—to produce fossil-free sponge iron using hydrogen from fossil-free electricity. Positioned as a cornerstone of the EU Green Deal and Sweden's green industrial transition, HYBRIT promised CO_2 reductions significantly exceeding Sweden's current total emissions, but entailed unprecedented technological, economic, and infrastructural challenges. The analysis situates HYBRIT within the broader trend of "moonshot" industrial policies, emphasizing their susceptibility to political enthusiasm, rent-seeking, and disregard for opportunity costs. Technologically, the project required large-scale hydrogen production, storage, and industrial adaptation unproven at commercial scale. Economically, profitability hinged on exceptionally low electricity prices and high CO_2 emission costs—conditions unlikely to persist—while facing intensifying global competition in green steel. Electricity supply constraints, particularly in northern Sweden, compounded feasibility concerns. Political, regional, and corporate interests aligned to advance HYBRIT despite these risks, aided by limited external scrutiny of state-owned firms. Growing criticism and competing priorities eventually led LKAB to defer its sponge iron ambitions indefinitely, reframing its strategy around high-grade ore and extraction of rare earth metals and phosphorus. The case illustrates the pitfalls of mission-oriented policies when technological and market realities are subordinated to political symbolism, underscoring the need for rigorous, independent evaluation of large-scale green industrial projects.

Keywords Green deals · Green steel · Hydrogen · Mission-oriented policies · Moonshots · Public choice · Rent-seeking

---

I am grateful for useful comments and suggestions from Christian Sandström, Mikael Stenkula, and David Sundén. I also acknowledge financial support from the Jan Wallander and Tom Hedelius Foundation (P2023-0186) and the Kamprad Family Foundation for Entrepreneurship, Research & Charity (P20220048).

M. Henrekson (✉)
Research Institute of Industrial Economics (IFN), Stockholm, Sweden
e-mail: magnus.henrekson@ifn.se

M. Henrekson et al. (eds.), *A Green Entrepreneurial State?*, International Studies in Entrepreneurship 49, https://doi.org/10.1007/978-3-032-15512-2_10

JEL Codes L20 · L52 · L70 · O38 · Q28 · Q48

Introduction

Roughly 80% of all iron ore in Europe comes from the Swedish government-owned mining company LKAB. Its high-quality ore is sold as DR pellets in the world market, and its annual production of some 80 million tonnes is used to produce 40 million tonnes of steel.[1]

Steel production is a significant contributor to global CO_2 emissions, accounting for roughly 8% of the world's total CO_2 emissions.[2] If all steel made from LKAB's iron ore could become fossil-free, that would have a sizable effect on total emissions reducing total CO_2 emissions by 56 million tonnes—some 20% more than Sweden's total CO_2 emission.[3]

Potential reductions of such a magnitude paved the way for political entrepreneurship both at the national and the EU level. The iron ore could be reduced to sponge iron, which is mixed with scrap to make steel in electric arc furnaces (EAFs) using hydrogen (H_2) instead of natural gas (CH_4). The waste product would then be water (H_2O) instead of carbon dioxide (CO_2).

Such a project would also fit like hand in glove in the EU Hydrogen Strategy,[4] adopted in July 2020, where it is laid down that the European Commission has identified hydrogen as a key enabler of a climate-neutral Europe by 2050. It is projected that a "potential ¼ of the EU's renewable electricity production will be used for hydrogen production, which in turn would account for up to more than 23% in the 2050 energy mix" (European Hydrogen Observatory 2025).

The purpose of this study is to describe and explore the mechanisms behind an extensive project in Sweden to implement the EU Green Deal in mining and metal production by analyzing an attempt to create a supply chain for steelmaking that eliminates all CO_2 emissions. The analysis will show how the confluence of a number of forces led to a situation where all realism and pragmatism was thrown overboard. Attaining "net zero" in one specific area was given priority over all other concerns

[1] DR pellets are iron ore pellets designed for use in direct reduction (DR) processes. DR pellets are a key raw material for producing direct reduced iron (DRI) using gas rather than the traditional blast furnace method that uses coal.

[2] https://worldsteel.org/data/world-steel-in-figures/world-steel-in-figures-2024/?utm_source=chatgpt.com. Estimates range from 7.2% (Carbon Brief) to 11% (Our World in Data) of total global carbon emissions (https://www.sustainable-ships.org/stories/2022/carbon-footprint-steel).

[3] Assuming that LKAB's iron ore is used to produce 40 million tonnes of steel per year using the natural gas-based Direct Reduced Iron–Electric Arc Furnace (NG DRI–EAF) method with an average CO_2 emission of 1.4 tonnes per tonne of steel. Assuming that oxygen is removed from part of the LKAB ore using coal in blast furnaces, the reduction in CO_2 emissions would be greater still.

[4] The hydrogen strategy looms large in the EU's Green Deal, where 43% (EUR 430 billion) of the total resources are earmarked for hydrogen-based technologies.

such as opportunity costs, possible crowding out of existing activities, technological risks, and business risks.

The study is organized as follows. I begin by providing a theoretical and empirical background to "moonshot policies" and Green Deals. This is followed by three sections where I present and analyze the project and critically evaluate its technological and economic feasibility. In the final section the main conclusions are drawn. In particular, I attempt to explain how this project could come as far as it did despite the many insurmountable obstacles for its execution.

Moonshots and Green Deals

The economic gap between Europe and the United States has been widening since the onset of the 2008 financial crisis. To reverse this trend and boost its competitiveness, the European Union has laid out on an ambitious path aiming to be in the international forefront toward achieving a sustainable "green" economy. To this end, European as well as other Western nations increasingly adopt large-scale industrial policies; hard-won lessons regarding the challenges of successfully implementing interventionist large-scale innovation policies seem to be largely forgotten (Lerner 2009).

The COVID-19 pandemic further cemented this trend from 2020 and onwards as the European Commission introduced a temporary framework for state aid to allow unprecedented flexibility. Direct grants, loans, tax breaks, and guarantees were now allowed. Following the pandemic and Russia's invasion of Ukraine in 2022, the EU further amended and extended the Temporary Crisis and Transition Framework (TCTF). This included increases in aid ceilings (i.e., magnitudes allowed for each company or sector) and a broadened mandate for offsetting high energy prices and subsidizing the green transition.

The framework, initially intended to end in 2020, has been extended several times and includes provisions effective at least until the end of 2025. The TCTF was replaced by the Clean Industrial Deal State Aid Framework (CISAF) in June of 2025 and remains in force until 31 December 2030. The CISAF "helps Member States to easily support the development of clean energy, industrial decarbonisation and clean technology" (European Commission 2025).

This renewed embrace of state-led capitalism deserves a thorough analysis within a broader economic context (Henrekson et al. 2024a; Wennberg and Sandström 2022), especially since such policies are skillfully marketed under terms such as "mission-oriented innovation policy" and "the entrepreneurial state."

Influential public intellectuals (e.g., Mazzucato 2021; Rodrik 2022) argue that, just as the Apollo program boosted the U.S. economy, similar "moonshot" projects should be launched in other areas, combining public and private resources to tackle issues such as homelessness or cancer. Henrekson et al. (2024b) identify several interrelated reasons why these large-scale top-down missions are likely to fail: missions cannot solve highly complex problems and are susceptible to rent-seeking and special interest capture; policymakers are subject to self-interest and lack essential information for effective mission planning; market competition is disrupted when targeted support creates harmful incentives and moral hazard; and opportunity costs tend to be ignored or underestimated.

HYBRIT and Green Steel

In 2020 LKAB (jointly with steelmaker SSAB and the government-owned electricity producer Vattenfall) inaugurated its pilot plant for direct reduction of iron ore using hydrogen.[5] The pilot plant was announced as the first step in the huge project named HYBRIT (Hydrogen Breakthrough Ironmaking Technology). EU President Ursula von der Leyen did not miss this opportunity to boost the project in her September 2020 State of the Union Address (European Commission 2020):

> Two weeks ago in Sweden, a unique fossil-free steel pilot began test operations. It will replace coal with hydrogen to produce clean steel. This shows the potential of hydrogen to support our industry with a new, clean, license to operate. **I want NextGenerationEU to create new European Hydrogen Valleys** (bold in original) to modernize our industries, power our vehicles and bring new life to rural areas.

For Swedish politicians, government agencies and LKAB's management team, the project was also extremely attractive. Politicians could praise themselves for a project that would result in huge reductions in CO_2 emissions, environmental agencies would have a project where they could join forces with the politicians, and the LKAB leadership saw an opportunity to be both virtuous and expansionary by adding an additional step in the value chain by making fossil-free sponge iron instead of DR pellets their end product. LKAB asserted that this would increase their turnover by 200% (LKAB 2022a). A major political advantage of the project was that it, despite its enormous scale, could be financed through a combination of retained earnings from LKAB's mining operations and earmarked subsidies from the EU.

There were several additional factors at play. Historically, the northernmost part of Sweden, rich in natural resources and hydroelectric power, has felt exploited by the south, and this project was said to be a key part of "the reindustrialization of Norrland."[6] Last but not least, the project required an enormous amount of fossil-free electricity, 70 TWh to be precise, which is more than half of total electricity consumption in Sweden (136 TWh in 2024). As a result, potential suppliers of machinery, equipment, and construction services saw enormous business opportunities and joined forces with the political sphere in pushing the project.

[5] SSAB is a public company and Sweden's largest steel producer. Since 2021 LKAB has a 16% voting share, which makes it the de facto controlling owner of SSAB.

[6] Norrland is the northernmost, largest, and least populated of the three traditional lands of Sweden. It cover almost 60% of the land area but harbors a mere 11% of Sweden's population.

The Project

The part of the value chain from mine to finished steel that currently emits the most CO_2 is the production step between iron ore and iron where the oxygen is removed from the ore. This step has predominantly been carried out in blast furnaces where coal is used both as an energy source and as a means of removing the oxygen from the ore. Approximately 70% of all steel globally is produced in this way. The method currently results in 2.3 tonnes of CO_2 emissions per tonne of raw steel produced (Somers 2022; Institute for Energy Economics and Financial Analysis 2022).

An alternative way to remove oxygen from iron ore is to use the NG DRI-EAF method using sponge iron, which consists of between 90 and 95% pure iron. The production process requires high-quality iron ore; the iron content must be at least 65% and preferably above 67%. Currently, natural gas is used in sponge iron plants. For this reason, most sponge iron plants are located in regions with good access to cheap natural gas, such as the Middle East, Iran and Russia (Midrex 2023). This process of removing oxygen from the ore causes CO_2 emissions of 1.4 tonnes per tonne of steel (the commonly cited industry average), which is 40% less than in blast furnaces. As the need to reduce carbon emissions has become more important, demand for sponge iron has increased.

LKAB's HYBRIT project (HYdrogen BReakthrough Ironmaking Technology) aims to revolutionize the iron and steel industry by replacing fossil fuels with hydrogen produced by means of fossil-free electricity. The project is a collaboration between LKAB, SSAB, and Vattenfall and was launched in 2016. The goal is to create a completely fossil-free value chain from iron ore to finished steel. By using hydrogen instead of natural gas in the reduction process, CO_2 emissions are significantly reduced, with water as the only byproduct. In 2020, a pilot plant was opened in Luleå (a city located at the very north of the Baltic Sea) to produce sponge iron using fossil-free hydrogen. The plant has shown that the process can work, at least on a small scale. However, whether it will work at an industrial scale remains to be seen.

The long-term plan that was launched meant that, over a period of 25 years, LKAB would transition from being a company whose end product was DR pellets to having sponge iron as its end product (LKAB 2021).

LKAB estimates the total cost of the project at SEK 400 billion when fully developed. This does not include the costs of investments in electricity production and the associated grid. These investments are at least of the same magnitude (Blomgren 2024). Together this makes it by far the most extensive project in Sweden's modern industrial history both in absolute terms and relative to the country's GDP. If the project fails, it is difficult to see any alternative use for the volumes of weather-dependent electricity in the region.

Technological Feasibility

LKAB has no experience whatsoever of any of the technologies in question or of running such extensive projects. If one lists the specifics of their overall plans for sponge iron production, the overall technical challenges and risks become abundantly clear.[7]

LKAB would commit itself to building hydrogen production based on electrolysis on a scale never achieved, nor proven to be technically feasible or economically viable. According to LKAB's own narrative, their process would be unique and thus highly valuable for the company as well as for Sweden. However, this was not the case at all. Two examples are sufficient to disprove any assertion of this sort.

ArcelorMittal, the world's third largest steel company with industry experience dating back to 1902, initiated its hydrogen-based steelmaking efforts in 2019. In June 2025, following six years of R&D and experimental production, ArcelorMittal announced the cancelation of their plans for hydrogen-based steelmaking, citing high energy costs, insufficient infrastructure, and uncertainties regarding the long-term profitability of hydrogen-based steelmaking (Zadeh 2025). The legendary German steelmaker ThyssenKrupp, whose history dates back to 1802, is pursuing fossil-free steel production using hydrogen through its flagship initiative, the tkH_2Steel project. In 2023 the company received EUR 2 billion funding from the EU for its decarbonization project (Thyssenkrupp 2023). However, in March 2025 the company paused its hydrogen procurement tender due to higher-than-expected price indications for hydrogen. Instead, they plan to use natural gas in the foreseeable future at least until 2037 (Bolotova 2025).

Since the industrial process is continuous, while the electricity required for hydrogen production was mainly intended to come from weather-dependent sources (in practice, wind power), a significant hydrogen storage facility is needed to cope with periods of deficient wind. LKAB's experimental storage facility is a mere 100 m^3 (e.g., a cube where each side is 4.54 m or a sphere with a diameter of 5.76 m). At a pressure of up to 250 bars the facility can store 2 tonnes of hydrogen. But if there is going to be sufficient hydrogen stored to withstand close to one week of little or no wind, a storage is needed that is at least 1000 times larger.[8] However, no hydrogen storage facility on such a scale has ever been built or demonstrated to be technically feasible or economically viable (Sundén 2023; Vattenfall 2022). Nevertheless, LKAB (2025a) announced in early 2025 that "HYBRIT's pilot project for hydrogen gas storage has now been completed and reported to the Swedish Energy Agency. The results show that it is technically possible to store fossil-free hydrogen gas for producing fossil-free iron and steel on an industrial scale" (HYBRIT 2025).

[7] A similar situation applies to Stegra (formerly H2 Green Steel), which is a start-up company with owners and management with no previous experience of the relevant technologies, steel production and iron and steel markets. This project is evaluated in this volume by Johansson and Kriström (2026).

[8] According to LKAB's own estimate (LKAB 2022b). Sundén (2023) estimates that the storage must be up to 3,000 times larger (at a temperature of 20 °C and a pressure of 250 bar).

A third major challenge is to build many capital-intensive sponge iron plants powered by hydrogen on a scale that has never been done before and with a technology that has not yet been demonstrated to be commercializable and industrializable. As yet, there exists no industrial scale sponge iron production equipment customized to use hydrogen instead of natural gas anywhere (Sundén 2023, 2024a).

Economic Feasibility

The prospects for LKAB to make its sponge iron production profitable are bleak. The challenges stem both from the raw material markets and from the product markets they will operate in. First, the various technological challenges described above translate into increased uncertainty regarding the project's economic viability.

Sponge iron is mainly produced in regions with good access to cheap natural gas. The use of natural gas leads to high CO_2 emissions. In the future, these emissions will incur costs as they are covered by EU emissions trading rules.[9]

It is more expensive to produce sponge iron using hydrogen than natural gas, even when the costs of CO_2 emissions are included (Sundén 2024a). Only if the price of CO_2 is very high and the price of electricity is very low can hydrogen-based sponge iron become competitive. Compared with regions with access to cheap natural gas, Norrbotten therefore has no decisive competitive advantage. A large number of new sponge iron factories are also being built and planned in regions with access to cheap natural gas. In some cases, they are being built with the option of using hydrogen should hydrogen become sufficiently cheap in the future. Other factories are planning to capture and store the CO_2 (Sundén 2024a).

Alternative Methods

There are a great many other projects and pioneering technologies with the aim of producing steel without giving rise to CO_2 emissions. The Green Tracker (Vogl et al. 2025) reported 99 publicly announced low-carbon steel projects worldwide in May 2025.

One method that is already widely used is the replacement of coal with biochar (a type of charcoal) from eucalyptus in blast furnaces. According to the company behind the technology, Aço Verde do Brasil, CO_2 emissions per tonne of steel are reduced by 99% (Rostas 2022; Iwarson 2023). In Sweden, for example, two technologies are

[9] To prevent production from moving outside the EU and prevent non-EU producers from gaining competitive advantages on the EU market, a border adjustment mechanism that prices the emissions of imported iron and steel products—the Carbon Border Adjustment Mechanism (CBAM)—will be introduced. This will function as an import tariff. The level of the tariff will be determined by the price difference of emission allowances within the EU and the region from which the products are imported.

being developed to become fossil-free. FerroSilva uses forestry residues, biogenic carbon, to produce synthesis gas, which in turn is used to produce fossil-free sponge iron. GreenIron H2 intends to use hydrogen gas in the same way as LKAB but states that the process will be significantly more energy and cost-efficient than the one LKAB is developing.[10]

Yet another example of a pioneering technology is smelting reduction and smelting electrolysis, which is still at the pilot stage. The advantage over other processes is that they can produce pure iron more or less directly from any type of iron ore. This chemically pure iron can then be fed to electric arc furnaces for precision production of all types of low- and high-quality steel. Unlike in the traditional process, CO_2 emissions can be significantly reduced, and unlike the technologies that rely on sponge iron, high-quality iron ore is not needed.

The pressure to make the blast furnace technology fossil-free has also intensified and will continue to intensify over time. There are many possibilities, but it has not yet been possible to demonstrate that the technology can be completely fossil-free. To reduce emissions, steel companies seek to change the composition of material inputs. This includes increasing the share of higher quality iron ore, using more scrap steel, mixing in hydrogen, or using biochar. Other companies are developing technologies to capture emissions for recycling, storage, or use in other processes. Whether and how quickly blast furnaces can reduce their emissions on a larger scale is still unclear.

In short, additional business risks arise from the fact that pioneering technologies have been shown to work at the pilot stage, and that research and development to reduce CO_2 emissions in blast furnaces is increasing and slowly demonstrating the feasibility of reducing emissions.

Electricity: Availability and Price

A major argument used by the project's advocates was an alleged surplus of fossil-free hydroelectric power in northernmost Sweden. However, the total annual production of hydroelectric power in Norrbotten County, which makes up 25% of Sweden's land area, averages a mere 14 TWh per annum and the electricity demand of the many "green" projects in the north is almost one order of magnitude greater. For instance, H2 Green Steel (renamed Stegra in 2024) is a startup planning to make fossil-free steel using hydrogen and the Spanish fertilizer company Fertiberia has plans to build a plant to produce fossil-free fertilizer in Luleå. If realized, those two projects would need roughly 20 TWh of electricity per year.

Sundén (2024b) analyzes the significant electricity demand arising from the planned operations of LKAB, SSAB (a new EAF steel works in Luleå), Stegra, and Fertiberia in Norrbotten County. Their combined electricity demand was expected

[10] See Jafri et al. (2022) for a research overview of different decarbonization technologies in the iron and steel industry.

to reach 20 TWh by 2026, rising to 40 TWh by 2030 and 90 TWh by 2050. The analysis shows that unless electricity production increases accordingly, electricity prices will rise sharply throughout the Nordic region. Sundén estimates that if the companies' plans for 2026 were realized without a corresponding increase in electricity production, electricity prices would rise sharply in all electricity areas in the Nordic region. The price increase would be greatest in northern Sweden. There, prices were expected to rise by just over 170%, while the price in the Nordic region as a whole was expected to increase by 77%. Such price increases would be far higher than the companies had anticipated in their calculations.[11]

Thus, it is clear that the argument of an alleged surplus of fossil-free hydroelectric power in northernmost Sweden is untrue. HYBRIT's entire electricity demand will have to be covered by investments in new capacity.[12]

In this context it is noteworthy that it was not until 2023 that Sweden changed its policy on nuclear power and decided that it could be a constituent part in the green transition. The change was codified into law effective from January 1, 2024.[13] This means that the implicit plan was to cover the required 70 TWh of electricity almost exclusively through a massive expansion of land-based wind power in northern Sweden.

Fahlén et al. (2026) estimate that the cost of electricity from land-based wind power will be at least double compared what is claimed in the analyses by the Swedish Energy Agency. Based on actual experience, they conclude that the investment cost is higher, the service life is shorter, maintenance is more expensive, and the capacity factor is lower than projected. This leads to a production cost at the power plant level that is approximately twice as high as estimated by the Swedish Energy Agency.

In addition, there are costs at the system level, where the differences between power types are significant: costs for connection to the grid, transmission costs, and costs for balancing power and energy storage systems such as batteries required when there is insufficient wind. When the share of wind power exceeds 20%, the system cost increases rapidly, and even at that level, the system cost can be as high as the power plant cost (Manzolini et al. 2024).

If electricity production from wind power were to increase by 70 TWh to cover HYBRIT's long-term need, this would dramatically increase the weather-dependent share in the production mix. It is far from clear that it would then be possible to guarantee the functioning of the system throughout the year (Fahlén et al. 2026).

[11] Profus' and Nordeuropeiska energiperspektiv's (Nepp) forecasts for electricity market prices also indicate a sharp rise, albeit slightly lower than Sundén's (Odenberger et al. 2024).

[12] In fact, Stegra has only managed to secure half of its future electricity need (as of August 2025), despite requiring a mere one-fifth of the electricity that HYBRIT will need (Energinyheter.se 2024).

[13] The most important change was that the energy policy target was changed from the electricity system being 100% renewable by 2040 to being 100% fossil-free. Hence, instead of being totally phased out by 2040, nuclear power is now considered a central part of Sweden's climate transition and future energy mix.

Which Factor(s) Will Absorb the Premium on Fossil-Free Steel?

Competition in the fossil-free segment of the steel market will be fierce when all companies make the transition. The premium for fossil-free steel is therefore not expected to be particularly high. Competition is also fierce for input goods. As European steel companies switch to scrap-intensive electric arc furnaces, demand for steel scrap is also expected to increase. To secure access to steel scrap, major global steel producers have started buying scrap companies. The supply of tradable steel scrap is therefore uncertain. This leads to price risks for steel companies such as SSAB and Stegra, as their access to scrap is outside their value chains.

High-quality ore and steel scrap are strategically important in the steel industry's transition to decarbonization. The demand for these raw materials will therefore increase over time (Sundén 2023). High-quality ore of the type LKAB produces is only available in limited quantities, which will lead to higher prices as demand increases. This is good news for LKAB. The company has streamlined the production of its ore over many years, and the premium of their ore will be increasingly higher and the profitability of continuing to sell only ore can be expected to be high. The resource that is most limited in supply will command the highest price or return in the market.

In essence, the principle of the scarcest factor getting the premium highlights the fundamental economic concept that limited resources drive up their value in the market. Thus, an economic analysis based on first principles strongly suggests that any premium on fossil-free steel will accrue to suppliers of scrap and the high-quality ore required to make sponge iron.

Analysis and Discussion

Given the many obstacles and risks I have discussed, the obvious question is to ask how the project could ever leave the drawing board.

Most importantly, the project was perfectly aligned with the *zeitgeist* of politicians and the respective agencies at all levels from the highest echelons in Brussels down to the municipalities concerned in northernmost Sweden. Second, as LKAB was expected to be able to largely finance its massive investment by means of positive cash flows from its mining operations and subsidies earmarked to the green transition (that would otherwise be granted to other companies), the central government budget would not be directly affected.

Third, numerous companies, including the highly influential wind power industry, saw huge business opportunities as suppliers of equipment and services in connection with the enormous investments required.

Fourth, since neither LKAB nor Vattenfall are public companies, they are not subject to the normal daily scrutiny of a large number of stock-market and equity analysts. As a consequence, the announced plans were not questioned, and the reasoning and calculations were not scrutinized in detail. Without a stock exchange listing, the public does not receive a market assessment of the companies' plans in the form of a share price that combines all the external assessments made by thousands of independent analysts and investors.[14]

The fact that LKAB is owned by the Kingdom of Sweden creates a double problem. First, LKAB has a significant informational advantage over the handful of bureaucrats at the Ministry of Finance who are responsible for overseeing the company. These officials neither have the time nor the competence to review LKAB's plans in the way that would have been the case had the company been public. Second, appointments to the board of LKAB are not to a sufficient degree based on the special knowledge required to run a highly competitive international mining or steel company. Especially when the crucial decisions regarding HYBRIT were taken, the competence and experience of LKAB's board members differed significantly from its competitors. It is particularly noteworthy that the Chairman of the Board at that point in time was a former Prime Minister. In 2024, he was succeeded by a former Minister of Finance.

Conclusions

The original plan to convert all iron ore produced by LKAB into sponge iron using hydrogen manufactured from water and fossil-free electricity in northernmost Sweden would have been the largest industrial project in Sweden's modern industrial history both absolutely and relative to GDP.

The analysis in this essay indicates that both the technological and business risks were unacceptable. Therefore, the plans should never have left the boardroom. The various factors raised in the second section together shed explanatory light on how the HYBRIT project could garner so much positive attention and political support despite the high technological and economic uncertainty.

Most importantly, the project turned out to fit perfectly as a flagship in the green transition for all parties involved. To no small extent, politicians and government officials are governed by self-interest (Muldoon and Yonai 2023). Given the *zeitgeist* and the adamancy by which the green transition was touted both at the EU and the national level, HYBRIT constituted a political opportunity of extraordinary proportions (Schnellenbach 2024).

Moreover, the northernmost part of Sweden, rich in natural resources and hydroelectric power, has felt unduly exploited by the south, and this government-owned project could be marketed as a way to repay part of the historical debt to the north. Doing so was facilitated by the fact that, despite the enormity of the investment, the government envisaged that the project could be financed by a combination of earmarked subsidies and positive cash flows from LKAB's mining operations.

[14] This is also true for Stegra.

Furthermore, potential suppliers of machinery, equipment, and construction services, who saw enormous business opportunities, joined forces with the political sphere. Finally, strong concern for the environment and climate change also paved the way for a public debate where few scholars, policymakers, and journalists raised concerns. A person who expressed skepticism ran the risk of being dismissed as a "climate denialist," which made dissent costly, socially, politically, and economically.

In light of the growing criticism leveled against the project,[15] policymakers were slowly becoming aware of the lack of realism and exorbitant risks involved. The challenge was to find a politically acceptable reason for terminating the project, preferably without saying so outright.

The government and thus the owner of the project, represented by State Secretary Lars Hjälmered, announced at a conference in May 2024 that LKAB was facing several difficult challenges: moving the Kiruna city center, start mining deeper than anyone has ever done (down to 2000 m), open a new mine containing both iron ore and rare earth metals, extract phosphorus from the cinder, and make all current processes fossil-free. Mr. Hjälmered then concluded that overcoming these challenges should be prioritized. In practice, this meant that the HYBRIT project had to be put on hold.[16]

LKAB has now also changed its strategy. Although they still talk about producing fossil-free sponge iron in the future, they no longer say when. The revised mission statement (July 9, 2025; LKAB 2025b) clearly reflects what Mr. Hjälmered said at the conference in May 2024: "The high-grade ore we already sell has a relatively high premium. This, combined with the valuable [rare] earth metals and phosphorus we also can produce, gives us the perfect conditions to lead the transformation towards a carbon-free iron, mineral and steel industry." The mission statement no longer contains any timeline and dates for the production of sponge iron using fossil-free hydrogen.

Hence, in the light of criticism, politicians have managed to save face, the company has been able to make an honorable retreat, and for the citizens of the Kingdom of Sweden a likely economic disaster has been averted.

References

Blomgren, J. (2024). Elförsörjning till de planerade industriprojekten i norra Sverige [Electricity supply to the industrial projects in northern Sweden]. In M. Henrekson (Ed.), *De norrländska stålsatsningarna—frälsare eller gökunge* (pp. 189–213). Stockholm: Samhällsförlaget. https://www.ifn.se/media/oyebba5z/2024-henrekson-de-norrl%C3%A4ndska-sta-lsatsningarna-fra-lsare-eller-go-kunge.pdf

Bolotova, J. (2025). ThyssenKrupp puts hydrogen tender for future DRI plant on hold due to high prices. *DJJ*, March 27. https://djj.com/thyssenkrupp-puts-hydrogen-tender-for-future-dri-plant-on-hold-due-to-high-prices/

[15] See the collection of contributions in Henrekson (2024).

[16] Scandinavian Institute for Public Policy (2024).

Energinyheter.se (2024). Uniper och Stegra ingår sexårigt elavtal för grön industriomställning [Uniper and Stegra sign six-year electricity agreement for green industrial transition]. November 27. https://www.energinyheter.se/20241127/32310/uniper-och-stegra-ingar-sexarigt-elavtal-gron-industriomstallning
European Commission (2020). State of the Union Address by President von der Leyen at the European Parliament Plenary. https://ec.europa.eu/commission/presscorner/detail/en/SPEECH_20_1655
European Commission (2025). Clean Industrial Deal State Aid Framework (CISAF). https://competition-policy.ec.europa.eu/about/contribution-clean-just-and-competitive-transition/clean-industrial-deal-state-aid-framework-cisaf_en
European Hydrogen Observatory (2025). EU Hydrogen Strategy under the EU Green Deal. https://observatory.clean-hydrogen.europa.eu/eu-policy/eu-hydrogen-strategy-under-eu-green-deal
Fahlén, P., Henrekson, M., & Nilsson, M. (2026). In pursuit of a green transition—electricity at any cost? In M. Henrekson, C. Sandström, & M. Stenkula (Eds.), *A Green Entrepreneurial State? Exploring the Pitfalls of Green Deals* (pp. 149–172). Cham. Springer.
Henrekson, M. (Ed.) (2024). *De norrländska stålsatsningarna—frälsare eller gökunge [The Steel Projects in Northern Sweden: White Knight or Cuckoo in the Nest?].* Stockholm: Samhällsförlaget.
Henrekson, M., Sandström, C., & Stenkula, M. (Eds.) (2024a). *Moonshots and the New Industrial Policy: Questioning the Mission Economy.* Cham: Springer. https://doi.org/10.1007/978-3-031-49196-2
Henrekson, M., Sandström, C., & Stenkula, M. (2024b). Seven reasons why mission-oriented innovation policies seldom work in practice. *Economic Affairs, 44*(2), 354–362. https://doi.org/10.1111/ecaf.12654
HYBRIT (2025). HYBRIT: Large-scale storage of fossil-free hydrogen gas successfully proven. https://www.hybritdevelopment.se/en/hybrit-large-scale-storage-of-fossil-free-hydrogen-gas-successfully-proven/
Institute for Energy Economics and Financial Analysis (2022). The facts about steelmaking: Steelmakers seeking green steel. https://ieefa.org/sites/default/files/2022-06/steel-fact-sheet.pdf
Iwarson, T. (2023). Brasilien—störst på träkol och först med fossilfritt stål [Brazil—world leading in fossil-free steel using charcoal]. *ATL*, May 26. https://www.atl.nu/brasilien-har-redan-fossil fritt-stal.
Jafri, Y., Ahlström, J. M., Furusjö, E., Harvey, S., Pettersson, K., Svensson, E., & Wetterlund, E. (2022). Double yields and negative emissions? Resource, climate and cost efficiencies in biofuels with carbon capture, storage and utilization. *Frontiers in Energy Research, 10*, Article 797529. https://doi.org/10.3389/fenrg.2022.797529
Johansson, P.-O., & Kriström, B. (2026). Green industrial megaprojects: A welfare economics perspective. In M. Henrekson, C. Sandström, & M. Stenkula (Eds.), *A Green Entrepreneurial State? Exploring the Pitfalls of Green Deals* (pp. 173–185). Cham: Springer.
LKAB (2021). Varför koldioxidfri järnsvamp? [Why carbon-free sponge iron?]. https://lkab.com/nyheter/varfor-koldioxidfri-jarnsvamp/
LKAB (2022a). Snabbare takt och högre mål i LKAB:s omställning mot en hållbar framtid [Faster pace and more ambitious targets in LKAB's transition towards a sustainable future]. https://mb.cision.com/Main/11419/3532814/1568943.pdf
LKAB (2022b). HYBRIT: Nästa milstolpe nådd—pilotanläggningen för vätgaslagring i drift [HYBRIT: Next milestone reached—pilot plant for hydrogen storage now operational]. https://lkab.com/press/hybrit-nasta-milstolpe-nadd-pilotanlaggningen-for-vatgaslagring-i-drift/
LKAB (2025a). HYBRIT: Storskalig lagring av fossilfri vätgas framgångsrikt bevisad [HYBRIT: Large-scale storage of fossil-free hydrogen successfully proven]. https://lkab.com/press/hybrit-storskalig-lagring-av-fossilfri-vatgas-framgangsrikt-bevisad/
LKAB (2025b). Our strategy for the future. https://lkab.com/en/what-we-do/our-strategy/.

Lerner, J. (2009). *Boulevard of Broken Dreams. Why Public Efforts to Boost Entrepreneurship and Venture Capital Have Failed—and What to Do about It*. Princeton, NJ: Princeton University Press.

Manzolini, G., Binotti, M., Gentile, G., Picotti, G., Pilotti, L., & Cholette, M. E. (2024). Actual cost of electricity: An economic index to overcome levelized cost of electricity limits. *iScience*, *27*, Article 109897. https://doi.org/10.1016/j.isci.2024.109897

Mazzucato, M. (2021). *Mission Economy: A Moonshot Guide to Changing Capitalism*. New York, NY: Harper Collins.

Midrex (2023). 2022 World Direct Reduction Statistics. Charlotte, NC: Midrex Technologies, Inc.

Muldoon, J., & Yonai, D. K. (2023). A wrong but seductive idea: Public choice and the entrepreneurial state. *Journal of the International Council for Small Business*, *4*(4), 1–11. https://doi.org/10.1080/26437015.2023.2182730

Odenberger, M., Unger, T., Kofoed-Wiuff, A., Gaballo, F., & Wråke, M. (2024). Modellanalyser av den svenska elprisutvecklingen till följd av en omfattande elektrifiering. Nordeuropeiska energiperspektiv. Nepp and Profu [Modelling the effects on Swedish electricity prices of an extensive electrification: A North European perspective]. https://energiforsk.se/media/33096/nepp-elprisutveckling-till-foljd-av-omfattande-elektrifiering-2024-01-30.pdf

Rodrik, D. (2022). An industrial policy for good jobs. Washington, DC: The Hamilton Project, Brookings. https://drodrik.scholar.harvard.edu/files/dani-rodrik/files/rodrik_-_an_industrial_policy_for_good_jobs.pdf

Rostás, R. (2022). Brazil at steel decarbonization crossroads: Charcoal, gas short-term options. *Fastmarkets*, 21 March. https://www.fastmarkets.com/insights/brazil-at-steel-decarbonization-crossroads-charcoal-gas-short-term-options/

Scandinavian Institute for Public Policy (2024). De norrländska stålsatsningarna: Frälsare eller gökunge? [The steel projects in northern Sweden: White knight or cuckoo in the nest?]. Malmö. https://www.youtube.com/watch?v=1UhjMb24a50&t=8328s

Schnellenbach, J. (2024). A behavioral economics perspective on the entrepreneurial state and mission-oriented innovation policy. In M. Henrekson, C. Sandström, & M. Stenkula (Eds.), *Moonshots and the New Industrial Policy: Questioning the Mission Economy* (pp. 61–76). Cham: Springer. https://doi.org/10.1007/978-3-031-49196-2_4

Somers, J. (2022). *Technologies to Decarbonise the EU Steel Industry*. Luxembourg: Publications Office of the European Union. https://publications.jrc.ec.europa.eu/repository/handle/JRC127468

Sundén, D. (2023). Från brunt till grönt—bedömning av satsningarna på fossilfritt stål i Norrland utifrån ett teknik- och marknadsperspektiv [From brown to green—Assessment of fossil-free steel initiatives in Norrland from a technology and market perspective]. Malmö: Scandinavian Institute for Public Policy. https://policyinstitutet.se/wp-content/uploads/2023/11/Rapport-Fran-brunt-till-gront-Final2.pdf

Sundén, D. (2024a). Lönsam eller kostsam? Lönsamhetsbedömning av de svenska satsningarna på fossilfritt stål i Norrland [Profitable or costly? Profitability assessment of Swedish investments in fossil-free steel in Norrland]. Malmö: Scandinavian Institute for Public Policy. https://policyinstitutet.se/wp-content/uploads/2024/01/Rapport-Lonsam-eller-kostsam-240115.pdf

Sundén, D. (2024b). Till vilket elpris som helst? Bedömning av effekterna på den nordiska elmarknaden av satsningarna på fossilfritt stål i Norrland [At any electricity price? Assessment of the impact on the Nordic electricity market of investments in fossil-free steel in Norrland]. Malmö: Scandinavian Institute for Public Policy. https://policyinstitutet.se/wp-content/uploads/2024/01/Policyinstitutet-Till-vilket-elpris-som-helst-1.pdf

Thyssenkrupp (2023). EU approves €2 billion funding for Thyssenkrupp's decarbonisation project. https://www.newcast.com/en/Media_News/News/EU_approves_%E2%82%AC2_billion_funding_for_Thyssenkrupp_s_decarbonisation_project

Vattenfall (2022). HYBRIT: Världsunikt bergrumslager för fossilfri vätgas invigs i Luleå [HYBRIT: World-unique underground storage facility for fossil-free hydrogen inaugurated

in Luleå]. https://group.vattenfall.com/se/nyheter-och-press/pressmeddelanden/2022/hybrit-varldsunikt-bergrumslager-for-fossilfri-vatgas-invigs-i-lulea
Vogl, V., et al. (2025). Green Steel Tracker. Stockholm: Leadership Group for Industry Transition (LeadIT). https://www.industrytransition.org/green-steel-tracker/
Zadeh, J. (2025). ArcelorMittal halts German green steel project amid economic challenges. *Discovery Alert*, June 25. https://discoveryalert.com.au/news/arcelormittal-green-steel-project-cancellation-2025/

Magnus Henrekson is a Professor of Economics and Senior Research Fellow of the Research Institute of Industrial Economics (IFN) in Stockholm, Sweden. He resigned as CEO of IFN in 2020 after 15 years of service. Until 2009, he held the Jacob Wallenberg Research Chair in the Department of Economics at the Stockholm School of Economics. He is also a member of the Royal Swedish Academy of Engineering Sciences (IVA).

He received his PhD in 1990 from Gothenburg University with his dissertation *An Economic Analysis of Swedish Government Expenditure*. Throughout the 1990s, he conducted several projects that aimed to explain cross-country growth differences. Since the turn of the new millennium, his primary research focus is entrepreneurship economics and the institutional determinants of the business climate. In this area, he has published extensively in scientific journals and contributed several research surveys to *Handbooks* in the field of entrepreneurship.

In addition to his academic qualifications, Henrekson has extensive experience as an advisor, board member and lecturer in many different contexts, in both the business and public sectors.

Explaining Northvolt's Bankruptcy and the Dilemma of Green Deals

Christian Sandström

Abstract This study analyzes how and why green deals may create failed companies by exploring the recent bankruptcy of Northvolt, Europe's most extensive effort to create an independent battery factory on the continent. By 2023, Northvolt had expanded to a staff of nearly 6,000. Yet, its efforts to reach industrial scale encountered major setbacks, leaving the company reliant on Chinese equipment and expertise, even though public funding had been justified on grounds of European self-sufficiency. Four reasons why Northvolt developed into one of the largest bankruptcies in modern European history are identified. Public support distorted corporate incentives, and Northvolt ended up taking too much risk. Capabilities take time to develop, but the political and financial logic pushed for more rapid expansion. At the same time, cognitive biases and a sense of urgency surrounding environmental concerns created a consensus landscape in Sweden where the headquarters and first plant were located.

Keywords Green deal · Northvolt · Batteries · Mission-oriented · Sustainability

JEL Codes H50 · L26 · L52 · O31 · O38 · P16

Introduction

Europe has embarked on an ambitious path toward sustainability, in part through the convergence of industrial and environmental policy into green deals. Large stimulus packages have been put forth by the European Commission (2020) via its various funding mechanisms for firms to accomplish a green transition.

In late 2024, Mario Draghi also underscored the need for substantial investments in Europe and reiterated that Europe is falling behind in competitiveness vis-à-vis China and the United States.

C. Sandström (✉)
Linnaeus University, Växjö, Sweden
e-mail: christian.sandstrom@lnu.se

M. Henrekson et al. (eds.), *A Green Entrepreneurial State?*, International Studies in Entrepreneurship 49, https://doi.org/10.1007/978-3-032-15512-2_11

This study explores the mechanisms at work in firms that take part in the EU Green Deal. It does so by describing the rise and subsequent fall of battery manufacturer Northvolt. The empirical part and some of the analysis draws upon my book published in Swedish (Sandström 2025). The Swedish firm was for many years the flagship of the EU's efforts to accomplish electrification and increased autonomy.

Drawing on both interviews and secondary data, the article uncovers how moral hazard and opportunism paved the way for rapid and unrealistic expansion. Northvolt is the most extensive bankruptcy in Sweden since the 1930s and provides a cautionary tale for the design of green industrial policy.

The study shows how government support results in the distortion of economic incentives (Sandström and Alm 2022) and how rent-seeking mechanisms, lobbying and regulatory capture are made more likely than not. Northvolt demonstrated considerable financial and political capabilities as the firm amassed both political support and copious funding, both public and private.

The next section provides a conceptual background to the notion of green deals and the role of industrial policy. The subsequent sections describe the Northvolt case in more detail—from its initiation via rapid expansion and dramatic bankruptcy. Next, policy implications are discussed, and lastly, some concluding remarks are provided.

Background: Missions and Moonshots

Since the global financial crisis of 2008, Western policymakers have leaned more heavily on expansive industrial strategies. These so-called "mission-oriented" approaches are promoted as ways to confront pressing societal challenges—from climate change to social issues such as homelessness (Lucas and Boudreaux 2024) or public health.

This resurgence of state-directed capitalism, manifested in extensive government programs, warrants careful examination within a broader economic and political framework (Wennberg and Sandström 2022; Henrekson et al. 2024a).

Scholars such as Dani Rodrik and Mariana Mazzucato argue that "moonshots" should be launched in other areas, uniting public and private efforts, and that government efforts should not just be about raising money but also about directing it toward transformative, mission-oriented investments that reshape the economy toward sustainability. Mazzucato (2022) emphasizes that public finance must play a leading role, not only de-risking private investment but actively steering markets in the public interest to further the common good.

In the process of doing so, it is argued that considerable knowledge externalities will materialize, creating a "supermultiplier" effect (Deleidi and Mazzucato 2019; cf. Boysen-Hogrefe 2025). Analyses touting mission-oriented innovation policies (MOIPs) have been invoked to motivate and shape the design of the European Union's Green Deal (e.g., Mazzucato 2018).

Findings on how and why such initiatives fail have been synthesized into a collection of factors (Henrekson et al. 2024b). One such factor concerns how missions tend to be captured by special interests (Muldoon and Yonai 2023). Moreover, public funds may create moral hazard as taxpayer money is made available for firms. Scholars interested in behavioral political economy have also underscored that both firms and policymakers engaged in MOIPs are subject to cognitive biases (Schnellenbach 2024), while others have emphasized that policymakers lack information to design missions effectively (Waldron and Coyne 2024).

This study shows how several of the aforementioned factors came together in the rapid rise and equally rapid fall of Northvolt. While attention has been devoted to the mechanisms behind industrial policy failures in general, less is known about green industrial policy failures, i.e., attempts to create both industrial renewal and increased competitiveness while at the same time contributing to sustainability. The reasons for failure might be similar in some regards, but also different in scale and scope.

The Northvolt Case

This section provides an empirical description of Northvolt's rise and fall, partly based on interviews and partly based on secondary data.[1]

Northvolt was launched by Peter Carlsson and Paolo Cerutti, with investors Harald Mix and Carl-Erik Lagercrantz from Vargas Holding joining as co-founders. Carlsson, who had previously worked at Ericsson and in semiconductors before moving to Tesla (2011–2015), soon acquired the media nickname "the Tesla Swede" when he returned to Sweden to establish the company. Mix and Lagercrantz had a background in the buyout form of private equity (PE) and as originators as well as owners of Vargas Holding. Vargas is an investment company explicitly focused on building new companies contributing to a green transition.

Upon having initiated the Northvolt venture, Carlsson asserted in several interviews that he was burnt out after his years at Tesla. At the same time, he was increasingly referred to as "Europe's battery Messiah."

Rapid Expansion

The business idea of Northvolt was to produce the world's greenest batteries. This would be done by accessing green electricity in northern Sweden, primarily hydro power. The first main production site was therefore located in Skellefteå, a city which controlled some of the most extensive hydro power capacity in the country. Recycling batteries was also a major priority for Northvolt.

[1] The description draws on Sandström (2025).

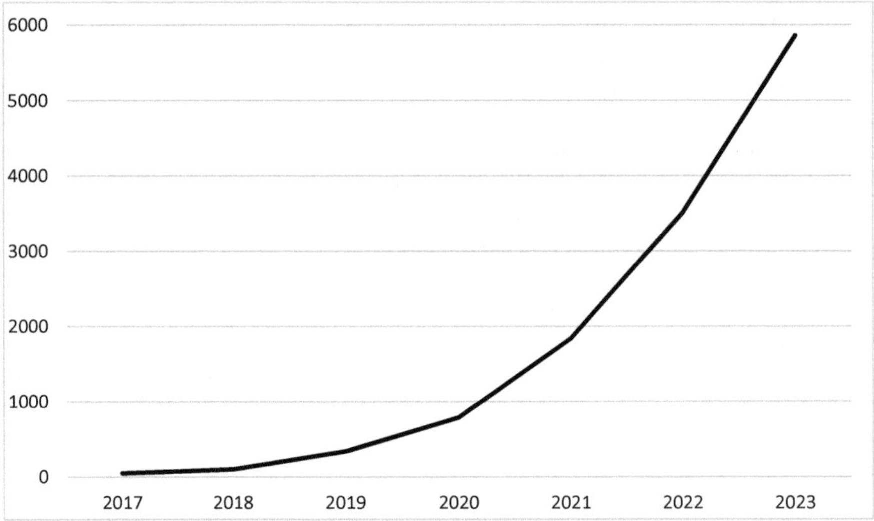

Fig. 1 Number of employees at Northvolt, 2017–2023 *Source* Northvolt Annual Report 2023

Northvolt was founded during a period when trade tensions between Europe and China had begun to increase. As China controlled most of the supply chain related to batteries, an important reason for Northvolt's inception was also to increase Europe's strategic autonomy vis-à-vis China. In a speech in Brussels in March 2020, co-founder Carl-Erik Lagercrantz said that Europe cannot rely solely on batteries from abroad and countries like China.[2] The president of the EU Commission, Ursula von der Leyen, also participated in the event. Lagercrantz argued that vertical integration was an integral part of creating both increased competitiveness and enhanced strategic autonomy for the union.

Focusing on lithium-ion batteries, the business was quickly scaled up in the following years. Northvolt was founded in 2017. Two years later, it had 50 employees—already with 25 different nationalities represented. In 2018, the company reached 100 employees, in the following year 340, and by 2020, the work-force had grown to 790 employees. The number of employees continued to almost double each year, reaching peak in 2023 at nearly 6,000 employees (Fig. 1).

This rapid expansion encountered considerable challenges. Production was plagued with delays and quality problems. One reason was lack of knowledge and experience in battery manufacturing. Another reason was related to the fact that Northvolt had become dependent on Chinese suppliers of production equipment. For several years, there were hundreds of Chinese guest workers at the Skellefteå plant. The Chinese workers installed and operated a substantial share of the machines.

One interviewee stated that "the Chinese were in complete control and did what-ever they wanted." According to the same source, some sections of Northvolt's plant

[2] Youtube (2020).

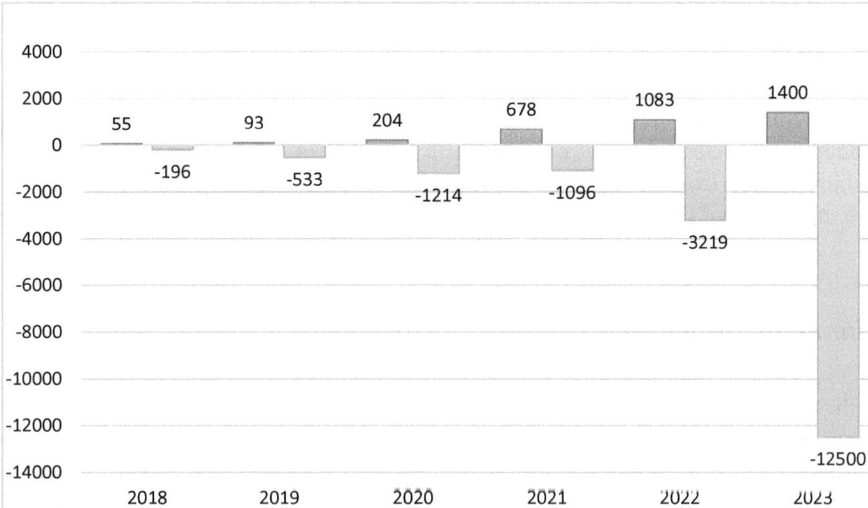

Fig. 2 Northvolt's turnover and operating profit (loss), 2018–2023 (in SEK million) *Source* Northvolt Annual Report 2023

contained up to 75% Chinese machines. The maintenance staff at Northvolt were frequently shocked by the poor quality of the Chinese equipment, stating that at times "it even looked like industrial sabotage."

Interviewees indicated that the equipment delivered by the main Chinese supplier Wuxi Lead Equipment was in fact based on a more than 30-year-old technology, and Swedish workers at the Skellefteå site had to use Google Translate in order to understand how to operate the equipment.

International Expansion

Instead of focusing solely on addressing operational challenges in Skellefteå, Northvolt continued to expand. In Sweden, they announced plans to set up a second plant in Borlänge as well as a joint venture with Volvo Cars in Gothenburg. Simultaneously, they launched an international expansion. Already in 2020, the firm was present in many parts of the world including Japan, Germany, Portugal and Poland. Later, Canada and California were added.

Upon a closer look at the incentives for Northvolt to engage in this expansion, it seems like public funds were made available in order to attract Northvolt to certain regions. Regional and federal agencies together offered more than USD 2.7 billion for Northvolt to establish a site in the province of Québec. In Germany, authorities pledged approximately SEK 9 billion (around EUR 0.8 billion) in total, with the majority in direct subsidies and the remainder in the form of state-backed loan guarantees.

One owner of Northvolt shares, former Social Democratic Minister of Industry Anders Sundström, stated in an interview in 2024 that "the German site is entirely funded by the German government. Northvolt owns it but has put in very limited resources of its own." For its operations in Gdansk, Poland, Northvolt received SEK 750 million from the EU Innovation Fund.

Financial Difficulties

In the annual report for 2023, published belatedly in July 2024, CEO Peter Carlsson did his best to convey a positive message, asserting that "[o]ur position is stronger than ever, and we are leading in setting the benchmark for sustainability in the battery industry." The Chairman of the Board, Jim Hagemann Snabe, writes in the annual report that "Northvolt is poised to emerge as one of the most significant companies of our time."

At the same time, the numbers in the annual report conveyed a very different message. They clearly showed that the combination of persisting operational challenges and the frenzied international expansion had resulted in mounting losses both in 2022 and 2023.

By 2023, revenues showed little movement while losses mounted to SEK 12.5 billion. At such a rate of capital depletion, insolvency became increasingly difficult to avoid without fresh injections of capital or a rapid move to profitability. Northvolt was never close to becoming a profitable and competitive battery producer.

But why did Northvolt fail to secure new funding from shareholders during the autumn of 2024? One important reason was Northvolt's debt financing. As of early 2024, Northvolt had accumulated more than SEK 80 billion in debt, paying interest of several billions per year with almost no revenue to match mounting interest payments.

Upon having reached this state, any new equity would be used to service the existing debt. Once the company finds itself in such a situation, banks and credit institutions are likely to pull back and it will be difficult to raise new equity. The only remaining option for the company to survive was to start generating its own revenues.

Chinese Competition

Northvolt was nowhere near catching up with its Chinese competitors, who had already dominated the global market for more than a decade. By 2020, China had established an unparalleled leadership in the global market for electric vehicles and batteries, controlling more than 70% of the world's production capacity for lithium-ion batteries as well as most parts of the supply chain from raw materials to finished vehicles. This scale and integration gave China a strategic advantage.

The Chinese share of global electric vehicle sales increased to about 60% in 2023. The following year, Chinese brands accounted for 76% of electric vehicle sales worldwide. Of the ten largest electric vehicle manufacturers in the world by sales volume in 2024, eight were Chinese.

In 2023, China accounted for roughly three-quarters of global lithium-ion battery output. By the following year, leading Chinese producers dominated the market: CATL (Contemporary Amperex Technology Co. Limited) held about 38% of global share, while BYD (Build Your Dreams) controlled around 17%. Regarding the production of anode materials, Chinese companies control nearly 90% of the global market, and more than 75% of the refinement of key natural resources such as lithium, nickel and cobalt is done by Chinese companies.

Taken together, Chinese companies had established market dominance prior to Northvolt's attempt to scale up its operations in 2020. In fact, an international group of senior battery scholars had warned Northvolt's top management against trying to compete with the Chinese in making lithium-ion batteries. In a recommendation to Peter Carlsson and senior management, these scholars declared that "given China's dominance and complete control over natural resources and refinement of lithium, its lack of environmental concern, subsidies, and advanced manufacturing equipment, our recommendation is not to proceed with lithium."

According to one interviewee, Peter Carlsson and Northvolt's management team were well informed about the risks and challenges related to lithium-based technology. By deciding to follow this path anyway, they in effect led the company to a dead end.

Political Connections

From its inception, Northvolt's founders had been strategic in cultivating strong political connections. Carl-Erik Lagercrantz stated in a speech at Business Europe in 2020 that the company has "a very close collaboration with the EU Commission."[3]

Among the shareholders of the company, conservative profile Anders Kempe, owner of the public affairs firm Bellbird, was both a shareholder, advisor and supplier of public affairs services. Mr. Kempe has been one of Sweden's most influential lobbyists over the past decades with close personal ties to the ruling Moderate Party and Prime Minister Ulf Kristersson. Former Social Democratic Minister of Industry, Anders Sundström, also owned shares in Northvolt and acted as an advisor to the company. Another member of his party and a former Minister (of Education and Industry), Thomas Östros, served as vice president of the European Investment Bank

[3] Youtube (2020).

(EIB) during these years. In 2023, Ibrahim Baylan, also a former Social Democratic Minister (of Energy and Industry), became a registered lobbyist in Brussels for Vargas, the investment company behind Northvolt.

These connections likely boosted Northvolt's ability to garner public support. As early as 2017, Northvolt reported in its annual filings that it had established collaborations with public bodies such as Vinnova and the Swedish Energy Agency. Other examples of public funding include EUR 5 billion in "green loans" that were announced in February 2024. As Northvolt failed to meet all contractual terms, most of that loan was never paid out. In the end, EIB contributed almost EUR 280 million.

Political Praise

Northvolt received considerable positive publicity. In hindsight, it is obvious that this was unwarranted. Cabinet ministers and EU representatives praised the project on numerous occasions. Media attention was particularly intense when the establishment of a new site was announced. Peter Carlsson was exposed in international press next to, e.g., Canadian Prime Minister Justin Trudeau and the German Chancellor Olaf Scholz only a few months before the bankruptcy. In Sweden, then Prime Minister Stefan Löfven praised the company, asserting that "the entire world can now see that the future is in Skellefteå and that these batteries will have a great impact on the green transition."

In Sweden, several other cabinet ministers and party leaders expressed hope and optimism related to Northvolt's expansion. The Social Democratic Minister for Business, Industry and Innovation, Karl-Petter Thorwaldsson spoke of a "rural revival" and stated that he had never before "encountered such optimism."

In May 2022, Mr. Thorwaldsson, together with two other Social Democratic ministers, authored an op-ed in Dagens Nyheter declaring that "northern Sweden is world-leading in the climate transition."

Upon announcing the establishment of a new site in Borlänge in 2023, Peter Carlsson declared: "We are delighted to contribute to the creation of this new chapter in Borlänge's history as a global industrial hub." One year later, Northvolt announced that this establishment had to be canceled due to financial difficulties.

Former Prime Minister Stefan Löfven, like his colleague Thorwaldsson, was enthusiastic. On October 18, 2021, he proclaimed (on national public service television) that "this is enormous, and progress has been relatively swift for a project of this complexity" and continued saying that "the world can see that the future lies in Skellefteå."

In a speech, the Prime Minister gave more praise: "I grew up in the 1960s and 1970s when people were moving south in droves. At that time there were few jobs here; now, the trend has reversed."

Upon the Prime Minister's visit to Skellefteå, Northvolt's then Head of Communications, Anders Thor, wrote on LinkedIn: "Today, Stefan Löfven is visiting Northvolt Ett. Cut flowers are not very sustainable, so we are welcoming him with two new circular factories in Skellefteå and Örnsköldsvik." Before joining Northvolt, Mr. Thor served as advisor and speechwriter to Prime Minister Löfven.[4]

Politicians from conservative parties were also enthusiastic about Northvolt's growth. It is worth noting, however, that the Northvolt boom took place during the years 2018–2022, when the Social Democrats governed in coalition with the Green Party.

In the summer of 2023, Conservative Prime Minister Ulf Kristersson described Swedish industry as "the new environmental movement." During his visit to Northvolt's experimental plant in Västerås on November 23, 2022, Kristersson asserted (on public service radio) that "this really is the technological frontier." On national public service television, he declared that "there are only a few countries in the world capable of these things, and we are becoming one of them."

Senior politicians in Brussels also paved the way for Northvolt. EU Energy Commissioner Maroš Šefčovič stated in 2017 that by 2025, the EU will be self-sufficient in electric vehicle batteries.

Positive Media Coverage

Using a media archive database, it is possible to obtain aggregate figures regarding media coverage. As shown in the Fig. 3 below, attention surrounding Northvolt increased significantly during the years 2018–2023.

Whether this attention was positive or negative can be further analyzed by examining the occurrence of keyword combinations. Figure 4 shows the number of press articles in Swedish media that include the term "Northvolt" as well as either "world-unique" or "world-leading." The number of such articles increased sharply in 2020–2021.

Media and the Northvolt Crisis

At the onset of the Northvolt crisis in autumn 2024, media and politicians seemed reluctant to express any critique concerning mismanagement. "There is nothing to be ashamed of," commented Frida Wallnor on *Dagens Industri's* editorial page on November 21, when the company initiated its Chapter 11 restructuring.

Conservative Minister for Energy, Business and Industry, Ebba Busch from the Christian Democrats, asserted on Swedish public service radio in November 2024 that "[t]his is a company with a unique product—one that is high quality, truly green,

[4] After leaving Northvolt, a few months before the bankruptcy, Anders Thor joined the Association for Swedish Energy Companies as Head of the Department for Energy and Policy with the aim of "driving the transition toward a fossil-free Sweden by 2045" according to his LinkedIn profile (September 2025).

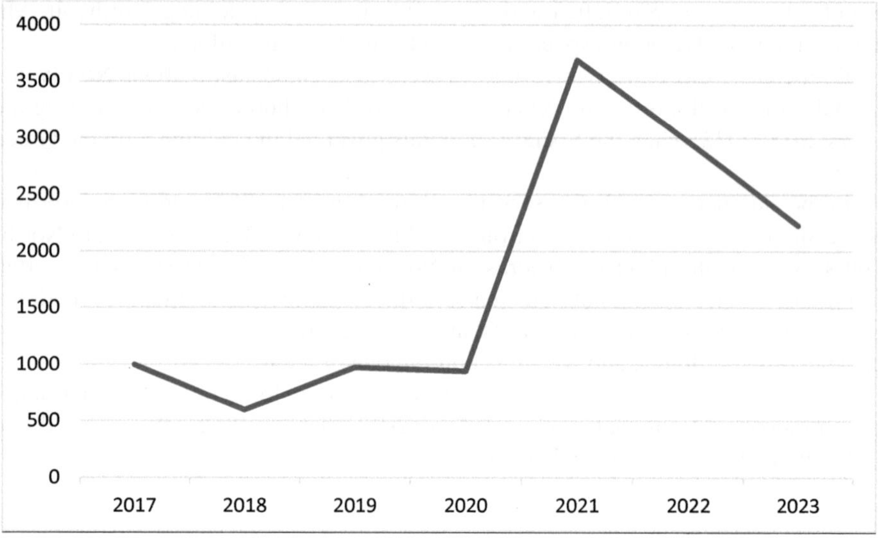

Fig. 3 Number of press articles concerning Northvolt, 2017–2023 *Source Mediearkivet,* 2017–2023

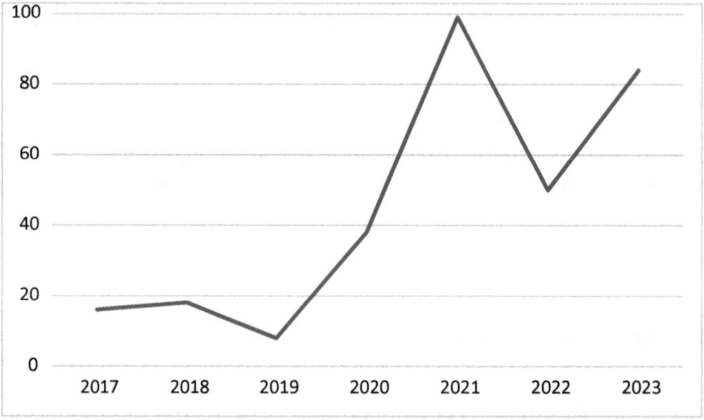

Fig. 4 Number of press articles where Northvolt is described as "world-leading" or "world-unique," 2017–2023 *Source Mediearkivet*, 2017–2023

and sustainable." Bearing in mind that Northvolt had hardly produced any batteries on their own due to severe operational problems, this assertion is remarkable.

Former Minister of Industry and Northvolt shareholder Anders Sundström said in an interview with *Affärsvärlden* (published November 16, 2024) that he would like to see state support for Northvolt.

Analysis and Discussion

This section analyzes how and why Northvolt failed and relates the case to the mechanisms of green industrial policy. Several factors contributed to the rapid rise and spectacular fall of the firm.

Lack of Capabilities

In the end, Northvolt could not compete against China as the firm lacked the requisite expertise in battery technology and manufacturing. Literature in both strategic management and innovation policy underscores that capabilities take time to develop and require considerable efforts (Alves 2024). To scale up and establish new sites across the globe without prior industry experience proved infeasible.

Interviewees confirm that Northvolt's CEO Peter Carlsson did not possess strong manufacturing knowledge. Co-founders Harald Mix and the Vargas group had extensive experience in the buyout sector but little knowledge and experience regarding the challenges related to starting new businesses in a sophisticated manufacturing industry facing competitors with decades of experience.

This persistent gap in capabilities was also present both in Sweden and at Northvolt's main production site in Skellefteå. The city had no previous experience of such megaprojects, and it had neither a university nor a labor market with relevant expertise. Northvolt worked hard to offset this lack of expertise and manpower by recruiting internationally. More than 50 nationalities were represented at the Skellefteå site. In the end, these efforts proved insufficient.

Rent Seeking and Political Capitalism

The Northvolt case also illustrates how rent-seeking mechanisms (Muldoon and Yonai 2023) enabled access to vast pools of public funding. The company skillfully crafted strategies to obtain R&D grants, "green loans" and other forms of funding.

Political allocation of resources faces the risk that companies that are better at lobbying end up getting most support. This seems to have been the case with Northvolt as it obtained large pools of capital that were not matched with corresponding technical and operational capabilities.

The fact that Northvolt could attract such extensive resources and grow to almost 6,000 employees despite lacking capabilities can be attributed to other skills. Northvolt and its founders possessed a unique combination of political and financial capabilities. Former cabinet ministers and other people with excellent political contacts took on roles as advisors and lobbyists and were offered shares before the company had attained a significant market value. In return, they seem to have used their political connections to help unlock large pools of public funding, both in Sweden, the EU and in other countries where Northvolt planned to locate new plants.

Moral Hazard

Moonshot policies have often been justified by an alleged "crowding in" of private capital. Mariana Mazzucato contends that public funding does not "crowd out" private funding but instead helps to mobilize it toward socially desirable objectives (Deleidi and Mazzucato 2019).[5]

The Northvolt case illustrates that this might very well be the case, at least at the level of an individual company. Northvolt would not have expanded so rapidly without public funding, which in turn attracted large amounts of private funds. Both quotes and data on Northvolt's public funding from, e.g., Germany and Canada suggest that public funding lured the company into these initiatives. In this sense, a "crowding in" effect did take place.

At the same time, this mechanism creates a dilemma. Moral hazard means that an economic actor takes on too much risk because the downside is born by someone else. While considerable amounts of shareholder equity from companies such as Volkswagen and Goldman Sachs were also invested, it seems that public funds attracted private money. This combination also induced Northvolt to assume too much risk. Efforts to set up manufacturing facilities became out of touch with the underlying technological and economic realities of Sweden and Europe as global expansion was fueled by government money.

In effect, the "crowding in" of private money meant that public resources fueled a bubble as more private equity was mobilized into an initiative which in hindsight seemed almost bound to fail.

Behavioral Biases

As domestic battery production became a political priority for decision-makers in Sweden and across Europe, the initiative was bolstered by strong public support. For years, neither the media nor policymakers and academics subjected Northvolt to serious scrutiny—until the crisis erupted with the first wave of layoffs in September 2024.

For politicians, each new press release announcing a new factory constituted an opportunity to instill a sense of progress and development among the public at large.

[5] Deleidi and Mazzucato's (2019, p. 319) claim that "mission-oriented policies have the potential to generate the largest positive effect on investments and output growth as well as on innovation processes and labor productivity growth" has been empirically rebutted by Boysen-Hogrefe (2025).

The opportunity for politicians and other interests to claim a share of the accolades was an additional benefit. The political logic of grand openings and inaugurations and rhetoric about reindustrialization is close to irresistible. Whether the production facilities ultimately materialize or whether there is any realism underpinning these announcements seems secondary, at least in the short term.

Combined with a growing sense of urgency over environmental matters, this logic paved the way for creating a "loss frame." A loss frame can be established when societal problems are considered to be of such a large magnitude that bold investments are warranted, however risky (Schnellenbach 2024). Charismatic leaders like Peter Carlsson thrive in such a consensus-oriented and alarmist media environment.

Conclusion: "Picking Winners" versus "Creating Losers"

The Northvolt crash is one of the most extensive bankruptcies in modern European history. As such, the case starkly illustrates how Green Deals may result in green bubbles.

Critics of industrial policy and government innovation efforts typically assert that governments cannot "pick winners." Rooted in evolutionary economics, this argument underscores the inherently uncertain and unpredictable co-evolution of businesses and technology and why policymaking cannot replace this evolutionary process by administrative decision-making.

The evidence suggests that the problem is not limited to the difficulty of governments "picking winners." Instead, green industrial strategies may actively foster firms that are ill-prepared to compete—in effect, they end up "creating losers." Put differently, green deal policies nurture behavior and capabilities among firms, which make them skilled at appeasing policymakers and obtaining public funds. But at the same time, they become uncompetitive actors in the marketplace.

A couple of mechanisms jointly contribute to the "creating losers" dilemma. Public support distorts incentives and gives rise to moral hazard. Firms become skilled at obtaining political favors rather than creating products that are competitive in the marketplace (Holcombe 2018). In effect, they become "subsidy entrepreneurs" (Gustafsson et al. 2020). As industrial megaprojects which are labeled as "green" tend to receive more positive attention and be subject to less scrutiny expectations rise. Behavioral biases kick in and steer public discussions toward favoring the mission (Schnellenbach 2024). Unless these patterns are understood and mitigated, the risk of turning green ambitions into costly failures will only grow.

References

Alves, A. C. (2024). The cost of missions: The case of shipbuilding in Brazil. In M. Henrekson, C. Sandström, & M. Stenkula (Eds.), *Moonshots and the New Industrial Policy: Questioning the*

Mission Economy (pp. 169–189). Cham: Springer. https://doi.org/10.1007/978-3-031-49196-2_10

Boysen-Hogrefe, J. (2025). Is the supermultiplier nil? A replication study of Deleidi and Mazzucato (2021). *Research Policy, 54*(3), Article 105176. https://doi.org/10.1016/j.respol.2025.105176

Deleidi, M., & Mazzucato, M. (2019). Putting austerity to bed: Technical progress, aggregate demand and the supermultiplier. *Review of Political Economy, 31*(3), 315–335. https://doi.org/10.1080/09538259.2019.1687146

European Commission (2020). The European Green Deal Investment Plan and Just Transition Mechanism explained. https://ec.europa.eu/commission/presscorner/detail/en/qanda_20_24

Gustafsson, A., Gustavsson Tingvall, P., & Halvarsson, D. (2020). Subsidy entrepreneurs: An inquiry into firms seeking public grants. *Journal of Industry, Competition and Trade, 20*(3), 439–478. https://doi.org/10.1007/s10842-019-00317-0

Henrekson, M., Sandström, C., & Stenkula, M. (Eds.) (2024a). *Moonshots and the New Industrial Policy: Questioning the Mission Economy*. Cham: Springer. https://doi.org/10.1007/978-3-031-49196-2

Henrekson, M., Sandström, C., & Stenkula, M. (2024b). Seven reasons why mission-oriented innovation policies seldom work in practice. *Economic Affairs, 44*(2), 354–362. https://doi.org/10.1111/ecaf.12654

Holcombe, R. G. (2018). *Political Capitalism: How Political Influence Is Made and Maintained.* Cambridge: Cambridge University Press.

Lucas, D. S., & Boudreaux, C. J. (2024). When "what works" does not work: The United States' mission to end homelessness. In M. Henrekson, C. Sandström, & M. Stenkula (Eds.), *Moonshots and the New Industrial Policy: Questioning the Mission Economy* (pp. 145–168). Cham: Springer. https://doi.org/10.1007/978-3-031-49196-2_9

Mazzucato, M. (2018). *Mission-Oriented Research & Innovation in the European Union: A Problem-Solving Approach to Fuel Innovation-Led Growth.* Luxembourg: Publications Office of the European Union.

Mazzucato, M. (2022). Financing the green new deal. *Nature Sustainability, 5*(2), 93–94. https://doi.org/10./s41893-021-00828-x

Muldoon, J., & Yonai, D. K. (2023). A wrong but seductive idea: Public choice and the entrepreneurial state. *Journal of the International Council for Small Business, 4*(4), 1–11. https://doi.org/10.1080/26437015.2023.2182730

Sandström, C. (2025). *Northvoltkraschen [The Northvolt Crash].* Stockholm: Timbro förlag.

Sandström, C., & Alm, C. (2022). Directionality in innovation policy and the ongoing failure of green deals: Evidence from biogas, bio-ethanol, and fossil-free steel. In K. Wennberg & C. Sandström (Eds.), *Questioning the Entrepreneurial State: Status-quo, Pitfalls, and the Need for Credible Innovation Policy* (pp. 251–269). Cham: Springer. https://doi.org/10.1007/978-3-030-94273-1_14

Schnellenbach, J. (2024). A behavioral economics perspective on the entrepreneurial state and mission-oriented innovation policy. In M. Henrekson, C. Sandström, & M. Stenkula (Eds.), *Moonshots and the New Industrial Policy: Questioning the Mission Economy* (pp. 61–76). Cham: Springer. https://doi.org/10.1007/978-3-031-49196-2_4

Waldron, K., & Coyne, C. J. (2024). You can't develop what you don't know: The realities and limitations of foreign aid missions. In M. Henrekson, C. Sandström, & M. Stenkula (Eds.), *Moonshots and the New Industrial Policy: Questioning the Mission Economy* (pp. 191–212). Cham: Springer. https://doi.org/10.1007/978-3-031-49196-2_11

Wennberg, K., & Sandström, C. (Eds.) (2022). *Questioning the Entrepreneurial State: Status-quo, Pitfalls, and the Need for Credible Innovation Policy*. Cham: Springer.

Youtube (2020). BUSINESSEUROPE Day 2020—5 March—Carl-Erik Lagercrantz. https://www.youtube.com/watch?v=XSYnXyZz5gs

Christian Sandström is Associate Professor of Technology Management from Chalmers University of Technology, where he also received his doctoral degree (2010). His research concerns innovation policy and the interplay between technological and institutional change. Sandström is one of the editors of *Questioning the Entrepreneurial State* (Springer) and *Moonshots and the New Industrial Policy* (Springer). He has published more than 30 papers in peer-reviewed academic journals, such as *Business History, Small Business Economics, Technological Forecasting & Social Change*, and *Industry & Innovation.*

Sandström wrote his PhD thesis on the topic of disruptive innovation. He has been a visiting scholar at the University of Cambridge and ETH Zürich in Switzerland. Sandström has received several awards for his pedagogical skills and is a frequently invited public speaker on the topic of technological change and industrial transformation.

The Planetary Diet: An Illusory Recipe

Stefan Hellstrand and Johan Gärdebo

Abstract In 2025, the Swedish Food Agency introduced dietary guidelines promoting a shift from meat and dairy to plant-based proteins, aligning with the global "planetary diet" concept to support a sustainable food system within planetary boundaries. This paper critiques the weak scientific basis of these guidelines, highlighting their potential to undermine food security and agricultural stability in Sweden amidst a geopolitical crisis. It examines the bureaucratic momentum behind the green transition, driven by the EU, NGOs, and research bodies such as the Swedish Climate Policy Council, which advocate phasing out animal husbandry despite its historical significance in Nordic diets. The guidelines, ignoring governmental directives to prioritize food security, propose drastic reductions in red meat (65–82%) and dairy (54–70%) consumption, risking increased import reliance and biodiversity loss. The paper contrasts historical Nordic diets, reliant on animal husbandry due to harsh climates, with the planetary diet's unfeasible reductions, arguing that such policies could lead to political upheaval, as seen in European farmer protests and rising populist movements. The Swedish Climate Policy Council's ideological approach, rooted in the planetary boundaries framework, is criticized for neglecting practical agricultural realities, potentially exacerbating food insecurity and societal unrest.

Keywords Dietary guidelines · Planetary diet · Green transition · Food security · Animal husbandry · Agricultural policy · Planetary boundaries · Populist nationalism

---

Johan Gärdebo gratefully acknowledges financial support from FORMAS, the Swedish Research Council for Sustainable Development (Grant: The mediated planet: Claiming data for environmental SDGs).

S. Hellstrand
Ekostrategi i Fryksdalen AB, Kil, Sweden
e-mail: stefan.hellstrand@ekostrateg.se

J. Gärdebo (✉)
Clare Hall, University of Cambridge, Cambridge, UK
e-mail: jg2077@cam.ac.uk

M. Henrekson et al. (eds.), *A Green Entrepreneurial State?*, International Studies in Entrepreneurship 49, https://doi.org/10.1007/978-3-032-15512-2_12

JEL Codes K32 · L32 · Q18 · Q28

Introduction

In the Spring of 2025, the Swedish Food Agency presented new national dietary guidelines (Swedish Food Agency 2025a). In terms of food production, it would mean shifting from meat and dairy toward plant-based protein. As a science policy, these guidelines are linked to an overarching green transition promoted by policymakers in Sweden, the European Union, and the United Nations, toward a sustainable food system, a "planetary diet," operating within planetary boundaries.

Sweden's new dietary guidelines, and by continuation of the planetary diet, is an illustrative example of science policy lacking roots in an actual agricultural system and food production. This green transition, we argue, falls short both in terms of scientific backing and policy efficiency.

What we are concerned with here are the underlying forces promoting the planetary diet, and what consequences such an illusory recipe for our food system would set in motion at this point in history.

Until very recently, the green transition was the stated singular ambition of the European Commission. In particular, the EU Green Deal launched in 2019 directed all subsequent policies toward an overriding goal: making Europe the first climate-neutral continent by 2050. These claims were first found in scientific contexts that identified the planetary diet as a necessary innovation to bring about a transformation of society as a whole (Sachs et al. 2019). These claims were then picked up by policymaking bodies, rapidly becoming fundamental to Europe's various climate regulations and framed as a credible basis for a sustainable food system. This is why the EU's Farm-to-Fork Strategy, adopted in 2020, relied on the rationales of the planetary diet and repeated its claims that livestock farming be drastically decreased. These new policy priorities were then administered at the national level, monitored by government agencies, and advocated by an international community of research institutes, media platforms, and NGOs.

Together, the above-mentioned actors provide impetus and momentum for bureaucratic bloat surrounding green transition policies—a green bubble—whose key performance indicators are still more green policies. What these actors have in common is a shared conviction that animal husbandry is a net negative to be phased out of the European agricultural system (European Commission 2023). In just a few years, then, the planetary diet has become central to green transition policies reshaping food systems in all EU member states, albeit with somewhat differing regional effects.

Importantly, for Sweden, this planetary diet is what the Swedish Climate Policy Council believes to be the best model for a sustainable agricultural food system in northern Europe. Their task is to evaluate "how well the Government's overall policy is aligned with the climate goals established by the Swedish Parliament" (Swedish Climate Policy Council 2025a). And the Council's members are promoted as representatives of Sweden's scientific consensus, speaking on behalf of its research community, with regards to climate knowledge, policy, and politics (cf. Dagens Nyheter 2025).

In its 2025 annual report, the Swedish Climate Policy Council provided an in-depth review of Sweden's agricultural system, examining how agriculture could contribute to society's climate transition, and suggested policy changes to bring about this transition (Swedish Climate Policy Council 2025b). In brief, the Council advocates for the enforcement of the planetary diet. If Sweden were to adopt the planetary diet, the national consumption and production of milk would drop by 80%. And red meat would be reduced by 90%.

Another example is how the Swedish Food Agency replicates the dietary guidelines of the Nordic Nutrition Recommendations 2023 (Blomhoff et al. 2023), which in turn closely follows that of the planetary diet.[1] These guidelines, recommendations, and diets are important because they steer public procurement of food supplies, e.g., to schools and municipal homes. This steers the demand for plant and animal products in the Nordics. And the background reports to the Nordic Nutrition Recommendations on environmental sustainability (see Blomhoff et al. 2023) are used as a tool for *informing* children about how their personal choice of food affects planetary health.

We argue that the planetary diet, including the recommendations of the Swedish Climate Policy Council and guidelines of the Swedish Food Agency to follow that diet, are illustrative of the above-mentioned green bubbles.

It is a bubble that bloats the bureaucracies of policymakers and researchers, who have proven unable to correct course on their proposed green transition. Rather than simply replacing one source of nutrients with another, the planetary diet reduces the overall production capacity of the food system and aggravates its vulnerabilities in times of crisis or war. When tested against real-world pressure, what people in the past had to do to put food on the Nordic table, this bubble bursts.

To understand how green bubbles are formed, we will here look closer at the Swedish dietary guidelines of the Swedish Food Agency, in addition to its connections to reviews of Swedish agriculture and diets by the Swedish Climate Policy Council. These two, we argue, serve as case studies of relevance to anyone concerned about green transition policies as a whole.

After the 2022 election Sweden's new center–right Government made attempts at course correcting the green transition. With regard to the Swedish dietary guidelines, the government clarified that these should be written so as to contribute to safeguarding national food security, including the preservation of dairy and meat production. As we will demonstrate in this study, these instructions were ignored, ridiculed, and opposed by the actors mentioned above, despite the planetary diet lacking sufficient scientific basis and societal support.

---

[1] The Nordic Nutrition Recommendations 2023 (NNR) were developed as part of a project supported by the Nordic Council of Ministers.

Europe's uncertain geopolitical situation as of September 2025 is a stark reminder of the importance of locally rooted food production. And that the *planetary* diet lacks this necessary ingredient of being rooted in a *particular* place.

In the following sections, we describe why Sweden, the Nordic region, and the European Union can ill afford the planetary diet. We argue that it is an illusory recipe, beginning with an examination of the "meal" itself—namely, the political upheavals that follow from implementing a planetary diet. Next, we review the diet's "ingredients," juxtaposing historical Nordic diets with present-day Swedish dietary guidelines in order to compare and contrast the scientific basis of the planetary diet with that of actual diets. Finally, we turn to "the chef": the Swedish Climate Policy Council, which represents the research community and its allies who, for well over a decade, have been avid proponents of the green transition and the main beneficiaries of the green bubble that is now about to burst.

The Meal—Planetary Diet Begets Political Upheaval

For starters, to understand what is at stake concerning Sweden's new dietary guidelines, pay attention to the central role that agricultural policies play in what is currently an ongoing political realignment throughout the Western world.

One striking indication of this political realignment is the emergence of national populist movements in a number of European countries as a reaction to the EU in 2019 declaring a state of climate emergency whereafter the Commission embarked on a number of ambitious green transition policies (European Parliament 2019).

In the Netherlands, the green transition involved close collaborations between activistic NGOs, the judiciary, and government officials who sought to limit agricultural nitrogen fertilizers in support of the aforementioned planetary diet. They mapped areas where nitrogen accumulated, highly correlating with agriculture relying on animal husbandry, and subsequently told farmers to decrease their input of fertilizers or be forced to close down. In effect, the Dutch Supreme Court's ruling meant phasing out meat and dairy and a shift toward plant-based protein. The center–right government, in turn, then moved ahead with implementing the court's ruling as part of the Netherland's policy for a green transition of its agricultural sector.

The reaction that followed was an unprecedented surge in populist nationalism in opposition to the Dutch government's transition policies. In the 2023 election, the newly formed Farmer-Citizen Movement secured 30% of votes in the upper chamber of parliament, followed by national electoral victory for Geert Wilders's populist Party of Freedom.

Then, throughout the Spring of 2024, European farmers all over Europe organized national protests, in addition to descending on Brussel. In large numbers, tractors blocked highways and forklifted barricades. Farmers sprayed manure onto government buildings. Riot police responded in kind by soaking farmers using water cannons. The sky turned black from smoke rising from piles of burning tires.

These clashes between protesting farmers and police took place in relation to the European Parliament passing its Nature Restoration Law. Similar to the court ruling in the Netherlands, the EU Nature Restoration Law risked disrupting EU's agricultural supply chains and drive-up food prices for consumers. The larger questions at play here concerned what until recently had been a cornerstone of the EU as a unifying political project, namely its common agricultural policy of subsidizing farmers to stimulate food production.

Hypocrisy on the part of the EU then added insult to injury. After years of logistically disruptive Covid mandates, farmers found themselves not only financially strained but also under pressure from cheap Ukrainian imports after the EU waived duties in 2022. It emerged that, until recently, European environmental regulations imposed on farmers in the EU were not applied to food imported from Ukraine—under the pretext of supporting the war effort. The cumulative effect of such policies has harmed European farmers, contributed to a continued decline in their numbers, and weakened overall preparedness against food shortages.

The Dutch court ruling demonstrates that policymakers have the volition and momentum to circumvent popular concerns regarding domestic food production as part of pursuing an internationally mandated green transition. And, in turn, it demonstrates how populist nationalists were able to build broad coalitions around the question of food sovereignty.

What is at stake in the years to come are food riots and subsequent political upheavals that may continue to spread across Europe. To help avert these risks, it is now relevant to examine more closely why certain diets succeed where others fail, and why certain research communities persist in promoting the scientific claims underpinning the planetary diet.

The Ingredients—The Nordic Diet

What constitutes dietary guidelines in a region or country in its original sense largely reflects the character of its agriculture. Anyone interested in policies aimed at transitioning from one form of agriculture to another must first examine, historically, which diets or food systems that were able to sustain life in that region. To illustrate this point in relation to the planetary diet and its influence on present-day Swedish dietary guidelines, we must first look to the history of the Nordic diet.

The first known writings on European agriculture, which featured Nordic conditions, were recorded by the geographer Pytheas of Marseille around 300 BCE. In the lands to the North, he had been told during his travels, nights would last half of the year. Seasons for growing crops were short and harsh. Rains were so frequent that harvested crops must be threshed indoors to avoid rotting away (Roseman 1994).

Pytheas' observation on northern Europe's agriculture, cited at the opening of a five-set volume on the history of Swedish agriculture, is that peoples and lands coevolved.[2] The harsh Nordic climate conditions meant large populations of humans could only be sustained by combining farming with animal husbandry (Myrdal 1998).

For thousands of years, Scandinavian settlements kept vast pastures in order for livestock to add a rich source of nourishment for both humans and the soil itself. In this way European agriculture could be seen as naturally transitioning, from crops growing in the south to cattle grazing in the north. Animals transform biomass from photosynthesis that is indigestible for humans, for example grasses and leaves, into high quality food. Scandinavians found a way to sustain larger populations through meat and dairy.

The genetic expression of Northern Europe's historical reliance on animal husbandry is that over 90% of Sweden's adults have the capacity to digest lactose (cf. Swedish Food Agency 2025b) while the degree of lactose tolerance in Central and Western Europe ranges from 60 to 90% (Itan et al. 2010). This is because most of these populations descend from people who evolved in environments that gave strong selection advantages to mutations for processing and tolerating lactose. A high share of lactose tolerance can be found in regions around the world where animal husbandry is of great importance to food security.

On a global level, 35–43% of adults have the capacity to digest lactose (Itan et al. 2010; Catanzaro et al. 2021). There are regions in Africa and Asia where people have similarly high levels of lactose tolerance as those in Northern and Western Europe. This is because the ecological conditions for agriculture in these places are similarly harsh. It is not easy to grow wheat, rice, maize, or soybeans in boreal Scandinavia, the Scottish Highlands, or along the deserts of Northwestern Africa and Saudi Arabia.

It was not until food production from plants was combined with animals that agriculture could progress into northern Europe. This took thousands of years and with long intervening periods before plants domesticated in the Levantine Crescent and Asia were transplanted to northern Europe and could be relied on for sustaining larger settlements in the Baltics and Scandinavia. Therefore, agricultural products have constituted a substantial part of the Nordic diet for a mere 4,000 years. And it did so because animal husbandry could produce sufficient amounts of manure needed to nourish and sustain a limited production of grains for direct human consumption (Stock et al. 2023).

In relation to the green transition and policies for a planetary diet, it is relevant to describe the historical impact that animal husbandry, and the lack thereof, have had on the Nordic diet. This can be traced archaeologically by measuring the average length and body size of northern Europeans and how that relates to dietary changes, for example as a result of a crisis, from war or a changing climate, that led to diminished food production and disrupted supply chains (Figs. 1 and 2).

During the early agricultural phase in what is today Sweden, beginning around 3300 BCE, the diet relied on a combination of food from animals and plants, with

[2] *The History of Swedish Agriculture* (Original in Swedish, *Fembandsverket: Det svenska jordbrukets historia*), edited by Janken Myrdal, consists of five volumes, totaling 2,109 pages and published between 1998 and 2001. All volumes can be accessed through the Royal Swedish Academy of Agriculture and Forestry, https://www.ksla.se/bibliotek/fembandsverket/.

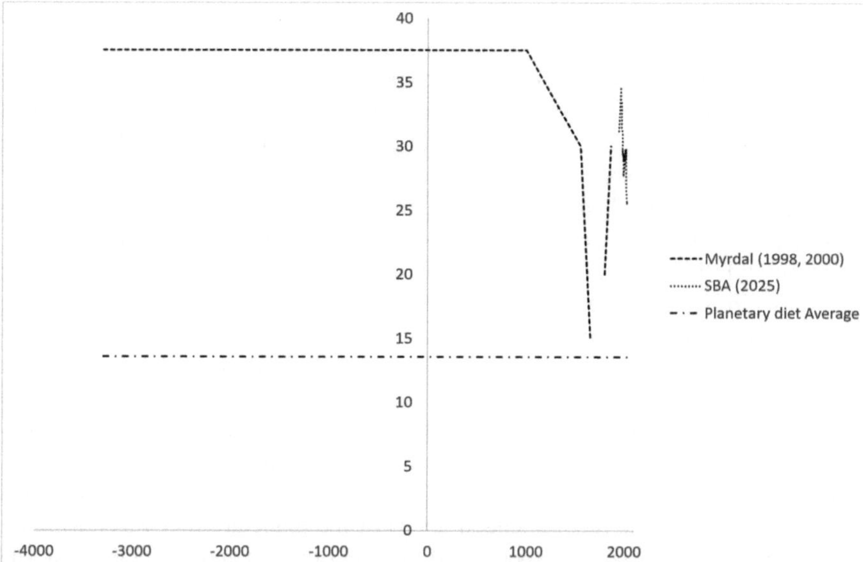

Fig. 1 Share of animal products (%) in the diet on an energy-basis from early agriculture until the present in Sweden, 3300 BCE to 2023 CE. *Source* Eurostat, authors' processing of data from Myrdal (1998, 2000), Morell (1987), and data from the Swedish Board of Agriculture (2025a)

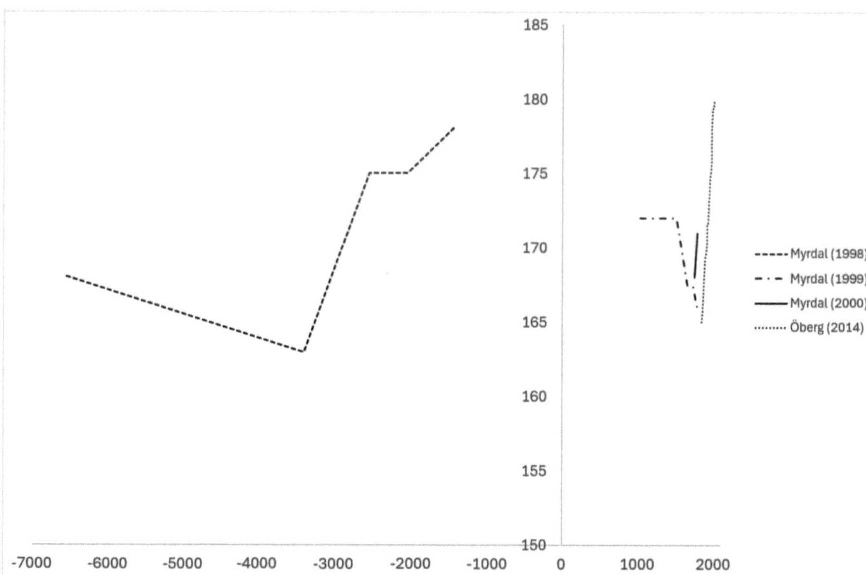

Fig. 2 Estimates of length of men in Sweden from before the introduction of agriculture until the year 2000 CE. *Source* Authors' processing of data from Myrdal (1998, 1999, 2000) and Öberg (2014)

35–40% derived from hunting and husbandry. During this period, populations across Europe were on average taller in the northern and western regions.

Then, in the early modern period from 1500 to 1800, the length of Swedish males declined by approximately 10 cm. During this period the fraction of animal products in the Nordic diet halved, from 30 to 15% of the total energy supply. This decrease was the result of less nutritious diets, which corresponded in part with the period's harsher climate, the so-called Little Ice Age, and numerous wars (Mann 2003). After this period, the fraction of animal products in the diet increased again. It is only just now, in modern times, that Nordic males on average reach the same length as their counterparts in Northern Europe during the Bronze Age (Fig. 2).

In Fig. 1 we have included a reference average for the planetary diet (cf. Springmann et al. 2018; Willett et al. 2019), which we will discuss in-depth below. The aim with juxtaposing this reference to the planetary diet next to historical dietary estimates is to clarify the degree to which the planetary diet differs from all diets that ever existed in Sweden—from 3300 BCE until the present.

Note that the only time when the estimated share of animal products in total energy supply was as low as the recommended levels of the planetary diet was during the 1500s to 1800s when Sweden experienced tougher climatic and societal conditions (cf. Morell 1987) and the length of adult men was at its lowest estimate during the period from 6,550 years BCE to the year 2000 CE (Fig. 2).

The estimate for male length around 1450 BCE was 178 cm, and around 172 cm during the 1500s. By the end of the 1700s it had dropped to 166 cm, while it began to increase in the early 1800s. This length increase is associated with what in economic history is often referred to as a sequence of agricultural revolutions, where crop rotations developed in symbioses with improvements in animal husbandry, especially milk production (Morell 2022). During the 1800s, total agricultural land in Sweden remained fairly constant, while permanent pastures were transformed to arable land.

When analyzing long-term trends of global and regional agriculture by the primary global data source for agriculture—that is, forestry and food from FAO-statistics covering the period 1961 until present—global agricultural developments demonstrate similar trends to that of Sweden during the 1800s and onward. To our judgment, global agriculture has since mid-1900s repeated a recipe for success that in the Nordic region withstood the test of time.

Outlining a longer-term perspective on the Nordic diet is important, as it provides the foundation for a more practical approach to what is today referred to as *sustainability*.[3] A sustainable food system, in essence, concerns how specific peoples have managed to sustain themselves in particular places over extended periods of time, including during times of crisis.

---

[3] *Our Common Future* by the United Nations World Commission on Environment and Development, published in 1987 (UN 1987), often referred to as the Brundtland Report, has long been foundational to debates on sustainability. In particular, it envisaged sustainable development as three interconnected dimensions: environmental, economic, and social. For a further discussion on the Brundtland Report and sustainability in relation to a variety of long-term environmental and social implications, see Fahlén et al. (2026).

When it comes to sustaining food production, what Pytheas observed about the ancient Nordic diet still resonated with policymakers drafting the first modern Swedish dietary guidelines in 1916. These guidelines were formulated in response to the disruptions of World War I, which posed new challenges for securing food production in an industrial society with large urban populations. With Sweden's supply chains severely disrupted, the concern was not only how to safeguard public nutritional health, but also how to avert food riots and maintain social order. Similar dynamics fueled tensions in neighboring Finland, ultimately culminating in civil war.

Having reviewed the history of Nordic diets and the origins of Sweden's modern dietary guidelines, we now turn to the present-day guidelines and to why their implementation would have far-reaching consequences for the country's food security.

The Swedish Food Agency's Dietary Guidelines

The Swedish Government's directive (SweGov 2023) to the Swedish Food Agency, issued on June 15, 2023, was "to analyze, based on the Nordic Nutrition Recommendations 2023, how environmental sustainability aspects may affect Swedish food production and update the Swedish dietary guidelines." The dietary guidelines should be crafted to support Swedish preparedness for food security in times of crisis and war, to increase food production, and do so based on foods that Sweden has good natural conditions to produce. A second directive, issued on December 19, 2024, demanded a deeper analysis of the consequences of new dietary guidelines on the consumption and production of red meat (SweGov 2024).

In brief, the Swedish Government conceived these updated dietary guidelines as being essential to establishing its national food strategy. These guidelines were intended to increase food production and do so in a way that could be sustained during times of trouble.

How, then, were public health and preparedness reflected in the Swedish Food Agency's updated guidelines? The new guidelines (Swedish Food Agency 2025a) imply an average intake of milk and milk products of 425 g milk equivalents per capita and day, and a maximum intake of red meat on an individual level of 350 g per week.

The Swedish Food Agency claimed these guidelines would have no or only minor impacts on domestic milk and red meat production. For milk, the Agency (2025a) presumed that the guideline was in line with current levels of consumption. For red meat, the Agency presumed that only a minority of Swedes would actually follow the guidelines (see also Swedish Food Agency 2025c).

We argue, on the contrary, that the impacts of these dietary guidelines are profound. To understand why this is, and why the Swedish Food Agency is mistaken in its conclusions, require some unpacking of the details in these guidelines.

The Swedish Food Agency (2025a) links its updated guidelines regarding milk to the dietary patterns of adults measured more than a decade ago. In a study from 2012, a representative sample of 5,000 Swedes between the ages 18 and 80 were invited to report on their food habits. Of these, 1,797 men and women chose to participate and, during four consecutive days reported everything they ate and drank using a web-based "food diary" (Swedish Food Agency 2012).

By way of statistical materials, this investigation is not strong enough to be used for drawing conclusions about consumption patterns at the level of Sweden's entire population level more than a decade later. These speculations on dietary guidelines, furthermore, say little about how one is to develop national food production that is fit for times of crisis or war.

A more reliable source on the production and consumption would be to use statistics provided by the Swedish Board of Agriculture. These allow for consideration of losses in overall consumption, as well as losses at the levels of retail distribution and households. Such calculations can be carried out at both regional and national scales, for example by estimating the extent to which a population's physiological requirements for energy, fat, and protein can be met from milk and red meat. Conversely, one can also estimate the impact of the planetary diet in terms of its inability to meet these physiological requirements. In turn, this outcome translates into lost income for farmers in the affected regions (cf. Hellstrand et al. 2024).

If we rely on recent statistics by the Swedish Board of Agriculture (2025b), their estimate of milk products consumed in Sweden implies a consumption of 1,027 g per capita and day. This is also the method used by FAOstat, the database from FAO that gives the official data internationally. When correcting for losses at the level of retail stores and households, the estimate of 1,027 g per capita and day transforms to an average intake of 950 g per capita and day. Taken together, this gives a reduction by 54% in the consumption and production of milk as a result of following the Swedish Food Agency's new dietary guidelines.

Regarding the estimates of the dietary guideline's impact on red meat, we argue that the Swedish Food Agency faces a similar significant methodological problem.

The task from the Swedish Government was to evaluate and formulate guidelines that could be adapted to the natural settings of Sweden when planning production of sufficient quantities and qualities of food. Furthermore, these guidelines should contribute to increased national food production also in times of crisis.

Moving on to meat, then: how much would the Swedish dietary guidelines reduce the consumption of red and processed meat at population level? One problem with assessing this is that the guidelines are formulated as a maximum individual intake. But at the population level, you have the case that people consume little or no meat at all, and others consume significantly more.

So where can a population average intake be in relation to the maximum individual intake set by the Swedish Food Agency? The answer is found in an appendix to a joint report by the Public Health Agency of Sweden and the Swedish Food Agency (2024). Here it is stated that in order to ensure no individual exceeds the recommended maximum, the average intake at population level should not surpass 60% of the individual limit.[4]

[4] In particular, see Public Health Agency of Sweden and Swedish Food Agency (2024, p. 121).

This means the new dietary guidelines that the consumption of red meat should not exceed 350 g per week de facto translates to a far lower amount. As an average at population level, the consumption per capita in Sweden amounts to no more than 210 g per week.

Similar to when we assessed Sweden's current consumption of milk, we again rely on the market-balances of the Swedish Board of Agriculture (2025b) to get the best possible estimate of the per capita consumption of red meat in Sweden. For the year 2024, the estimate provided by the Board is a consumption of 519 g red meat per capita and week.

We then arrive at a reduction of red meat by ca 60%, which stands in critical contrast to claims by the Swedish Food Agency that the updated dietary guidelines would only reduce Swedish production by ca 1–3% (cf. 2025c, p. 86).

Up until now, we have discussed the impact of the Swedish dietary guidelines in quantitative terms, i.e., grams of dairy or meat. But the Swedish Food Agency also includes a general recommendation to avoid animal fats, such as lard and tallow.

These discrepancies are not minor details. The Swedish Food Agency claims that the effects on animal production are negligible, when in fact they will have major consequences for Swedish animal husbandry and, by extension, for national preparedness in the event of crises or wartime supply disruptions.

Reducing domestic production of milk and red meat would inevitably increase reliance on imports of plant-based alternatives. Based on FAOstat's publicly available data on food production and consumption from 2022, an increased Swedish demand for plant-based substitutes would place additional pressure on 1.5 million hectares of cropland in Brazil. The corresponding figure for the EU is 65 million hectares. All else being equal, this would aggravate global deforestation by precisely these amounts. If we use the same methods for estimating carbon dioxide released from clearcutting one hectare of forest (cf. FAO 2006), the one-time emission from deforestation as a result of Sweden adopting the planetary diet would equal 22 times that of Sweden's total annual emission in 2022. If the planetary diet were to be adopted at the EU level, the one-time emissions generated would have exceeded 13 times that of the Union's total greenhouse gas emissions in 2022.[5]

This can be understood as a quantification of the "green bubble" generated by the new Swedish guidelines—expressed in terms of biodiversity loss, destruction of tropical forests, and increased greenhouse gas emissions.

Such increases in import dependency, particularly outside the EU, represent a significant security risk in an increasingly unstable geopolitical climate. Yet, this is exactly what is proposed: a 54–70% reduction in milk consumption and production, and a 65–82% reduction in the consumption and production of pork, beef, lamb, poultry, and reindeer meat.

The lower range of these estimates reflects only the effect of reduced consumption quantities, while the higher range incorporates the additional effect of choosing low-fat meat and avoiding all animal fats. Taken together, the impact on the energy supply from milk products and red meat would reduce availability by 74% for energy, 85%

[5] For further details on methodology for these estimates, see Hellstrand (2013).

for fat, and 55% for protein when accounting for both reduced quantities and the requirement to choose low-fat products and substitute animal fats with plant-based alternatives.

It is worth reiterating that the Swedish Food Agency fail to report on these impacts. And they fail to do so despite having access to, and even cite, the official sources where such impacts are described.

When providing recommendations on the consumption of milk and milk products, the Swedish Food Agency (2025a) advises that a greater share should come from domestic production for environmental reasons. The same recommendation is given for red meat.[6] However, this reasoning is misleading. First, while choosing Swedish meat may work for the average family, this option is not available to the large-scale households such as schools and hospitals since it violates public procurement laws in both Sweden and the EU. These laws forbid giving preference to domestically produced milk and meat over products from other EU countries. Secondly, beyond Sweden's own dietary guidelines, the EU has instituted several regulations aimed at further reducing milk and red meat consumption.

One example of these regulatory preferences is the European academies' science advice for policy (Science Advice for Policy by European Academies 2020, 2023) that serve as scientific foundation for EU's climate agricultural policies (European Environment Agency 2023). These science advisories advocate using the planetary diet as a guide for the EU food system as a whole. This would reduce Europe's animal husbandry by 75% over the period 2019 and 2050.[7] If combined with data from the Science Advice for Policy by European Academies (2023), enforcing the planetary diet would shift 50% of agricultural land now used for food production in the EU—82 million hectares, which equals the total land area of Denmark, Sweden, and Finland—toward mainly producing biofuels, around 55 million hectares. The remaining 27 million hectares of Europe's agricultural land would then be used for nature restoration, including forest that for decades would serve as a carbon sink.

The purpose of these dietary regulations, in brief, is to make the planetary diet the norm for European public procurement laws. These are policy priorities touted by various researchers that shine through in the Swedish Food Agency's dietary guidelines. The impact of the dietary guidelines is a reduction in consumption and production of red meat (by 65–82%) and dairy (by 54–70%), respectively. This would cause a significant economic loss for Swedish farmers. At the national level, it would weaken the food supply chain. As game and reindeer are parts of red meat, this would also limit the means for reindeer husbandry by the Sápmi community. At the local level, the consequences would be equally severe or even greater, as smaller farms already struggle economically.

The government's directive to the Swedish Food Agency was clear: the dietary guidelines should consider Sweden's ability to feed its population in times of crisis and war. Had this been the case, the dietary guidelines would have been designed in a way that could increase national production. Instead, they reduce it. In addition to

[6] For details, see Swedish Food Agency (2025a, p. 92 and 103).

[7] For details on this reduction, see European Environment Agency (2023, fig. 29).

Table 1 Percentage changes in the intake of energy, fat, and protein by adopting the planetary diet

	Denmark	Finland	Iceland	Norway	Sweden	The Nordic region	EU	US
Energy	−41	−33	−37	−24	−25	−30	−29	−27
Fat	−89	−68	−77	−51	−49	−62	−60	−53
Protein	−48	−51	−61	−35	−44	−45	−45	−55

Note Values represent a reduced supply of animal products, expressed as a percentage of the total physiological requirements of energy, fat, and protein at population level.[9] *Source* Authors' calculations based on data from FAOstat

being detrimental to Sweden's food security, the Food Agency failed to make this transparent.

The Planetary Diet from Local to EU Level

Is the problem then that the planetary diet is not adapted to Nordic conditions, but perhaps could be suitable in other parts of Europe, or the Western world more broadly? Again, the answer is no. Table 1 demonstrates how the planetary diet would reduce the fulfillment of nutritional requirements for energy, fat, and protein if applied in Denmark, Finland, Iceland, Norway, Sweden, the Nordic Region, the EU, and the United States.[8]

If we take the EU as an example, the planetary diet's reduction of animal products would reduce the intake of energy corresponding to 29% of the total requirements of the population. The intake of fat is reduced by as much as 60% of total requirements, and the intake of protein via animal products is reduced by an amount corresponding to 45% of the population's total physiological needs.

Table 2 lists changes in the food supply due to planetary diet. The numbers are the percentage changes in the food supply, measured in kcal per capita and day for different sorts of animal products. These measures of the decline in energy supply

[8] Our analysis is based on the first version of the planetary diet (Willett et al. 2019). In October 2025, after our manuscript was finalized, an updated version was published (Rockström et al. 2025). This goes even further. In the 2019 version, the recommended daily intake of milk and milk products was 153 kcal per capita. For red meat including lard and tallow, the recommendation was 66 kcal. In total, recommended daily intake of animal products was 340 kcal per capita. In the planetary diet 2.0, the recommended intake of milk and milk products is 145 kcal per capita and day, and the recommended intake of red meat including lard and tallow is 45 kcal per capita and day. The total recommended intake of animal products is 295 kcal, a 13% reduction from the first version. Thus, the problems we have identified in the planetary diet 1.0 are now greater.

[9] The recommendations by Blomhoff et al. (2023) for planning the food security of an entire national population differ only slightly from the nutritional guidelines defined by the Nordic Council of Ministers (2014). For example, they call for a 1% increase in energy intake, a 1% decrease in fat, and a 3% increase in protein. These recommendations apply to adults aged 18–70, expressed as a weighted average across two sexes, three age groups, and three levels of physical activity.

Table 2 Percentage changes in animal production in Northern Europe, the European Union, and the United States due to the planetary diet, 2022

	Denmark	Finland	Iceland	Norway	Sweden	EU	US
Milk and milk products	−78	−77	−77	−60	−71	−70	−60
Ruminant meat	−85	−88	−91	−87	−87	−88	−89
Ruminant products	−79	−79	−79	−65	−73	−72	−67
Animal fats minus butter and cream	−92	−42	−44	−83	−12	−82	−67
Pigmeat	−85	−88	−91	−87	−87	−88	−89
Red meat	−85	−88	−91	−87	−87	−88	−89
Poultry meat	0	−23	−40	−14	9	−19	−65
Meat including offals	−65	−72	−79	−70	−69	−71	−79
Eggs	−64	−42	−36	−52	−57	−57	−59
Fish, Seafood	−14	−21	−73	−47	−14	10	99
Red meat including animal fats	−89	−83	−87	−86	−81	−86	−85

by branch of animal production also serve as a direct percentage-based indicator of the planetary diet's economic impact on specific countries or regions expected to implement it.

The assessments in Table 2 are in good agreement with the results expressed in a report from the European Scientific Advisory Board on Climate Change that details the scientific basis for the EU Climate Law (European Environment Agency 2023). The same report uses this as a potential option. To substantially increase the production of bioenergy, agricultural land previously dedicated to producing food for humans could in the near future be shifted toward growing fuel for machines. And the European Commission expresses a similar sentiment in its descriptions of animal production systems as being fundamentally harmful for the environment.[10]

One of the ironies of the planetary diet, contrasting to the self-understanding of its proponents, is how it would result in a loss of biodiversity. This is true not just in the Nordic countries but also in Europe and other parts of the world. The reason is that one of the major threats to biodiversity is the loss of grazing animals such as cattle, sheep, and goats.

Eide et al. (2020) found that in total, 4,746 species in Sweden were threatened. They discussed the problem of exporting biodiversity loss, through changed food habits from food that can be produced to food that cannot be produced in Sweden. The increase in consumption of imported food to Sweden can on the margin increase biodiversity loss in other parts of the world. In terms of loss of biodiversity within Sweden, it is the discontinued use of arable land and pastures for animal husbandry that constitute the main reason behind a negative impact on 830 species.

[10] See European Commission (2023, p. 58).

The reduction in the food consumption and production in Sweden following from these dietary guidelines are profound. And the Swedish Food Agency failed to report this to the government despite clear instructions to do so. In addition, the planetary diet will severely reduce biodiversity in Sweden and large parts of the European Union, and the increased dependency on plant-based alternatives will lead to a loss of biodiversity in other parts of the world.

The Planetary Diet's Weak Scientific Basis

Before moving on to discuss why the Swedish Food Agency failed to provide credible Swedish dietary guidelines, it is relevant to further review the research behind the planetary diet, so as to evaluate the scientific basis of this concept.

Let us first look more closely at the link between the planetary diet and the overarching concept of planetary boundaries. As a matter of fact, these boundaries define what the diet can include. In particular, the planetary boundaries include a cap on reactive nitrogen. The cap is set at such a low level that no agriculture is possible to conduct, neither conventional nor organic (cf. Rockström et al. 2009). The only known food system to have operated below this cap at global scale is the hunter-gathering system. This supported 1–10 million people globally, to be contrasted with the food system relying on husbandry and farming that supports the current global population of close to 10 billion people (cf. Hellstrand 2013).

Let us now return to the planetary diet. The concept was first introduced by Rockström et al. (2016) and further elaborated by Springmann et al. (2018) and Willett et al. (2019). Subsequent attempts were made by Wood et al. (2019) to adapt the planetary diet to Nordic conditions.

Methodologically, the planetary diet relies on quantifying the ecological consequences of dietary choices. It can be understood as a form of life-cycle assessment, as defined by ISO 14040 and ISO 14044, combined with the concept of planetary boundaries (Rockström et al. 2009). However, neither life-cycle assessment nor planetary boundaries can adequately evaluate the sustainability performance of integrated ecological-economic systems. This is a major concern when analyzing food supply systems, particularly those based on ruminant production, i.e., systems involving cattle, sheep, and goats (cf. Hellstrand 2015).

This results in a situation where the planetary diet does not reflect the historical, real-world conditions of food production. Nor does it account for local variations, as it is based on global averages. In doing so, the diet prioritizes abstract models over actual agricultural realities.

For example, in their attempt to analyze the environmental impacts of agricultural food production, Springmann et al. (2018) excluded land classified as permanent pasture, which constitutes 70% of all global agricultural land. Their analysis also omitted the top-soil layer of agricultural land. Furthermore, when assessing climate impacts, they considered only methane and nitrous oxide, while excluding carbon dioxide.

When you omit a large part of all agricultural land from the analysis you will not be able to analyze the land-use consequences of agricultural systems and the food they can produce. When you omit the top-soil layer you cannot analyze the impact of diet choices through the demand they impose on the agricultural production system, and whether they are possible given the local agroecological production conditions. Among them are the possible carbon sinks of carbon emissions from the same agricultural land, pending the way the agricultural system is managed. But it is also a matter of supplying nutrients for coming years' food production. By omitting the top-soil layer from the analysis, Springmann et al. (2018) is analytically blind to these important aspects in the agricultural food system.

At this point, having reviewed the planetary diet's weak scientific basis, it is relevant to level critique not only against the Swedish dietary guidelines but also against the research community that has seemingly provided a strong scientific basis for these guidelines and their implications for European agriculture and food supply, not least in times of crisis.

The Chef—The Swedish Climate Policy Council

Why has the Swedish Food Agency not previously been required to clarify the conflicts arising from the updated dietary guidelines? One explanation is that it shares the perspectives, conclusions, and interests of the research community that currently constitutes the Swedish Climate Policy Council, tasked with reviewing the Swedish Government's contributions to EU's green transition.

Members of the Swedish Climate Policy Council are researchers whose contributions were central to formulating the internationally influential concepts of planetary boundaries and the planetary diet. This scientific foundation underpins the political imperative of the green transition. Within the EU, this is evident in the legislative process for building a sustainable food system. The Farm-to-Fork Strategy, the Climate Law, and the Green Deal are all based on the logic of planetary boundaries and are strongly influenced by the planetary diet.

An illustration of this shared alignment between researchers and policymakers can be found in the Council's own description of its chair, Åsa Persson: "Her research focuses on the interplay between international and national policies for climate and sustainability. Her earlier research has addressed the choice of policy instruments, coherence in environmental policy, and international politics on climate adaptation, planetary boundaries, and the UN's Sustainable Development Goals" (Swedish Climate Policy Council 2025c).

Persson, along with Carl Folke and colleagues of the Stockholm Resilience Centre co-authored the concept of planetary boundaries. The Centre has also been central to the subsequent creation of the planetary diet (Stockholm Resilience Centre 2019). In brief, this is how a specific research community can push its own positions into a national government body—the Swedish Climate Policy Council—and influence the still larger European green transition.

In the Swedish Climate Policy Council's annual report (2025b), where it reviewed Sweden's agricultural policies, they argue that the key to Sweden's green transition is to reduce production and consumption of milk and meat from cattle, sheep, poultry, and reindeer. These recommendations, similar to those presented about the same time by the Swedish Food Agency, became the focus of support groups directed against the Swedish Government's instructions that the dietary guidelines should prioritize national food security. Protest lists, involving over a thousand academics and published in major Swedish newspapers (Dagens Nyheter 2025), argued that the actions of the Swedish Government made it guilty of climate denial. By questioning the Swedish Food Agency's expertise, and in continuation the research of the Swedish Climate Policy Council, the researchers concluded that the Swedish Prime Minister and his government posed a threat to democracy itself.

What stands out, however, is that in their reports, and in the scientific bases on which these rest, neither the Swedish Food Agency nor the Swedish Climate Policy Council has attempted to describe Swedish agriculture in its local context, whether in relation to historical Nordic diets or to contemporary developments. A simple explanation for this is that the Council's members lack expertise in agriculture and forestry.

This omission of sector-specific knowledge about Sweden's national conditions is a consistent feature of the Swedish Climate Policy Council's work. Since its establishment in 2019, the Council has reported favorably on a number of green transition initiatives, focusing initially on the industrial sector and more recently on agriculture.

Once criticism against these initiatives began mounting around 2023, notably against failed fossil free steel projects in northern Sweden (e.g., Henrekson 2024), the Swedish Climate Policy Council in its annual reports interpreted this as a sign that the green transition required even stronger and faster government support. When these transition projects finally did fail, the Council left these events uncommented and moved on to other aspects of the green transition, of which the planetary diet and Swedish dietary guidelines is the most recent one.

In this respect, the Swedish Climate Policy Council does not assess the scientific basis or feasibility of the green transition. Their work is not practical but principled, in the sense that it is self-servingly idealistic. The solutions it offers concerns commitments and a willingness to dedicate resources to the transition, rather than assessing what has been the actual outcome of their work thus far. In this sense, the climate crisis becomes less of a problem to be solved and more of a solution in and of itself. The crisis provides opportunities for the research community responsible for drafting policies, guidelines, and recommendations to further promote the green transition.

Conclusion

The Swedish dietary guidelines were meant to answer a new set of urgent questions haunting Europe's ruling elites—how to secure national food sovereignty in an increasingly uncertain multipolar world order. But instead of addressing Sweden's food security, such as avoiding local famine in the event of crisis or war, these dietary guidelines ended up reflecting global concerns of avoiding a climate crisis. These clashes between advocates of planetary diets vs. traditional diets illustrate the Western world's failure in science policy. In brief, preoccupation with culture wars hamper any serious attempt to prepare for actual wars.

Neither the Swedish Food Agency nor the Swedish Climate Policy Council demonstrate any deeper understanding of the Nordic societies whose diet they now seek to alter. Instead, they propose, without evidence, to embark on a full-scale experiment to revolutionize Sweden's diet and agriculture. This would radically break with the dietary patterns shaped by an evolutionary process over 5,000 years, where the interplay between humans and animals, culture, and cultivation has been tested under constant selection pressure in real-world ecosystems. The planetary diet is an illusory recipe, predicated on ingredients that do not grow in our soil, and prepared by chefs neither able nor willing to cook Nordic food.

It is worth reiterating the strong influence that the planetary diet have had on policies and policy processes: The Swedish Dietary Guidelines by the Swedish Food Agency; review of Sweden's agricultural policies by the Swedish Climate Policy Council; the Nordic Nutrition Recommendations by the Nordic Council of Ministers; in addition to numerous EU regulations relating to sustainable food systems, farm to fork strategies, climate laws, the Green Deal, and impetus for the green transition as whole.

In all of the above cited policies, the planetary diet has laid a misleading foundation for how Europe is to undertake its green transition. What the planetary diet illustrates is how green bubbles are generated by a combination of a weak scientific basis and the proximity to—and power of—policymaking. The end results are strong incentives for a professed sustainable development, but in reality, it undermines it.

The major cost of the planetary diet is that it undermines food security; increases loss of biodiversity dependent on agriculture with husbandry, especially ruminants; causes loss of tropical forests; causes major increases of emission of carbon dioxide due to loss of tropical forests.

Both current experience and that of previous generations show that what climate policy researchers propose will not work. Their policymaking experiment, regardless of its initial intentions or stated aims, has produced a bureaucratic bloat incapable of course correction. The "green bubble" has instead expanded to the point where it now undermines national food security. This is a development that neither Sweden nor Europe can afford in today's geopolitical climate.

If we keep adding the proposed, allegedly scientifically based, ingredients, and allow these chefs to stir the pot, then these bubbles will continue to grow. For Sweden, this means that more than half of its agricultural land would be taken out of production, resulting in reduced food production. The planetary diet is literally an illusory recipe for putting food on the table as well as for preserving biodiversity in the Nordic region and the European Union.

References

Blomhoff, R., Andersen, R., Arnesen, E. K., & Christensen, J. J. (2023). Nordic nutrition recommendations 2023: Integrating environmental aspects. Nordic Council of Ministers. https://norden.diva-portal.org/smash/get/diva2:1769986/FULLTEXT06.pdf

Catanzaro, R., Sciuto, M., & Marotta, F. (2021). Lactose intolerance: An update on its pathogenesis, diagnosis, and treatment. *Nutrition Research, 89*, 23–34. https://doi.org/10.1016/j.nutres.2021.02.003

Dagens Nyheter (2025). Vår forskning kan inte viftas bort som åsikter [Our research cannot be dismissed as opinions]. May 6. https://www.dn.se/debatt/var-forskning-kan-inte-viftas-bort-som-asikter/

Eide, W., et al. (Eds.) (2020). Tillstånd och trender för arter och deras livsmiljöer—rödlistade arter i Sverige 2020 [Status and trends for species and their habitats—red-listed species in Sweden 2020]. SLU *Artdatabanken rapporterar, 24*. Uppsala: SLU Artdatabanken.

European Commission (2023). *Towards Sustainable Food Consumption—Promoting Healthy, Affordable and Sustainable Food Consumption Choices*. Luxembourg: Publications Office of the European Union. https://data.europa.eu/doi/10.2777/29369

European Environment Agency (2023). *Scientific Advice for the Determination of an EU-Wide 2040 Climate Target and a Greenhouse Gas Budget for 2030–2050*. Luxembourg: Publications Office of the European Union. https://data.europa.eu/doi/10.2800/609405

European Parliament (2019). The European Parliament declares climate emergency. 29 November. https://www.europarl.europa.eu/news/en/press-room/20191121IPR67110/the-european-parliament-declares-climate-emergency

Fahlén, P., Henrekson, M., & Nilsson, M. (2026). In pursuit of the green transition—Electricity at any cost? In M. Henrekson, C. Sandström, & M. Stenkula (Eds.), *The Green Entrepreneurial State? Exploring the Pitfalls of Green Deals* (pp. 149–172). Cham: Springer.

FAO (2006). *Livestock's Long Shadow*. Rome: Food and Agriculture Organization of the United Nations. https://www.fao.org/4/a0701e/a0701e.pdf

Hellstrand, S. (2013). Animal production in a sustainable agriculture. *Environment, Development & Sustainability, 15*(4), 999–1036. https://link.springer.com/article/10.1007/s10668-012-9423-z

Hellstrand, S. (2015). *On the Value of Land*. PhD thesis. Västerås: Mälardalen University Press Dissertations, No. 182. http://www.diva-portal.org/smash/get/diva2:814613/FULLTEXT01.pdf.

Hellstrand, S., Herlin, A., & Sverdrup, H. (2024). *Sustainability and Resilience in Norwegian Agriculture and Food Systems: The Role of Animals Combined with Crops in the Norwegian Food Supply—and an Assessment of the Consequences of Different Potential Changes in the Primary Production System*. Manuscript. Hamar: Inland Norway University of Applied Sciences.

Henrekson, M. (Ed.) (2024). *De norrländska stålsatsningarna—frälsare eller gökunge* [*The Green Steel Initiatives in Northern Sweden: Savior or Millstone*]. Stockholm: Samhällsförlaget. https://www.ifn.se/publikationer/bocker/2024/2024-henrekson-de-norrlandska-sta-lsatsningarna-fra-lsare-eller-go-kunge/

Itan, Y., Jones, B. L., Ingram, C. J., Swallow, D. M., & Thomas, M. G. (2010). A worldwide correlation of lactase persistence phenotype and genotypes. *BMC Evolutionary Biology, 10*, Article 36. https://doi.org/10.1186/1471-2148-10-36

Mann, M. (2003). Little Ice Age. In M. C. MacCracken & J. S. Perry (Eds.), *Encyclopedia of Global Environmental Change, Volume 1, The Earth System: Physical and Chemical Dimensions of Global Environmental Change*. New York, NY: John Wiley & Sons.

Morell, M. (1987). Eli F. Heckscher, the 'food budgets', and Swedish food consumption from the 16th to the 19th century. *Scandinavian Economic History Review, 35*(1), 67–107.

Morell, M. (2022). *Agrar revolution: Jordbruksproduktionen i Uppsala och Västmanlands län 1750–1920*. Uppsala Studies in Economic History No. 121. Uppsala: Department of Economic History, Uppsala University.

Myrdal, J. (1998). *Det svenska jordbrukets historia—Band 1: Jordbrukets första femtusen år 4000 f.Kr.–1000 e.Kr.* [*The History of Swedish Agriculture—Volume 1: The First Five Thousand Years of Agriculture 4000 BCE–1000 CE*]. Stockholm: Natur & Kultur.

Myrdal, J. (1999). *Det svenska jordbrukets historia—Band 2: Jordbruket under feodalismen 1000–1700* [*The History of Swedish Agriculture—Volume 2: Agriculture under Feudalism 1000–1700*]. Stockholm: Natur & Kultur.

Myrdal, J. (2000). *Det svenska jordbrukets historia—Band 3, Den agrara revolutionen: 1700–1870* [*The History of Swedish Agriculture—Volume 3, The Agrarian Revolution: 1700–1870*]. Stockholm: Natur & Kultur.

Nordic Council of Ministers (2014). Nordic nutrition recommendations 2012: Integrating nutrition and physical activity. Copenhagen.

Öberg, S. (2014). *Social Bodies: Family and Community Level Influences on Height and Weight, Southern Sweden 1818–1968*. Gothenburg Studies in Economic History 10. Gothenburg: Unit for Economic History, Department of Economy and Society, School of Business, Economics and Law, University of Gothenburg.

Public Health Agency of Sweden and Swedish Food Agency (2024). En hållbar och hälsosam livsmedelskonsumtion [A sustainable and healthy food consumption]. https://www.livsmedelsverket.se/globalassets/publikationsdatabas/rapporter/2024/2024-en-hallbar-och-halsosam-livsmedelskonsumtion.pdf

Rockström, J., Steffen, W., Noone, K., Persson, A., Chapin, F. S., Lambin, E. F., et al. (2009). A safe operating space for humanity. *Nature, 461*, 472–475. https://doi.org/10.1038/461472a

Rockström, J., Stordalen, G. A., Horton, R. (2016). Acting in the Anthropocene: The EAT–Lancet Commission. *The Lancet, 387*(10036), 2364–2365. https://doi.org/10.1016/S0140-6736(16)30681-X

Rockström, J., Thilsted, S. H., Willett, W. C., Gordon, L. J., Herrero, M., Hicks, C., et al. (2025). The EAT–Lancet Commission on healthy, sustainable, and just food systems. *The Lancet, 406*(10512), 1625–1700. https://doi.org/10.1016/S0140-6736(25)01201-2

Roseman, C. H. (1994). *Pytheas of Massalia: On the Ocean: Text, Translation and Commentary*. Palos Heights, IL: Ares Publishers.

Sachs, J. D., Schmidt-Traub, G., & Mazzucato, M., et al. (2019). Six transformations to achieve the sustainable development goals. *Nature Sustainability, 2*, 805–814. https://doi.org/10.1038/s41893-019-0352-9

Science Advice for Policy by European Academies (2020). *A Sustainable Food System for the European Union*. Berlin: SAPEA. https://www.ksla.se/bibliotek/fembandsverket/

Science Advice for Policy by European Academies (2023). *Towards Sustainable Food Consumption*. Berlin: SAPEA.

Springmann, A. M., Clark, M., & Mason-D'Croz, D., et al. (2018). Options for keeping the food system within environmental limits. *Nature, 562*, 519–525. https://doi.org/10.1038/s41586-018-0594-0

Stock, J. T., Pomeroy, E., Ruff, C. B., & Wells, J. C. K. (2023). Long-term trends in human body size track regional variation in subsistence transitions and growth acceleration linked to dairying. *PNAS, 120*(4), e2209482119. https://www.pnas.org/doi/10.1073/pnas.2209482119

Stockholm Resilience Centre (2019). The planetary health diet. https://www.stockholmresilience.org/research/research-news/2019-01-17-the-planetary-health-diet.html

Swedish Board of Agriculture (2025a). *Jordbruksverkets statistiskdatabas* [Board of Agriculture's Statistical Database]. https://statistik.sjv.se/PXWeb/pxweb/sv/Jordbruksverkets%20statistikdatabas/?rxid=5adf4929-f548-4f27-9bc9-78e127837625

Swedish Board of Agriculture (2025b). Marknadsbalans för kött, mejeriprodukter och ägg [Market balance for meat, dairy products and egg]. https://jordbruksverket.se/mat-och-drycker/handel-och-marknad/priser-och-marknadsinformation-for-livsmedel#marknadsrapporter-for-kott-mejeriprodukter-och-agg.

Swedish Climate Policy Council (2025a). Our mission. August 24. https://www.klimatpolitiskaradet.se/en/our-mission/

Swedish Climate Policy Council (2025b). *Klimatpolitiska rådets rapport 2025* [*Annual Report of the Swedish Climate Policy Council*]. Stockholm: Klimatpolitiska rådet. https://www.klimatpolitiskaradet.se/wp-content/uploads/2025/03/klimatpolitiskaradetsrapport2025.pdf

Swedish Climate Policy Council (2025c). Åsa Persson Chair, Swedish Climate Policy Council, August 21. https://www.klimatpolitiskaradet.se/en/ledamot/asa-persson-2/

Swedish Food Agency (2012). *Riksmaten—vuxna 2010–11: Livsmedels- och näringsintag bland vuxna i Sverige.* Uppsala: Livsmedelsverket. https://www.livsmedelsverket.se/globalassets/publikationsdatabas/rapporter/2011/riksmaten_2010_20111.pdf

Swedish Food Agency (2025a). Livsmedelsverkets generella kostråd för den vuxna befolkningen [The Swedish Food Agency's general dietary guidelines for the adult population]. www.livsmedelsverket.se/globalassets/publikationsdatabas/rapporter/2025/l-2025-nr-04-livsmedelsverkets-generella-kostrad-for-den-vuxna-befolkningen.pdf

Swedish Food Agency (2025b). Hur vanligt är laktosintolerans? [How common is lactose intolerance?]. https://www.livsmedelsverket.se/matvanor-halsa--miljo/sjukdomar-allergier-och-halsa/allergi-och-overkanslighet/mjolk-och-laktos

Swedish Food Agency (2025c). Fördjupad konsekvensanalys av kostrådet om rött kött och chark [In-depth impact analysis of the dietary recommendation on red meat and processed meat products]. https://www.livsmedelsverket.se/globalassets/publikationsdatabas/rapporter/2025/r-2025-fordjupad-konsekvensanalys-av-kostradet-om-rott-kott-och-chark-allt.pdf

SweGov (2023). Regeringsbeslut L12023/02733 [Government decision]. Landsbygds- och infrastrukturdepartementet. https://www.regeringen.se/contentassets/2888af734a9c4254825d026b4805e4a6/uppdrag-till-livsmedelsverket-att-uppdatera-de-svenska-kostraden.pdf

SweGov (2024). Ytterligare analys behövs i det fortsatta arbetet med nya kostråd [Further analysis is needed in the continued work on new dietary guidelines]. https://regeringen.se/pressmeddelanden/2024/12/ytterligare-analys-behovs-i-det-fortsatta-arbetet-med-nya-kostrad/

UN (1987). *Report of the World Commission on Environment and Development: Our Common Future.* New York, NY: United Nations. https://sustainabledevelopment.un.org/content/documents/5987our-common-future.pdf

Willett, C. W., Rockström, J., Loken, B., et al. (2019). Food in the Anthropocene: the EAT–*Lancet* Commission on healthy diets from sustainable food systems. *The Lancet, 393*(10170), 447–492. https://doi.org/10.1016/S0140-6736(18)31788-4.

Wood, A., Gordon, L. J., Röös, E., Karlsson, J. O., et al. (2019). Nordic food systems for improved health and sustainability: Baseline assessment to inform transformation. Stockholm: Stockholm Resilience Centre. https://www.stockholmresilience.org/publications/publications/2022-02-15-nordic-food-systems-for-improved-health-and-sustainability.html

Stefan Hellstrand is a Researcher and Consultant with a PhD in Energy and Environmental Engineering, a PhLic in Systems Ecology—Natural Resource Management, and an MSc in Agriculture (Animal Husbandry) from the Swedish University of Agricultural Sciences (SLU). He is recognized for his interdisciplinary approach to sustainable development, integrating economic, social, and ecological perspectives in resource management.

Hellstrand has over 40 years of experience as an advanced consultant, using real-world systems to test and refine his research, focusing on how to integrate ecological and economic systems for the purpose of increasing sustainability and economic efficiency in local communities, in milk farms, as well as in healthcare.

Johan Gärdebo is Research Fellow of Clare Hall, University of Cambridge, and an Associate of the Cambridge Centre for History and Economics, and affiliated with the Ratio Institute, Stockholm. He received his PhD in 2019 from the KTH Royal Institute of Technology in Stockholm. His PhD thesis details Sweden's role in promoting environmental diplomacy, climate politics, and dual use-industries. He has published research papers and popular pieces on green transition policies, earth observation technologies, European industrial and agricultural policies, and its role in the West's political realignment.

Gärdebo has held positions as a researcher and visiting scholar at a number of universities in Sweden and abroad. His works appear in monographs, a dozen edited and co-authored collective volumes, journal articles, in addition to corporate white papers. He frequently writes for international magazines, national newspapers, and hosts the Manifesto Podcast.

Italy's Superbonus and the Capture of Climate Policy by Modern Monetary Theory

Luciano Capone and Carlo Stagnaro

Abstract In 2020, Italy introduced an unprecedented incentive scheme for residential renovations as part of a broader stimulus package aimed at promoting economic recovery from the COVID-19 crisis. The measure, known as the *Superbonus*, remained in effect from late 2020 through 2023. It allowed households to claim a tax credit of 110% on expenditures related to retrofitting properties to improve energy efficiency and/or seismic resilience. The tax credit was fully transferable to third parties or could be used as an invoice discount. Together with other home-renovation incentives, the Superbonus generated an estimated fiscal cost of approximately EUR 220 billion, exceeding the initial projections by about 150 billion. In its final year (2023), the cost of the program reached 4.2% of GDP, making it one of the largest industrial-policy initiatives in Italian history and arguably the most significant budgetary shock in Europe since World War II. Although the Superbonus enjoyed broad bipartisan support, its intellectual origins can be traced to a heterodox economic school of thought known as *Modern Monetary Theory* (MMT). This study examines the Superbonus through that theoretical lens, demonstrating how a small group of MMT advocates assumed influential roles within the government in 2020 and advanced their policy agenda by capitalizing on the exceptional circumstances and fiscal leniency that followed the pandemic. It further assesses the outcomes of the Superbonus across multiple dimensions—including its effects on economic growth, fiscal sustainability, and environmental performance.

Keywords Energy efficiency · Buildings · Energy transition · Green deal · Public spending · MMT

JEL Codes E62 · H23 · L52 · Q48

L. Capone
Roma, Italy
e-mail: capone@ilfoglio.it

C. Stagnaro (✉)
Istituto Bruno Leoni, Milano, Italy
e-mail: carlo.stagnaro@brunoleoni.org

M. Henrekson et al. (eds.), *A Green Entrepreneurial State?*, International Studies in Entrepreneurship 49, https://doi.org/10.1007/978-3-032-15512-2_13

Introduction

In the early months of 2020, Italy was among the first and most severely hit countries by the coronavirus pandemic. The government reacted by implementing strict lockdown measures and far-reaching restrictions on personal lives and economic activities (Roser 2021). These exceptional measures, aimed at curbing the spread of the virus, had a profound economic impact: GDP contracted by 8.9% in 2020. Policymakers struggled to design relief packages that could simultaneously prevent a further economic downturn, foster recovery, and enhance resilience to COVID-19 at a time when vaccines were not yet available.

At the time, Italy was governed by a left-of-center coalition led by Prime Minister Giuseppe Conte, supported by the Democratic Party, the populist Five Star Movement, and smaller parties on the far left. Among the various measures introduced, one stood out for its scale and design: the so-called *Superbonus*. This was an unprecedented incentive scheme for home renovations, including retrofitting to improve energy efficiency and resilience to seismic events.

The Superbonus had two defining features:

1. A subsidy rate of 110%, to be claimed in four or five equal annual installments to offset tax obligations; and
2. unlimited transferability, or eligibility for invoice discounts.

This peculiar design aimed to enable low-income households to benefit from the incentive by removing economic and liquidity constraints. The subsidy covered not only the entire cost of home renovations (the 100% component) but also financing costs (the additional 10%) and the need for upfront payment. Beneficiaries could transfer their tax credit to third parties—construction firms, banks, or financial intermediaries—which further expanded access.

Initially scheduled to expire by mid-2021, the measure was repeatedly extended and remained in force, with limited modifications, until 31 December 2023. In the meantime, the Conte Government was succeeded first by a broad-based technical government led by Mario Draghi (2021–2022), and after the September 2022 election by a right-wing administration under Giorgia Meloni (still in office as of January 2026). Although Mr. Draghi had voiced concerns about the Superbonus, his parliamentary majority rejected almost every attempt to curtail its size and scope. Ms. Meloni, who had previously supported the policy, was later forced to reduce its generosity and eventually suspend it altogether in the interest of financial stability and fiscal discipline.

The Superbonus soon became associated with several perverse effects, including inflated invoicing due to the elimination of the natural "conflict of interest" between buyers and sellers, widespread tax fraud, and insufficient oversight. In retrospect, it is unsurprising that "four years since its inception, the Superbonus has left an outsized mark on Italy's fiscal accounts and public debt, while the benefits for construction activity and energy efficiency have been more limited" (IMF 2024).

While it may appear to be just another case of poorly designed public spending, the Superbonus has deeper intellectual roots. It did not emerge spontaneously. Rather, it was conceived and promoted by a small group of economists influenced by *Modern Monetary Theory* (MMT). They managed to secure influential advisory positions in government, including proximity to Prime Minister Conte himself.

MMT is a heterodox economic theory that posits that a government issuing its own currency faces no default risk:

> The most important conclusion reached by MMT is that the issuer of a currency faces no financial constraints. Put simply, a country that issues its own currency can never run out and can never become insolvent in its own currency. It can make all payments as they come due… for most governments, there is no default risk on government debt. (Mitchell et al. 2019, pp. 13–15)

Taking advantage of the extraordinary conditions of the pandemic—most notably, the temporary suspension of EU fiscal rules—a small group of MMT proponents pushed Italy as far as possible toward circumventing institutional limits on deficit spending. The experiment demonstrated that MMT offers no useful guidance for public finance. Outcomes aligned closely with mainstream economic predictions: limited impact on growth, significant fiscal deterioration, and a contribution to the inflationary wave of 2022–2023.

What is most striking, however, is that a small group of ideologues managed to shape the fiscal policy of the world's eighth-largest economy. The episode vividly illustrates the enduring influence of ideas—and the destructive potential of misguided ones—as long emphasized by economists and philosophers alike (Keynes 1936; Weaver 1948; Hayek 1949).

The remainder of this essay is structured as follows. The next section traces the evolution of Italy's incentives for home renovation and explains the rationale behind the Superbonus. This is followed by a concise discussion of Modern Monetary Theory and its intellectual role in shaping the policy. The subsequent section analyzes the consequences of the Superbonus and compares them with both MMT-based expectations and forecasts from mainstream economics. The final section concludes with a summary and policy implications.

The Superbonus and Other Incentives for Home Renovations in Italy

This section provides a concise history of Italy's pre-Superbonus incentives for energy efficiency and the political dynamics that led to the introduction and subsequent extension of the Superbonus until the end of 2023. Most of the information is drawn from Capone and Stagnaro (2024a).

Italy has a long history of tax credits for home renovations dating back to the late 1990s. Initially conceived as a support measure for the construction sector, these tax credits also sought to combat tax evasion, a persistent problem in the Italian economy.

The subsidy rates of the first "bonuses" ranged from 36 to 41%, depending on the year.

Beginning in 2007, the design of these tax credits evolved to pursue broader objectives, notably energy efficiency and seismic resilience. Renovations that met specific technical criteria qualified for higher subsidy rates, rising to between 65 and 75%. At the time, these were the most generous, broad-based, and non-means-tested subsidies for home renovations in both the EU and the UK (Amenta and Stagnaro 2021). Over the years, additional bonuses were introduced—some minor and narrowly targeted (e.g., the "faucet bonus," the "curtains and mosquito nets bonus," and the "furniture bonus"), others more substantial. The most important among them was the "façade bonus," offering a 90% subsidy, introduced in 2019.

When the government sought measures to accelerate post-pandemic recovery in May 2020, it appeared natural to build on this well-established system of incentives, which had already proven relatively effective in stimulating construction activity. Two further considerations strengthened the case for a large renovation incentive. First, it allowed Italy's recovery strategy to align with the political goal of the energy transition—an identity-defining issue for the governing left-wing coalition and a central component of the emerging Next Generation EU program. The European Union subsequently approved the inclusion of the Superbonus in the National Recovery and Resilience Plan (NRRP), allocating approximately EUR 14 billion—by far the largest share of funds dedicated to energy efficiency (European Commission, n.d.). Second, promoting private building retrofits was expected to revive a construction sector which had endured years of stagnation and underinvestment, while also creating employment opportunities as temporary pandemic support schemes were phased out.

The Superbonus, introduced in May 2020, was initially intended to remain in force only until mid-2021. Its objective was to provide a short-term boost to economic activity rather than to establish a permanent measure. However, the initial uptake was disappointing. In the second half of 2020, implementation lagged because beneficiaries faced substantial bureaucratic obstacles. Public spending on home-renovation incentives in that year was driven mainly by the façade bonus, which, despite its lower rate (90% compared to the Superbonus's 110%), imposed virtually no restrictions on the type or scope of eligible projects. Moreover, when the Superbonus was introduced, all existing home-related tax credits, including the façade bonus, were made transferable, further expanding their appeal.

In December 2020, the Parliament amended the government's budget law, extending the Superbonus from mid-2021 to mid-2022. This extension resulted from bipartisan pressure: both the left-leaning majority and the right-wing opposition proposed amendments to increase the scheme's scope and duration. The measure was politically popular. Homeowners were pleased by the prospect of renovating their properties "for free," while business associations, trade unions, and environmental groups alike endorsed the Superbonus as a source of jobs and energy efficiency.

After a period of political instability, Prime Minister Conte resigned on 26 January 2021 and was succeeded by a technical government led by former European Central Bank president Mario Draghi. The new coalition brought together parties from across the political spectrum, leaving Giorgia Meloni's Brothers of Italy as the sole major opposition force. Initially, Draghi viewed the Superbonus favorably, seeing it as a tool to promote growth and leverage EU funding through the NRRP. His first interventions aimed to simplify administrative procedures and accelerate the program's implementation, which indeed gained momentum in the first half of 2021.

However, Draghi soon recognized that the fiscal cost of the Superbonus was far greater than expected. The Ministry of Economy and Finance had underestimated the behavioral response of households to a measure that removed all financial constraints. As evidence of fraud and inflated invoicing mounted, Draghi proposed several reforms to tighten eligibility and limit transferability of the tax credits. Yet, only a few of these were approved. By December 2021, the Parliament again extended the measure, postponing its expiry first to the end of 2022 and later to the end of 2023.

By mid-2022, disagreements within the governing coalition deepened—including over the Superbonus, whose fiscal burden had become unsustainable. Draghi resigned on 20 July 2022, prompting new elections in September. The right-wing coalition won a large majority, and Giorgia Meloni became Prime Minister. Although she had previously supported the Superbonus, she soon recognized its impact on public finances. In 2022, Italy—a heavily indebted country—recorded a budget deficit equal to 8.1% of GDP, more than twice the EU average of 3.2%.

The new government ended further extensions of the program and reduced the tax credit from 110 to 90% beginning in April 2023, introducing for the first time income-based eligibility thresholds. The Minister of Economy, Giancarlo Giorgetti—who had long expressed skepticism about the measure—played a central role in this policy reversal. In February 2023, the government declared the program's fiscal cost still excessive and imposed new restrictions on the transferability of tax credits and on invoice discounting. Despite these efforts, the Parliament introduced multiple loopholes that diluted the reform.

As a result, 2023 became the year of the Superbonus's greatest fiscal toll. The total value of tax credits generated by the Superbonus and related renovation incentives reached an unprecedented EUR 90 billion. Confronted with this unsustainable burden, the government suspended the program in February 2024, abolished transferability of tax credits, and progressively reduced the subsidy rates to 65% in 2024, 50% in 2025, and 36% in 2026–2027 (further reduced for second homes). Thus ended the brief but turbulent history of the Superbonus.

Government expenditure for incentivizing home renovations was steady as a share of GDP in the late 1990s and early 2000s at around 0.12%. As shown in Fig. 1, it began to grow more rapidly after 2005 with an increase to some 0.8% of GDP. In 2021 expenditures skyrocketed, peaking at EUR 90 billion or 4.2 percent of GDP in 2023.

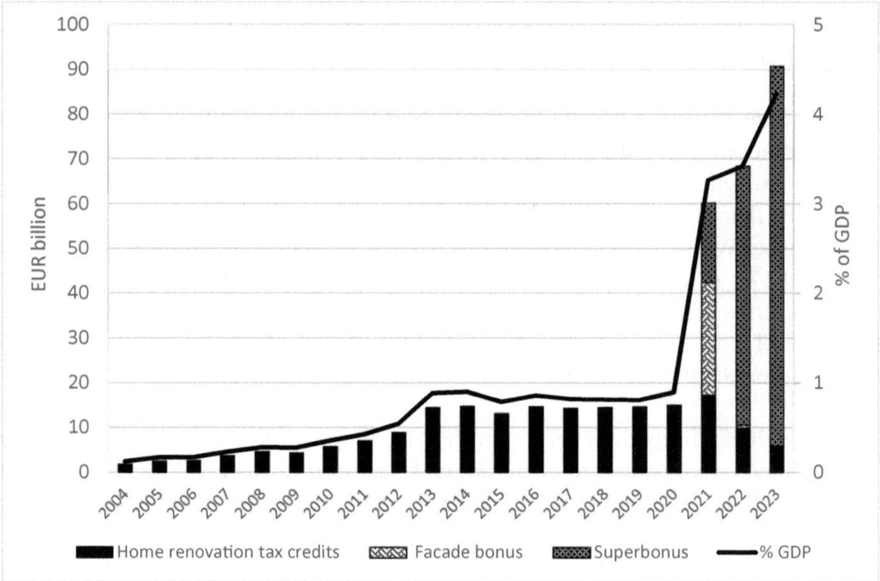

Fig. 1 Total expenditure in Italy for the tax credits for home renovations, 2004–2023 (EUR billion and as a share of GDP). *Note* The 2021 data may be slightly overestimated because it includes the Superbonus expenditures related to 2020. The big jump between 2020 and 2021 is driven mainly by the "facade bonus" scheme and other already-existing bonuses that benefited from the possibility to transfer the tax credit to third parties. *Source* 2004–2020: Camera dei Deputati (2023); 2021–2023: own calculations based on data from the Italian Ministry of Economy and Finance.

The Modern Monetary Theory and the Superbonus

The political history of the Superbonus cannot provide a key information: Who did invent such a measure? Answering this question may unveil the intellectual influence prevailing in the Italian government in 2020. But it will also show how a small group of determined intellectuals can advance their ideas and indeed gather the support from all across the political spectrum, without most "practical men" even realizing that they are just "hear[ing] voices in the air" and "distilling their frenzy from some academic scribbler of a few years back" (Keynes 1936).

While the Superbonus was originally announced by then Prime Minister Conte at a press conference in May 2020, the very idea did not come from the Presidency of the Council, nor did it come from any relevant minister (such as the Minister of Economy and Finance or the Minister of Economic Development). As Mr. Conte admitted, the idea came from an under-secretary to the Presidency, Riccardo Fraccaro. Mr. Fraccaro was not (and is not) a prominent politician. Mr. Fraccaro gave several interviews at the time, explaining that "the Superbonus pays for itself"[1] by generating positive

[1] "Il Superbonus si ripaga da sé, non è una spesa. E vi spiego perché," in ripartelitalia.it, 8 November 2021: https://www.ripartelitalia.it/riccardo-fraccaro-superbonus-si-ripaga-da-se-non-e-una-spesa/.

spillovers on economic growth, employment, and sustainability. This very idea soon became a major selling point for the Superbonus: the notion, widely endorsed by politicians left and right, was that the Superbonus would stimulate the economy so much that the additional economic activity—and the underlying fiscal revenue—would eventually offset the negative budget impact, while reducing CO_2 emissions and dependence on imported natural gas for residential heating.

Mr. Fraccaro drew this idea from his own belief in the so-called Modern Monetary Theory (MMT), a heterodox economic theory that "is not a theory and indeed is not even modern" (Bisin 2021). In a nutshell, MMT posits that "fiscal deficits don't matter; monetary policy should be subordinate to fiscal policy; and the monetary authorities should be willing to issue base money to finance government spending" (Dowd 2020; see also Edwards 2019; Mankiw 2020; Castañeda 2021). Or, to paraphrase the title of an influential book by MMT theorist Stephanie Kelton, the public deficit is a myth.

Interestingly, the Italian edition of Kelton's book (Kelton 2020) included a laudatory endorsement by Mariana Mazzucato, a former advisor to Prime Minister Conte: "Kelton's revolutionary book is both theoretically rigorous and empirically engaging. It reminds us that money is not scarce and that the only limit is our imagination" (quoted in Kelton 2021). Fraccaro, a lawyer from Trento, came to know MMT via three young scholars from the University of Trento, namely Giacomo Bracci, David Lisetti, and Daniele Della Bona, who are themselves followers of Warren Mosler, a self-described founder of MMT (see, e.g., Mosler 2010, 2024). Bracci, Lisetti, and Della Bona (BLDB) used to organize seminars in Trento with Fraccaro and Mosler himself, through associations such as Trentino MMT[2] and FEF Academy, of which Mosler himself is a founder together with BLDB and others.[3]

As Fraccaro gained a Parliamentary seat and, later, a position in the Conte Administration, he brought BLDB to Rome. Bracci became his chief of staff and Della Bona his economic adviser. Bracci, in particular, became increasingly important. Together with Pasquale Tridico—then chairman of Italy's National Institute for Social Security and now a MEP for the Five Star Movement—he was the father of Italy's version of the universal basic income (so-called citizenship income; Bracci et al. 2021). Later, as economic advisor to Prime Minister Conte, he was one of the main opponents of the ratification of the ESM Treaty reforming the European Stability Mechanism (Capone and Stagnaro 2024a). BLDB—who self-describe themselves as the Trento Boys, echoing the Chicago Boys—tell their version of the story in a presentation held at the Leeds University MMT Conference on July 15, 2024 (Lisetti et al. 2024).

BLDB rightly claim credit for the "largest fiscal expansion of the Italian economy in the last 30 years." They quote Mosler's assertion that "[t]oday's currencies are simply tax credits, the thing needed to pay taxes" (quoted in Lisetti et al. 2024) and explain the Superbonus as the consistent attempt to do the opposite. If, under MMT, currencies are simply tax credits, then tax credits can be turned into currencies. This is what is called "fiscal money," which can have no legal tender under Article 128 of

[2] http://www.trentinommt.it/.

[3] https://www.fef.academy/.

the Treaty on the Functioning of the European Union (TFEU) and Articles 2, 10, and 11 of Council Regulation (EC) No 974/98 (Bank of Italy 2017). However, BLDB understood that COVID-19 created exceptional circumstances, thanks to the combination of the General Escape Clause to the Stability and Growth Pact (that temporarily reduced or annulled budget restrictions) (Delivorias 2020) and the commitment of the European Central Bank to guarantee macroeconomic stability by continuing its pursuit of non-conventional monetary policy measures.

According to BLDB, the first and main goal of the Superbonus was to "reduce the impact on the government deficit while maximizing the fiscal space within EU rules." By allowing the tax credit transferability, MMT theorists in the Italian government understood they would attract the banks and other financial entities that would eventually buy credits and turn them into a quasi-currency that could be sold multiple times and eventually be used to settle fiscal liabilities, which is exactly what the theory predicts.

BLDB claim that the Superbonus resulted in outstanding economic growth, a booming construction sector, an improved debt/GDP ratio, and a more sustainable economy. We will discuss the actual outcome of the Superbonus in the next section. Before we do so, however, it is important to emphasize that the entire operation could work if, and only if, Eurostat—the EU's statistics agency—treated the Superbonus tax credits as "non-payable tax credits," i.e., "which are those limited to the amount of the tax liability. All amounts of tax credit that exceed the taxpayer's liability in the period in force are 'lost'" (Eurostat 2023a, p. 85). Therefore, non-payable tax credits "are treated as negative tax revenue and not as expenditure, they will be recorded when they are used to reduce the tax liability, impacting the accounts for the exact amount used each year, instead of recording the whole amount in one single year, as will be the case for payable tax credits" (ibid., p. 88). In this case, the expected income from the Superbonus would be accounted for in four or five equal installments, greatly reducing its impact on the deficit and creating the illusion that its benefits, which accrue as investments in the year they are made, outweigh the costs, which are spread out over subsequent years. The key bet of BLDB is that by then the investment has already generated its own effects on economic growth. Thereby, the Superbonus shall effectively pay for itself.

This narrative became the conventional wisdom in Italy. It was spread by the Government, endorsed by political parties across the political spectrum, and shared by most opinion-makers. The ideas of the Trento Boys had massive consequences. They triggered a large fiscal expansion, blessed by national and EU institutions (that were happy to see more investments in energy-saving). Then came a time when reality testeds ideas and determined whether or not they were correct.

The Effects of the Superbonus

The clash with reality happened as two key expectations became deluded: the statistical treatment of the Superbonus and its actual budget impact.

From an accounting perspective, BLDB were well aware that their operation rested on the Italian and European Statistical Offices, Istat and Eurostat, treating the Superbonus as a non-payable tax credit. In that case, its deficit impact would have been split in four or five annual installments (depending on the specific bonus). Since the beginning, though, both Istat and Eurostat raised the issue that transferability made the Superbonus qualitatively—and not just quantitatively—different from any other home-related tax credit that in the past had been considered a non-payable. Due to transferability, no amount of the tax credit could be expected to go "lost," because the beneficiary would always have an implicit incentive to sell it to third parties if her tax liabilities are lower than the tax credit itself.

When this is the case, Eurostat considers the tax credit as payable, i.e., "the full amount of the tax credit is paid out to the beneficiary in any case, implying the payment of the excess when the tax relief is greater than the tax liability. In a payable tax credits system, payments or obligations of payment are awarded independently of the size of the tax liability, even in the case where no tax liability exists. Payable tax credits are thus non-contingent government liabilities; they represent a present obligation for government" (Eurostat 2023a, p. 85). That a transferable tax credit should be accounted as payable is plainly stated in Eurostat's *Manual on Deficit and Debt*: "if the tax credit can be transferred to third parties, such tax credit is thus to be deemed as a payable tax credit and has to be recorded in national accounts as an asset of the taxpayer and a liability of government" (Eurostat 2023a, p. 86).

If a tax credit is payable, its deficit impact should be recorded entirely in the same year of issuance. Even though things were plain and clean from the beginning, the Italian government insisted that the Superbonus should be recorded as non-payable. Given the extraordinary situation created by the pandemics, the discussion took a few years, during which Italy incorrectly recorded the Superbonus as non-payable. But eventually, Eurostat required Istat to issue a correction and impute the entire spending as deficit accruing to the same year of issuance (Eurostat 2023b, 2023c, 2024). This forced the Government to issue a correction of its public accounting, recording a much higher deficit and reducing its fiscal space for other measures. This was happening at the time the General Escape Clause was being deactivated and therefore the usual budget constraints were being reintroduced. Therefore, the Government had to stop the issuance of new payable tax credits, which it did by reducing the subsidy rate well below 100% and by canceling transferability.

The second major delusion emanated from the unexpectedly high budget impact of the Superbonus and other transferable tax credits. In every single year since 2021, the ex-post impact of the Superbonus was many times greater than forecasted by the Ministry of Economy and Finance (MEF). The MEF systematically underestimated the fiscal impact of the Superbonus, because it had no macroeconomic model fit for a tax credit with those outlandish features—a subsidy rate exceeding 100% and unlimited transferability. There was also no transparency regarding the methodology employed so no public scrutiny over the estimate. The methodology was later disclosed by the Parliamentary Budget Office, an independent agency:

> The Technical Report does not specify the assumptions underlying the quantifications, referring to the Technical Report accompanying the original legislation, which in turn adopts the method adopted in the Technical Reports of previous legislation in this area.
>
> In order to assess the cost of renewing the increased tax credit, the Technical Reports regarding past extensions of the Ecobonus referred to expenditure carried out in the previous years of the programme. In order to assess the differential cost attributable to the extension of the increased rate, it was assumed that if the measure had not been renewed, eligible expenditure would have decreased by 50 per cent. This prudential assumption required that only 50 per cent of the tax credits granted at the pre-increase rate be assessed as a cost under current legislation (and therefore be deducted from the overall cost of the extension). The evaluation of the costs of the superbonus programme (in the Technical Report accompanying Decree Law 34/2020), expressly adopting this approach, assumed that expenditure would double compared with subsidised spending under the 65 and 50 per cent Ecobonus mechanism. In this case, however, the context was significantly different, given that for the introduction of a new measure it was not possible to refer to an ex ante expenditure level in which this subsidy was available. (UPB 2021, p. 61)

In practice, the MEF estimated the impact of the Superbonus based on the observed impact of previous tax credits, whose subsidy rate, however high, was well below 100% and that were not transferrable. These mistakes drove the director of the State General Accounting Department to resign. They explain why the Government had to react sharply. The Eurostat decision forced it to record the entire cost of the Superbonus in the year of issuance, and the forecasting error resulted in a much higher impact than expected.

While the cost overrun posed a fiscal problem for the Government, from the MMT perspective it should be viewed as a pro: under the MMT assumptions, the fiscal deficit is a "myth." The greater public spending, the more significant its impact on GDP growth. As already quoted above, BLDB in their presentation praise it as "the largest fiscal expansion of the Italian economy in the last 30 years."

Unfortunately, things turned out quite differently. The contribution of the Superbonus and other home-related tax credits was limited, as compared to the enormous resources spent (equal to roughly 10% of Italy's GDP in the median year, 2022). Table 1 shows the outcome of several analyzes ex-post, performed by both vested interests (such as the Centro Studi Confindustria, i.e., the Italian Business Confederation) and institutional bodies (such as Italy's National Statistical Office, the Court of Auditors, the Bank of Italy, the Parliamentary Budget Office, and the IMF).

To summarize, most estimates find an implied multiplier below 1, and only one source (Istat) finds a multiplier around 1. As mainstream economists would have expected based on the past evidence of incentives to the construction sector, borrowing money to subsidize the retrofitting of buildings, whatever its merits, will not deliver economic growth (see, e.g., Warmedinger et al. 2015). This disproves one key expectation of MMT.

The other key expectation was that massive public spending would not result in inflation. In fact, while Italy experienced a dramatic growth in the construction activity after the pandemic, the construction costs remained consistently below the euro area average. Corsello and Ercolani (2024) contribute to solve this puzzle. The different severity of bottlenecks across country (with Italy relatively less impacted)

Table 1 Economic impact of the superbonus and other home-related tax credits

Source	Period	GDP Impact	Implied fiscal multiplier
Confindustria (2023)	2021–22	1.2%	0.5
Corte dei Conti (2023)	2021–22	1.8%	0.7*
Istat (2023)	2021–22	1.4–2.6%	0.7–1,3
Accetturo et al. (2024)	2021–24	2%	0.7–0.9
MEF (2023)	2021–22	3%	0.9
IMF (2024)	2021–23	2.5%*	0.25–0.33

*Own estimate based on the data provided by the sources

and the depressed condition of the construction sector in the country (with significant idle capacity) explain why the sector could absorb a demand spike without significant increases in the construction costs (and, most notably, in the cost of labor). Keeping these factors in mind, the authors find that the Superbonus:

> has a statistically significant and positive effect on the construction costs. We further show that about half of the total increase in these costs observed between September 2021 and December 2023 (amounting to an overall rise of about 13%) can be attributed to the S[upper]B[onus]. (Corsello and Ercolani 2024, p. 6)

This result is consistent with the observation that construction companies increased their markups and improved their financial situation between 2019 and 2023 (Capone and Stagnaro 2024a; based on data from ANCE, Italy's confederation of construction companies).

The Superbonus also had other undesirable consequences. From a distributional point of view, it implied a massive transfer of resources from low-income taxpayers to high-income homeowners (UPB 2023), while only a small share of the funds (approximately 2%) went to social housing apartments (Capone and Stagnaro 2024b). From an environmental perspective, it is unlikely that this unprecedented tax-funded scheme to promote energy efficiency, that involved only about 500 thousand buildings (a mere 4% of the residential building stock; Enea 2024) will ever pay off, even under generous assumptions regarding the social cost of carbon (Alpino et al. 2022).

Conclusion

The Superbonus scheme in Italy offers a compelling case study to test two propositions: first, that ideas have consequences; and second, that Modern Monetary Theory (MMT) provides a poor guide for political economy.

Introduced in the context of the emergency measures that followed the COVID-19 outbreak in 2020, the Superbonus was largely shaped by a small group of economists influenced by MMT principles. This group managed to secure key advisory roles within government institutions and exerted substantial influence over major policy decisions, including the design of Italy's *citizenship income*, the decision not to ratify the European Stability Mechanism (ESM) reform, and, most notably, the Superbonus itself. Conceived as a massive fiscal stimulus, the scheme effectively operated as a form of parallel currency creation through the issuance of a vast volume of transferable tax credits. Between 2021 and 2023, the Superbonus and related incentives generated an estimated EUR 220 billion in tax credits corresponding to more than 10% of annual GDP.

Although MMT economists claimed the Superbonus as evidence of their theoretical framework in action—and as the largest fiscal expansion in Italy's recent history—the results fell far short of their own expectations. The policy produced a significant deterioration in public finances while delivering only modest effects on economic growth. It contributed to inflationary pressures, exacerbated income inequalities, and yielded limited environmental benefits—to the point that it was called "one of the dumbest fiscal policies in recent memory" (Garicano, 2025).

By embedding the Superbonus within Italy's broader climate and recovery strategy, policymakers effectively shielded it from institutional and political scrutiny. The combination of expansive fiscal latitude, due to temporarily relaxed EU budgetary rules, and the perceived legitimacy of environmental goals eliminated most constraints on its adoption and continuation. In retrospect, the policy not only undermined fiscal stability but also weakened the credibility of Italy's long-term decarbonization strategy. It stands as a cautionary example of how misguided economic ideas, when translated into policy under exceptional circumstances, can harm both economic performance and the pursuit of rational climate objectives.

References

Accetturo, A., Olivieri, E., & Renzi, F. (2024). Incentives for dwelling renovations: Evidence from a large fiscal programme. Questioni di Economia e Finanza. Occasional Papers No. 860. Rome: Bank of Italy.

Alpino, M., Citino, L., & Zeni, F. (2022). Costs and benefits of the green transition envisaged in the Italian NRRP. An evaluation using the Social Cost of Carbon. Questioni di Economia e Finanza (Occasional Papers) no 720, Bank of Italy.

Amenta, C., & Stagnaro, C. (2021). Quanto è efficiente l'ecobonus? *Energia*,*4*, 62–69.

Bank of Italy (2017). The functions of money and proposals for 'fiscal money'. https://www.bancaditalia.it/media/approfondimenti/2017/moneta-fiscale/index.html?com.dotmarketing.htmlpage.language=1

Bisin, A. (2021). La Modern Monetary Theory non è una teoria e non è moderna. *Il Foglio*, January 2.

Bracci, G., Paternesi Meloni, W., & Tridico, P. (2021). Output gap, participation and minimum income: A proposal for Italy. *Journal of Post Keynesian Economics, 44*(4), 643–676. https://doi.org/10.1080/01603477.2021.1913752

Camera dei Deputati (2023). Il recupero e la riqualificazione energetica del patrimonio edilizio: una stima dell'impatto delle misure di incentivazione (dati aggiornati al 2021). Documentazione e ricerche, Rapporto 2020, 32(3).

Capone, L., & Stagnaro, C. (2024a). *Superbonus. Come fallisce una nazione*. Soveria Mannelli, Italy: Rubbettino.

Capone, L., & Stagnaro, C. (2024b). Superbonus: Rubare ai poveri per dare ai ricchi. *Eco, 9*, 63–65.

Castañeda, J. E. (2021). Modern Monetary Theory. Why it can't provide sustained economic growth and low inflation. IEA Current Controversies No. 77. https://iea.org.uk/publications/modern-monetary-theory-why-it-cant-provide-sustained-economic-growth-and-low-inflation/

Confindustria (2023). Audizione nell'ambito dell'indagine conoscitiva sugli effetti macroeconomici e di finanza pubblica derivanti dagli incentivi fiscali in materia edilizia.

Corsello, F., & Ercolani, V. (2024). The role of the Superbonus in the growth of Italian construction costs. Questioni di Economia e Finanza. Occasional Papers No. 903. Rome: Bank of Italy.

Corte dei Conti (2023). Memoria nell'ambito dell'indagine conoscitiva sugli effetti macroeconomici e di finanza pubblica derivanti dagli incentivi fiscali in materia edilizia. https://documenti.camera.it/leg19/documentiAcquisiti/COM05/Audizioni/leg19.com05.Audizioni.Memoria.PUBBLICO.ideGes.29873.15-02-2024-15-12-51.602.pdf

Delivorias, A. (2020). The 'general escape clause' within the Stability and Growth Pact. European Parliamentary Research Service Briefing PE 649.351. https://www.europarl.europa.eu/RegData/etudes/BRIE/2020/649351/EPRS_BRI(2020)649351_EN.pdf

Dowd, K. (2020). The deficit myth: Modern Monetary Theory and the birth of the people's economy. *Cato Journal, 40*(3), 795–809.

Edwards, S. (2019). Modern Monetary Theory: Cautionary tales from Latin America. *Cato Journal, 39*(3), 529–561.

Enea (2024). Report dati mensili. October 31. https://www.efficienzaenergetica.enea.it/images/detrazioni/Avvisi/Report_31_10_2024.pdf

European Commission (n.d.). Superbonus—Strengthening of the Ecobonus and Sismabonus for energy efficiency and building safety. https://commission.europa.eu/projects/superbonus-strengthening-ecobonus-and-sismabonus-energy-efficiency-and-building-safety_en

Eurostat (2023a). *Manual on Government Deficit and Debt—Implementation of ESA 2010*. 2022 Edition. Luxembourg: Publications Office of the European Union.

Eurostat (2023b). Statistical recording of Superbonus 110%, Transition 4.0 and other renovation tax credits. ESTAT/D-2/LA/GB/DI/pr D(2023).

Eurostat (2023c). Statistical recording of Superbonus according to new legislation adopted in 2023. ESTAT/D-2/LA/VG/DI/pr D(2023).

Eurostat (2024). Statistical recording of Superbonus—follow up including new legislation adopted since September 2023. ESTAT/D2/RJ/MS/DI/pr D(2024).

Garicano, L. (2025). How to torch 220 billion euros. *Silicon Continent*, February 14. https://www.siliconcontinent.com/p/how-to-incinerate-220-billion-euros

Hayek, F. A. (1949). The intellectuals and socialism. *University of Chicago Law Review, 16*(3), 417–433.

IMF (2024). Italy. Article IV Consultation. IMF Country Report 24/240. https://www.imf.org/en/Publications/CR/Issues/2024/07/23/Italy-2024-Article-IV-Consultation-Press-Release-Staff-Report-and-Statement-by-the-552191

Istat (2023). Indagine conoscitiva sugli effetti macroeconomici e di finanza pubblica derivanti dagli incentivi fiscali in materia edilizia. Audizione dell'Istituto nazionale di statistica. https://www.istat.it/wp-content/uploads/2023/05/Istat-Audizione-Incentivi-edilizi-24-maggio-2023.pdf

Kelton, S. (2020). *The Deficit Myth: Modern Monetary Theory and How to Build a Better Economy*. London: Public Affairs.

Kelton, S. (2021). *Il mito del deficit. La teoria monetaria moderna per un'economia al servizio del popolo*. Rome: Fazi Editore.

Keynes, J. M. (1936). *The General Theory of Employment, Interest and Money*. London: Macmillan & Co.

Lisetti, D., Bracci, G, & Dalla Bona, D. (2024). MMT in Italy: A journey of activism and government policy making. Presentation held at the Leeds University MMT Conference, July 15, 2024. https://gimms.org.uk/wp-content/uploads/2024/07/LEEDS-PRESENTATION-Final-Version.pdf

Mankiw, G. (2020). A skeptic's guide to Modern Monetary Theory. *AEA Papers and Proceedings, 110*(2), 141–144. https://doi.org/10.1257/pandp.20201102
MEF (2023). Audizione nell'ambito dell'indagine conoscitiva sugli effetti economici e di finanza pubblica degli incentivi fiscali in materia edilizia. https://documenti.camera.it/leg19/documentiAcquisiti/COM05/Audizioni/leg19.com05.Audizioni.Memoria.PUBBLICO.ideGes.29877.15-02-2024-15-45-00.366.pdf
Mitchell, W., Wray, R. L., & Watts, M. (2019). *Macroeconomics.* 10^{th}edition. New York, NY: Worth Publishers.
Mosler, W. (2010). *Seven Deadly Innocent Frauds of Economic Policy.* St. Croix, VI: Valance Co Inc.
Mosler, W. (2024). *Soft Currency Economics.* St. Croix, VI: Valance Co Inc. https://moslereconomics.com/mandatory-readings/soft-currency-economics/
Roser, M. (2021). What is the COVID-19 Stringency Index? https://ourworldindata.org/metrics-explained-covid19-stringency-index
UPB (2021). *2022 Budgetary Balance Report.* Rome: Parliamentary Budget Office. https://en.upbilancio.it/wp-content/uploads/2022/02/2022_Budgetary-Policy-Report.pdf
UPB (2023). Audizione della Presidente dell'Ufficio parlamentare di bilancio nell'ambito dell'indagine conoscitiva sugli effetti macroeconomici e di finanza pubblica derivanti dagli incentivi fiscali in materia edilizia. https://www.upbilancio.it/audizione-sugli-effetti-macroeconomici-e-di-finanza-pubblica-derivanti-dagli-incentivi-fiscali-in-materia-edilizia/
Warmedinger, T., Checherita-Westphal, C. D., & Hernández de Cos, P. (2015). Fiscal multipliers and meyond. ECB Occasional Paper No. 162. Frankfurt: European Central Bank.
Weaver, R. M. (1948). *Ideas Have Consequences.* Chicago, IL: University of Chicago Press.

Luciano Capone is a journalist and chief economics reporter for the Italian newspaper *Il Foglio.* He holds a master's degree in political science and international relations from the Catholic University of Milan and a degree from the university's School of Journalism.

Together with Carlo Stagnaro, he published the book *Superbonus. Come Fallisce Una Nazione* [*The Superbonus: How a Nation Fails*] (Soveria Mannelli: Rubbettino, 2024).

Carlo Stagnaro is Research and Studies Director of Istituto Bruno Leoni, Italy's leading free-market think tank. He is also a member of the scientific committee of the quarterly journal *Energia* and a member of the Academic Advisory Council of the Institute of Economic Affairs in the UK, as well as a research fellow of Epicenter. Prior to that he was Chief of the Minister's Technical Staff at Italy's Ministry of Economic Development.

He holds an MSc in Environmental Engineering from the University of Genoa and a PhD in Economics, Markets, and Institutions from IMT Alti Studi Lucca. He is a regular contributor on economic affairs to the Italian daily newspaper *Il Foglio.*

Together with Luciano Capone he has published the book *Superbonus. Come Fallisce Una Nazione* [*The Superbonus: How a Nation Fails*] (Soveria Mannelli: Rubbettino, 2024).

Alternative Paths

A Silent Transition: Growth with Less Environmental Weight

Jonas Grafström

Abstract Across Europe, environmental performance has improved alongside economic expansion. Since 1990, most EU countries have seen a steady decline in territorial CO_2 emissions, improved energy-efficiency, and reductions in pollution, enabled by common instruments such as emissions trading, product regulations, and renewable energy targets. While the broad pattern is visible across member states, some cases demonstrate especially sustained and measurable decoupling. Sweden offers one such example. Between 1990 and 2023, the country reduced territorial CO_2 emissions by 38% while GDP more than doubled. Air pollutants fell across nearly all tracked categories, energy intensity declined, and hazardous chemical use decreased despite rising population and output. These outcomes emerged gradually—not through disruption or centralized intervention, but through quiet steps. This essay examines how those long-term shifts unfolded. It draws on empirical indicators of emissions, energy use, and resource flows to illustrate how Sweden reduced its environmental weight while maintaining economic growth.

Keywords Decoupling · Environmental policy · Carbon emissions · Resource efficiency · Technological change · Economic growth · Sweden

***JEL* Classifications** O44 · O52 · Q56 · Q58 · Q01

Introduction

What if a country could grow richer while using fewer resources, emitting less pollution, and consuming less energy per unit of output?

I thank Christian Sandström and Magnus Henrekson for useful comments and suggestion on earlier versions of this essay.

J. Grafström (✉)
Luleå University of Technology, and the Ratio Institute, Stockholm, Sweden
e-mail: jonas.grafstrom@ltu.se

M. Henrekson et al. (eds.), *A Green Entrepreneurial State?*, International Studies in Entrepreneurship 49, https://doi.org/10.1007/978-3-032-15512-2_14

EU countries' greenhouse gas emissions decreased by 29% between 1990 and 2021. Emissions decreased in 24 out of 27 member states. At the same time, the union's real GDP increased by 62%. In relation to GDP growth, greenhouse gas emissions have decreased in all EU member states since 1990.

This essay examines decoupling between economic growth and environmental pressure by delving deeper into the example of Sweden (based on data from Statistics Sweden and the Swedish Environmental Protection Agency). Over the last three decades, the country has quietly pursued that path (Grafström and Sandström 2021). Between 1990 and 2023, Sweden's population rose by almost 25% and real GDP nearly doubled. Yet, over the same period, total carbon dioxide emissions declined by over 38% while energy use remained unchanged (Swedish Energy Agency 2025). Air and water pollution has declined across most categories. Of the 26 tracked air pollutants, 24 showed reductions.

Sweden tells a story not of grand transformation, but of cumulative shifts—thousands of incremental changes in technology, behavior, policy, and industrial design. Cleaner vehicles, more energy-efficient buildings, electrified infrastructure, and smarter logistics have all played a role. So too have stable institutions and a policy environment that rewarded long-term thinking over short-term gain.

This essay focuses on observed empirical shifts and their implications for the resource intensity of growth. Using national data from 1990 onward, it traces trends in CO_2 emissions, energy and water use, industrial inputs, transport fuels, and air pollutants. It also includes less visible indicators—such as consumption-based emissions and the use of hazardous chemicals—that capture the environmental impact embedded in imports and production. Together, these metrics reveal a society that has managed to produce more output with less environmental strain.

Sweden's experience does not offer a universal blueprint, but it provides a compelling case study. The observed pattern of progress challenges the assumption that economic growth and ecological degradation must always go hand in hand. Decoupling—while incomplete and uneven—is already happening.

None of these shifts were inevitable. Each depended on a combination of policy, innovation, and private response. When viewed together, they form a picture of material change: a society growing wealthier and larger, yet placing less strain on air, water, and material resources (McAfee 2019).

More from Less

What people consume, how they travel, and how buildings are heated have undergone substantial changes since the early 1990s—but not always in ways that are immediately visible. Most of the shifts have occurred quietly: one instance of efficiency improvement at a time, one regulatory change at a time or just responses to relative price changes. The result is not a sudden transformation, but an accumulation of adjustments that show up in national statistics. Across energy systems, vehicle fleets,

Table 1 Changes in key environmental and resource indicators for the European Union

	Period	Change (%)
CO_2 emissions	1990–2021	−28
Methane	1990–2021	−38
Arsenic	1990–2021	−90
Lead	1990–2021	−95
Sulfur Dioxide	1990–2021	−93

Source Eurostat (2024)

industrial processes, and emissions profiles, the numbers suggest a society that has learned to operate with less environmental weight per unit of output.

As shown in Table 1, the European Union provides many examples of this trend.

In what follows, emissions, fuel use, electricity demand, chemical inputs, and water consumption are examined in relation to economic growth. Although the data do not suggest uniform progress, they do reveal a general direction. As output has expanded, the intensity of resource use has fallen. Some indicators declined slowly, others sharply while a few increased. Together, they offer a picture of how environmental pressure has evolved across sectors—and how the material basis of growth has shifted.

The overall pattern of "more from less" in Sweden is illustrated clearly in Table 2, which shows the changes in emissions, energy, water, and hazardous chemical use, adjusted for economic growth. The figures reveal a broad-based decoupling between environmental impact and GDP.

The pattern presented in Table 3 is most evident in the trajectory of CO_2 emissions. In 1990, emissions stood at 71.6 million tonnes. By 2023, emissions had declined to 44.4 million tonnes, even as GDP more than doubled. That shift did not result from an economic slowdown, but from structural and technological changes across multiple sectors. Energy systems became less carbon intensive. Industrial processes grew more efficient. Transport fuels diversified, and heating shifted away from oil.

Consumption-based emissions reflect the greenhouse gases generated in the production of goods and services consumed domestically, regardless of where those emissions occur. This includes imports such as electronics, food, industrial materials, and transport services. This approach is complementary to territorial accounting, which only measures emissions within national borders.

As shown in Fig. 1, Sweden's domestic consumption-based CO_2 emissions declined from 39.6 to 29.6 million tonnes, equivalent to a 25% drop between 2008 and 2022. The reduction suggests changes in the composition of imports, improvements in production efficiency abroad, and shifts in domestic consumption patterns.

Car ownership continued to rise, yet average fuel consumption per kilometer fell. From 1990 to 2024, the number of passenger cars in traffic in Sweden increased from approximately 3.6 million to nearly 5 million while average fuel consumption per vehicle declined substantially (Trafikanalys 2025). New gasoline-powered cars sold in 1990 consumed an average of around 9 L per 100 km. By 2018, consumption had

Table 2 Percentage changes in key environmental and resource indicators relative to GDP in Sweden, 1990–2024

	Period	Change	GDP Growth	Change per unit of GDP
CO_2 emissions	1990–2023	–38	101	–69
Consumption-based CO_2 emissions	2008–2022	–25	28	–42
Greenhouse gases from domestic transport	1993–2022	–27	101	–64
Use of liquefied petroleum gas	1993–2023	–49	101	–75
Greenhouse gases from cars	1993–2024	–33	101	–67
Energy consumption	1993–2024	–5	101	–53
Electricity consumption	1993–2024	–3	101	–52
Use of water	1995–2020	–6	73	–79
CFC emissions (freons)	1993–2024	–92	101	–96
Use of health- and environmentally hazardous chemical products (incl. export)	2008–2020	–5	19	–24

Source Grafström and Sandström (2024), Swedish Environmental Protection Agency (2024a, 2024b, 2024c) and Statistics Sweden (2025)

Table 3 Absolute change in CO_2 emissions and economic growth in Sweden, 1990–2023

Year	CO_2 emissions (million tonnes CO_2-equivalents)	GDP (billion USD, 2023 prices)
1990	71.6	259.9
2023	44.4	584.96

Source Swedish Environmental Protection Agency (2024a) and Statistics Sweden (2025)

dropped below 6 L per 100 km for comparable gasoline models and even further for hybrids. For the fleet as a whole, the Swedish Environmental Protection Agency estimated a reduction in average CO_2 emissions from new cars from over 200 g per kilometer in the early 2000s to 120 g by 2018. In 2024, the average was 63 g.

Figure 2 captures a key contradiction turned into a success: a transportation sector that has grown in volume while shrinking in terms of emissions.

In the early 1990s, Stockholm's skyline was not what it was today. Diesel engines rattled through city centers, and few questioned the inevitability of pollution as the price of modernity. Sweden's emissions of nitrogen oxides had fallen by more than half since 1990 (Grafström and Sandström 2021). In transportation, similar developments occurred. Road transport continues to dominate domestic logistics, but

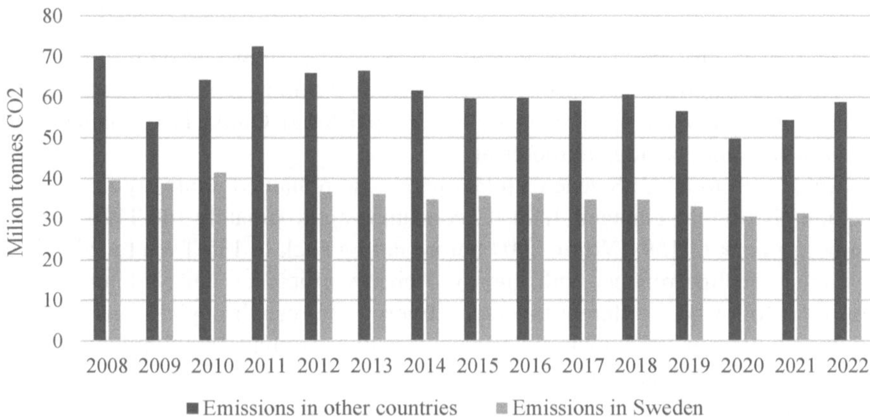

Fig. 1 Sweden's consumption-based CO_2 emissions, 2008–2022 (million tonnes). *Source* Swedish Environmental Protection Agency (2025)

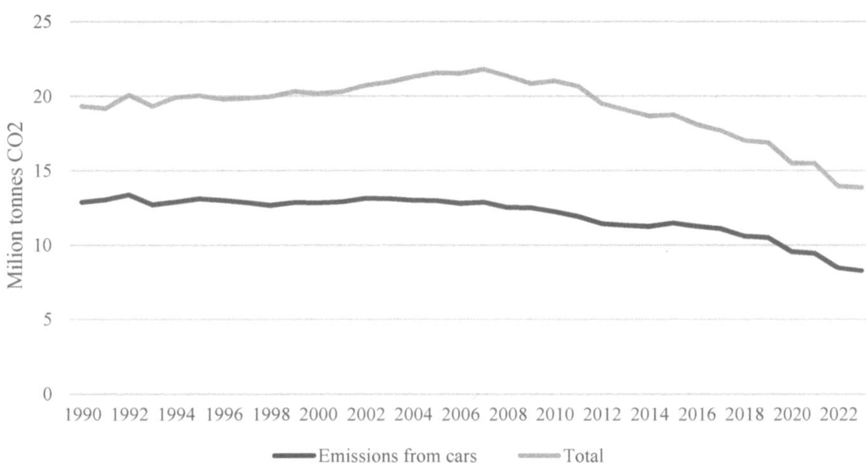

Fig. 2 CO_2 emissions from cars and total emissions from the transportation sector in Sweden, 1990–2023 (million tonnes). *Source* Swedish Environmental Protection Agency (2024b)

improvements in fuel economy, logistics planning, and vehicle design have moderated emissions growth. Railway electrification expanded, and more efficient intermodal hubs were established. Fewer trucks returned empty across the country, and delivery routes were optimized.

Between 1993 and 2018, energy use per unit of industrial output declined by more than 30%. Investments in combined heat and power, automation, and internal energy recovery reshaped the industrial energy profile. The objective was not to scale down production, but to reduce the energy required per unit of value.

Paper production illustrates this transition. Long associated with high environmental impact, the sector adopted closed-loop water systems, waste heat recovery, and steam reuse. Mills that once relied on linear flows now recirculate process water and capture energy that was previously lost (Bajpai 2015). Output has remained high, but with a smaller ecological footprint.

From 1990 to 2023, Sweden's total energy use remained relatively flat, but the sectoral distribution changed. Industry consumed approximately 140 TWh in 1990, rising to a peak of 159 TWh in 2007 before falling back to 135 TWh by 2023. The post-crisis decline reflects both improved energy-efficiency and structural shifts. Transport followed a different trajectory. Energy use rose through the early 2000s, reaching a peak in 2004, then declining gradually to around 78 TWh—close to the 1990 level. Electrification remains limited in total energy terms but is increasingly visible in new vehicle registrations and fleet performance.

In 1990, housing and services consumed nearly 150 TWh—more than any other sector. Despite rapid population growth and an expanding building stock, energy use declined to 139 TWh in 2023. The decline reflects more efficient heating, widespread district heating systems, and improvements in insulation and appliances. Changes in household energy use predate the period. In the 1970s, oil dominated residential heating (Di Lucia and Ericsson 2014). By the 2010s, heat pumps and thermal networks had displaced fossil fuels. The result is a sector where energy demand has decoupled from both floor area and income. Figure 3 shows how this shift in sectoral composition unfolded over time.

Air quality also improved across several dimensions. Emissions of nitrogen oxides dropped by more than half since the early 1990s (Grafström and Sandström

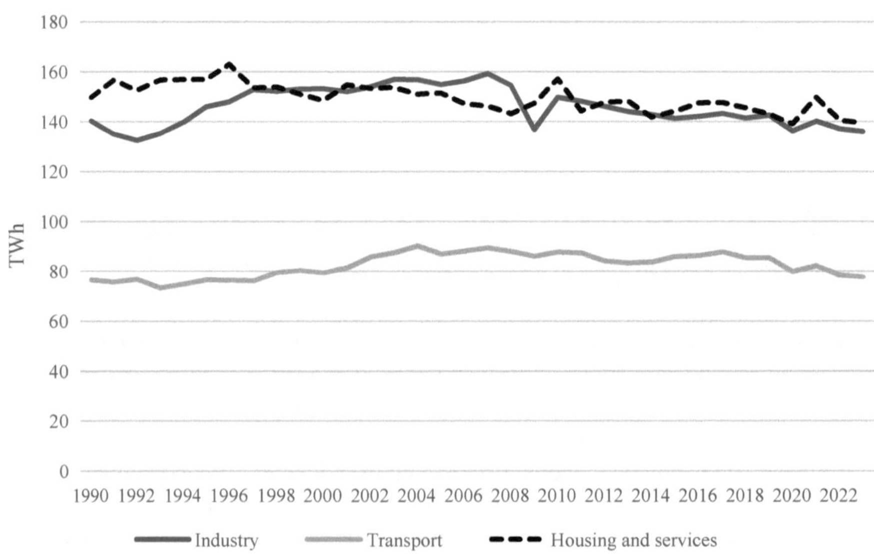

Fig. 3 Sectoral energy use in Sweden, 1990–2023 (TWh). *Source* Swedish Energy Agency (2025)

2021). The shift occurred not through singular policy action, but through a series of embedded changes: catalytic converters, cleaner fuels, and vehicle standards. In the industrial sector, similar improvements took shape. In Luleå, for example, steel output was maintained while cutting emissions per ton of steel, through fuel substitution and process redesign (Pei et al. 2020). Table 4 summarizes these developments, showing that most tracked air pollutants fell by over 50% in absolute terms, and even further when adjusted for economic growth.

Between 1993 and 2022, emissions of air pollutants in Sweden declined across nearly all major categories. The steepest reductions occurred in substances linked to fossil fuel combustion and industrial processes. Sulfur dioxide emissions fell by

Table 4 Percentage changes in air pollutant emissions and intensity Sweden, 1993–2022

Air pollutants 1993–2022	Change emissions	Emissions per GDP unit
Nitrogen oxides	–38	–69
Volatile organic compounds, excl. methane	–53	–77
Sulfur dioxide	–79	–90
Ammonia	–18	–60
PM2.5	–59	–80
PM10	–39	–70
Total suspended particulates—TSP	–29	–65
Soot/Black carbon	–62	–81
Carbon monoxide	70	–86
Lead	–94	–97
Cadmium	–53	–77
Mercury	–61	–81
Arsenic	–61	–81
Chromium	–58	–79
Copper	–30	–66
Nickel	–46	–73
Selenium	–0.6	–51
Zinc	–48	–74
Dioxins	–62	–81
Benzo(a)pyrene	–68	–84
Benzo(b)fluoranthene	–64	–82
Benzo(k)fluoranthene	–71	–86
Indeno (1,2,3-cd) pyrene	–67	–84
PAH 1–4	–65	–83
HCB	–84	–91
PCB	3	–49

Source Swedish Environmental Protection Agency (2024c)

79%, and emissions per unit of GDP declined by 90%. Lead emissions dropped by 94%.

Particulate matter also decreased. Emissions of PM2.5 and black carbon fell by 59 and 62%, respectively, contributing to improved urban air quality. Volatile organic compounds, excluding methane, declined by over 50%. Emissions of heavy metals—including cadmium, mercury, arsenic, and chromium—decreased by 50 to 60% as a result of tighter discharge standards and cleaner production technologies.

Several complex organic compounds, such as dioxins and polycyclic aromatic hydrocarbons, declined by 60 to 85%. These pollutants are commonly associated with combustion, waste incineration, and industrial by-products. Carbon monoxide was the only major pollutant to increase in absolute terms, rising by 70%. In relative terms, though, emissions per unit of GDP declined by 86%, indicating that the rise in total emissions was outweighed by economic growth.

Discussion

The reductions in emissions, pollutant discharge, and resource intensity observed in Sweden since 1990 are not the result of any single reform. They reflect a set of overlapping shifts in both economic structure and technological capability. Taken together, these adjustments have altered the environmental profile of production and consumption.

One major factor is the changing composition of the Swedish economy. Over the past three decades, the share of output generated by knowledge- and service-based sectors increased, while the relative importance of heavy industry declined (Segerfeldt 2025). This shift aligns with broader trends in advanced economies and was not primarily driven by environmental goals (Felipe and Mehta 2016). The result has been a gradual movement toward sectors with lower energy and material intensity per unit of value added.

Within industry, process redesign and technological substitution contributed to lower resource intensity. Energy use per unit of output declined, supported by automation, digital control, and equipment upgrades (Lundgren et al. 2016). The energy system itself changed in parallel. A stable supply of low-carbon electricity, dominated by hydro and nuclear power, enabled both industrial and household transitions without triggering an increase in fossil energy demand. Combined heat and power systems, district heating, and improved building insulation all helped moderate total energy use despite population growth and rising floor space (Åberg and Henning 2011).

Incremental technological improvements have had cumulative effects (Grafström 2018). Gains in motor efficiency, building standards, and industrial equipment design contributed to a measurable decline in emissions and energy intensity. These improvements occurred without reducing output. The volume of goods and services produced continued to grow, but each unit required fewer physical inputs. Although decoupling is not complete, the Swedish case illustrates that rising GDP does not inherently require proportional increases in environmental pressure (McAfee 2019).

Policy shaped many of the conditions under which Sweden's environmental performance improved. Although structural change and technological development account for much of the observed decoupling, institutional stability and policy design helped steer both the timing and direction of those shifts.

One of the most influential instruments was carbon pricing. Introduced in the early 1990s, the carbon tax raised the cost of fossil energy and encouraged substitution toward electricity, district heating, and biofuels (Knaggård and Hildingsson 2025). The effect was particularly visible in heating systems, where oil use declined sharply. The tax was introduced alongside reductions in labor and capital taxation, creating a revenue-neutral structure that redistributed the tax burden without raising overall fiscal pressure (Köppl and Schratzenstaller 2023).

Other pricing and regulatory instruments reinforced the shift. Landfill taxes, producer responsibility rules, and deposit-refund systems reshaped behavior across waste systems (Hage 2007). Industrial emissions faced direct limits, but firms retained flexibility in how to comply. The approach focused on outcomes, not uniform methods. Informational tools also played a role. Appliance labeling, public reporting on energy use, and green procurement criteria shaped reputational and normative expectations (Emmelin and Lerman 2008).

Rather than choosing between centralized control and market liberalism, Swedish policy relied on structured signals and gradual adjustment. Instruments were designed to align long-term incentives without prescribing specific technologies or pathways. Over time, environmental pricing became an integrated part of economic governance, shaping decisions without dominating them.

Technological and economic shifts are shaped by the institutional context in which decisions occur (Berggren and Bjørnskov 2017). In Sweden, institutional stability and relatively high levels of social trust have supported environmental improvements over time (Marbuah 2019). Political consensus on long-term goals has helped maintain continuity in environmental governance, even as political coalitions changed.

The policymaking process has often emphasized procedural credibility over administrative discretion. Agencies responsible for environmental regulation operate within broadly accepted mandates. This has enabled regulatory frameworks to persist even when there have been government changes. Although policy details are contested, the direction of change has remained consistent (Bergh and Erlingsson 2025).

Coordination among public and private actors has further reduced the friction of environmental adjustment. Employers' organizations, labor unions, and industry associations have long participated in structured dialogue on energy systems, industrial development, and workforce transitions. These arrangements lower the transaction costs of compliance and adaptation.

Urban infrastructure developed gradually but measurably. New buildings were required to meet increasingly strict efficiency codes, and retrofitting accelerated across both public and private building stocks (Niskanen and Rohracher 2020).

Public lighting systems transitioned from sodium vapor to LED. Traffic signals and ventilation systems became sensor-regulated.

Sweden's material consumption, measured by domestic extraction, remained broadly stable over time (Grafström and Sandström 2020). Packaging materials became thinner, buildings increasingly used recycled inputs, and energy was recovered from waste-connected material for use in local heat production. The result was a gradual move toward more circular flows of resources across the board.

Conclusions

There are examples of how countries have been able to combine economic growth with environmental concern. This essay outlined the case of Sweden as well as some statistics for the European Union as a whole.

Sweden's environmental record since 1990 does not follow a dramatic trajectory, nor does it hinge on a singular breakthrough. Instead, it reads more like a slow reengineering of everyday systems—how homes are heated, how steel is made, how waste becomes heat, and how power reaches sockets without concomitant emissions. The numbers tell part of the story: a 38% drop in territorial CO_2 emissions, a 25% reduction in consumption-based emissions, air pollutants falling across the board during a period when real GDP doubled. But behind those figures lies something quieter and harder to replicate: a society that changed course without making a show of it.

There was no moratorium on growth, no sweeping ban on consumption. The economy expanded and living standards rose rapidly. Yet, energy use flattened, emissions per unit of output dropped, and toxic releases shrank. This happened not because anyone flipped a switch, but because multiple parts of the system evolved in a loosely coordinated rhythm. Industrial engineers found ways to reuse heat; households phased out oil tanks; appliance standards nudged manufacturers to trim energy demand; policy kept the direction steady.

Much of this, at its best, rested on trust—not just in institutions, but in the idea that gradual change would be rewarded. When a carbon tax was introduced, it was coupled with reductions in other taxes. When standards were tightened, this was done predictably and gradually over many years. Environmental reform in Sweden was rarely urgent or dramatic, but it was hard to reverse.

Coordination helped, too. Industry groups, labor unions, regulators—none had to agree on everything, but most shared a sense that predictability mattered. It made compliance less adversarial and change less risky. A city could retrofit lighting across its public housing stock without waiting for a subsidy. A steel plant could plan a ten-year upgrade knowing that energy prices would nudge it in the same direction.

This model is not easily exported. Sweden had advantages—a low-carbon electricity grid, high institutional trust, and a policymaking culture that rewards consensus. But it offers a counterpoint to two extremes: that environmental progress requires heroic disruption or that it emerges naturally from growth and innovation.

In the Swedish case, neither story fits. What mattered was a sustained alignment of incentives, expectations, and capacity to adapt.

References

Åberg, M., & Henning, D. (2011). Optimisation of a Swedish district heating system with reduced heat demand due to energy efficiency measures in residential buildings. *Energy Policy, 39*(12), 7839–7852. https://doi.org/10.1016/j.enpol.2011.09.031

Bajpai, P. (2015). *Management of Pulp and Paper Mill Waste*. Cham: Springer International.

Berggren, N., & Bjørnskov, C. (2017). The market-promoting and market-preserving role of social trust in reforms of policies and institutions. *Southern Economic Journal, 84*(1), 3–25. https://doi.org/10.1002/soej.12209

Bergh, A., & Erlingsson, G. Ó. (2025). Retrenchment without liberalisation: Making sense of Sweden's shift away from consensual and evidence-based politics. *Scandinavian Political Studies, 48*(2), e70000. https://doi.org/10.1111/1467-9477.70000

Di Lucia, L., & Ericsson, K. (2014). Low-carbon district heating in Sweden: Examining a successful energy transition. *Energy Research & Social Science, 4*, 10–20. https://doi.org/10.1016/j.erss.2014.08.005

Emmelin, L., & Lerman, P. (2008). Environmental quality standards as a tool in environmental governance—the case of Sweden. In M. Schmidt, J. Glasson, L. Emmelin, & H. Helbron (Eds.), *Standards and Thresholds for Impact Assessment* (pp. 463–486). Berlin and Heidelberg: Springer.

Eurostat (2024). Air pollutants by source sector. Brussels. https://ec.europa.eu/eurostat/databrowser/view/env_air_emis__custom_8249852/default/table?lang=en

Felipe, J., & Mehta, A. (2016). Deindustrialization? A global perspective. *Economics Letters, 149*(C), 148–151. https://doi.org/10.1016/j.econlet.2016.10.038

Grafström, J. (2018). International knowledge spillovers in the wind power industry: Evidence from the European Union. *Economics of Innovation and New Technology, 27*(3), 205–224. https://doi.org/10.1080/10438599.2017.1328778

Grafström, J., & Sandström, C. (2021). More from less? Economic growth and sustainability in Sweden. Ratio Working Paper No. 352. Stockholm: Ratio Institute.

Grafström, J., & Sandström, C. (2024). *Mer för mindre: Hållbarhet och tillväxt i EU*. Stockholm: Ratio Institute.

Hage, O. (2007). The Swedish producer responsibility for paper packaging: An effective waste management policy? *Resources, Conservation and Recycling, 51*(2), 314–344. https://doi.org/10.1016/j.resconrec.2006.10.003

Knaggård, Å., & Hildingsson, R. (2025). The adoption of the Swedish carbon tax: Influences and interactions across multiple political levels, jurisdictions, and policy areas. *Policy Studies Journal, 52*(2), 414–435. https://doi.org/10.1111/psj.70011

Köppl, A., & Schratzenstaller, M. (2023). Carbon taxation: A review of the empirical literature. *Journal of Economic Surveys, 37*(4), 1353–1388. https://doi.org/10.1111/joes.12531

Lundgren, T., Marklund, P. O., & Zhang, S. (2016). Industrial energy demand and energy efficiency: Evidence from Sweden. *Resource and Energy Economics, 43*, 130–152. https://doi.org/10.1016/j.reseneeco.2016.01.003

Marbuah, G. (2019). Is willingness to contribute for environmental protection in Sweden affected by social capital? *Environmental Economics and Policy Studies, 21*(3), 451–475. https://doi.org/10.1007/s10018-019-00238-6

McAfee, A. (2019). *More from Less: The Surprising Story of How We Learned to Prosper Using Fewer Resources—and What Happens Next*. New York, NY: Simon & Schuster.

Niskanen, J., & Rohracher, H. (2020). Passive houses as affiliative objects: Investment calculations, energy modelling, and collaboration strategies of Swedish housing companies. *Energy Research & Social Science, 70*, 101643. https://doi.org/10.1016/j.erss.2020.101643

Pei, M., Petäjäniemi, M., Regnell, A., & Wijk, O. (2020). Toward a fossil free future with HYBRIT: Development of iron and steelmaking technology in Sweden and Finland. *Metals, 10*(7), 972. https://doi.org/10.3390/met10070972

Segerfeldt, F. (2025). *Efter industrin: Friare, rikare, grönare*. Stockholm: Timbro förlag.

Statistics Sweden (2025). Nationalräkenskaper: Kvartals- och årsberäkningar. Stockholm: Statistiska centralbyrån. https://www.scb.se/hitta-statistik/statistik-efter-amne/nationalrakenskaper/nationalrakenskaper/nationalrakenskaper-kvartals-och-arsberakningar/

Swedish Energy Agency (2025). Användning av energi. Eskilstuna: Energimyndigheten. https://www.energimyndigheten.se/energisystemet/energianvandning/

Swedish Environmental Protection Agency (2024a). Sveriges utsläpp och upptag av växthusgaser. Stockholm: Naturvårdsverket. https://www.naturvardsverket.se/data-och-statistik/klimat/sveriges-utslapp-och-upptag-av-vaxthusgaser/

Swedish Environmental Protection Agency (2024b). Utsläpp av luftföroreningar. Stockholm: Naturvårdsverket. https://www.naturvardsverket.se/amnesomraden/luft/statistik--utslapp-och-halter/utslapp-av-luftfororeningar/

Swedish Environmental Protection Agency (2024c). Växthusgaser: Utsläpp från inrikes transporter. Stockholm: Naturvårdsverket. https://www.naturvardsverket.se/data-och-statistik/klimat/vaxthusgaser-utslapp-fran-inrikes-transporter/

Swedish Environmental Protection Agency (2025). Växthusgaser: Konsumtionsbaserade utsläpp i Sverige och andra länder. Stockholm: Naturvårdsverket. https://www.naturvardsverket.se/data-och-statistik/konsumtion/vaxthusgaser-konsumtionsbaserade-utslapp-i-sverige-och-andra-lander/

Trafikanalys (2025). Fordon i län och kommuner 2024. Statistik 2025:2. Stockholm: Trafikanalys. https://www.trafa.se/globalassets/statistik/vagtrafik/fordon/2025/fordon-i-lan-och-kommuner-2024.pdf

Jonas Grafström is a PhD in Economics and a Senior Research Fellow at the Ratio Institute in Stockholm, Sweden. He received his doctoral degree in 2017 from Luleå University of Technology, where he defended his dissertation *Technological Change in the Renewable Energy Sector: Essays on Knowledge Spillovers and Convergence.* He is also affiliated with Luleå University of Technology, where he has taught courses in environmental economics and energy policy.

His research explores the intersection of technological change, energy systems, and environmental performance, with a particular focus on how institutions and policy shape the transition toward lower resource and emissions intensity. He has published academic articles on innovation diffusion in the energy sector, economic decoupling, and circularity in industrial systems. In addition to his academic work, he is an experienced public commentator on energy and climate policy and has contributed regularly to Swedish policy debates through reports, op-eds, and media appearances.

Nuclear Technology Transition Towards SMR and Generation-IV

Ernest Mund

Abstract Concern about climate warming is a strong driving force for reduced fossil fuel consumption. European leaders want to reduce greenhouse gas releases to nearly zero by 2050 and extend the electrification of final energy use as much as possible. Nuclear energy should be a primary choice in this perspective. Unfortunately, hostility towards nuclear energy persists despite past successful achievements. The arguments of deniers are based on economic viability, risks of accidents and long-lived nuclear wastes. None of these arguments—partially justified for today's light-water technology—is a showstopper in the long term. Technologies have something in common with the living world: they are in constant evolution. The process is slow, taking almost a century to produce disruptive changes. Starting in 1950, nuclear technology should be very different in 2050 as a result of current R&D. Factory-made modules with reduced power sizes known as SMR (*Small Modular Reactors*), will address some of the economic and safety concerns. Emergent technologies dubbed Generation-IV will considerably enlarge the applications towards water desalination, high temperature heat and naval propulsion. Adoption of different reactor coolant fluids (helium gas, liquid heavy metals or molten salts) instead of water should reduce the safety concerns. Combining specific choices of reactor fuels with adequate neutron spectra might contribute to the elimination of long-lived nuclear wastes. Ignoring the intricacies of technology change and persisting blindly in today's hostile attitude can lead to environmentally detrimental choices.

Keywords Technology transition · Time factor · SMR · Generation-IV · Molten salt reactors (MSR) · Lead-cooled fast reactors (LFR)

***JEL* Codes** O33 · Q42 · Q48 · L94

Professor Ernest Mund passed away in late 2024 after having delivered a draft of this manuscript. This is a slightly edited and updated version of the originally submitted manuscript, which is published with the permission of Professor Mundt's immediate family. https://bnsorg.be/passing-away-of-prof-ernest-mund/

E. Mund (✉)
FNRS, Université Catholique de Louvain, Louvain-La-Neuve, Belgium

M. Henrekson et al. (eds.), *A Green Entrepreneurial State?*, International Studies in Entrepreneurship 49, https://doi.org/10.1007/978-3-032-15512-2_15

Introduction

The European Green Deal adopted in 2020 should drastically reduce the continent's greenhouse gas releases (GGR) by 2030 and lead to carbon neutrality in 2050. With member states such as Austria, Germany and Luxembourg fiercely against nuclear energy, this policy scheme means the adoption of essentially 100% renewable energy, a detrimental choice for environmental reasons as shown in Furfari and Mund (2021). The arguments of nuclear deniers run essentially against high building costs, the fear of potential accidents and the legacy of long-lived nuclear wastes (Sovacool and Cooper 2008). Considering the present state of the technology, these arguments are partially justified. However, there is such a large variety in selecting the basic elements to build a neutron chain-reacting system that the technology could soon become very different from its current state inherited from the Cold War (Ud-Din Khan and Nakhabov 2020).

Though not strictly Darwinian, the evolution of technologies has much in common with the evolution of the living world (Arthur 2009). Both evolve on their own time scales according to similar principles.[1] The emergence of a new technology usually corresponds to the satisfaction of social needs not yet covered or to the implementation of recent scientific discoveries. As soon as a new technology emerges, it is coupled in some way or another to existing technologies to form a new branch of a tree structure. Structural deepening and internal replacement are two important mechanisms presiding over the evolution of a new technology. Trial-and-error mechanisms allow at any time the adoption of the most efficiently performing auxiliary tools.

The evolutionary process is *autopoietic* in the sense that a technology fully participates in its own transformation.[2] Once different varieties of a new technology get access to the market, the latter selects the variety that most fully satisfies its needs. But, unlike the Darwinian biological world where long-term domination is exercised by the most robust elements, technologies do not necessarily obey the same rule. Some suboptimal version of a technology may achieve market dominance. As soon as a technology exerts dominance over its competitors for whatever reason, one speaks of *lock-in*. Instances of suboptimal technological lock-ins abound on the market (Cowan and Hulten 1996).

In the nuclear field, we will first have a look at the light-water (LWR) technology, a felicitous example of suboptimal dominance (Cowan 1990) and afterward explain the reasons why optimism must prevail.

---

[1] See Edquist and Henrekson (2006) for an in-depth discussion of the time-lag involved in the adoption of new general purpose technologies from the steam engine through the ICT revolution.

[2] *Autopoietic* is a Greek word borrowed from biologists, describing the property allowing systems to transform themselves.

The Present Lock-In of Nuclear Power

On December 2, 1942, a team of physicists led by Enrico Fermi at the University of Chicago performs the first neutron chain reaction in a graphite-moderated pile called CP-1. This chain reaction is based on nuclear fission of uranium-235, a physical phenomenon discovered in Germany four years earlier. A new technology emerges with physical processes releasing extremely large amounts of thermal energy. At that time, the United States top priority is a rapid ending of World War II. Obviously, the new technology has many military applications. These are immediately developed in the frame of the so-called Manhattan Project leading to the destruction of Hiroshima and Nagasaki in August 1945. After the end of WWII, a new threat emerges that also asks for military strategy: Soviet imperialism. At that time some high commanders of the US Navy envisaged nuclear propulsion for submarines as a main deterrent, allowing long term underwater immersion. Similar prospects arise at the US Air Force although, from the start, they look more difficult to achieve.

Early on physicists were aware of the variety of possible chain-reacting systems depending on the choice of moderator (a light element such as hydrogen, deuterium or carbon for the slowing down of high energy fission neutrons) and coolant (light or heavy water [D_2O], gas, or liquid metals). The graphite-moderated CP-1 reactor offered an excellent neutron balance, but graphite-moderation results in less compact facilities than water-moderated reactors. On the other hand, light water reactors (LWR) have a less favorable neutron economy than graphite- or heavy water-moderated reactors. But reactor size being imperative for submarine propulsion systems, LWRs were chosen for the US Navy (Weinberg 1994). As industry giants such as Westinghouse and General Electric were soon involved in the naval program, the commercial power reactors that would follow would naturally belong to the same technology, requiring slightly enriched uranium in U^{235} ($\leq 5\%$). The United Kingdom and France initially opted for natural uranium (U_{nat}) and graphite, while Canada chose U_{nat} and heavy water for its CANDU line. Over time, only CANDU reactors among the varieties based on U_{nat} were maintained, the British and French graphite-moderated and gas-cooled reactors being gradually supplanted by the suboptimal LWRs, enforcing lock-in (Cowan 1990).

Shippingport, the first civilian pressurized water reactor (PWR) (Generation-II) was launched in 1957 with a 60 MWe power output.[3] Five years later came BR3, the first PWR installation outside the US, built at SCK CEN in Mol, Belgium. Shippingport was a landmark in many respects. In particular, it demonstrated the possibility to breed (produce fissile nuclei in excess of nuclei consumption entailed by energy production) U^{233} from Th^{232} with thermal neutrons. However, thermal neutron breeding was not exploited; at that point in time, R&D being focused essentially on fast neutron breeding.

The first LWR commercial units built in the early 1970s were rated well above 400 MWe to optimize investments and reduce energy costs.[4] A basic feature of the

[3] In a PWR, light water is used both as a neutron moderator and as coolant fluid for the reactor core.

[4] Approximately one-third of the capacity of today's standard reactors.

embryonic industry—with obvious economic consequences—was that no two power plants were identical. This practice has not changed, although technical elements are progressively put in place that could modify LWR concepts within the next decade. Major advances in LWR technology were achieved at Oregon State University (OSU) in Portland during the 1990s: The development of so-called integral PWRs, having their steam generators (SG) inside their pressure vessels, which considerably reduces the risk of loss-of-coolant accident (LOCA). These advances provided the start of a new industrial paradigm: factory-made units of much smaller power size (~75MWe), the so-called *Small Modular Reactor* (SMR) concept. NuScale, an offspring of the OSU nuclear R&D team, will likely be the first SMR designer to install a power plant comprising six 77 MWe power modules at the Idaho National Laboratory (INL) before the end of the decade.[5] Other light-water SMR systems with integrated steam generators (SG) will soon appear on the market in China (ACP100), France (Nuward) and the UK. In the latter case, Rolls-Royce—better known for its luxury cars—is the architect-engineer of British nuclear submarines developing a 470 MWe pressurized water SMR. In March 2023, it signed a letter of intent with the Polish group Industria to deploy three SMRs to decarbonize the company's energy infrastructure.

The economic competitiveness of SMRs versus large conventional reactors is a key topic. It was extensively studied in the early 2000s (Boarin et al. 2012) and still is (Mignacca and Locatelli 2020), but so far no definitive conclusion has transpired. Most authors agree that the scale effect is not the only factor to be considered: co-siting economies, modularity and construction time are relevant parameters that must also be reckoned with. Finally, there is agreement on the need for an analysis of the decommissioning cost of SMR sites compared to the decommissioning cost of large power plants. Decommissioning multiple smaller installations could be less costly, but whether this is so needs to be properly assessed.

Early Activities in Advanced Reactor Systems

At the time the US Navy endorsed nuclear propulsion for its submarines, the US Air Force was looking for aircraft nuclear propulsion (ANP). Water reactors being unable to provide temperature levels needed for aircraft propulsion (~750 °C), physicists at Oak Ridge National Laboratory (ORNL) suggested an alternate neutron chain-reacting system based on molten salts providing high temperatures. The first system known as ARE (Aircraft Reactor Experiment) had too many snags, including the molten salt corroding the reactor metal, leading to its abandonment in 1954. It was followed by the Molten Salt Reactor Experiment (MSRE) in 1965, which was operated for four years. Both systems were very successful. The technology differed fundamentally from Fermi's original one, with a uranium tetrafluoride fluid fuel instead of a uranium metallic one.

[5] Approximately 15 such units would be needed to produce the same amount of electricity as a newly built conventional reactor.

At that time, Alvin Weinberg and Eugene Wigner were fascinated by homogeneous nuclear systems, easy to model mathematically. At Oak Ridge National Laboratory (ORNL), they promoted the development of two systems using a highly enriched uranium oxide sulfate aqueous solution: the Homogeneous Reactor Experiment (HRE) and Homogeneous Reactor Test (HRT). These four successful facilities—ARE, MSRE, HRE, and HRT—are perhaps the most important ones among the 13 that were built at ORNL. Regarding the design of future nuclear systems these systems are called Generation-IV (Rosenthal 2010).

Nuclear Energy of the Future

In 2001, the US Department of Energy (USDOE) launched an initiative to identify nuclear technologies that meet stringent safety, economic, environmental, and non-proliferation criteria for future primary energy production. A study group called Generation-IV International Forum (GIF) was created. Several countries responded to the call.[6] Six technologies that met these requirements were identified: gas cooled fast reactors (GFR), sodium cooled fast reactors (SFR), super-critical water reactors (SCWR) very high temperature reactors (VHTR), lead cooled fast reactors (LFR) and molten salt reactors (MSR). The molten salt technology that was tested at ORNL during the 1950s in the ARE and MSRE experiments was considered by the GIF experts as one of the most attractive and safe nuclear technologies for the following reasons:

- The absence of water in the reactor core eliminates the risk of a loss-of-coolant accident (LOCA), as was the case in the Three Mile Island accident in 1979. It also eliminates the risk of hydrogen explosion from zirconium/water reactions that can occur on exposed high-temperature fuel rods cladding (the thin-walled metal tube that forms the rod's outer jacket)—an event that occurred at Fukushima in 2011.
- The absence of sodium eliminates the risk of highly exothermic chemical reactions.
- A pressure close to atmospheric pressure, the liquid state of the fuel and favorable neutron properties (strongly negative temperature reactivity coefficient) also contribute to safety.
- The fact that at operating temperatures (~700 °C) the fuel for MSRs is in the liquid phase, makes it easier to feed fresh fuel than in solid fuel systems. Although this is a delicate operation, a regular supply is possible, which is not the case for solid fuel systems. Therefore, there is no need for a long-term reactivity reserve, which eliminates the risk of a Chernobyl-type accident.

[6] Argentina, Brazil, Canada, France, Japan, South Korea, South Africa, the United Kingdom, and the United States, later joined by Switzerland, the European Union, China, Russia, and Australia.

- The composition of the molten salt is such that the liquid state can be maintained up to 1400 °C, well above operating values. If, for any reason, the temperature of the salt falls below 459 °C, the melting temperature of the lithium beryllium fluoride (LBF) of which it is composed, solidification occurs with mass retention of the non-volatile fission products.

All of these aspects were outlined in detail in the first Generation-IV technology roadmap (U.S. DOE NERAC 2002).

MSR's reduced accident risks have a positive impact on the reactor economy, by reducing the need for active systems to guarantee the safety of the installations, such as those used in current LWR plants. Finally, molten salt installations with fast neutron spectra would open the way to a reduction in the nuclear "liabilities" of current reactors (plutonium and minor actinides with very long half-lives)[7] that are unmanageable in the latter. Inserting these waste products as a fuel source in these MSRs would simultaneously tap their residual energy content and eliminate a highly problematic environmental presence of radioisotopes having half-lives of several hundred thousand years.

The conclusions of the Generation-IV Roadmap resulted in a revived interest throughout the world in a technology that had been lethargic since the early 1980s. Many current MSR R&D projects can be expected to produce prototypes within the next 15 to 20 years (Furfari and Mund 2022; IAEA 2020). Figure 1 displays some of the most advanced ones in various countries.

Attention should be paid to the Moltex, Elysium, TerraPower and Mosart projects. These are four fast reactor projects specifically designed to exploit not only conventional resources (^{235}U and ^{239}Pu produced from the conversion of ^{238}U) but also the existing stock of spent fuel from current LWR and CANDU reactors with a significant range of actinide nuclei. While doing so, they transform an environmentally unsustainable by-product—for the most ardent opponents of nuclear power—into an energy resource that can be used until all fissile nuclei are exhausted. TMSR, as its name indicates, is oriented towards the exploitation of the thorium fuel cycle, an important mineral asset in China. TMSR is the only facility developed along two different technological tracks: a molten salt fuel version or a solid fuel version using pebbles with TRISO particles (Zhang et al. 2018).

Most installations enter into the SMR category, with electric power units less or equal to 300 MWe. Depending on the intended applications, the power unit effect may be as low as 45 MWe. This is the case, for instance, of Terrapower's MCFR that has been selected by Core Power, a British maritime company to decarbonize naval propulsion (Furfari and Mund 2022).

Future MSR systems will coexist with Generation-II and Generation-III LWRs with power sizes exceeding 1.6 GWe. Their nuclear fuel cycles will be in synergy as illustrated in Fig. 2. Basically, all will depend on uranium mining, but MSRs with fast neutron spectra will eliminate minor actinides generated in LWRs and reduce

[7] Actinides are radioactive metallic elements whose atomic numbers start from 89 (actinium) and end at 103 (lawrencium). Because of their unstable nucleus, they decay into other elements and other simple particles.

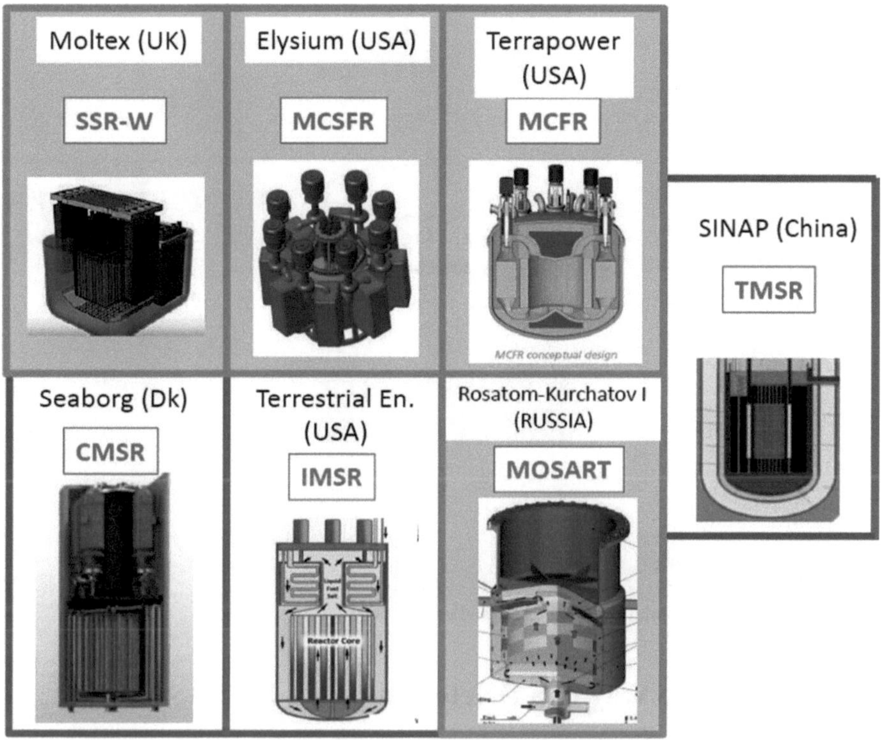

Fig. 1 MSR systems with thermal- and fast neutron spectra, in various stages of progress. *Note* SSR-W = Stable Salt Reactor Waste burner, MCSFR = Molten Chloride Salt Fast Reactor, MCFR = Molten Chloride Fast Reactor, CMSR = Compact Molten Salt Reactor, IMSR Integral = Molten Salt Reactor, and TMSR = Thorium Molten Salt Reactor

the long-lived nuclear waste stockpile. All facilities will provide electricity, but in addition MSR will also deliver high temperature heat for industrial uses (district heating, water desalination) and final energy for naval propulsion.

Industrial heat production is of the utmost importance (Furfari and Mund 2020). In current energy policies, the use of heat is often neglected. The 2022 crisis in Germany highlighted this fundamental need for "final energy," which the chemical industry badly needs. More than 90% of the natural gas used in Germany is used for thermal purposes.

The MSR heat may also become an energy source for the thermal decomposition of water for hydrogen production. An EU Green Deal requirement for accelerated hydrogen production from variable and intermittent renewables may lock-in this hydrogen production despite its economic and environmental disadvantages shown below.

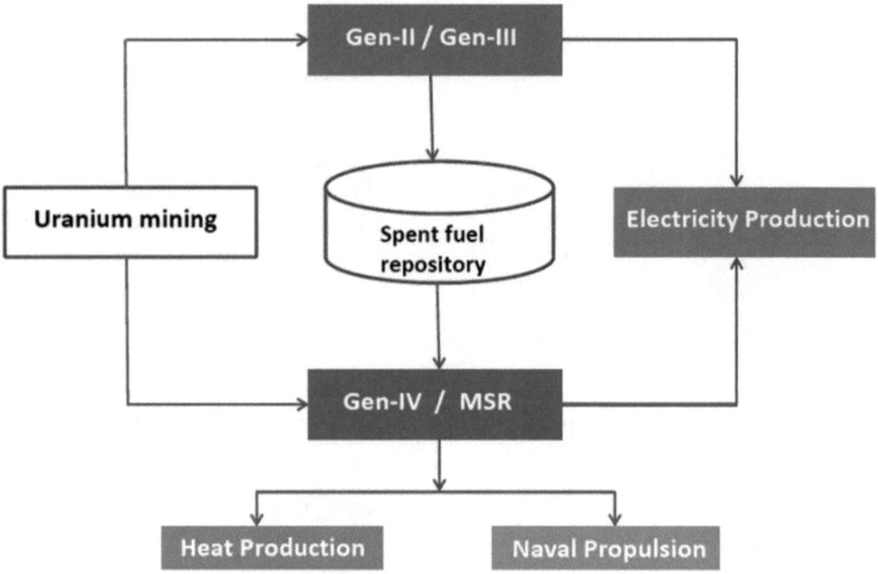

Fig. 2 Flexibility and benefits of Generation-IV

Is Europe on the Way to a Deleterious Lock-In?

The European Union was born on the basis of the European Coal and Steel Community (ECSC) and Euratom treaties in 1951 and 1957, respectively. These treaties aimed to create an internal market for coal and steel and to promote civil nuclear energy. Until recently, the European Commission was the guardian and promoter of the latter. Under the influence of Germany's hostility towards nuclear energy, the Commission has gradually withdrawn from the promotion of civil nuclear energy.

By choosing to promote renewable energies "whatever it takes" and by abstaining from taking a pro-active position in favor of nuclear energy as required by the Euratom Treaty, the European Commission is weakening further continental development of the technology, instead promoting variable and intermittent renewable energy sources. Preconditions for future locking in of the latter are thus in place despite the fact that several environmental indicators are in favor of nuclear energy such as power plant footprints, material requirements (concrete, metals, cement, glass and more) and system costs.

These are the most obvious factors, but there are more subtle elements involved as well. Unlike variable and intermittent renewables, nuclear reactors do not create geopolitical dependence on China, which dominates the market for rare earths and other metals that renewables equipment require, as we will see below. Renewable energy source lock-in would not only be detrimental for environmental but also for geopolitical reasons.

Table 1 compares the power footprints (expressed in m^2/GW) of nuclear plants and intermittent renewable energy sources on the basis of data collected in a very large geographical area (Deshaies 2020). Intermittent renewable energy sources have very low power densities compared to nuclear energy. This implies much larger footprints than nuclear plants. The ratio depends on both location and technology and approximately ranges from 200 to 1000.

Table 2 shows the basic material requirements (excluding fuel resources) for the implementation of energy technologies for nuclear pressurized water reactors, solar and onshore wind energy. These requirements are expressed in thousands of tons per TWh. Here again, nuclear power has advantages over variable and intermittent renewables. Despite the considerable quantities of concrete that are invested to guarantee the safety of the nuclear installations, these quantities are only one-fourth of those required by wind power (and much lower still than those invested in the construction of dams) and even lower than those required for solar photovoltaic panels. The differential in the use of core metals is much larger. The need for steel, aluminum and copper per TWh is at least one order of magnitude larger for solar and wind compared to nuclear.

Moreover, the lifespans differ greatly. A sixty-year lifespan of a nuclear plant is probably an underestimation. Today's plants are more likely to last for at least 80 years. When it comes to wind turbines, the only independently conducted study I am aware of, shows that new generations have turned out to have shorter lifespans and higher operating costs than the previous ones (Hughes 2021). The 30-year lifespan maintained by the World Nuclear Association (2024) may thus be too optimistic.

Table 1 Footprints of three types of primary energy installations

Primary Source	Power units (GW)	Power footprint (m^2/GW)	Ratio to nuclear
Nuclear	1 to 5	5×10^5 to 10^6	1
PV solar park	0.005 to 0.8	10^8 to 5×10^8	200–1000
Thermal solar park	0.01 to 0.4	10^8 to 2×10^8	200–400
Wind park	0.01 to 0.5	$2 \bullet 10^8$ to 5×10^8	400–1000

Source Deshais (2020)

Table 2 Major materials for different generating technologies, tonnes per TWh

	Nuclear PWR	Solar PV	Onshore wind
Concrete	1060	1220	4450
Steel	130	940	1450
Aluminum	0.3	287.5	17.4
Copper	2.5	68	39.1
Lifespan	60	30	30

Source World Nuclear Association (2024)

Last but not least, the cost of these technologies has been extensively studied by the OECD's Nuclear Energy Agency (NEA). In a report entitled *The Full Costs of Electricity Provision*, the agency reviews the different components of the cost of production (Keppler et al. 2018). This is particularly important for intermittent generation (wind, solar PV), which faces supply difficulties in the event of a prolonged intermittency. To guarantee the supply of demand, variable and intermittent renewable energy sources must be replaced by controllable means which themselves represent a cost and whose profitability is not necessarily optimal. All these elements guaranteeing security of supply are to be classified (from a cost point of view) in what the NEA calls the *system cost*. More than the costs of production, operation and maintenance, it is the system costs that make the difference between these different technologies (controllable and intermittent). The NEA report estimates the system cost (in USD/MWh) for controllable (fossil, nuclear) and intermittent (wind, solar PV) technologies for two penetration rates (10 and 30%) of the latter in the electricity system. The system cost is made up of several elements, namely connection, transmission and distribution, grid balancing and usage costs.

While it should be acknowledged that uncertainties are considerable, most estimates recognize that the grid-level system costs associated with variable renewable energy integration are large and increase disproportionately with the share in electricity generated (i.e., the penetration level). In comparison, system costs of dispatchable technologies, such as coal, gas, nuclear power or hydro, are at least one order of magnitude lower (Fahlén et al. 2026). Thus, it comes as no surprise that controllable production such as nuclear is the most economically favorable.

All three elements of comparison (footprint, materials, and costs) point in the same direction: nuclear technology is preferable to variable and intermittent renewables. Of course, in the studies referred to, Generation-II technology was used to assess the various parameters. The forthcoming arrival of Generation-IV should not fundamentally change the conclusions. And, as mentioned earlier, the inherent safety of future nuclear power should make the technology more attractive. The biggest hurdle to overcome will be the psychological one, as an instinctive fear of radiation permeates the public mind.

Conclusion

Evolution and transition of technologies are processes that take time. There are many reasons for this state of affairs, technical, commercial as well as political. The great successes of the past make us forget today that at the time they took place, things were far from simple, resistance to change being always present for many reasons, including commercial ones. This was particularly the case in Colonel Drake's time (1859), at the beginning of the industrial era of rock oil, a competitor to coal oil, turpentine and whale oil, especially for lighting (Rhodes 2018). The use of this commodity eventually took off in the transport sector.

In the case of Generation-IV nuclear power discussed in this essay, the time needed for future deployment of this technology is related to its fine-tuning. Its advantages over Generation-II and Generation-III technologies are known, and previous successful implementation only reinforces the attractiveness of the new technology. The biggest hurdle to overcome will be psychological, as an instinctive fear of radiation permeates the public mind in the West.

This fear is far from universal: What will the European Union do if it is confirmed that in 20 years' time the rest of the world, having not taken part in the "monoculture" of variable and intermittent renewables, will have taken a serious lead in these new technologies, which are free of the main shortcomings of current installations—accident risks, long-lived waste—and have eminent environmental qualities? To ignore this opportunity would be to set up a pernicious lock-in that future generations are likely to regret. Paradoxically, for reasons that are essentially environmental.

References

Arthur, B. W. (2009). *The Nature of Technology—What It Is and How It Evolves*. New York, NY: Penguin.

Boarin, S., Locatelli, G., Mancini, M., & Ricotti, M. E. (2012). Financial case studies on small- and medium-size modular reactors. *Nuclear Technology, 178*(2), 218–232. https://doi.org/10.13182/NT12-A13561

Cowan, R. (1990). Nuclear power reactors: A study in technological lock-in. *Journal of Economic History, 50*(3), 541–567.

Cowan, R., & Hulten. S. (1996). Escaping lock-in: The case of the electric vehicle. *Technological Forecasting and Social Change, 53*(1), 61–79.

Deshaies M. (2020). Geographical problems of energy transitions: What perspectives for the evolution of the energy system? *Mondes en Développment, 2020/4*(192), 25–44.

Edquist, H., & Henrekson, M. (2006). Technological breakthroughs and productivity growth. In A. J. Field, G. Clark, & W. A. Sundstrom (Eds.), *Research in Economic History*, Vol. 24 (pp. 1–53). Bingley: Emerald.

Fahlén, P., Henrekson, M., & Nilsson, M. (2026). In pursuit of a green transition—Electricity at any cost? In M. Henrekson, C. Sandström, & M. Stenkula (Eds.), A Green Entrepreneurial State? Exploring the Pitfalls of Green Deals (pp. 149–172). Cham. Springer.

Furfari, S., & Mund, E. (2020). Renewable energy in the EU: From perception to reality. *Energy Literacy*, 27–11–2020. https://www.connaissancedesenergies.org/tribune-actualite-energies/energies-renouvelables-dans-lue-de-la-perception-aux-realites

Furfari, S., & Mund, E. (2021). Is the European green deal achievable? *European Physics Journal Plus, 136*(11), Article 1101. https://doi.org/10.1140/epjp/s13360-021-02075-7

Furfari, S., & Mund, E. (2022). Advanced nuclear power for clean maritime propulsion. *European Physics Journal Plus, 137*(6), Article 747. https://doi.org/10.1140/epjp/s13360-022-02980-5

Hughes, G. (2021). Costs, performance and investment returns for wind power. School of Economics, University of Edinburgh, and Renewable Energy Foundation. https://www.ref.org.uk/attachments/article/369/GH20210621.pdf

IAEA (2020). *Advances in Small Modular Reactor Technology Developments*. A Supplement to: IAEA Advanced Reactors Information System (ARIS), 2020 Edition. Vienna: IAEA. https://aris.iaea.org/publications/smr_book_2020.pdf

Mignacca, B., & Locatelli, G. (2020). Economics and finance of Small Modular Reactors: A systematic review and research agenda. *Renewable and Sustainable Energy Reviews, 118*(February), 109519. https://doi.org/10.1016/j.rser.2019.109519

Keppler, J. H., et al. (2018). *The Full Costs of Electricity Provision*. NEA No. 7298. Paris: Nuclear Energy Agency (NEA), OECD. https://www.oecd-nea.org/upload/docs/application/pdf/2019-12/7298-full-costs-2018.pdf

Rhodes, R. (2018). *Energy – A Human History*. New York, NY: Simon & Schuster.

Rosenthal, M. W. (2010). *An Account of Oak Ridge National Laboratory's Thirteen Nuclear Reactors*. ORNL/TM-2009/181. Oak Ridge, TN: Oak Ridge National Laboratory, US Department of Energy. https://info.ornl.gov/sites/publications/files/Pub20808.pdf

Sovacool, B. K., & Cooper, C. (2008). Nuclear nonsense: Why nuclear power is no answer to climate change and the world's post-Kyoto energy challenges. *William & Mary Environmental Law and Policy Review, 33*(1), Article 2. https://scholarship.law.wm.edu/wmelpr/vol33/iss1/2

Ud-Din Khan, S., & Nakhabov, A. (2020). *Nuclear Reactor Technology Development and Utilization*. Amsterdam: Elsevier.

Weinberg, A. M. (1994). *The First Nuclear Era: The Life and Times of a Technological Fixer*. New York, NY: Springer.

U.S. DOE NERAC (2002). *A Technology Roadmap for Generation IV Nuclear Energy Systems*. Paris: OECD-NEA. https://www.gen-4.org/gif/upload/docs/application/pdf/2014-03/gif-tru2014.pdf

World Nuclear Association (2024). *Nuclear Energy and Sustainable Development*. London. https://world-nuclear.org/information-library/energy-and-the-environment/nuclear-energy-and-sustainable-development.aspx

Zhang, D., Liu, L., Liu, M., et al. (2018). Review of conceptual design and fundamental research of molten salt reactors in China. *International Journal of Energy Research, 42*, 1834–1848. https://doi.org/10.1002/er.3979

Professor Ernest Mund passed away on November 12, 2024. At that point in time, he was Honorary Research Director of FNRS and Emeritus Professor at Université Catholique de Louvain, Belgium.

He was a world-renowned figure in the field of nuclear engineering and reactor physics. Over the past decade, he turned his interest to the economic and societal aspects of nuclear energy, aiming to contribute to the factual evaluation of this energy source and to the societal debate on the contribution of nuclear energy to the energy transition.

"State-ification" of the Entrepreneur—Or "Entrepreneurialization" of the State? How Singapore Challenges Both Mazzucato and Her Critics

Jacob Hjortsberg

Abstract This article reviews the debate over the "entrepreneurial state" by examining Singapore as a case that both confirms and challenges Mariana Mazzucato's vision. Rather than adopting the entrepreneurial role while retaining conventional features of statehood, Singapore reframes governance itself as an entrepreneurial activity—what I term the "entrepreneurialization" of the state. Through an exploration of elite investment via sovereign wealth funds, mass homeownership as a tool of citizen buy-in, and the strategic deployment of "dual state legality," the article shows how Singapore aligns both elite and popular incentives with long-term national economic performance. The result is a model in which the state does not "pick winners," but creates an environment that attracts them. While this model is deeply context-specific and normatively contentious, it offers broader insights into how traditional domains of governance—housing, law, and public administration—can be reconceived through an entrepreneurial lens. The article concludes by suggesting that, rather than seeking to replicate Singapore wholesale, policymakers might explore how to embed entrepreneurial thinking into state functions, especially in domains like green innovation, where long-term success requires public commitment without sacrificing institutional credibility.

Keywords Industrial policy · Government policy · Asia including Middle East · Criminal law · Contract law · Social security and Public pensions

***JEL* Codes** O25 · O35 · O53 · K12 · K14 · H55

This work was supported by funding from the European Research Council (ERC) under the European Union's Horizon 2020 research and innovation program (Grant Agreement No. 101054237) for the project Global Value Chain Law: Constituting Connectivity, Contracts and Corporations.

J. Hjortsberg (✉)
Copenhagen Business School, Department of Business Humanities and Law, Copenhagen, Denmark
e-mail: jahj.bhl@cbs.dk

M. Henrekson et al. (eds.), *A Green Entrepreneurial State?*, International Studies in Entrepreneurship 49, https://doi.org/10.1007/978-3-032-15512-2_16

Introduction

In debates over the entrepreneurial state, both Marianna Mazzucato and her critics share a common premise: that the entrepreneurial state involves a "state-ification" of the entrepreneurial role. When the state acts as an entrepreneur in the market, the thinking goes, it does so while retaining its defining characteristics, most notably the power to levy taxes backed up by the monopoly on the legitimate use of force. Where proponents and detractors diverge is on the question of whether such an actor will exert a positive or negative influence on market dynamics: whether it can deliver beneficial outcomes that private entrepreneurs cannot (acting as a "lead risk-taker" and "market-shaper"), or whether it is more likely to distort market incentives and misallocate resources.

In this article, I will take a closer look at this debate from the vantage point of Singapore. My argument is that Singapore, on the one hand, lends support to proponents of the entrepreneurial state, as it represents a highly successful example of a state that acts as an entrepreneur in the market. But rather than following the model proposed by Mazzucato, I suggest, Singapore represents a different kind of entrepreneurial state: one that does not seek to "state-ify" the role of the entrepreneur, but instead approaches governance itself as a marketable service to be offered "for sale" on the global market—in other words, by "entrepreneurializing" the role of the state.

This argument has important implications for how to think about the state's role in driving technological change. Advocates of the entrepreneurial state often argue that governments should act as drivers of innovation in areas like green technology, where the risks involved are too high for private actors. Based on the discussion in this article, we should be cautious about such claims. This does not imply, however, that the state must retreat to a minimalist role of merely upholding the rule of law or correcting market failures. On the contrary, this article envisions a more proactive state—one that does not attempt to "pick winners" in the market, but instead adopts an entrepreneurial posture in traditional domains of governance: infrastructure, housing, and the legal system. Here, the state can act not by competing with other entrepreneurs, but by strategically shaping the conditions in which market actors operate.

Mazzucato's Core Thesis

In her 2013 book, *The Entrepreneurial State: Debunking Public vs. Private Sector Myths*, Mariana Mazzucato calls for a fundamental rethinking of the relationship between the state and the market in capitalist economies. According to the dominant, neoclassical conception, the state has a legitimate role to play in the economy, but it is narrowly confined to two core functions: (1) upholding the rule of law and protecting property rights and (2) correcting market failures, such as those involving public goods, externalities, or information asymmetries. Beyond these functions, neoclassical economists tend to view state intervention with skepticism, often characterizing it as inefficient, overly bureaucratic, or distortive of otherwise self-regulating market forces.

According to Mazzucato, however, the role of the state in a capitalist economy should be understood as far more expansive and active. This claim is both empirical and normative. Empirically, she argues, many of the innovations that underpin the modern economy were not the result of private entrepreneurs operating in the market, but of state-led investments and initiatives. Take, for example, the iPhone, she writes:

> [A]ll of the technologies that make [Steve] Jobs' iPhone so 'smart' were government funded (Internet, GPS, touch-screen display and the recent SIRI voice activated personal assistant). Such radical investments – which embedded extreme uncertainty – did not come about due to the presence of venture capitalists, nor of 'garage tinkerers'. It was the visible hand of the State which made these innovations happen. Innovation that would not have come about had we waited for the 'market' and business to do it alone – or government to simply stand aside and provide the basics. (Mazzucato 2013, p. 3)

So from an empirical standpoint, Mazzucato argues, it is simply not true that the only legitimate or productive role of the state in a market economy is to uphold the rule of law and correct market failures. On the contrary: without the "visible hand of the state," many of the breakthrough technologies we attribute to private entrepreneurs and the "invisible hand" of the market would simply not exist (Mazzucato 2013, p. 3).

From a normative point of view, in turn, this implies that the state should be much more confident in its role. Why is it, Mazzucato asks, that private entrepreneurs get to reap all the benefits from technologies whose development was largely enabled by public risk-taking? The state assumes much of the risk, but the rewards are privatized, justified by the "myth" that private actors alone took the risks and did the innovating. But if the state has in fact borne much of the uncertainty and investment, and done so much of the innovating, should it not also share more directly in the returns?

In fact, Mazzucato says, not only is the state an entrepreneurial actor among others—it is a "lead risk-taker" (Mazzucato 2013, chapters 8 and 9) and a "market shaper" (Mazzucato 2013, chapter 4). This means that the state does more than simply invest in innovative technologies; it takes on the kinds of high-risk, high-uncertainty investments that private entrepreneurs typically avoid. For example, Mazzucato writes, while the state may fund the development of radical new therapies, pharmaceutical companies often prefer to invest in safer "me too"-drugs that offer minor variations on existing treatments (ibid., pp. 108–110). Similarly, while the state has been central in funding the development of breakthrough technologies like the touch-screen or GPS, private entrepreneurs have largely focused on commercializing these technologies once the risk has been absorbed by the public sector (Mazzucato 2013, chapter 5).

So not only is the state entrepreneurial; it is the *most important entrepreneur of them all*, willing to invest in technologies that fundamentally transform how we live. And by consciously embracing this role and securing a fair share of the returns, Mazzucato argues, the state could ensure that the benefits of innovation are shared more broadly—enabling a more inclusive and equitable distribution of rewards, rather than "socializing risks and privatizing gains."

The Critics' Response

If Mazzucato's vision seems too good to be true, her critics argue, that is because it is. Here, my aim here is not to catalogue all of their objections (see instead Wennberg and Sandström 2022; Henrekson et al. 2024), but rather to highlight what many of them describe as a central contradiction in her argument—namely, that Mazzucato's case for the entrepreneurial state rests on the impossible assumption that there can exist a category of investments that are simultaneously too risky for private entrepreneurs to pursue, yet consistently successful enough to generate returns that outweigh the state's losses. But such a category cannot exist, critics argue—because if it did, private investors would pursue it too!

If state bureaucrats truly had knowledge of investments that, like the internet, could reliably produce high returns despite high-uncertainty, then why would they not be immediately hired by private investment firms? The answer, critics contend, is that state bureaucrats do not, in fact, possess any special foresight that allows them to consistently "pick winners." Instead, the only categories of investments that the state alone can undertake are: (a) investments that are typically not profitable within any reasonable time frame, but nevertheless socially valuable (such as basic research or investments in infrastructure), or (b) investments so risky that only a state insulated from financial failure would be willing to fund them.

Revealingly, critics point out, Mazzucato herself struggles to provide convincing examples of investments that truly fall into the first category. Instead, she often cites examples that fit one of the other two, while treating them as evidence of the first. For instance, she points to public funding of basic science that later enabled commercial breakthroughs. But from a neoclassical perspective, this is a textbook example of a public good, and thus an area where state intervention is already well justified. Worse yet, she celebrates state-led investments that, in hindsight, proved to be economically disastrous, and could only have been made by an actor shielded from market discipline. A case in point is Germany's *Energiewende*, which she treats as bold and visionary, despite its widely criticized costs and outcomes (see Mazzucato 2013, p. 185).

Thus, the entire argument appears to be based on a bait-and-switch. First, Mazzucato boldly claims that the state must go beyond its traditional roles of upholding the rule of law and correcting market failures, and instead act in the market as an entrepreneurial agent pursuing high-risk, high-reward investment. But when it comes to specifying exactly what kinds of investments these are, she tends to fall back on either investments in public goods (which, from a neoclassical point of view, are already accepted as legitimate), or investments so risky that only a state insulated from financial losses would undertake them (which, from a neoclassical point of view, are precisely the reason why the state should not undertake entrepreneurial activities in the first place). Nevertheless, Mazzucato treats all these examples as evidence of her basic claim, concluding that the state can fund its future entrepreneurial activities through returns on past investments, despite having offered little actual evidence that such a model can consistently generate those returns.

State-Ification or Entrepreneurialization?

In this article, my primary aim is not to side with Mazzucato's critics—though, as the reader can tell, my theoretical sympathies generally lie in that direction. Rather, my goal is to suggest that, while critics are likely right about the unfeasibility of the entrepreneurial state as conceptualized by Mazzucato, this does not mean that such a thing as an entrepreneurial state could never exist at all.

This is where Singapore enters the picture. Since at least 1974, when journalist Louis Kraar published his *Fortune* article, "Singapore, the country run like a corporation," observers have noted that the Singaporean state resembles a corporation much more than a traditional nation-state. As political scientist Michael Barr writes, it is "a lot easier to understand Singapore if you put aside notions of modernity and ordinary governance, let alone democracy, and begin from the premise that it is a Chinese family business, complete with a patriarch, an eldest son, *guanxi* networks and questions of cross-generational continuity" (Barr 2014, p. 108). Similarly, when science fiction writer William Gibson visited Singapore in 1993—famously describing it as "Disneyland with the death penalty"—he came away with the impression that the country is "micromanaged by a state that has the look and feel of a very large corporation," speculating that "If IBM had ever bothered to actually possess a physical country, that country might have had a lot in common with Singapore" (Gibson 1993). And when senior Singaporean diplomat Kishore Mahbubani was asked what the "secret sauce" of Singapore consists of, he pointed to the fact that Singapore's civil service had originally been modeled on the Shell Oil corporation:

> Singapore did not invent meritocracy. The leaders of Singapore simply asked which organizations in the world were most successful and why. The answer they got was that private sector companies were often more successful. At that time, Shell Oil Company offered a useful example. They were successful because they promoted their staff on merit, not seniority. It was on this basis that the Singapore civil service became the first ex-British colony to switch its promotion policies away from the British civil system to that of a British oil corporation system. (Mahbubani 2018)

To conceptualize the Singaporean state as an entrepreneurial state is therefore not much of a leap. Indeed, the Singaporean state is often referred to as "Singapore Inc" (see also Ong 2006, pp. 177ff; Balding 2012; Singh 2019). What crucially distinguishes Singapore's version of the corporate state from Mazzucato's vision, I will argue, is how each understands the relationship between the state and the market.

In Mazzucato's conception, the defining feature of the entrepreneurial state is precisely that it is *not* a private actor, but a state—meaning, a sovereign actor that has *power over* the market. This is why the entrepreneurial state is able to pursue long-term, socially oriented goals that are not constrained by short-term profit-motives: it can use taxes to fund its investments, which means that it is not constrained by narrow profit-motives. According to Mazzucato, of course, once the entrepreneurial state has made successful high-risk investments, it can reinvest the returns into further rounds of innovation, thus no longer having to rely on taxation. Nevertheless, what allows the state to act as the lead risk-taker in the first place is that it is spending public money, which insulates it from the financial constraints that govern private-sector behavior.

In this way, we might think of Mazzucato's conceptualization of the entrepreneurial state as a *state-ification* of the entrepreneurial role: the state assumes the function of the entrepreneur while leveraging its distinct capacities as a state—chiefly, its ability to collect taxes and channel public funds into high-risk investments. In Singapore, by contrast, this model is effectively reversed. Rather than the state adopting the role of the entrepreneur while retaining all the characteristic features of a state, Singapore represents what I will call an *entrepreneurialization* of the state itself—meaning, a state that approaches the project of governance itself as an entrepreneurial activity, rather than seeking to compete with private entrepreneurs in the market.

This understanding of the relationship between state and market was present from the very beginning in Singapore. In 1961—four years before Singapore became an independent nation—the United Nations sent a mission to the island to assess its prospects for surviving as an independent state. The mission was led by Dutch economist Albert Winsemius. In his report, commonly known as the Winsemius Report, he laid out what he saw as the basic conditions for economic development in Singapore. "In a small country with a large population, which has to live on exports," he wrote,

> it is in the long run not the government which can lay down working hours and conditions, not the trade unions and the employers who can fix wages and fringe benefits, but it is the foreign customer. [...] Capital can go to other countries, as it has already done. Enterprise can quiet down or escape, as it has done in recent years. Labour has no escape possibilities. It needs employment here and has no time to wait. (Winsemius 1963, pp. 200–201)

According to Winsemius, in other words, Singapore's only path to economic success was to position itself as a partner to global entrepreneurs—offering an attractive environment for international capital and enterprise. In this view, the market was not something over which the state could exert control or shape at will; on the contrary, it was the state that had to adapt to the imperatives of the global market, over which it had no power.

In what follows, I will outline three key features of Singapore's entrepreneurial state that are central to its success. In each case, the crucial point is that the Singaporean state does not attempt to compete with private entrepreneurs in the market. Instead, it applies an entrepreneurial mindset to traditional domains of governance—such as infrastructure, law, and public administration—reframing statecraft itself as a form of entrepreneurial activity.

Wealth Fund Elites

Besides its similarity to a corporation, the most well-known feature of the Singaporean state is its authoritarian, illiberal style of governance. At first glance, this presents observers with something of a paradox: how has Singapore managed so effectively to combine political illiberalism with economic liberalism? How has it become one of the world's most open, trade-dependent economies, while maintaining a fairly closed political system—governed by the same political party, and, for most of its history, by the same family?

In a recent article, economist Tegan Truitt tackles this question head-on. His answer lies in Singapore's distinctive approach to corporate governance. In most authoritarian regimes, he says, the lack of democratic accountability tends to foster corruption, as governing elites are incentivized to consolidate power, protect allies, and extract national wealth. "In general", he writes,

> we should expect state agents with massive amounts of discretionary power to use their power to enrich themselves. Government officials operating corporate enterprises might seek to impose heavy regulations on local businesses, once again to insulate themselves from competition, or take bribes from rent-seeking businessmen who seek such protection. Or we might expect the state to threaten to impose burdensome policies on private businesses in order to extract rents. We should probably expect very high tax rates, and perhaps a fair amount of trade protectionism. In short, the conventional literature on rent-seeking would suggest that elites of a functionally autocratic government would use their discretionary power more or less corruptly. (Truitt 2024, p. 6)

Incidentally, this is also one of the main criticisms leveled at Mariana Mazzucato's concept of the entrepreneurial state: giving bureaucrats control over public investment in high-risk ventures is more likely to encourage protectionism and rent-seeking than genuine innovation, since bureaucrats typically act based on political incentives and institutional self-interest rather than the public good. In Singapore, however, you find very little of this. Despite its leaders having far more discretionary power than most of their counterparts in other places, the country has remarkably low levels of corruption and rent-seeking. Now, how is this possible? Truitt offers a compelling explanation: rather than allowing elites to hold personal stakes in specific industries or firms, Singapore's political leadership is collectively invested in the country's two sovereign wealth funds—Temasek and GIC—both of which are diversified across the entire economy.

Temasek, on the one hand, holds majority stakes in all of Singapore's "government-linked corporations" (GLCs), which are state-owned enterprises that operate with a high degree of autonomy. Crucially, the government does not interfere in the management of either Temasek or the GLCs under its control. This, Truitt explains, was the main reason Temasek was established in the first place: "[I]n order to sustain investor confidence, [the government] created Temasek in 1974 as a holding company to deliberately insulate corporate governance from regulatory interference and vice versa" (ibid., p. 14). In addition to its control over GLCs, Temasek also holds minority stakes in nearly all companies listed on the Singapore Stock Exchange, reinforcing its broad, economy-wide investment strategy. GIC, by contrast, is tasked primarily with managing Singapore's foreign reserves and investing them in international capital markets. Most importantly, GIC also owns nearly 90% of all land in Singapore, much of which has been used for public housing, where the majority of Singaporeans live.

Beyond their indirect ownership through these funds, Singapore's political elites are barred from holding other profit-seeking positions. This, Truitt argues, is the key to Singapore's success: because "the government [...] is composed, essentially, of the owners of most of the land and most of the businesses" (ibid., p. 15), elites have no compelling reason to favor any particular special interest. Instead, their most rational self-serving strategy is to ensure the overall health of the national economy. This, in turn, requires strong property rights, the rule of law, and low levels of corruption—both in the public and private sectors. In other words, because their incomes are tied to the overall performance of the economy, Singapore's elites have a vested interest in promoting good governance and staving corruption, not out of moral virtue, but because it aligns with their own material interests. As Truitt puts it: "The key, and to my knowledge, unique feature of Singapore's SWF management is that the de facto owners of the funds have tied each of their income to the success of the funds, and have minimal special interests in the success of any part" (ibid., p. 16).

Crucially, this structure also creates a powerful incentive for internal accountability. If a single member of the ruling People's Action Party (PAP) were to abuse the system to benefit a particular company or sector—or worse, if such behavior became systemic—it would undermine the broader economy, in which all other PAP members are financially invested. As a result, Truitt writes,

> Each elite wants to be able to easily monitor and harshly discipline each other elite, because his income so heavily depends on minimizing the abuse of discretionary power. He is thus willing to submit himself to the same monitoring mechanisms. As a result, Singapore ends up governed by a group of self-watching watchers. Ministerial rent-seeking is radically curtailed because the Cabinet of Ministers collectively owns the country's national assets. (ibid., p. 16)

In this, then, we begin to see the synthesis that Singapore represents between Mazzucato's vision of the entrepreneurial state and the concerns raised by her critics. On the one hand, Singapore clearly exemplifies a state that adopts an entrepreneurial approach to governance. Its institutional structure resembles that of a holding company or investment firm, with ruling elites collectively invested in national development through their oversight of sovereign wealth funds. These elites are not merely bureaucrats or civil servants—they function, in effect, as stewards of national capital, tasked with maximizing the long-term value of Singapore as an economic entity. Perhaps most notably, the Singaporean state has achieved precisely the kind of independence from tax reliance that Mazzucato envisions for the entrepreneurial state, as both of its sovereign wealth funds rank among the ten largest in the world (taken together, they would rank at number three, surpassed only by the Norwegian Oil Fund and the Abu Dhabi Investment Authority), providing a powerful financial base from which to pursue long-term strategic investments.

At the same time, Singapore's model is carefully designed to avoid precisely the dangers critics associate with Mazzucato's formulation. Rather than empowering government bureaucrats to make direct, high-risk bets on individual entrepreneurial ventures, Singaporean elites are incentivized to improve one overarching asset: the nation itself. This is the main effect of their exclusive investment in the sovereign wealth funds: instead of backing specific technologies or individual companies, Singapore's ruling elites are incentivized to treat governance itself as an entrepreneurial enterprise. In this, their core question becomes: How can the traditional domains of governance be managed as if they were entrepreneurial ventures, designed to deliver measurable, compounding returns for society as a whole?

In the following, I will examine two such domains of governance, in which the Singaporean state's entrepreneurial approach is particularly evident: public housing, on the one hand, and law, on the other.

Public Housing as "Stake in the Country"

As mentioned above, the Singaporean government owns the majority of land in the country, and much of this has been used to build public housing for citizens. This is a central feature of Singapore's model of governance.

When Singapore gained independence in 1965, most of its population lived in so-called *kampong*s, meaning informal, self-built urban villages on the outskirts of the city center ("kampong" is the Malay word for village). These settlements were seen by the government as unsanitary and incompatible with its vision of transforming Singapore into a modern, high-income nation-state. The government therefore launched a large-scale effort to rehouse the population in modern, high-rise apartment blocks (see Loh 2013).

Singapore's model of public housing is highly unusual. Most of the housing stock, where the majority of the population lives, is built by the Housing and Development Board (HDB), a government agency. When a new HDB building is constructed, the government issues 99-year leases for the apartments in it. These leases are then sold at a subsidized price to citizens, who typically finance the purchase using savings from their pension accounts, which are managed by another government agency, the Central Provident Fund (CPF). The CPF is otherwise invested by the government in one of the two wealth funds (see Chua 1997).

Through this system, Singapore has gradually become a society in which the vast majority of citizens—around 80%—own their homes. From the beginning, this was seen by the ruling elite as a crucial strategy for securing public buy-in to the broader project of national development. As the first Prime Minister, Lee Kuan Yew, explained:

> My primary preoccupation was to give every citizen a stake in the country and its future. I wanted a home-owning society. I had seen the contrast between the blocks of low-cost rental flats, badly misused and poorly maintained, and those of house-proud owners, and was convinced that if every family owned its home, the country would be more stable [...] I had seen how voters in capital cities always tended to vote against the government of the

day and was determined that our householders should become homeowners, otherwise we would not have political stability. (Lee 2000, p. 160)

What matters most here is Lee's notion that housing will give citizens "a stake in the country and its future." Through homeownership, Lee believed, Singaporeans would gain a tangible, financial interest in the nation's long-term economic performance, as the value of their apartments would rise alongside overall growth. And this, in turn, would foster continued support for PAP rule, since Singapore's success as a global business hub depends heavily on maintaining a stable social and political environment (see Castells 1988; Chua 1997). As Lee put it in 2011: "As Singapore prospers, the value of their HDB homes also appreciate. Home ownership motivates Singaporeans to work hard and to aspire for a better future for their family, to upgrade to better and bigger flats" (Lee 2011). Thus, homeownership would forge a lasting bond of loyalty and identification between citizens and the state—in other words, a social contract—centered around economic development and political stability.

In terms of understanding Singapore as an entrepreneurial state, what is most striking about this set-up, I would say, is how clearly it resembles the kind of social relation found between employers and employees in a traditional company town. As Crawford describes this in her excellent book on the subject:

> The steel companies' major innovation was to sell houses to their workers. [...] [S]teel workers could buy houses at below-market prices or with special mortgage plans. [...] The welfare director of a steel firm summarized the companies' logic: "get workers to invest their savings in their homes and own them. Then they won't leave and they won't strike. It ties them down so they have a stake in our prosperity." (Crawford 1995, p. 52)

This, then, is what I mean by the *entrepreneurialization* of the state. The Singaporean government's approach to public housing—a traditional domain of welfare policy—is not framed primarily in terms of social rights or redistribution, but as a mechanism for aligning the economic interests of citizens with those of national economic development.

Crucially, as with the governing elite's investment in the sovereign wealth funds, the point is not to tie individuals to a particular asset or enterprise. Rather, it is to give them a generalized stake in the broader economic trajectory of the nation, since the value of their homes rises alongside Singapore's prosperity. As then-Minister of Labor Shanmugam Jayakumar put it in a 1984 speech: "With homes, our citizens have a stake in the well-being and future of the country. Thus, CPF has been an instrumental factor in bringing about a sense of belonging, where citizens have real interests to safeguard" (Jayakumar 1984, p. 3).

In this way, the public housing program mirrors the logic behind elite investment in the wealth funds, only directed at the general population. And just as elite investment reduces the risk of corruption, homeownership acts as a check against the opposite danger, namely populism. By ensuring that most citizens are invested in an asset whose value depends on the long-term health of the national economy, the system discourages political support for short-term redistributive policies—such as heavy taxation of the wealthy—that might undermine Singapore's status as a destination for foreign investment. In a home-owning society where national prosperity is closely tied to global capital flows, policies that threaten investor confidence are likely to be seen as threats to personal financial security as well.

To reinforce this alignment, HDB estates are intentionally organized around the principle of social mixing—both ethnic and economic. Each estate is subject to demographic quotas that ensure its residents reflect the national makeup: roughly 70% Chinese, 15% Malay, and 7% Indian. A similar logic applies to income levels, with households of different socioeconomic backgrounds living side by side. This design ensures that HDB estates offer something close to equal shares in the nation itself: since there are no "bad" neighborhoods or enclaves of concentrated privilege or exclusion, each citizen's stake in national success is broadly comparable, making it more likely that the population as a whole will prioritize long-term growth and stability over short-term populist gains.

Dual State Legality

The second area in which the Singaporean state transforms a traditional domain of governance into an entrepreneurial activity is also the most controversial—namely, its approach to law.

In her work, Singaporean legal scholar Jothie Rajah has described Singapore's legal system in terms of "dual state legality." By this, she means that the Singaporean state "matches the 'law' of the liberal 'West' in the commercial arena while repressing civil and political individual rights" in the political arena. "The bifurcation of Singapore's legal system," she writes, "is so distinct that the Canadian courts have recently specified that Singapore courts have parity with Canadian courts in commercial matters, a specification that might be seen as implicit acknowledgement of different standards in other realms of 'law'" (Rajah 2012, p. 23). Similarly, Jayasuriya observes that although Singapore's leaders often claim that rule of law "is one of the defining features of the Singapore state," this claim "applies selectively to the economic or commercial sphere," whereas the political arena "is regulated by executive prerogative power" (Jayasuriya 2001, p. 121).

According to Rajah, the best way to understand Singapore's legal system is in terms of a suspension of rule of law in the political arena, in favor of rule *by* law. As Hayek explained this distinction, rule of law does not simply mean that the state acts in accordance with laws, since that could easily include a law declaring that anything the state does is legal, thereby effectively legalizing what "to all intents and purposes remains arbitrary action" (Hayek 2001, p. 86). Instead, Hayek argued, rule of law must mean "that the government in all its actions is bound by rules fixed and announced beforehand—rules which make it possible to foresee with fair certainty how the authority will use its coercive powers in given circumstances, and to plan one's individual affairs on the basis of this knowledge" (ibid., p. 75). Rule by law, by contrast, is precisely when the state legalizes arbitrary action.

Broadly speaking, there are two main ways in which rule by law replaces rule of law in Singapore. The first is encapsulated in a single statute: the Internal Security

Act (ISA), which grants sweeping powers to the government to detain individuals indefinitely without trial. Historically, this law has been used liberally against the political opposition. The two most well-known instances of this are Operation Coldstore (1963) and Operation Spectrum (1987). During Operation Coldstore, more than a hundred opposition figures were imprisoned, including Lim Chin Siong, leader of the Barisan Sosialis, the main opposition party at the time (see Poh et al. 2013). Operation Spectrum, on the other hand, involved the detention of 16 individuals from various backgrounds, many of them former student activists, on accusations of orchestrating a "Marxist conspiracy" to "subvert the existing system of government and seize power in Singapore" (Barr 2010; see also Chng et al. 2017). The longest-serving political prisoner under the ISA was Chia Thye Poh, who was detained in 1966 and spent 32 years in custody, five years longer than Nelson Mandela.

The second way rule of law is undermined in Singapore is through a suite of vague and broadly defined laws that are near-impossible to enforce universally, as doing so would likely criminalize large segments of the population. These include: a Public Order Act that defines a "public assembly" as any gathering of one person or more; a Sedition Act that criminalizes any material with a "seditious tendency"; an Internet Code of Practice that bans content deemed objectionable "on the grounds of public interest, public morality, public order, public security, national harmony, or is otherwise prohibited by applicable Singapore laws"; a law against "wounding the religious or racial feelings of others"; and a Films Act that prohibits "party political films," defined broadly as any film "made by any person and directed toward any political end in Singapore"; among others (see Human Rights Watch 2017).

According to Hayek's definition, these laws clearly fail to meet the standard of rule of law, as they do not provide the kind of clear and predictable "rules of the game" that allow individuals to anticipate how the state's coercive powers will be applied (Hayek 2001, p. 86). Instead, they establish rules that are difficult—or in some cases impossible—to consistently follow or even interpret, giving the state wide discretion to selectively enforce them. Rather than limiting state power, they expand it, allowing authorities to intervene whenever they wish under the guise of legality.

The rationale behind this model of "dual state legality" is straightforward: it maximizes Singapore's attractiveness to foreign investors. On the one hand, foreign investors seek strong assurances that their commercial dealings with the state will be governed by clear, stable, and predictable rules—that is, rule of law. They want guarantees, for example, that their assets will not be suddenly seized by the state, a problem often faced in authoritarian regimes. At the same time, one of Singapore's greatest appeals, beyond its business-friendly policies, is its political stability, cleanliness, and exceptionally low crime rate—features that are, in large part, maintained precisely by allowing the government to bypass the rule of law in favor of rule by law in its relationship with its own citizens. The challenge for Singapore's legal system, then, is how to appear as a "rules-based order" in dealings with the outside world, while reaping the domestic advantages of a suspension of rule of law in the political realm. The model of "dual state legality" accomplishes exactly that.

For our purposes, what is most important to note about Singapore's legal order is how clearly outward-facing it is. Unlike most traditional legal systems, it does not primarily seek to maximize what legal sociologist Poul Fritz Kjaer (2018) calls "coherency norms" and "possibility norms." These are the classical ideals of law: coherency norms refer to the expectation that the legal system should be non-contradictory and consistent in its description of how society actually works (e.g., "taxes are 30%"). Possibility norms, by contrast, are counterfactual: they express how society ought to behave, regardless of actual conduct (e.g., "thou shall not kill"), and therefore remain valid even when continuously violated. Crucially, both types of norms assume a largely closed legal system, aiming to define how a given community (e.g. a nation-state) does and should act.

Singapore's legal order, by contrast, is much more geared toward maximizing what Kjaer calls "connectivity norms." These are legal norms that aim not to reflect or prescribe a particular social or moral order, but to enable coordination and exchange *between* different normative and legal systems. This, then, is what the model of "dual state legality" is ultimately about. In order to maximize Singapore's appeal to foreign investors, the legal system has split into two spheres that operate according to different and contrasting legal logics. The point, however, is that this arrangement is only "incoherent" if we begin from the assumption that the legal system *should* prioritize internal consistency over external compatibility. If, instead, we begin from the premise that the primary goal is external connectivity, then Singapore's legal system is in fact perfectly coherent—precisely because it reflects the preferences of foreign investors, who want both: the predictability that rule of law brings to commercial transactions, and the social stability that rule by law helps secure in domestic politics. It is this productive relation between inside and outside—rather than the internal moral or legal consistency of the system itself—that Singapore's legal architecture is primarily designed to maximize.

To that end, another way of conceptualizing Singapore's legal order may be through the lens of Ronald Coase's theory of the firm (1937). Coase posed what he saw as a fundamental puzzle for neoclassical economics: if markets are the most efficient means of allocating resources, as neoclassical theory assumes, then why do firms exist at all? Coase's answer was that firms emerge not in spite of market efficiency, but because of the costs involved in using the market—what he called "transaction costs." When the cost of coordinating through prices, contracts, or external suppliers exceeds the cost of managing the same activities internally, it becomes rational to create a firm. In this way, the firm functions as a bounded sphere of authority and coordination, nested within a broader market economy, yet governed by different rules.

From this perspective, Singapore—and in particular its legal order—can be understood much like a Coasean firm, only scaled to the level of a sovereign state. Externally, Singapore presents itself as an open, liberal market economy, embedded in global value chains and aligned with international norms of legal predictability, property rights, and commercial arbitration. Internally, however, the state maintains a tightly managed political-legal domain, characterized by executive discretion and limited avenues for participatory contestation—features that clearly diverge from liberal-legal expectations. From the standpoint of classical rule-of-law theory, this duality may appear incoherent or even contradictory. But from a Coasean perspective, it can be seen instead as a rational, entrepreneurial response to the "transaction costs" of global governance, as Singapore's "dual state legality" offers precisely the kind of environment global investors seek: liberal and rules-based when it comes to commerce, providing predictability and legal certainty, but illiberal and tightly controlled in political matters, ensuring social stability and security. Crucially, as a sovereign state, Singapore offers a service that no private firm can: a legal infrastructure that guarantees cross-border commercial reliability while simultaneously maintaining internal political order.

Here, then, we find another area where the Singaporean state approaches a traditional domain of nation-state governance as an entrepreneurial venture. For Singapore, the primary function of law is not to reflect the moral values of the demos or to offer a coherent account of social behavior. Instead, law is treated pragmatically as a tool for making Singapore maximally attractive to global capital. In this, the national legal system becomes a marketable global product: curated, adaptable, and strategically deployed to provide global investors precisely the legal environment they prefer, even if it comes at the cost of internal legal coherence.

Conclusion: What Can—And Cannot—Be Learned from Singapore

In this article, I have approached Singapore's version of the entrepreneurial state from a value-neutral perspective, aiming to describe how it works without making any normative judgments about whether it *should* work that way. My argument has simply been that, in contrast to the entrepreneurial state as envisioned by Mariana Mazzucato, Singapore's model actually delivers results. While Mazzucato's version of the entrepreneurial state may not work, this does not mean that such a thing as an entrepreneurial state cannot exist at all. It just needs to take a different form.

The model I have described rests on three pillars. The first is elite buy-in: the challenge of aligning the self-interest of an autocratic leadership with the long-term economic interests of the nation. Singapore addresses this by giving its political elites a collective, diversified stake in the national economy through its sovereign wealth funds, thus tying elite prosperity to national performance and disincentivizing rent-seeking or corruption. The second pillar is citizen buy-in. This is achieved through a system of mass homeownership, which the government describes as giving each citizen "a stake in the country and its future." Just as elite incentives are structured around the success of sovereign investment portfolios, citizens' economic well-being is closely tied to national growth, especially via property values. The third pillar is Singapore's system of dual state legality: the division between rule of law in the commercial sphere and rule by law in the political sphere. This bifurcation allows

Singapore to offer global investors the predictability and protections they demand, while preserving a high degree of domestic control over political life.

Crucially, these three pillars reinforce one another. The legitimacy of suspending rule of law in domestic politics ultimately depends on a shared perception—among both elites and citizens—that the trade-off yields concrete and broadly distributed benefits. This balance is maintained, first, by ensuring that elites are collectively and structurally invested in the long-term performance of the national economy, thereby aligning self-interest with public outcomes. Second, citizen consent is grounded less in formal participatory rights than in the tangible rewards of economic growth, asset appreciation, and social stability. The system holds together only as long as these two forms of buy-in remain intact. Remove any one of the pillars, and the model begins to unravel. Without elite buy-in, corruption would likely take root, eroding the institutional integrity required for sustained growth—and with it, the legitimacy of the "dual state legality." And without citizen buy-in, the social contract begins to fray, making the political trade-offs required by the model far more difficult to justify or sustain.

The question I suspect many readers are left with, however, is how to think about the normative implications of all this. For those raised in traditions that prize civil liberties, political pluralism, and participatory governance, much of what makes the Singaporean model effective also seems deeply troubling. What, then, can other states take from this model?

Few liberal democracies could probably replicate the elite investment structures embedded in Singapore's sovereign wealth funds; even fewer would benefit from importing its legal bifurcation. The political culture, institutional design, and historical contingencies that sustain Singapore's model are deeply context-specific and not easily transplanted. Indeed, this is a point often emphasized by Singaporean officials in response to Western criticism over the country's limited civil liberties: differences in governance are not primarily a matter of ideology or values, but of local conditions and strategic necessity. In Singapore's case, they argue, its small size, lack of natural resources, and deep integration into global value chains demand a model that prioritizes discipline, stability, and competitiveness over liberal pluralism.

What can be learned, however, is something more general but potentially transformative: a shift in how we conceive of governance itself. Singapore's success, I would argue, lies less in its authoritarianism than in the entrepreneurial mindset it brings to statecraft—particularly in policy domains that are typically treated as non-market or purely administrative, such as housing, law, and public service. Rather than treating state functions as fixed or normatively inviolable, the Singaporean government treats them as instruments to be optimized, iterated upon, and strategically aligned with the country's long-term competitiveness.

Taking this broader perspective, we can distil some key lessons from each domain of governance explored in this article. In terms of elite incentives, Singapore offers an interesting example of how to cultivate an entrepreneurial mindset among political leaders without turning them into entrepreneurs in the conventional sense. Rather than encouraging state actors to compete directly in the market or to invest in specific startups—such as those developing new green technologies—the Singaporean model incentivizes them to act as stewards of the national economic environment. Crucially, their role is not to "pick winners" themselves, but to create the conditions that attract winners—namely, successful firms that have already been "picked" by the global market—to operate within Singapore. In this way, the entrepreneurial activity of political elites lies in shaping and managing the broader ecosystem in which market actors thrive, not in competing with them.

The public housing program offers a parallel insight. Rather than treating housing purely as a matter of social welfare or redistributive justice, Singapore reimagines it as a mechanism for aligning citizen interests with long-term national economic performance. Public housing thus becomes a key domain in which governance is entrepreneurialized—not by generating profit for the state, but by cultivating citizen buy-in to national success. Crucially, instead of shielding citizens from market dynamics, as is often the case with public housing elsewhere, Singapore uses housing to do the opposite: to embed citizens more deeply within the logic of the market, giving them a direct and material stake in the project of long-term national economic development. A similar logic could be applied to green policy: rather than presenting sustainability as a matter of sacrifice or moral duty, governments might instead explore how to design systems in which green outcomes align with citizens' personal and financial interests.

The last and most controversial area—Singapore's "dual state legality"—may also be the most conceptually instructive. Here, the key lesson lies in distinguishing between two distinct functions of law: its role in generating internal social and political order ("coherency norms" and "possibility norms"), and its role in enabling external connectivity with the global economic system ("connectivity norms"). Especially in the context of green transition—where legal harmonization across jurisdictions, investment treaties, and cross-border intellectual property rights are key—the Singaporean model invites us to consider how legal infrastructure can be adapted not only to reflect internal values, but to interface productively with a globalized regulatory environment. Even if the substantive content of Singapore's legal regime is not replicable, its structural orientation toward legal connectivity over legal purity may hold broader significance for any state navigating the complexities of green industrial transformation.

Across these three domains of governance, one key pattern recurs: the state is treated not just as a manager of national affairs, but as an enterprise—one in which both elite incentives and public legitimacy are tied to performance. Elections are held, but legitimacy stems much more from Singapore's success in global markets, than from democratic contestation. In line with this logic, public servants in Singapore are among the highest paid in the world. This serves a dual purpose: to attract top talent from the private sector, and, equally important, to eliminate incentives for public officials to exploit their positions for private gain.

Rather than attempting to replicate the Singapore model wholesale, the lesson other states can take is that many traditional functions of the modern state can be reimagined—and, under the right conditions, repurposed—through an entrepreneurial lens. Instead of state-ifying the entrepreneur, perhaps we should begin thinking about how to entrepreneurialize the state.

References

Balding, C. (2012). *Sovereign Wealth Funds: The New Intersection of Money and Politics*. New York, NY: Oxford University Press.

Barr, M. (2010). Marxists in Singapore? Lee Kuan Yew's campaign against catholic social justice activists in the 1980s. *Critical Asian Studies, 42*(3), 335–362. https://doi.org/10.1080/14672715.2010.507389

Barr, M. (2014). *The Ruling Elite of Singapore: Networks of Power and Influence*. London: I.B. Tauris.

Castells, M. (1988). The developmental city-state in an open world economy: The Singapore experience. Working Paper 31. Berkeley, CA: University of California.

Chng, S. T., Low, Y. L., & Teo, S. L. (2017). *1987: Singapore's Marxists Conspiracy 30 Years on*. Singapore: Function 8.

Chua, B. H. (1997). *Political Legitimacy and Housing: Stakeholding in Singapore*. London: Routledge.

Coase, R. H. (1937). The nature of the firm. *Economica, 4*(16), 386–405. https://doi.org/10.1111/j.1468-0335.1937.tb00002.x

Crawford, M. (1995). *Building the Workingman's Paradise: The Design of American Company Towns*. London: Verso.

Gibson, W. (1993). Disneyland with the death penalty. *Wired Magazine*. Retrieved August 14, 2025. https://www.wired.com/1993/04/gibson-2/

Hayek, F. A. (2001 [1944]). *The Road to Serfdom*. New York, NY: Routledge.

Henrekson, M., Sandström, C., & Stenkula, M. (Eds.) (2024). *Moonshots and the New Industrial Policy: Questioning the Mission Economy*. Cham: Springer. https://doi.org/10.1007/978-3-031-49196-2

Human Rights Watch (2017). *Kill the Chicken to Scare the Monkeys: Suppression of Free Expression and Assembly in Singapore*. https://www.hrw.org/sites/default/files/report_pdf/

Jayakumar, S. (1984). The evolution of CPF: From a mere old age provident fund to an institution giving Singaporeans a stake in the nation's future. Government Press Release No. 45. September 22.

Jayasuriya, K. (2001). The exception becomes the norm: Law and regimes of exception in East Asia. *Asian-Pacific Law & Policy Journal, 2*(1), 108–124.

Kjaer, P. F. (2018). Constitutionalizing connectivity: The constitutional grid of world society. *Journal of Law and Society, 45*(S1), 114–134. https://doi.org/10.1111/jols.12106

Kraar, L. (1974). Singapore, the country run like a corporation. *Fortune*. Retrieved August 14, 2025. https://fortune.com/2015/03/23/singapore-leekuanyew-corporation-1974/

Lee, K. Y. (2000). *From Third World to First: The Singapore Story: 1965–2000*. New York, NY: HarperCollins.

Lee, K. Y. (2011). Speech by Minister Mentor Lee Kuan Yew at the Launch of Tanjong Pagar Town Council's Five-Year Masterplan and Opening of ABC Waters at Alexandra Canal, 19 March 2011. Prime Minister's Office. Retrieved August 14, 2025. https://www.pmo.gov.sg/Newsroom/

Loh, K. S. (2013). *Squatters Into Citizens: The 1961 Bukit Ho Swee Fire and the Making of Modern Singapore*. Singapore: Asian Studies Association of Australia in association with NUS Press and NIAS Press.

Mahbubani, K. (2018). The Secret Sauce of Singapore. *Dubai Policy Review*. Retrieved August 14, 2025. https://dubaipolicyreview.ae/the-secret-sauce-of-singapore/

Mazzucato, M. (2013). *The Entrepreneurial State: Debunking Public vs. Private Sector Myths*. London: Anthem Press.

Ong, A. (2006). *Neoliberalism as Exception: Mutations in Citizenship and Sovereignty*. Durham, NC: Duke University Press.

Poh, S. K., Tan, K. F., & Lysa, H. (Eds.) (2013). *The 1963 Operation Coldstore in Singapore: Commemorating 50 Years*. Petaling Jaya: Strategic Information and Research Development Centre.

Rajah, J. (2012). *Authoritarian Rule of Law: Legislation, Discourse and Legitimacy in Singapore*. Cambridge: Cambridge University Press.

Singh, R. (2019). In the company of citizens: The rhetorical contours of Singapore's neoliberalism. *Communication and Critical/Cultural Studies*, *16*(3), 161–177. https://doi.org/10.1080/14791420.2019.1637009

Truitt, T. (2024). Self-Watching Watchers: The Case of Singapore. *GMU Working Paper in Economics* No. 24–46.

Wennberg, K., & Sandström, C. (Eds.) (2022). *Questioning the Entrepreneurial State: Status-quo, Pitfalls, and the Need for Credible Innovation Policy*. Cham: Springer.

Winsemius, A. (1963). *A Proposed Industrialization Programme for the State of Singapore*. New York, NY: United Nations.

Jacob Hjortsberg is a Postdoctoral Research Fellow at the Department of Business Humanities and Law, Copenhagen Business School. He is part of the ERC-funded project "Global Value Chain Law: Constituting Connectivity, Contracts and Corporations," where he examines the global value chain of insulin from production in Denmark to patient access in Southeast Asia.

He received his PhD in Social Anthropology from the University of Bergen in 2022. Based on extensive ethnographic and historical research in Singapore, his dissertation develops the concept of the "middleman minority state" to conceptualize Singapore's distinctive form of state-making, arguing that its success lies in scaling up the strategies of classic middleman minorities to the level of the state.

MIX
Papier aus verantwortungsvollen Quellen
Paper from responsible sources
FSC® C105338

If you have any concerns about our products,
you can contact us on
ProductSafety@springernature.com

In case Publisher is established outside the EU,
the EU authorized representative is:
Springer Nature Customer Service Center GmbH
Europaplatz 3, 69115 Heidelberg, Germany

Printed by Libri Plureos GmbH
in Hamburg, Germany